Policing Life and Death

Policing Life and Death

RACE, VIOLENCE, AND RESISTANCE IN
PUERTO RICO

Marisol LeBrón

UNIVERSITY OF CALIFORNIA PRESS

University of California Press, one of the most distinguished university presses in the United States, enriches lives around the world by advancing scholarship in the humanities, social sciences, and natural sciences. Its activities are supported by the UC Press Foundation and by philanthropic contributions from individuals and institutions. For more information, visit www.ucpress.edu.

University of California Press
Oakland, California

Library of Congress Cataloging-in-Publication Data

Names: LeBrón, Marisol, author.
Title: Policing life and death : race, violence, and resistance in Puerto Rico / Marisol LeBrón.
Description: Oakland, California : University of California Press, [2019] | Includes bibliographical references and index. |
Identifiers: LCCN 2018040129 (print) | LCCN 2018044143 (ebook) | ISBN 9780520971677 (ebook) | ISBN 9780520300163 (cloth : alk. paper) | ISBN 9780520300170 (pbk. : alk. paper)
Subjects: LCSH: Discrimination in law enforcement—Puerto Rico—History—20th century. | Discrimination in criminal justice administration—Puerto Rico—History—20th century. | Police-community relations—Puerto Rico—History—20th century.
Classification: LCC HV8174.A3 (ebook) | LCC HV8174.A3 L43 2019 (print) | DDC 363.2/3097295—dc23
LC record available at https://lccn.loc.gov/2018040129

Manufactured in the United States of America

28 27 26 25 24 23 22 21 20
10 9 8 7 6 5 4 3 2

For my mother—this would not have been possible without you.

CONTENTS

List of Tables ix
Acknowledgments xi

Introduction: They Don't Care If We Die 1

1 · A War against the Victims 23

2 · Colonial Projects 52

3 · Underground 83

4 · The Continued Promise of Punishment 114

5 · Policing Solidarity 144

6 · #ImperfectVictims 176

7 · Security from Below 202

Postscript: Broken Windows and Future Horizons
after the Storm 232

Notes 241
Bibliography 279
Index 287

TABLES

1. *Delitos Tipo 1* Recorded in Puerto Rico, 1990–2000   *43*
2. Discrepancies in the Reporting of Homicides in
   Puerto Rico, 1990–2000   *44*

ACKNOWLEDGMENTS

I have been fortunate to have many brilliant and thoughtful accomplices as I worked on this book. Researching and writing this book has been a truly collaborative process, which grew from desires to imagine and work collectively toward a more just world. I am grateful to everyone who pushed me to articulate the stakes of this project and think about it as part of a larger anti-colonial and abolitionist intellectual project.

This project would not have been possible without everyone in Puerto Rico who shared their thoughts and struggles with me for nearly a decade. Thank you to Giovanni Roberto, Xiomara Caro, Waldemiro Vélez Soto, Lourdes C. Santiago Negrón, Pedro Lugo Vázquez, Abner Y. Dennis Zayas, Roberto Thomas, Alana Feldman Soler, and Zinnia Alejandro for sharing your stories with me. I am constantly inspired as I continue to follow the important work you all are doing to rethink and transform what it means to really live in Puerto Rico. Maritza Stanchich has been a tremendous source of support, and I always look forward to our conversations as we walk around Old San Juan when I'm in town. Gary Gutiérrez, José Raúl Cepeda, Judith Berkan, Osvaldo Burgos, Fernando Picó, Dora Nevares-Muñiz, and Ileana Colón Carlo all provided me with invaluable information and insights into the history of *mano dura contra el crimen*, the Rosselló administration, and contemporary human rights violations in Puerto Rico. Thank you also to the staff at the Colección Puertorriqueña at the University of Puerto Rico—Rio Piedras, the Biblioteca Legislativa Tomás Bonilla Feliciano, Comisión de Derechos Civiles, and Archivo de la Fundación Sila M. Calderón for helping me locate important documents and materials.

This project began as a doctoral dissertation in American studies at New York University and continues to be nurtured by the mentors, colleagues, and friends I met there. Arlene Dávila, I am eternally grateful for your rigor, kindness, engagement, and support. I can't even begin to express how important your mentorship has been to me. Your intellectual commitments and contributions are a constant source of inspiration. Lisa Duggan, Nikhil Singh, and Cristina Beltrán, thank you for encouraging my scholarship both in and out of the classroom. I was fortunate to go through graduate school with a cohort of brilliant scholars of color. Emily Hue, Eva Hageman, Carmen Phillips, Liza Keānuenueokalani Williams, and Marlon Burgess, I can't think of better people to have gone through this process with. Special appreciation to Leticia Alvarado, Ariana Ochoa Camacho, Johanna Londoño Roy Pérez, Karen Jaime, Sandra Ruiz, and Albert Sergio Laguna for all of the "Team Exito" love and support; I'm lucky to have you all as interlocutors. Conversations about empire, war, and policing with Stuart Schrader have animated my thinking since our seminar days together. Elliott Hunter Powell has helped me to think through questions of music, identity, and social resistance in ways that have deeply influenced my work. Justin Leroy, Christy Thornton, Jan Padios, Zach Schwartz-Weinstein, Rana Jaleel Elizabeth Mesok, Zenia Kish, Emma Kreyche, A.J. Bauer, Manijeh Moradian, Claudia Garriga-López, James Rodríguez, Jessica N. Pabón, Miles Grier, Andy Cornell, and Emmy Williamson all made my time at NYU infinitely better and continue to be amazing friends and colleagues.

Gina Pérez has been a mentor to me since I was an undergraduate at Oberlin College first dipping my toes into Latinx studies and American studies. Her work was a revelation to me when I first encountered it and was in many ways what made me want to go on and become an academic. I always wrote with Gina in mind, so I was thrilled when I found out she was one of the reviewers for this book. I'm appreciative of her analysis and suggestions, which have made this work stronger. Laura Briggs and Carlos Alamo-Pastrana also read this book for the University of California Press and offered critical feedback and guidance that helped me clarify and strengthen my central claims and interventions. The comments they both provided pushed me to clarify and strengthen my claims, and this book is much better as a result. Yarimar Bonilla also read a draft of this book and offered valuable feedback during the revision process. While I was a Postdoctoral Associate in Latina/o Studies in the Global South at Duke University in 2016, I invited Zaire Dinzey-Flores, Dan Berger, Sally Deutsch, and Wahneema Lubiano to read an earlier version of this book during a manuscript workshop. They spent hours carefully engaging with my work, pushing my thinking further, and demonstrating what radical mentorship and collegiality look like. Jordan T. Camp, Christina Heatherton, Chris Agee, and Themis Chronopoulos all read and commented on earlier versions of the first chapter and helped me think through how Puerto Rico fits into larger regimes of urban policing. I've also presented pieces of this project at a number of venues and am grateful to the countless folks who engaged with the work during invited talks and conference presentations.

The writing process can be incredibly isolating and daunting, especially when academia tends to encourage competition over collaboration. I'm grateful to all of the people who provided me with love, friendship, and camaraderie as I worked on this project and reminded me that we can (and should) do academia differently. Ruth Wilson Gilmore has been a staunch advocate of this project since its earliest days, and I am grateful for her constant reminders to always reach for abolitionist horizons in our work and everyday lives. I am indebted to Deborah R. Vargas, Erica Edwards, Kirstie Dorr, Sara Kaplan, and Marisol Negrón for their support, not just of this project but also of me as a scholar and as a person. I can't think of anyone else I'd rather be building community and *familia* with. Nick Mitchell, you are a constant source of joy, and our text chains about everything from antiracist feminist politics to memes are often the highlight of my day. In just the two short years I was at Duke, Jecca Namakkal, Eli Meyerhoff, Elizabeth Ault, Yuridia Ramírez Rentería, Felicia Arriaga, and Danielle Purifoy all helped to make sure that Durham will always feel like a second home. Mark R. Villegas made my time in central Pennsylvania much more manageable with writing dates, trips to seek out good food, and lots of cat videos. Emily Hue, Josen Masangkay Diaz, Davorn Sisavath, and Ashvin Kini have been a source of friendship, support, and accountability. I can't wait to start the next book if it means planning another writing retreat with you all.

A number of intellectual homes nurtured this project and helped me bring it to fruition. I am grateful to the community of Latinx and Puerto Rican studies scholars who provided me with necessary guidance, encouragement, and friendship. Many thanks to Petra Rivera-Rideau, Hilda Lloréns, Irene Garza, Jonathan Rosa, Daniel Nieves, Vanessa Díaz, Jennifer Harford Vargas, Javier Arbona, José Fusté, Jade Sotomayor, Michael Rodríguez Muñiz, Raquel Z. Rivera, Ana Ramos-Zayas, Stephen Pitti, Alicia Schmidt Camacho, Larry La Fountain, Sarah Molinari, Rudy Aguilar, Magdalena Barrera, Raúl Coronado, Sandy Placido, Deborah Paredez, Emma Amador, Inés Casillas, Sandy Soto, Jorge Matos Valldejuli, Margaret Power, and Sara

Awartani. I also have been lucky to be in conversation with a number of scholars doing critical work on the carceral state and abolitionist praxis, including Lydia Pelot-Hobbs (since our Oberlin days!), Elissa Underwood Marek, Elizabeth Hinton, David Stein, Sarah Haley, Judah Schept, Jenna Loyd, Naomi Paik, Craig Gilmore, Max Felkor-Kantor, Gilberto Rosas, Rebecca Hill, Micol Seigel, Christina Hanhardt, Michael Hames-García, and Steven Osuna.

Thank you to my former departmental colleagues in American studies at Dickinson: Jerry Philogene, Amy Farrell, Sharon O'Brien, and Cotton Seiler. I also want to thank the friends and colleagues I met during my time at Dickinson College, including Crystal Marie Moten, Poulomi Saha, Mitchell Bernard Patterson, Helene Lee, Erik Love, Lynn Johnson, Bronte Jones, Cynthia Burleigh, Jessica Howard, Julie Vastine, Vanessa Tyson, Emily Pawley, Roger Turner, Patricia Van Leeuwaarde Moonsammy, Sarah Niebler, Melissa Garcia, Sarah Kersh, Naila Smith, Amaury Sosa, and Say Burgin. As I was finishing this book, I joined the faculty at the University of Texas at Austin, where I look forward to working alongside new colleagues and long-time friends. Thanks especially to Cary Cordova, John McKiernan González, Simone Browne, Eric Tang, Mónica Jiménez, Laura Gutiérrez, Karma Chávez, Julie Minich, Rachel González-Martin, Belem López, and the rest of the folks in Mexican American and Latina/o Studies for offering such a warm welcome before I even set foot in Austin.

Working with the folks at the University of California Press has been an incredible experience. My editor, Kate Marshall, showed great excitement about this project from the moment I very clumsily described it to her as a newly minted PhD many years ago. She saw the potential in the project, pushed me to think more broadly in generative ways, and found readers who would do the same. Bradley Depew provided me with expert editorial assistance during the preproduction process. Many thanks to Tom Sullivan, Jessica Moll, and Sabrina Robleh, who all worked with me on the production and marketing of this book. Cathy Hannabach and the wonderful folks at Ideas on Fire helped me with the indexing for this book. Sharon Langworthy expertly copyedited the manuscript, and Nicholle Robertson coordinated key aspects of the production process.

This project would have been impossible without the love and support of my family. Perhaps one of the best parts of researching and writing this book was the opportunity to spend extended periods of time in Puerto Rico, which afforded me some much-needed time with my family there. My father, Efraín, and stepmother, Noemi, went out of their way to make this research more feasible, including making sure I had a car to drive and a place to stay. My father and I haven't always seen eye to eye politically, and we did get into quite a few disagreements during my time in Puerto Rico, but I look forward to the many conversations we will have when he reads this book about what needs to change in the archipelago, and I am eager to see all the ways we will continue to find common ground. It has been an absolutely beautiful experience to watch my sister, Solimar, and brother, Joel, come of age and become talented, intellectually curious, and independent adults over the decade that I've been doing this project. I wasn't there when they were growing up, so it meant the world to me for them to open their lives to me and let me be their big sister. In many ways this project is for them, because I want them, and other young people like them, to be able to live a just and dignified life in Puerto Rico. I hope that in some small way this project helps contribute to that. This work is dedicated to my mother, Maria, who has supported me every step of the way and in every way possible. Mom, all the words I can think of seem too small to appropriately capture everything you have done for me. You believed in me and in the project with an unwavering faith, reminding me of my commitments to this work when I felt like I had chosen an impossible career path. I always know how proud you are of me, and of this work, and that has meant everything to me.

My deepest and most heartfelt thank you goes to my partner, friend, and coconspirator, Jennifer Lynn Kelly. Jenny should really be listed as a coeditor, since she's read and reread every single word of this book (in all of its various instantiations) dozens upon dozens of times over the past decade. She never tired of engaging with my work and always showed great enthusiasm, patience, and attention to detail at moments when I was at my most exhausted and couldn't stand to keep thinking through this project or write another word. Your passion, thoughtfulness, radical empathy, and commitment to working toward a more just and free world constantly leave me in awe. I am fortunate to be able to grow as a scholar and person with you, and I look forward to sharing a better future with you and our little family.

Introduction

THEY DON'T CARE IF WE DIE

ON THE MORNING OF JANUARY 31, 2012, I met with local activist Giovanni Roberto at La Chiwinha, a small café a few blocks away from the University of Puerto Rico's (UPR's) main campus in the Río Piedras area of San Juan. Over a few cups of tea, he told me about his role in the student mobilizations that had shut down the university system for much of the 2010 and 2011 academic years. He explained the social, political, and economic contexts that drove students to strike for a more equitable and accessible educational system, as well as the incredible violence that students experienced at the hands of police and private security forces determined to "restore order" to the campus. Eventually our conversation turned to the question of self-defense. Toward the end of the strikes, students were increasingly criticized in the media for fighting back against the police. Images of students aggressively engaging law enforcement officials and committing acts of vandalism circulated widely, souring some Puerto Ricans' perceptions of the student movement. When I asked Roberto about this, without hesitation he said, "I believe in self defense. I believe that students have the right to defend themselves if they feel threatened by cops."[1] He paused before adding, "And with what is recently approved, a cop can kill you if he or she has the perception that you are dangerous or are going to put their life in danger."[2]

Shaping Roberto's response that afternoon were the recently announced changes to the guidelines concerning lethal force for the Puerto Rico Police Department (PRPD). On September 5, 2011, the Civil Rights Division of the US Department of Justice (DOJ) issued a damning report that declared the PRPD "broken in a number of fundamental and critical respects."[3] According to the DOJ report, the PRPD regularly used excessive, and sometimes deadly, force during routine stops and arrests. To remedy the PRPD's unlawful use of force and what it called a "deliberate indifference to the public's safety," the DOJ recommended that the PRPD work toward general standards of accountability by establishing written guidance regarding use of force, making officers aware of effective alternatives to force, offering ongoing professional training, and conducting thorough investigations when force is deployed.[4] Promising to drastically overhaul police procedure regarding the use of force in the wake of the DOJ's findings and recommendations, the PRPD had finally unveiled its response on January 30, 2012, the day before my meeting with Roberto.

In a perverse twist, the PRPD addressed the DOJ's concerns over a lack of standardized protocols regarding the use of force by issuing a general order that allowed the use of lethal force if an officer had a "reasonable perception" that his or her life or the life of another was threatened.[5] William Ramírez, director of the local chapter of the American Civil Liberties Union (ACLU), noted that this ambiguously framed order was troubling because an individual officer's "reasonable perception" of threat is often informed by bias and prejudice. According to Ramírez, "An officer can think that a young, Black man coming out of public housing with his hand in his pocket is dangerous. It could be a cell phone or a weapon [in his pocket], but after the officer can say: I shot him because I perceived that I was in danger."[6]

Roberto expressed a similar sentiment during our conversation in La Chiwinha. He said that police officers, like many other Puerto Ricans, have been conditioned to associate poverty, Blackness, and spatial location with criminality and danger. Indeed, more than two decades of violent police incursions into low-income and Black communities had helped to shape such popular conceptions of danger while seemingly justifying the need for more and more punitive measures to manage Puerto Rico's "dangerous classes." For Roberto, the previous day's announcement that a police officer could justifiably kill someone if he or she believed that person posed some sort of danger merely formalized what had already been long-standing police practice, especially toward low-income and Black people living in Puerto Rico.

Roberto connected both the recent changes to the PRPD's lethal force regulations and the deadly racialization of crime to *mano dura contra el crimen* (iron fist against crime), an anticrime measure that deployed police and military forces in public housing and other low-income spaces around the archipelago during the 1990s in an effort to eliminate drug trafficking.[7] He explained: "And that's what we see, the consequences of wrong politics, of *mano dura*. It's not the solution. At the same time, what they're doing now is increasing [mano dura], because they want to gain more social control. They don't fucking care if we die or experience violence. They feel secure because they live apart, they don't hang out in the same spaces that we hang out or live in the same spaces."[8] With this, Roberto articulated the very central role that policing plays in distributing harm and death according to hierarchies of difference and belonging. His comments also pointed to the segregation of Puerto Rican society and the idea that some Puerto Ricans may tolerate high levels of police violence because it is seen as being exercised somewhere else, against others who need to be contained and controlled in order to keep everyone else safe. As we spoke, I wondered exactly what role mano dura contra el crimen played in producing and justifying the notion that harm and death were natural, and in some cases desirable, outcomes of police work. In other words, how did policing initiatives like mano dura help bring us to the point where some Puerto Ricans, in Roberto's words, "don't fucking care" if their fellow citizens "die or experience violence?"

Policing Life and Death: Race, Violence, and Resistance in Puerto Rico answers that question by tracing the rise of punitive governance in contemporary Puerto Rico. By *punitive governance* I mean the ways in which the Puerto Rican state has reasserted itself in the lives of Puerto Ricans through technologies of punishment such as policing and incarceration, as well as the violence (state sanctioned and other) they often provoke.[9] Punitive governance also refers to the ideological work undertaken by the state to promote an understanding that punishment, justice, and safety are intrinsically linked.[10] In this book I demonstrate that punitive governance has left an indelible mark on how life and death are understood and experienced in Puerto Rico and has done so in a way that reinforces societal inequality along lines of race, class, spatial location, gender, sexuality, and citizenship status.

Punitive governance functions through an unequal distribution of resources and life chances that affects those populations occupying some of the most tenuous positions in Puerto Rican society.[11] It has hardened existing discriminatory attitudes and structures that target low-income, Black, queer, and residentially marginalized Puerto Ricans living in Puerto Rico in ways that have normalized and in some instances increased their vulnerability to harm at the hands of the state and their fellow citizens. As ethnic studies scholar Lisa Marie Cacho argues, the practices of criminalization that animate punitive governance make structures of human value "intelligible through racialized, sexualized, spatialized, and state-sanctioned violences" that target the most vulnerable, especially those who experience overlapping forms of marginalization.[12] Within punitive regimes, vulnerable populations experience a form of "social death" that renders them "targets of regulation and containment," subject to the law's discipline but excluded from its protection when confronted with violence.[13]

Yet Puerto Ricans also challenge deadly punitive logics and practices by working toward alternative understandings of justice, safety, and accountability in ways that are both spectacular and quotidian. This book follows a range of efforts by Puerto Ricans to critique punitive governance and imagine new ways of living in Puerto Rico. From public housing residents strategically using the press to provide their own accounts of the havoc policing has caused in their communities, to underground rappers skewering the absurdities of the war on drugs, to university students trying to build social movements across racial and class differences, to community activists implementing local solutions to violence that decenter policing, the story about punitive governance told in this book is as much one of resilience and resistance as it is one of repression.

I situate the growth of punitive governance in Puerto Rico within the ongoing colonization of the archipelago by the United States. Over the course of the late twentieth century and into the present, the Puerto Rican state has strengthened its security apparatus in an attempt to manage a range of social, economic, and political crises stemming from its continued incorporation into the United States as a commonwealth territory. By the late 1970s the once unprecedented levels of social and economic improvement experienced by Puerto Ricans were in steady decline, and personal insecurity increased as US-led development strategies had seemingly run their course. As the limitations of the commonwealth arrangement between the United States and Puerto Rico made themselves more intensely felt on Puerto Ricans, policing emerged as the state's primary means of responding to an array of resultant social problems such as high unemployment, chronic poverty, and a growing drug-based, informal economy. I demonstrate how a refusal on the part of both the US and Puerto Rican political establishments to fundamentally alter Puerto Rico's colonial status, which prevents Puerto Rico from meaningfully shaping its own policy, helps us understand why it is in the realm of biopolitical calculation—the policing of life and death— that we encounter the contemporary Puerto Rican state at its most robust.

While Puerto Rican elites and technocrats have conceptualized and implemented a range of punitive solutions to societal problems from the late-twentieth century to the present, this book focuses on the emergence and legacies of mano dura contra el crimen to explore Puerto Rico's punitive turn. Mano dura contra el crimen was a series of crime-reduction measures introduced by Governor Pedro Rosselló in 1993, which deployed police and military forces within public housing and other low-income spaces around the archipelago, but primarily across the big island, during the 1990s in an effort to eliminate drug trafficking. Although mano dura was short-lived, lasting from approximately 1993 to 2000, for many Puerto Ricans with whom I spoke, it marked a turning point when the state increasingly relied on punitive power to demonstrate its capacity and maintain social control. This is not to imply that punitive power had previously played no role in how either the US or the Puerto Rican state maintained social control, but it is to note that for many Puerto Ricans, mano dura fundamentally altered public discourse and attitudes around issues of crime, violence, victimhood, and the responsibility of the state—and continues to do so more than twenty years later.

In addition to charting the rise of mano dura contra el crimen, I am also interested in what has recently come to be discussed as *el fracaso de la mano dura*, or the failure of mano dura, which has encouraged some activists to seek out and attempt to implement nonpunitive solutions to social problems. Many Puerto Ricans, especially those who have borne the brunt of punitive policy in their communities, will point out that mano dura did not succeed in reducing drug-related crime and violence, but it did succeed in strengthening existing patterns of race- and class-based segregation. In addition, through both rhetoric and practice, mano dura normalized violent, premature death as an acceptable punishment for criminal behavior or social transgression. The emergence and implementation of mano dura contra el crimen illuminates how punitive measures became some of the few state-sanctioned solutions on offer to Puerto Ricans dealing with a wide range of social problems. Activists and ordinary Puerto Ricans are now pushing against punitive governance and the normalization of mano dura in order to build communities that are safe and secure for everyone in a meaningful way.

What has occurred in Puerto Rico over the past thirty years mirrors the growth of carceral and neoliberal regimes of dispossession both in the United States and globally. Although its status as a colonial possession of the United States played a central role in how and when punitive governance developed there, Puerto Rico nonetheless provides a clear example of much larger global trends. The growth of punitive governance in Puerto Rico demonstrates the ways in which governments have increasingly come to rely on policing, incarceration, and enclosure to manage the populations most affected by racist and capitalist inequality. This is a crucial point to underscore, as I work throughout the book to avoid either exceptionalizing Puerto Rico or denying it any specificity. Puerto Rico is not an isolated archipelago divorced from the rest of the world. Instead, what has occurred and is occurring in Puerto Rico both reflects and has implications for larger global processes that are both taking root and unfolding all around us. In other words, while this book acknowledges and engages the apparent peculiarities of Puerto Rico as a colonial site, examining the growth of punitive governance in Puerto Rico helps to expand our understanding of existing and emerging structures of domination throughout the Americas and beyond. In Puerto Rico, as in other sites, the consolidation of punitive solutions to social problems has hardened inequality while simultaneously inciting marginalized populations into forms of creative and sustained resistance against the vulnerability that shapes their lives. In this way, *Policing Life and Death* turns to Puerto Rico not only to understand punitive governance and its effects on vulnerable populations, but also to trace how those very communities are reimagining their own futures in ways that expand the meanings of safety and justice in the contemporary period.

COLONIAL CRISIS MANAGEMENT

In Puerto Rico as elsewhere, punitive governance functions as a form of crisis management that masks an inability or unwillingness to radically transform social relations and institutions in order to address pressing societal problems. Critical geographer Ruth Wilson Gilmore makes this point clear: "Crisis means instability that can be fixed only through radical measures, which include developing new relationships and new or renovated institutions out of what already exists."[14] In Puerto Rico the strictures of colonial rule explicitly prevented radical transformations within the official political or economic realms. As a result the Puerto Rican state turned to punitive governance to manage how structural instabilities were felt at the population level and promote the image of a strong and active state.

The crises that prompted Puerto Rico's punitive turn during the late twentieth century have their roots in the US-led development efforts that accelerated following World War II. During the postwar period, the United States responded to international calls for decolonization, as well as political unrest, in the archipelago by putting into place measures that would extend a limited self-governance to Puerto Rico while preserving US military and capitalist interests. In 1948 Luis Muñoz Marín of the Partido Popular Democratico (PPD), or Popular Democratic Party, became Puerto Rico's first democratically elected governor. According to geographer Déborah Berman Santana, by the time Muñoz Marín assumed the governorship there was already an overwhelming sense of Puerto Rico's "nonviability" as a sovereign nation. As Berman Santana notes, "Puerto Rico was seen as too small, too overpopulated, and too lacking in natural resources to survive as an independent country. It followed, therefore, that there was no option but to continue economic and political dependence on the United States."[15] Since many political elites perceived independence as unfavorable and statehood unlikely, Muñoz Marín promoted a seemingly third way forward for Puerto Rico, which would allow local politicians to govern local affairs while keeping the territory politically and economically incorporated within the United States.

In 1950 the US Congress enacted legislation that allowed Puerto Rico to draft its own constitution. The new constitution, of which Muñoz Marín was a chief architect, identified Puerto Rico as an *Estado Libre Asociado* (Associated Free State), or commonwealth of the United States, which would grant the latter ultimate authority over the archipelago but would give the local government a greater degree of autonomy in local affairs. The commonwealth constitution was enacted on July 25, 1952, the anniversary of the landing of US troops in Puerto Rico in 1898, signifying the endurance of American rule. To complement Puerto Rico's new political status, Muñoz Marín strategically utilized close ties with the United States to reinvigorate the local economy.

With Puerto Rico widely regarded as the "poorhouse of the Caribbean," Muñoz Marín sought to improve economic conditions for Puerto Ricans by transforming the economy from one based primarily on sugar production to an industrial one based on manufacturing. Muñoz Marín and his team of New Deal–trained technocrats, with the support of the US government, initiated Operación Manos a la Obra (Operation Bootstrap), which promoted rapid development and modernization through export-led industrialization. This strategy, which would come to be dubbed "industrialization through invitation," relied heavily on US capital to invest in labor-intensive manufacturing. The commonwealth government stimulated investment in the archipelago's new economy by providing tax holidays, subsidies, loans, and a guaranteed pool of low-wage workers to US corporations.[16] While the commonwealth government boasted of new factories opening almost daily during the early years of Operation Bootstrap, it was clear that the number of jobs generated through manufacturing was not sufficient for the local population.

This transformation of Puerto Rico's economy displaced rural workers and spurred a massive migration to the United States. Migration functioned as a "safety valve" for a development program that even in its early stages was already proving unable to generate sufficient employment. As political economist Emilio Pantojas-García notes, "The colonial relation that allowed Puerto Ricans to enter freely into the United States thus provided an artificial source of stability to a structurally unbalanced economic strategy; migration became an escape valve for employment pressures."[17] The migration of these surplus laborers also crucially helped to squelch political dissent as the commonwealth arrangement was consolidated during the mid-twentieth century. Scholars have noted that the economic achievements of Operation Bootstrap and the commonwealth arrangement would have been much less impressive than they appeared without Puerto Rico's ability to exile its surplus laborers and political dissidents.[18]

Massive out-migration and the neutralization of political dissidents through repression paved the way for Operation Bootstrap's "golden era" during the 1950s and 1960s. Puerto Rico was internationally celebrated as a modern miracle state, and many Puerto Ricans experienced improved living standards in the two decades following the program's implementation. However, unemployment, particularly among working-aged men, remained a recurrent problem. Although the Puerto Rican and US governments undertook well-documented efforts to enact population controls through migration and sterilization campaigns, large numbers of Puerto Ricans were still rendered redundant by the strategies and calculations of colonial capitalism.[19] During the heyday of Operation Bootstrap, unemployment never fell below 10 percent, while labor force participation numbers never rose above 50 percent. The displacement of workers, persistently high levels of unemployment, entrenched poverty, and an overdependence on US capital investment were thus central facets of Puerto Rico's "great transformation" and "modernization" efforts.

The 1970s marked the first significant moment of crisis for the commonwealth and US-led development in Puerto Rico. Starting in 1965, the Puerto Rican government stimulated the development of the petrochemical industry in order to take advantage of US oil import quotas, which gave special concessions to American oil refineries operating in Puerto Rico. In April

1973, however, US president Richard Nixon eliminated the oil import quotas, effectively ending the favorable conditions for the petrochemical industry in Puerto Rico. This situation was made worse by the 1973 OPEC oil embargo and subsequent price increases.[20] The blow to the economy represented by the oil crisis was compounded by the devaluation of the dollar and the spread of the US recession to Puerto Rico, both of which also occurred in 1973. In many ways the Puerto Rican economy was unable to recover from the numerous hits to its economy that struck in 1973. The economy stagnated, with annual economic growth rates slowing to an average of only 1.7 percent from 1974 to 1984.[21] As the economy faltered, unemployment levels steadily increased. Following the events of 1973, unemployment rose to 18.1 percent in 1975. This upward trend continued until 1985, when unemployment increased to a startling 21.8 percent.[22]

Puerto Rican and US officials scrambled to halt the economic crisis threatening to engulf the archipelago. The federal government responded with two policies in 1976. First, Congress increased federal transfer payments, for instance, increasing Puerto Rico's share in the US food stamps program. Second, Congress enacted Section 936 of the Internal Revenue Code, which provided attractive tax incentives for US corporations operating in Puerto Rico. Section 936 regulations shifted the economy once again, attracting capital-intensive, high-tech industries such as pharmaceuticals, precision instruments, and electronics.[23] The growth of this knowledge-intensive sector, however, failed to generate many new jobs. Puerto Ricans were faced with fewer and fewer options in the formal labor economy following the collapse of the agricultural, manufacturing, and petrochemical sectors.

It is within this context that we see the growth of Puerto Rico's informal economy. The informal or "underground" economy captures a range of semi-legal and illegal income-generating activities.[24] The informal economy can refer to street peddling, off-the-books construction work, and unlicensed childcare, as well as to illicit organizations dedicated to drugs, robbery, sex work, and gambling. Although extremely difficult to quantify, a number of economists and criminologists believe that the informal economy has played a key role in absorbing surplus laborers and stabilizing the Puerto Rican economy.[25] And while Puerto Ricans may be employed in a range of underground jobs, there is no denying that the traffic in illegal drugs provides a necessary source of income for a number of Puerto Ricans, particularly those in communities that have suffered significant economic disinvestment and neglect.

The rise of an explosive informal drug economy in Puerto Rico is intimately tied to the failures of US-led development, which had serious consequences for how Puerto Ricans came to understand what it meant to live (and die) in Puerto Rico. As the façade of the Puerto Rican miracle came crumbling down, Puerto Ricans found themselves in desperate need of solutions to the economic and social crises that they felt now shaped everyday life. The informal drug economy emerged as one response, particularly for young people from economically and racially marginalized communities who were confronted with dwindling opportunities for social and economic advancement. Punitive solutions promoted and enacted by the state emerged as another response, one that promised middle- and upper-class Puerto Ricans, in particular, relief from the vulnerability and insecurity that the informal economy, in their view, had ushered into their lives.

While Puerto Rico did witness elevated rates of violent crime over the course of the 1980s and 1990s, the expansion of punitive measures and logics over this period cannot be solely understood as a reaction to increased crime and violence. Indeed, as evidenced in other contexts, including the United States and England, punitive attitudes and policies have often proliferated in moments when crime rates were relatively stable or decreasing.[26] The rise of punitive governance in Puerto Rico has been less about halting high levels of crime (whether real or imagined) than it has been about shoring up political, economic, and social relations of power during moments of intense flux and crisis.

When existing political economic structures are faltering or being called into question, political elites have strategically mobilized fears about crime and violence to increase their reach and consolidate power. Stuart Hall and his colleagues outlined this process in the foundational text *Policing the Crisis: Mugging, the State, and Law and Order*, in which they noted that when society seems to be "slipping into a certain kind of crisis," panic over crime and violence can "serve as the articulator of the crisis, as its ideological conductor."[27] Panic about crime allows for the existing social order, and the unequal power dynamics that it produces, to be stabilized or strengthened through the "slow build-up to a 'soft' law-and-order society."[28] Under the guise of public safety, political elites are able to promote repressive policies that would normally receive tremendous pushback from various sectors of society. The Puerto Rican state strengthened its security apparatus and promoted a punitive common sense that treated violent crime as the central problem confronting the archipelago in order to elide the role of colonial capitalism in producing the insecurity experienced by many Puerto Ricans.

Accepting the colonial lie of Puerto Rico's "nonviability," the Puerto Rican government did not challenge the model of continued incorporation within the United States. Rather, left with the ruins of a failed development model and few options to affect political and economic change, the Puerto Rican state turned to punitive governance to suture the ruptures of colonial capitalism. In particular, the state has turned its punitive apparatus against racially and economically marginalized Puerto Ricans, who are the most likely to suffer the effects of Puerto Rico's social and economic crises.

POLICING RACE, CLASS, AND SPACE

Under neoliberal and colonial capitalism, punitive governance functions to contain the effects of a social order that is marked by extreme racial and economic inequality. Literature on the intersections between neoliberal governance and carceral expansion has focused on the ways in which these regimes of accumulation and dispossession have intensified conditions of precarity, particularly for already marginalized subjects.[29] Puerto Rico is no exception to this trend. The rise and consolidation of punitive governance in Puerto Rico have reproduced hierarchies based on race, class, spatial location, gender, sexuality, and citizenship. In particular, the securitization of urban space and the proliferation of gated residential communities segregated along lines of race and class have resulted in the exposure of economically and racially marginalized communities to greater harm at the hands of the state and their fellow Puerto Ricans.[30]

Punitive governance as a response to crisis has not led to greater public safety for many Puerto Ricans. Rather, it has only created the illusion of safety at the expense of low-income and racially marginalized populations, who experience elevated levels of insecurity, discrimination, violence, and death in their communities, much as Giovanni Roberto suggested during our conversation. The ways in which punitive governance targets the most vulnerable populations in Puerto Rico are of central concern to this work. Throughout this book I detail how punitive governance functions through the reification of already existing hierarchies of value at work in the archipelago, which largely target those Puerto Ricans who find themselves at the margins. In particular, this book demonstrates the ways in which punitive governance plays a central role in producing and reinforcing discriminatory understandings of race, which associate Black and dark-skinned Puerto

Ricans with crime and subsequently expose them to greater levels of exclusion and harm.

Revealing how policing and other punitive technologies produce and reproduce race in Puerto Rico is a necessary task, as Puerto Rico is often imagined as a "racial democracy" free of the kinds of violence and animus associated with race relations in the United States.[31] Puerto Ricans have been taught to understand themselves as products of the harmonious mixture of indigenous Taínos, Africans, and Spaniards—a family tree nurtured by three roots. Cultural nationalist discourses maintain that the absence of racial strife is a direct result of this racial mixing and is something that marks a distinct Puerto Rican cultural identity. As a result, efforts to discuss race and racism in Puerto Rico are often dismissed as attempts to import US racial problems and apply US racial analytics to the Puerto Rican context. As historian Ileana Rodríguez-Silva notes, there is no more effective strategy to shut down conversations about historical and contemporary expressions of racialized marginalization than to "deem race, racialization, and racism as foreign matters, specifically as U.S. phenomena" or to question the speaker's "commitment and love to the Puerto Rican nation."[32]

Racial formation in Puerto Rico has been structured by the histories of plantation slavery, indigenous genocide, serial colonization, and capitalist exploitation, as well as the resistance to these practices. The specific manner in which these historical processes unfolded in Puerto Rico makes the archipelago's racial formation distinct from that of the United States, although we should understand white supremacy as something that connects Puerto Rico to the United States, as opposed to something that is simply exercised upon Puerto Ricans by the United States. White supremacy in Puerto Rico was formed through histories of Spanish and US colonization at the same time that it emerged as a way to resist US colonial efforts by emphasizing cultural difference. Although Puerto Ricans are positioned as a racially and culturally mixed people, Puerto Rican elites have consistently emphasized a white, Hispanic identity in order to create a unified Puerto Rican identity under colonization. As anthropologist Hilda Lloréns points out, in response to Americanization projects and continued US colonial rule, "the upper classes were invested in representing the Puerto Rican nation as white, but they claimed that Puerto Ricans inherited their whiteness from the 'Iberian race' as opposed to the 'Anglo-Saxon race' of the American colonizers."[33] Similarly, according to Carlos Alamo-Pastrana, "Both nationalists and annexationists use racial democracy as an anticolonial strategy from which Puerto Rican cultural and political formations are disentangled from those in the United States."[34] The result is an ideology of racial exceptionalism that positions the United States as the "sole arbiter of racial violence and exclusion" and Puerto Rico "as a racially tolerant society," "effectively disavow[ing] Puerto Rico's own history of legally (i.e., slavery) and socially (i.e., segregation) sanctioned racial exclusions."[35] Elite (and with time, popular) discourses therefore positioned whiteness as central to the elaboration of a respectable and distinct Puerto Rican cultural identity under US rule at the same time that discourses of racial mixing functioned to distance Puerto Rico from the US racial regime and silence discussions of anti-Black racism within Puerto Rican society more generally.

The twinned structures of colonization and white supremacy in Puerto Rico have resulted in a color-blind discourse of racial mixing, which obscures the way that Blackness is managed and sublimated in contemporary Puerto Rican society. Thus, while Black and dark-skinned Puerto Ricans are the populations who perhaps have the most frequent contact with the state's security apparatus, the policing they experience is often discussed and justified by law enforcement officials, as well as members of the public, in racially neutral ways. In other words, while Blackness is policed by state and nonstate actors operating in Puerto Rico, how exactly Blackness is policed can be difficult to explain given the adherence to color-blind, racist discourses and ideologies in the public sphere.[36] Analyzing how discourses of spatial location and class function as coded ways to invoke Blackness provides a means of documenting how policing produces and reproduces ideas about race and Blackness in Puerto Rico. In particular, we see that spaces that are supposedly race neutral but are commonly associated with economically marginalized Puerto Ricans have been constant targets of oppressive surveillance and policing.

If dominant discourses of racial mixing and racial harmony serve to bury explicit references to racism and its effects in Puerto Rico, an analysis of spatial inequalities, particularly as they cohere around class position, provides a means of excavation. As American studies scholar George Lipsitz asserts, "Race is produced by space," and "it takes places for racism to take place."[37] Pointing out how "seemingly race-neutral urban sites contain hidden racial assumptions and imperatives" about "who belongs where and about what makes certain spaces desirable," Lipsitz highlights how racial subordination is often achieved through the segregation and policing of space.[38] This is true in Puerto Rico, where ideas about space and how it intersects with levels of socioeconomic inclusion or exclusion have been central to the creation and expansion of racial meaning.

In Puerto Rico, Blackness has long been tethered to particular spaces while rendered invisible or "out of place" in others. For instance, coastal regions are often understood as spaces of Blackness, due to their role in Puerto Rico's plantation economy under both Spanish and US rule, while the big island's rural interior has been figured as isolated and whiter and thus more authentically representative of Puerto Rican culture and identity. While there is a racialized dichotomy between Puerto Rico's rural interior and its coastal regions, racial difference becomes further delineated within localized contexts. For instance, according to cultural anthropologist Arlene Torres, the opposition between *caseríos* (public housing complexes) and *arrabales* (very poor neighborhoods and informal settlements) on the one hand, and *urbanizaciones* (suburban-style developments) on the other hand, has become a key way of understanding and making sense of race in contemporary Puerto Rico.[39] Torres explains that despite the wide range of phenotypical variation found in these residential areas, urbanizaciones are understood as white spaces, while public housing and other low-income communities are considered Black spaces.[40] In other words, Puerto Ricans are racialized through their association with particular classed residential spaces. Racialized associations with space are so powerful that they can sometimes override the racial self-identification or the perceived phenotypical difference of people who inhabit particular spaces. In this sense, in the Puerto Rican spatial imaginary, money, and the access that it buys, whitens, while its absence blackens. Spatial location and class position, and the way they intersect, are thus essential for understanding the way that many Puerto Ricans understand and discuss race without making explicit reference to it.

As Blackness is considered spatially bounded within certain low-income and urban locations suffering the effects of structural discrimination, those boundaries and the people within them are subjected to intense conditions of formal and informal policing in an effort to keep the "social ills" they encounter from spreading. According to Black studies scholar Petra R. Rivera-Rideau, the "emplacement" of Blackness within low-income urban areas grappling with structural inequality and disinvestment serves to "perpetuate common stereotypes of blackness, such as violence and hypersexuality."[41] Speaking about mano dura contra el crimen's incursions into public housing, or *caseríos*, Rivera-Rideau notes, "Mano Dura thus depicted caseríos as sites of abjection, the loci of urban blackness defined by various 'immoral' characteristics that differentiated them from the presumably more 'respectable' Puerto Rico, all while ignoring the larger structural policies that produced the adverse conditions affecting caseríos residents."[42] For anthropologist Isar Godreau, the emplacement of Blackness functions to circumscribe Black people and Afro-Puerto Rican culture to very specific places, which problematically "conveys the sense that blackness is different or exceptional from the context of the larger 'mixed nation'" and implicitly marks the broader national context as not Black.[43] Punitive power is deployed by state and nonstate actors, then, to contain the racialized and classed dangers of public housing while reifying spaces understood as white as worthy of protection from the state.

Policing and other punitive technologies have functioned as a way of reaffirming and reproducing racial ideologies in Puerto Rico under the guise of public safety. At the same time, punitive policing also functions to contain the negative effects of failed development. It first manages the populations most likely to be affected: those who, because of systemic discrimination, are already vulnerable to economic contraction. Second, punitive policing positions racially and economically marginalized populations as the key generators of societal insecurity due to the supposedly pathological and deficient culture bred in spaces like public housing. Examining how punitive governance targets particular spaces associated with Black and low-income Puerto Ricans allows us to understand not only how policing reifies racial inequality but also how the supposedly race-neutral policing of space functions to occlude the ways in which policing is complicit in, and in fact central to, racial discrimination and violence.

POLICING AS STRUCTURE

Often when I discuss my research, one of the first questions I get during question-and-answer sessions is: Who are the police? Members of the public and my academic colleagues want to know about the composition of the PRPD, I suspect, in an attempt to make sense of officers' inclination toward using violence against some of Puerto Rico's most vulnerable people. There is a desire to mark them as somehow different and distinct from the Puerto Ricans they police. For the most part, however, the police in Puerto Rico are similar to the populations they police. They are a racially diverse group of men and women who tend to be individuals of modest economic means, for whom joining the police force is a path toward economic stability. As policing increasingly became positioned as the solution to a wide range of social crises, the ranks of the police force swelled. Currently, the PRPD is comprised of approximately thirteen thousand officers and is one of the largest departments under US jurisdiction.[44] For thousands of middle- and low-income Puerto Ricans trying to envision a future for themselves while the archipelago is awash in economic uncertainty, the police force represents a stable and dignified career.

While there is much to be said about why joining the police, much like joining the military, is seen as one of the few paths toward upward mobility and economic stability in contemporary Puerto Rico, that is not the focus of this book. This book is less about the police as individual and collective actors and more about how policing functions as a structure that shapes various aspects of Puerto Rican society and impacts a range of social institutions and relationships, as well as the norms that often undergird them. By understanding policing as a structure as opposed to simply the work of individuals, we move away from seeing police violence as the actions of aberrant individuals within the police force—"a few bad apples"—to instead focus on how violence is inherent to police work and the colonial, capitalist, gendered, and racial order that it reproduces and maintains. As David Correia and Tyler Wall succinctly point out, "Capitalism and colonialism cannot exist without a state willing and able to defend colonial domination, private property, the wage relation, and the ongoing patterns of dispossession that characterize all of these. Ain't no colonialism and ain't no capitalism without cops."[45]

What makes the police different from ordinary citizens is that they are tasked with using force to maintain political order and the smooth functioning of capital.[46] We must understand violence as central to the functioning of state power and the police as "violence workers" empowered to use their discretion to exact state-sanctioned violence on individuals and populations deemed threatening or noncompliant.[47] As historian Sam Mitrani notes, professional police forces were created during the mid- and late nineteenth century to "use violence to reconcile democratic politics with the deeply exploitative industrial capitalist order that developed in late-nineteenth-century cities."[48] Although the police officers who populated these newly created forces often came from the working class and were "poorly paid and expected to work long, dangerous hours, like other workers," police were not "ordinary workers."[49] Rather, police officers were expected to maintain order among the working class and encouraged to use force when necessary in order to do so, creating a deep divide between the police and the working class.[50] Mitrani's description of the composition and function of the police remains relevant today. Attempts to divorce the police from the key role they play in perpetuating economic exploitation and class hierarchies, solely because individual offers are enmeshed within a capitalist (or colonial) social order, ignores how policing functions as a structure that protects and promotes processes of capital accumulation and racial differentiation.

In the context of the United States, Puerto Rico, and other societies founded on slavery and settler colonialism, native and other racially oppressed populations are criminalized in order to maintain a set of unequal power relations based on the theft of land and labor. According to historian Nikhil Singh, the history and function of policing within slaveholding and settler societies demand that policing be understood as an institution of whiteness that upholds white supremacist racial hierarchy and unequal property relations.[51] The whiteness of the police and the criminalization of Blackness are not strictly reducible to specific white people or Black people. Rather, these racial forms emerge as subject positions within racial capitalism.[52] The multiracial composition of a police force, in this case the PRPD, does not make the police as an institution any less racist or deadly; it merely demonstrates how "racial orders must be institutionalized, that is, managed by personnel who are recruited, invested in, and subjectively constituted for this purpose."[53] Thus the police, regardless of the racial makeup of a given police force, function as a race-making institution that upholds white supremacy while criminalizing racial and ethnic others who fall outside of the normative bounds of full citizenship.

This book is not interested in the individual race and class positions of the officers who serve in the PRPD or the justifications they provide for what they do. Instead, *Policing Life and Death* is chiefly concerned with how policing creates, maintains, and reinforces deeply exclusionary structures within contemporary Puerto Rican society. As a result, I prioritize accounts that detail the impact and outcomes of policing as experienced by those populations exposed to the harms of police violence, rather than the intentions of police officials. Following legal scholar Dean Spade's reminder that we should be wary of the stories that the law and its agents of enforcement tell us about themselves, in this book I amplify the voices of those Puerto Ricans who are often silenced in official narratives: the policed.[54] When we listen to, and indeed privilege, the voices of those who bear the brunt of punitive governance—those Puerto Ricans who have been rendered criminal and exposed to state intervention—we are able to better grasp what effects the state actually has on people's lives as opposed to what it says it does.

For this reason, this book centers interviews with activists, participant observation of protests, and informal conversations with a range of Puerto Ricans about how they understand policing, as well as the narratives marginalized and criminalized Puerto Ricans use to represent themselves in news outlets, expressive culture, and social media. Treating policing as a structural force challenges the individual and collective statements emanating from the police force, which seek to justify the various forms of harm and inequality that policing maintains, and focuses instead on the work that policing actually does in contemporary Puerto Rican society.

ARCHIVING POLICING

In order to chart the rise of punitive governance in contemporary Puerto Rico, *Policing Life and Death* deploys a radically transdisciplinary approach that is attentive to how Puerto Ricans enact and negotiate relations of power and hierarchies of difference in the context of ongoing crisis. Committed to an "exceedingly, rudely feral transdisciplinarity," to borrow from queer theorist Mel Y. Chen, this book brings together insights and approaches from the fields of American studies, Latinx studies, Black studies, carceral studies, feminist studies, queer studies, and critical ethnic studies, blurring the boundaries among them through a focus on race, resistance, and punitive power in contemporary Puerto Rico.[55] As a result, I turn to a range of sometimes incongruous sources to document punitive governance and its effects on how people live and die in the archipelago. I draw, for instance, from external investigations and evaluations of the Puerto Rican police department, internal police memos, federal and local governmental records, court documents, political speeches, US and Puerto Rican press accounts, demographic data, informal conversations, participant observation, interviews, song lyrics, and social media, among other sources, throughout this book.

I pay particular attention to media accounts and expressive cultural texts in order to construct a narrative of how mano dura contra el crimen unfolded as well as how it was experienced and continues to be understood by a range of Puerto Ricans. I recognize that mainstream media coverage related to issues of race, crime, and social protests is somewhat flawed and incomplete. As historian Donna Murch has noted, reliance on press accounts for data can be "particularly troublesome because, as anyone who writes about crime knows, 'what bleeds leads.'"[56] She adds that "newspapers have a vested interest in reporting sensationalized crime stories, and the press has often been a central instigator of moral panics."[57] Although I agree with Murch that the main-stream press does not supply its readers with unbiased accounts when it comes to crime reporting, I still find press accounts to be important sources for track-ing carceral growth and the expansion of punitive solutions to social crisis in contemporary Puerto Rico. In particular, media accounts provide crucial insights into how racialized panic over crime is constructed and spreads in ways that allow it to infiltrate the social and political common sense.

In this book I also look to mainstream and alternative press accounts for the voices of the policed and to glean information about how they under-stand the impact of punitive power in their lives. While remaining attentive to the literal and implied messages present in mainstream media accounts, I employ what Stuart Hall has called "an oppositional code" to read (or decode) these sources for alternative messages from below.[58] In many ways, the Puerto Rican state utilized the media to "send a message" about its stance on crime to "the law-abiding public" and instill fear among criminalized populations about the kinds of violence in store for them. I look at press coverage in order to understand not only how the state framed its punitive actions but also how those who experienced them spoke back to the state and tried to share their experiences with other members of the Puerto Rican public. Newspaper, television, and radio reports performed a mediating role between the state and the public, becoming a key venue for how they addressed and responded to each other, as well as a key venue for how Puerto Ricans communicated with each other across an increasingly fortified and segregated landscape. This book analyzes mainstream and alternative media accounts, alongside social media and popular culture, for what they reveal about how policed populations articulate their experience of the punitive logics of the state.

My focus on media and expressive culture also arose in response to the difficulties I encountered while conducting my research due to the incredibly secretive nature of the police force and my position as an outsider. As legal scholar Paul Chevigny and anthropologist Didier Fassin have both noted, it is extremely difficult to conduct research on the police because of their desire to contain public criticism, especially as police forces around the globe engage in increasingly militaristic and abusive strategies of social control in margin-alized communities.[59] For me, the inaccessibility of the police was com-pounded by my own outsider status as a queer, gender-nonconforming woman *de afuera* (literally from the outside, referring to diaspora/US), who spoke a kind of Spanish that could only be generously described as *matao* (murdered). The situation within the police force and my own embodiment indelibly shaped the access to information I had while conducting the research for this book.

I began the research for this book in 2011, just a short while before the DOJ's damning report on the widespread corruption and abusive behavior of the PRPD. The release of the report put the PRPD under a very public microscope and prompted an "information lockdown" in order to contain damage to the force's reputation. While I had expected resistance from government and law enforcement officials, the report essentially dead-bolted the few doors that might have been open to me. The wall of silence that I confronted forced me to decenter official law enforcement narratives in this book, ultimately, I believe, for the better. I built an alternative archive of policing in Puerto Rico filled with sources that document how people experience punitive measures in their everyday lives; how policing works through cultural ideologies and social inequalities; and how Puerto Ricans internalize, negotiate, or reject the forms of safety and justice promoted by punitive policing. This capacious approach was not about getting at the "real story" about policing in Puerto Rico, but rather about uncovering the ways punitive governance makes itself felt in the everyday lives of those Puerto Ricans subjected to its violence.

WHAT COMES NEXT

Policing Life and Death: Race, Violence, and Resistance in Puerto Rico is organized chronologically and moves through a series of flashpoints to detail the state's implementation of punitive measures and show how Puerto Ricans have experienced, negotiated, and resisted policing as a solution to crisis. The first three chapters follow the emergence and consolidation of mano dura contra el crimen over the course of the 1990s. The remaining chapters trace the afterlife of mano dura, from how its practices and logics have become further entrenched and normalized to how activists and everyday citizens are pushing for new understandings of justice and safety.

Chapter 1 argues that rather than salvation for communities in peril, mano dura promoted an uneven distribution of risk, harm, and death by tacitly allowing the proliferation of violence within and against economically and racially marginalized communities. The second chapter details attempts by political elites and technocrats to position Puerto Rico as a model for the policing and privatization of American public housing. While the international press and policy circles celebrated Puerto Rico as exemplary, public housing residents worked to expose the violence that drove this "experiment" in public housing reform. The third chapter analyzes the policing of young people, primarily through racialized categories of style and music associated with underground rap. Underground rap came under increased public scrutiny during the mid-1990s, and practitioners and fans became police targets due to the genre's association with public housing. Underground rappers and fans pushed back against the racist and classist logics of mano dura and used music to critique racial profiling and the war on drugs.

Mano dura contra el crimen was promoted as "modern" and "community-oriented" policing, despite abundant evidence that its direct impact on the crime rate was minor and that it actually caused serious upheaval in vulnerable communities. Although mano dura did not officially continue after Rosselló left the governor's mansion, it became the blueprint for what policing meant and looked like in contemporary Puerto Rico. Chapter 4 examines how the policing and crime reduction measures that followed mano dura during the 2000s reinforced a central assumption of punitive policing, namely that poor and working-class people were the key generators of violence and crime and that their communities needed constant surveillance and intervention. This continued reliance on the strategies associated with mano dura occurred despite a rhetorical shift that sought to mark an explicit break with it and its patterns of discriminatory policing.

Starting with the fifth chapter, the book pivots to critically examine the ways in which Puerto Ricans are dealing with the effects of over two decades of punitive policy in their communities and the kinds of alternative futures they envision. Chapter 5 examines how the state violence that student protesters experienced during the 2010–2011 strikes at the UPR drew from strategies of containment solidified, in part, through the policing of racially and economically marginalized populations during the mano dura era. While criminalization formed a powerful basis for solidarity between students at Puerto Rico's premier academic institution and residents of low-income communities often excluded from it, there were also moments when students reinforced logics of racialized criminalization promoted by the state. This chapter underscores the complex legacies left by mano dura that activists are forced to negotiate in their efforts to transform Puerto Rican society.

In the sixth chapter I show how activists in the diaspora and the archipelago are using social media to reshape understandings about the relationship between violence and human value. In particular, I discuss how activists have taken to social media sites like Twitter, Facebook, and Instagram to challenge the idea that violence and death are acceptable punishments for social transgression or involvement in illicit economies. The final chapter focuses on Taller Sauld, a feminist public health organization in the town of Loíza that worked toward violence reduction and prevention through its program Acuerdo de Paz, which identified and intervened in conflicts with the potential to end in violence and worked with community members to transform social norms around gender and the use of violence as a solution to conflict. I position Acuerdo de Paz as a salient example of a growing movement in Puerto Rico that is working to create alternative visions of justice that do not rely on punitive governance and the intensification of conditions of vulnerability for already marginalized communities.

I conclude with a postscript reflecting on how Puerto Rico's so-called debt crisis and the devastating effects of Hurricane María have intersected with and amplified the deadly effects of punitive governance in the lives of Puerto Rico's most vulnerable populations. I use this space to highlight how activists are working to create strong, self-sufficient communities based on principles of solidarity in order to counteract a colonial capitalist regime that encourages little beyond exploitation, punishment, and harm in the lives of so many Puerto Ricans.

Policing Life and Death: Race, Violence, and Resistance in Puerto Rico shows how the Puerto Rican state has turned to punitive governance in response to transformations in the colonial reality of the archipelago. Tracing the growth of punitive governance in Puerto Rico provides an alternative means of charting transformations in the relationship between Puerto Rico and the United States, as well as its effects on Puerto Ricans in their everyday lives. Together, the various chapters of this book show how punitive modes of governance have emerged as the central way that many Puerto Ricans encounter the state. These pages weave together stories about how Puerto Ricans understand the role of the state and moments when the state is complicit in their deaths. Refusing to accept the tenuous safety promised by state violence against Puerto Rico's most vulnerable, more and more Puerto Ricans are contesting punitive governance and working toward a future grounded in justice and freedom.

ONE

—————

A War against the Victims

DURING THE SPRING OF 1994 a controversial, state-sponsored television advertisement appeared, in which Puerto Ricans saw footage of the "war" taking place around the archipelago. The advertisement, originally intended for internal use as a motivational video for the police department, showed officers storming public housing complexes, arresting residents, and standing over young people as they lay spread-eagled with their faces to the ground. The two-minute television spot was set to the sound track of Carl Orff's haunting *Carmina Burana*, a selection that made clear the extent to which Puerto Rico's war on drugs had become a horror show for some public housing residents. The ad featured a series of statistics meant to showcase the achievements of the government's anticrime plan, mano dura contra el crimen, one year after its implementation. For instance, viewers were told that car thefts, burglaries, robberies, and sexual assaults all decreased in 1993 following the introduction of the new crime plan. Coupled with these statistics were rapid-fire shots of police running into public housing complexes, scaling the sides of buildings, jumping off the backs of Humvees, getting into helicopters, and even riding horses—almost always with weapons drawn—all in search of illegal drugs and weapons. As the music frantically built, the viewer was meant to get a sense that these men (and a few women) in uniform were all that was keeping "ordinary" and "decent" citizens safe from the constant threat posed by those within Puerto Rico's public housing complexes who wished to do them harm.

Soon after it aired, the advertisement drew criticism for its glorification of militarized force and its negative depiction of public housing residents.[1] Asked to account for the advertisement, police superintendent Pedro Toledo admitted that the video, which was part of a costly publicity campaign by the

PRPD totaling more than $700,000, was a little over the top, but claimed it was ultimately necessary to convey the reality of the war on crime the police were fighting.[2] Toledo remarked, "All we were trying to do was show the people of Puerto Rico that we are fighting crime on the front lines wherever we find it. We're not picking on just the people in the housing projects."[3] Alberto Goachet, director of the Government Communications Office, defended the advertisement by encouraging the public to think of Puerto Rico as a patient diagnosed with cancer. According to Goachet, the patient needed an immediate surgical intervention to remove the tumor and stop its malignancy from spreading to the rest of the body.[4] Such responses from state officials failed to curtail growing criticism of the advertisement, and in the case of Goachet's statements, likely added fuel to the fire. The advertisement was pulled after a limited run and replaced by another, which featured doves sitting on the newly constructed perimeter fence of an occupied public housing complex, with Beethoven's *Ode to Joy* playing in the background.[5]

Both the advertisement and its defense by state officials illuminate much about the logics and practice of mano dura contra el crimen. First, the remarks made by Superintendent Toledo aimed to inoculate law enforcement officials against claims of race and class animus in their targeting of public housing residents. In a rhetorical move common to color-blind justifications for discriminatory policing, Toledo argued that the police were simply doing their jobs, going where the crime was.[6] His comments naturalized the idea that spaces of concentrated poverty and those associated with Blackness, such as public housing, are also spaces of crime and violence. Toledo's comments justified police intervention in racially and economically marginalized areas while obscuring the structural forces that account for violence and criminalized activities in those areas. In a sense, then, the reduction of drug use and violence was made synonymous with intervention in low-income and racially marginalized communities. His comments justified the use of violence and force against poor people and Black and brown people, treating this violence as merely the reality of police work and crime fighting, not some petty form of "picking on people."

Second, Goachet's metaphor of disease also reveals the extent to which logics of dehumanization, contagion, and elimination undergirded law enforcement efforts and predetermined deadly outcomes for some of Puerto Rico's most vulnerable. Goachet's comments, echoing Toledo, located the problem of drugs and violence squarely within public housing, a cancerous site within the national body. In this formulation, the function of policing was largely reduced to containing and eliminating the threat emanating from public housing and other racially and economically marginalized communities. The fact that those threats were not abstract problems, but rather living, breathing people, was seldom mentioned or recognized. Public housing residents were figured not as people struggling to deal with the deleterious effects of state disinvestment and a violently competitive, drug-based, informal economy in their community, but rather as vectors of harm that had to be eliminated in order to protect everyone else.

Rather than providing safety, punitive policing has in many ways deepened existing societal inequalities and further limited life chances in Puerto Rico's racially and economically marginalized communities. Further, it has often done so in a way that has reproduced and reinvigorated social hierarchies of value and belonging in the name of public safety. This chapter traces the implementation of mano dura contra el crimen to show how punitive policing has rendered racially and economically marginalized populations vulnerable to harm and premature death through logics and practices of dehumanization and criminalization.[7] Mano dura promoted an uneven distribution of risk, harm, and death not only by creating situations that fostered an environment of police brutality, but also by tacitly allowing the proliferation of violence within and against economically and racially marginalized communities. While law enforcement agents enacted violence against public housing and *barrio* residents as part of mano dura contra el crimen, police and other state officials also positioned the alarmingly high levels of drug-related violence and death occurring within the confines of these classed and racialized spaces as a necessary by-product of Puerto Rico's "war on drugs." In this way, police intervention–both those initiatives hailed as "successful" in protecting *el pueblo puertorriqueño* (the Puerto Rican people) and those moments when police deliberately "failed" to prevent violence related to the informal drug economy—resulted in greater exposure to harm and death for low-income and racially marginalized populations.

STATES OF ABANDONMENT

The anticrime logics, measures, and rhetoric associated with mano dura arose during a moment of intense insecurity. By the late 1980s Puerto Rico was described in the local press as a nation besieged by crime. Fear of carjackings, armed robbery, and stray bullets from drug-related shootouts punctuated everyday conversations, and news of bloody "massacres" over *puntos* (drug points) dominated the headlines.[8] This sense of encroaching crime was in some ways exacerbated by the mixed-income layout of Puerto Rico's built environment, particularly in large urban centers like San Juan and the southern coastal city of Ponce.

Luis Muñoz Marín, who served from 1949 to 1965 as Puerto Rico's first democratically elected governor, emphasized the need for mixed-income housing and neighborhoods during the height of industrialization and urbanization efforts. Muñoz Marín believed that if the poor and working classes were placed in close proximity to the middle and upper classes, the latter's supposedly strong work ethic and morals would help to lift their fellow Puerto Ricans out of poverty.[9] His impact on the built environment not only resulted in drastic socioeconomic differences within close spatial proximity, but also reinforced the idea that low-income people were culturally deficient and in need of moral reform. As ethnic studies scholar José I. Fusté notes, through such social and spatial engineering, "the Puerto Rican state has literally cemented the discursive rendering of economically dispossessed Puerto Ricans as incorrigibly 'disordered.'"[10] This spatial engineering positioned low-income Puerto Ricans, and particularly public housing residents, as social burdens in need of constant surveillance and intervention on the part of both the state and their fellow citizens. Further, as sociologist Zaire Dinzey-Flores notes, "Plans to remove the stigma of public housing by placing it next to neighborhoods of the middle and upper classes backfired by angering those in private housing who feared the stigma would simply spread to them."[11] While the state sought to increase cross-class spatial proximity in the hopes of turning low-income Puerto Ricans into ideal urban citizens, the middle and upper classes looked toward privatized solutions to maintain social hierarchies of difference and prevent the downward mobility and moral deterioration they associated with integration. As the informal drug economy expanded over the course of the 1980s, leading to rising rates of crime and violence, securitization and crime prevention became sites for the reification of racialized and classed difference articulated through space.

Although the violence associated with the booming informal drug economy was most acutely felt in low-income and predominantly Black areas, there nonetheless existed a prevailing sense that crime was "out of control" and that everyone was at risk. The presumed involvement of low-income Puerto Ricans with the criminalized activities that comprised the informal economy led the upper and middle classes to hold the urban poor largely responsible for rising rates of crime. At the same time, affluent Puerto Ricans were growing increasingly dissatisfied with the state's public security efforts, which they felt left them vulnerable to the violence occurring in adjacent low-income communities. With legislative support, middle-class and wealthy Puerto Ricans turned to private security firms to fortify their homes and keep potential threats at bay.

On May 20, 1987, the Puerto Rican legislature approved Law 21, known as the Controlled Access Law, which allowed municipalities to grant permits to residential communities to restrict pedestrian and vehicular traffic. These permits allowed for the construction of gates and controlled access points that would monitor entry and exit as a crime control measure. Civilians were encouraged to collude with law enforcement to police their fellow Puerto Ricans, as fortified enclaves proliferated in an attempt to identify, screen, and exclude those perceived as dangerous and undesirable. According to anthropologist Ivelisse Rivera-Bonilla, between 1987 and 1997 more than one hundred middle- and upper-middle-class San Juan neighborhoods totally or partially restricted street access through the construction of gates and controlled access checkpoints.[12] Such changes followed apace in other cities and towns as the fear of crime and violence spread throughout the archipelago. Gates and guards, alongside police interventions in low-income areas, would become central to mano dura's strategy of containment and isolation of the urban poor as a means of combating crime.[13]

Contributing to the general sense of an uncontrollable crime wave was a perception of diminished state capacity. As historian Fernando Picó notes, "Nothing better symbolizes the lack of trust in the instruments of the state than the closed urbanizations."[14] Indeed, the state's encouragement of controlled access enclosures and other privatized security measures as a way to reduce crime indicated to many Puerto Ricans that they could not and should not depend on the state for protection. According to a poll conducted in 1991 by the local daily newspaper *El Nuevo Día*, approximately 63 percent of Puerto Ricans had no confidence in the police's ability to protect them.[15] A series of high-profile attacks on police stations that same year helped to strengthen the public's perception of a weak state security apparatus. Drug dealers operating out of Las Acacias, a public housing complex across the street from San Juan's Puerta de Tierra police station, blasted the exterior of the station house with high-powered assault rifles for three consecutive days, leaving the edifice riddled with bullet holes and the police terrified. Police officials responded by putting steel barriers on the windows and minimizing work in open areas to avoid being shot at.[16]

The PRPD's own turn to enclosure in the face of drug-related violence reinforced the general public sentiment that the police were completely ill-equipped to deal with the crime problem posed by the drug trade. The Puerto Rican ska band Los Pies Negros expertly described this moment in the song "Niño de sangre azul" (1992):

Niño de sangre azul	Blue-blooded boy
del que todo el mundo habla,	that the whole world's talking about,
ya nadie cree en él.	nobody believes in him anymore.
Porque a la gente no respalda?	Why don't people support you?
¿Dónde está ese niño	Where is that boy
que nos estás haciendo mucha falta?	that we're really missing?
La criminalidad social	Social crime
cada día es más alta.	every day is worse.
¿Niño de sangre azul	Blue-blooded boy
dónde estás metido?	where are you hiding?
Quieren asesinarte.	They want to kill you.
Pegarte un tiro,	To shoot you,
pegarte un tiro.	to shoot you.

As captured by Los Pies Negros, a sector of the Puerto Rican public was under the impression not only that the police had retreated in the face of the drug gangs, but that they were in hiding at precisely the moment when crime seemed at its worst.

On June 6, 1991, in the wake of escalating skepticism about police performance, 230 officers raided Las Acacias, arresting suspected drug dealers and confiscating drugs and weapons. This show of force was an attempt to show the public that, in the words of police superintendent Ismael Betancourt Lebrón, "no place in Puerto Rico is exempt from police presence."[17] After this spectacle, however, snipers continued to taunt police by firing upon squad cars and station houses. This targeting of police officers and property by drug dealers gave rise to an epidemic of the "blue flu," in which scores of demoralized officers called in sick or simply failed to report for work. In November 1991 police once again raided Las Acacias, but this time they did not withdraw. Following this operation, the police established a permanent minicuartel (mini police station) to house officers who would patrol and surveil the complex twenty-four hours a day. Based on the blueprint of Las Acacias, on February 26, 1992, police stormed Nemesio Canales in the Hato Rey section of San Juan, which boasted a drive-through, open-air drug market within yards of police headquarters. As in the operation in Las Acacias, police followed the operation in Canales by establishing a minicuartel, installing an access checkpoint at the main entrance, and building a perimeter gate around the complex. This was the start of a full frontal, and escalating, assault on public housing that would become a central component of mano dura contra el crimen.

That the police would respond in this way was not a foregone conclusion but had much to do with the perceived illegitimacy of the state during this time, as well as growing demands from various sectors of Puerto Rican society that the state do *something* to reduce the violence threatening to engulf the archipelago. On one level, the sniper attacks on police stations in the San Juan area revealed the weakness of the Puerto Rican state at this moment through a literal attack on state representatives. At the same time, the sniper attacks illuminated the extent to which the government had abandoned many low-income communities, allowing a parallel economic and political structure to take root and thrive. The puntos evidenced a perverse inversion of state capacity at the time. In contrast to the withering state that many Puerto Ricans encountered both directly and indirectly in their daily lives, the puntos commanded authority and displayed a keen ability to generate capital and employment—traits that could no longer be said to characterize the commonwealth government following the collapse of Operation Bootstrap (discussed in the introduction). *Bichotes*, a Spanglish play on "big shots," referring to drug kingpins, stepped in where the government fell short by providing jobs, clothing, medicine, food, and entertainment to public housing residents in exchange for complicity and silence. Against this backdrop, the police raids functioned to conjure forth an image of a strong state, manifested through its security apparatus, capable of managing the social problems arising largely from the political constriction and economic contraction of the commonwealth government. Failing to meet the economic and social needs of many Puerto Ricans, particularly low-income families and individuals, the state reasserted itself in the lives of these citizens through punitive interventions and shows of force. Puerto Rico, in this respect, echoed similar transformations in governance occurring around the globe as states attempted to respond to the effects of global economic restructuring by greatly reducing social service expenditures and increasing punitive power.

The displays of police power witnessed in Las Acacias and Canales, and those that would follow in dozens of public housing complexes as part of mano dura, served a strategic function at a moment when the capacity and power of the Puerto Rican state were greatly reduced as a result of neoliberal restructuring and continued colonization. The raids were an attempt to strengthen the legitimacy of the Puerto Rican state in the eyes of citizens despite the fact that political and economic power remained severely limited, especially after the failure of Operation Bootstrap. Political elites utilized and appealed to populist impulses to justify the relegitimization of the state during this moment of crisis. The police operations in public housing were framed as necessary to save the decent, hard-working people of Puerto Rico, especially those trapped in public housing and terrorized by the scourge of drugs and gang violence. Policy makers mobilized public housing residents' demands for the state to help put an end to the unchecked violence generated by the puntos in order to justify anticrime measures that further isolated and criminalized those residents and did little to improve conditions of safety where they lived.

Governor Rafael Hernández Colón and members of his administration pointed to stories of elderly people scared to leave their apartments, whole families who had to sleep on the floor in order to avoid the stray bullets that came in through their windows at night, and children who could not play outside because their parents feared that they would become collateral damage in the drug wars. Indeed, this was the reality for a number of families and individuals living in public housing and other low-income communities during the late 1980s and early 1990s. What was left out of this narrative, however, was the extent to which the government itself had created the conditions for such violence by eliminating many of its social and economic responsibilities to its most vulnerable citizens. Government neglect and the segregation of racialized, low-income communities played a significant role in generating the conditions of economic instability and socio-spatial isolation that allowed the violence of the puntos to flourish.

While public housing residents were demanding that the state help them to create safer living conditions, public officials and other political elites determined that assistance should come primarily in the form of policing. As African American studies scholar Keeanga-Yamahtta Taylor notes in the context of urban Black communities on the mainland United States, "Politicians were quick to manipulate crime numbers that showed the disproportionate burden of Black communities as an excuse to expand the powers and reach of the policing state; they did so using public funds that were needed to develop the kinds of public institutions and civil infrastructure that could mitigate poverty and criminal activity."[18] Similarly, historian

Elizabeth Hinton points out that in the wake of dramatic cuts to the American welfare state during the 1980s, the police emerged as one of the few, and in some cases the only, state agencies the urban poor could call upon for help with issues of violence and drug use in their communities. As Hinton puts it, "For those neighborhoods lacking comprehensive rehabilitative or social welfare programs, when law enforcement and criminal justice institutions became the last public agencies standing, the police were the service that could be summoned when help was needed."[19]

In a context of profound discrimination, disinvestment, and underresourcing, people living in racially and economically marginalized areas realized that greater police presence was the only assistance they were likely to receive from the state and asked the state to send police to protect them. Still, it is important to remember that police presence is not an equivalent "service" to the resources that they may have *desired* to access in order to reduce crime and violence in their communities. In addition, requests from residents of low-income housing and racially marginalized communities for greater law enforcement presence and government intervention should not draw attention away from the fact that structural forces and deliberate policy decisions created the conditions that made punitive policing seem like the only reasonable response to a complex range of social problems affecting Puerto Ricans.

Following a bloody shoot-out at the Puerta de Tierra public housing complex that left five residents dead and six wounded on October 14, 1992, the front page of the *San Juan Star* the next day carried a headline that screamed, "Please help us, we are not garbage." The headline quoted a resident imploring the governor to take action. While then governor Rafael Hernández Colón, and later Pedro Rosselló and his administration, would point to cries like this as a justification for the extraordinary measures needed to "rescue" public housing residents, these cries, more than anything else, demonstrate the inefficacy of the Puerto Rican state and the degree to which many low-income communities had been left on their own to deal with the devastating effects of an increasingly violent informal drug economy. Public housing residents, in the eyes of many Puerto Ricans, had come to embody human refuse: potentially contaminating, but ultimately superfluous and disposable. Within this context, the shouts that "we are not garbage" were not calls to further segregate public housing residents by enclosing them with gates and constant police surveillance, but rather an attempt to highlight the ways in which discrimination and abandonment—*the act of discarding humans like garbage*—had dramatically heightened poor people's exposure to harm relative to the rest of the population.

Following and expanding on these precedents set by Hernández Colón and his administration, Pedro Rosselló launched mano dura contra el crimen in 1993. With mano dura, Rosselló and his administration deployed a similarly populist discourse about the security of the population—often configured as *la gente trabajadora y decente*, or the hard-working and decent people of Puerto Rico—in order to marshal support for measures that would further segregate low-income and racially marginalized populations and expose them to even greater levels of violence, particularly state violence, in the name of saving them.

WE WANTED TO SEND A MESSAGE

Growing public concern over violence and crime reached a crescendo at the close of 1991, when Puerto Rico experienced record numbers of robberies, carjackings, assaults, and murders. In the 1992 gubernatorial race, Pedro Rosselló, a former pediatric surgeon, ran on a promise to wield a "mano dura" against crime. Rosselló pledged to institute a series of legal reforms and new law enforcement policies, including allocating more funds to the police department and doubling the size of the force, limiting the constitutional right to bail, federalizing crimes involving a firearm (thereby making them eligible for the federal death penalty), and even activating the Puerto Rican National Guard to help combat the crime wave assailing the archipelago.[20] Rosselló seized upon the "talk of crime" that was circulating among citizens and in the popular media in order to cement his position as a law-and-order candidate.[21]

Rosselló justified his hard-line approach by positioning violent crime as infiltrating all aspects of daily life and touching every family. He declared, "We live in a Puerto Rico where every day more Puerto Ricans are killed, and where even in our own homes our families are not safe. In essence, we are living in a crisis, an emergency. Faced with this crisis we must act firmly, with extraordinary measures."[22] Rosselló's rhetoric redefined daily life in Puerto Rico as marked by victimization or potential victimization at the hands of violent criminals. His rhetorical reconceptualization of the citizen as a victim of crime not only redefined the legal process and the appropriate conditions for government intervention, but also created consensus by appealing to existing hierarchies of value regarding who is deserving of state protection versus state intervention.[23]

Although Rosselló's discourse was decidedly race and class neutral, he appealed to the fears and concerns of many white and economically well-off Puerto Ricans who understood themselves as under attack from *ese gente*— *those people* living in public housing or other low-income communities, who endlessly preyed upon "decent and hardworking people." As Stuart Hall and his colleagues note in reference to the moral panic that erupted over mugging in 1970s London, "The image of the 'mugger' erupting out of the urban dark in a violent and wholly unexpected attack or penetrating right into apartment blocks became, in many ways, the precipitate for what were in fact much larger fears and anxieties about the racial issue in general."[24] We see a similar phenomenon in Puerto Rico during the late twentieth century as crime served as an aggregate for a whole host of economic, racial, and social issues and conflicts. Political elites centralized the experiences and interpretations of white, more affluent Puerto Ricans regarding the problem of crime and imposed solutions that deepened the exploitative and exclusionary social structures that most profoundly affected racially and economically marginalized populations. Rosselló's promises of a swift, mano dura approach to crime that would improve the lives of all Puerto Ricans provided populist cover for an increasing fortification of the urban landscape driven by racist and classist underpinnings. At the same time, mano dura marked criminalized populations as outside the bounds of appropriate citizenship and ultimately as threats to the peace of the nation.

Shortly after Rosselló was elected governor, he and Superintendent Toledo unveiled Operation Centurion, the most visible component of mano dura contra el crimen, in which they deployed the National Guard to assist in civilian policing efforts. On February 25, 1993, Rosselló signed an executive order activating the National Guard to assist police in maintaining public security and quelling drug-related crime.[25] Rosselló saw the National Guard as an underutilized force that could provide police with the essential technological assistance and extra manpower needed to win the war against drugs. The National Guard "is not here," Rosselló emphasized, "to prevent the Russians from invading us, but to fight the enemies of Puerto Rico . . . and the worst enemy Puerto Rico has is crime."[26] With this comment, Rosselló not only captured the shift in risk assessment following the end of the Cold War, which cast drug trafficking as one of the most serious threats to global security, but also solidified the notion of criminals as internal enemies of the state.

During the last weekend of May 1993, National Guard soldiers were deployed to patrol public recreational areas, including beaches, movie theaters, and shopping centers. According to the adjutant general of the Puerto Rican National Guard, Emilio Díaz-Colón, the sight of armed military personnel in fatigues patrolling the ritzy streets of Condado and corridors of Plaza Las Américas, the archipelago's largest shopping center, was supposed to "send a message to the people that we want[ed] to protect the citizens of Puerto Rico."[27] Similarly, Superintendent Toledo remarked, "We wanted to send the message to the people of Puerto Rico that we meant business, that we wanted to protect them, that we would use all the resources that we had to protect the people from criminals."[28] Operation Centurion was first unveiled within elite spaces of consumption and leisure to show Puerto Ricans, whether they saw it firsthand or through the media, that the state was doing something about the crime problem. Further, considering that spaces of leisure like beaches and malls are not accessible to all Puerto Ricans and are often informally segregated by race and class, it is obvious that the visibility of National Guard and police in these spaces was meant to assuage the fears of white and well-off sectors of the population. Soon after this strategic initial outing, the police began raiding and occupying supposed drug "hot spots." The police and National Guard quickly became concentrated in public housing and other racially marginalized and low-income spaces. This targeting of already marginalized communities had been the plan from the beginning.

Four days before the signing of the executive order authorizing the National Guard's activation, guardsmen and police were already preparing to do battle in racially and economically marginalized communities. On February 19, 1993, approximately one hundred police officers and National Guard soldiers participated in a simulated raid of a public housing complex at the police academy in Gurabo.[29] Soon thereafter, Rosselló and Toledo confirmed that public housing projects were to be the primary target for the joint military-police interventions because they housed many of the archipelago's drug distribution spots, which were seen as the principal generator of crime and violence.[30] The training exercises carried out at the police academy were put into practice on June 5, 1993, when police and National Guard forces occupied the Villa España public housing complex. The predawn raid at Villa España was the first of approximately eighty-two raids carried out between June 1993 and March 1999.[31] During these raids, police conducted searches, confiscated contraband, and interrogated residents while the National Guard provided logistical and tactical support in the form of soldiers, helicopters, military vehicles, technology, and weapons. The National

Guard was also responsible for setting up surveillance, establishing checkpoints, and constructing a perimeter fence around the newly occupied housing complex. The police and National Guard soldiers occupied these public housing complexes for weeks, even months, until a security force of part-time police and private security guards was able to establish a permanent presence.

The perimeter fences built during mano dura incursions into public housing, coupled with the simultaneous rise in private gated communities, further enclosed low-income Puerto Ricans and concentrated the violence of the war on drugs. It also put on full display the explicitly racialized and classed dimensions of state crime control efforts. There were clear differences between the reasons behind installing controlled-access gates in middle- and upper-class urbanizaciones and the purpose of the gates installed in public housing complexes in the aftermath of the raids. Criminologist Lina Torres argues, "In public housing, controlled access is so that people from the projects don't leave and in the urbanizaciones it's so they [people from public housing] don't enter. They have different meanings because controlled access results in a state of siege, practically turning public housing into a prison."[32] Unlike the gating of urbanizaciones, the gating of public housing did not come at the request of residents, but rather was dictated by the Puerto Rican government, in effect violating the Controlled Access Law. According to the Controlled Access Law, before a community is gated, the majority of residents must first agree to the gating, the municipality is required to hold hearings, and traffic studies must be conducted. However, the Puerto Rican government was able to sidestep such legal restrictions by citing immediate public safety concerns.[33]

Combined with the booming security industry, the interventions associated with mano dura transformed Puerto Rico's physical landscape, turning urban centers into walled cities and eliminating many possibilities for cross-class and cross-racial interaction.[34] Regardless of class status, as a result of mano dura, more and more Puerto Ricans found themselves sequestered behind gates, and the logic of spatial separation became further entrenched in the Puerto Rican social imagination. This has resulted in what some critics have termed *el apartheid boricua*, or Puerto Rican apartheid. "The difference between apartheid and the public housing interventions and communities with controlled access is minimal," suggests Puerto Rican criminologist Dora Nevares-Muñiz.[35] According to Nevares-Muñiz, the result of mano dura has been "a generation of children that live in a community under military occupation, where violence and drugs have not been eradicated and where the civil rights of residents are respected less and less."[36] Similarly, in 1994 activist Irmarilis González Torres noted:

> The invasions [of public housing] and closures of the urbanizations, with all intention, are blocking the possibilities for us to deal with the social differences between us. And there are fewer and fewer places in which people encounter each other. We are witnessing what some people have started to call "el apartheid boricua": a disgusting "project" of social segregation. Where can we encounter each other—any of us—in this moment? Our best chance of seeing each other is in traffic or maybe finding each other in Plaza Las Américas, at the hospital, or in any municipal cemetery.[37]

For many critics, mano dura contra el crimen exacerbated racial and class divisions and created new spaces of enclosure within an already intensely segregated urban terrain. For proponents, however, enclosure and spatial separation was not something to be belabored, but rather central to what made mano dura's crime control strategy "work."

The war on drugs waged by the Rosselló administration was implicitly a war on social contact zones. The overt race and class bias embedded within mano dura policing is perhaps best illustrated by a scandal that erupted shortly after the raids began. While soldiers and police were busting down doors in public housing to search for drugs and weapons, police were sending affluent drug users polite letters telling them that their cars had been spotted in "dangerous areas" and that they should stay away for their own safety.[38] Explaining the campaign, Superintendent Toledo said that the lawyers and doctors whose luxury cars were seen in proximity to public housing deserved to be warned because they might have driven by "innocently."[39] This incident confirmed for public housing residents, as well as social justice activists, civil rights attorneys, and other sympathetic observers, that mano dura contra el crimen had to do less with stamping out the drug trade and more with using the police to manage the threat of violence written onto public housing residents through racist and classist assumptions.

Rosselló dismissed outright the various concerns about discrimination and civil rights violations that arose over the course of the operations. He accused his critics of colluding with the criminal element, charging them with deploying "a strategy to get us to stand around with our arms crossed; it's a strategy to get us to do nothing. It is a strategy that simply may be promoting the criminal element because, for whom is this not convenient? This is not convenient for the criminal."[40] On June 5, 1993, during a meeting between residents of Villa España and representatives from various government agencies following the raid, Joaquina Cruz Pizarro, president of the Villa España Residents' Council, brought up the harassment experienced by residents during the raid. She said, "Today they broke 42 doors, and there are children here. This isn't a zoo. They had the right to search but not to hurt people."[41] Later, during a press conference and in reference to complaints about the police unnecessarily breaking down apartment doors, terrorizing residents, and conducting illegal searches, Rosselló responded, "I don't understand how anyone in Puerto Rico can make such superficial objections regarding an action that the majority of people have demanded. If we have to break down 37 doors or break down 74 doors to bring peace to the Puerto Rican family we are going to keep doing it."[42]

Rosselló attempted to fold criticisms of his crime-fighting approach back onto themselves by accusing people of being more invested in criticizing his administration and protecting the rights of criminals than in truly improving the lives of public housing residents who were being affected by drug-related crime and gang violence. He attributed criticism of mano dura to criminals and radicals, who had no attachment to the low-income communities they were ostensibly interested in defending. In doing so, Rosselló dismissed the very real apprehensions and objections coming from public housing residents, as well as concerned members of the public, about the corruption and violence that characterized these militarized interventions.

"I REMEMBER THERE WAS A LOT OF ABUSE"

As the joint police and National Guard interventions spread to public housing complexes around the archipelago, reports from residents and legal observers of excessive force, impropriety, and illegality on the part of soldiers and police began to circulate through word of mouth and the news media. Residents spoke about officers quick to hassle tenants and their guests and even quicker to draw their sidearms. León Santiago, a resident of Las Gladiolas in San Juan, recalling his military service, said, "I was a platoon sergeant in Vietnam, and when we entered villages we never pointed our guns at civilians—and that was a war."[43] Santiago's comments highlight the ways in which a war waged against drugs easily transformed into a war on economically marginalized populations, particularly young people living in public housing. Juan José Pérez, a resident of the Monte Hatillo public housing complex in Río Piedras, recalled, "I remember there was a lot of abuse. The National Guard didn't know how to treat people. They would step on 13 and 15-year-old boys with their boots, and if you said anything they would stomp on you harder."[44] Carmelo Zambrana, a resident of Las Gladiolas, remarked following the raids there, "Civil rights violations against residents are especially bad. We get stopped and searched without cause all the time."[45]

Children and teenagers experienced a disproportionate exposure to illegal searches and harassment at the hands of the police, in part because dealers sometimes employed minors as drug mules due to less stringent juvenile sentencing laws. This perception of young people in public housing as little more than potential mules made them particularly vulnerable targets of police power during the police occupation of public housing. For instance, residents reported that police officers would stop children on their way home from school without pretense or justification and force them to open their backpacks to see if they were transporting drugs. José Luis Rivera, a resident of La Perla, a low-income community in Old San Juan that was raided by police during March 1994, complained, "When kids come out of school at 3, they search them. Why? They're not selling drugs."[46] A particularly stark example occurred during the March 2, 1994, takeover of El Trebol, a public housing complex in Carolina, when police detained two young boys and a young girl, forcing the two boys to lie face down on the ground while the young girl sat beside them and leaned against a wall. The youths stayed like this for an hour and a half until a reporter on the scene finally asked Superintendent Toledo why the three were on the ground and flanked by heavily armed police. The superintendent asked one of the attending officers whether the youths had been found with drugs, and when the officer admitted that they hadn't, he released them.[47] One has to wonder how many times scenes like this played out when the press wasn't around to document and question them.

Residents also reported instances when police unnecessarily drew and discharged their service weapons, intimidating and occasionally injuring residents. In February 1995, following the police occupation of Las Gladiolas, Ada Estel Morales heard a commotion coming from the ground floor of the complex. Morales peered over the railing of her balcony on the eleventh floor to see if her son "was involved in the *bochinche* [ruckus]" below.[48] Instead of her son, she caught sight of a friend engaged in a heated argument with a police officer. As Morales continued to watch the events unfold, she suddenly heard a few shots ring out: "I don't know where they came from. That's when the officer took out his gun and shot wildly into the air."[49] One of the bullets fired from the officer's gun wounded Morales, striking her in the bladder. "I spent four weeks in intensive care at Centro Medico. And now I have to use this bag to go to the bathroom," she told reporters following the shooting.[50] Rosselló and Toledo responded to incidents like this by casting them as anomalous and urging public housing residents to see police and guardsmen stationed in public housing as a community resource rather than an occupying force.

The murder of José Rosario Díaz, a twenty-two-year-old resident of the José Celso Barbosa housing project in Bayamón, by an on-duty police officer illuminated the deadly contradictions of "community policing" that mano dura represented. Police and National Guard forces occupied the Barbosa public housing complex in Bayamón on June 8, 1993. Following the raid at Barbosa, like at many other projects, the National Guard constructed a perimeter fence around the complex, and a police-manned, controlled-access entrance was established. On September 8, 1993, exactly three months after the initial occupation and barely a week after the withdrawal of the National Guard from the complex, police officer Miguel Díaz Martínez was assigned to guard duty at Barbosa's vehicle-only controlled-access entrance. When twenty-two-year-old José Rosario Díaz arrived home from work that evening, he was stopped by Officer Díaz Martínez and asked for his identification to enter the complex. Rosario Díaz explained that he lived in an apartment with his grandmother, Bienvenida Lafontaine, but did not have his identification on him. Rosario Díaz asked the officer to let him enter his apartment to retrieve the necessary identification. Officer Díaz Martínez refused, and the two began arguing. Hearing the commotion, Rosario Díaz's sister, María Rosario Díaz, and aunt, Rosario María del Pilar Ramos, walked over to the guardhouse, which was near their apartment, to try to reason with the officer. Officer Díaz Martínez claimed that Rosario Díaz then physically assaulted him, although eyewitness accounts from Barbosa residents claimed that the officer verbally assaulted Rosario Díaz's sister María and shoved her to the ground. Residents reported that when Rosario Díaz approached the officer in an attempt to protect his sister, Díaz Martínez took out his service revolver, pushed it into Rosario Díaz's chest, and pulled the trigger. Díaz Martínez then shot María Rosario Díaz in her right leg. After shooting both siblings, Díaz Martínez pointed his revolver at their aunt, struck her, and threw her to the ground. Following the tragic incident, residents noted that the officer had acted out violently before but remained on active duty at the housing complex. Indeed, this was only one in a string of brutal acts that punctuated Officer Díaz Martínez's career.

Over a span of five years, Díaz Martínez engaged in numerous acts of violence toward civilians and fellow law enforcement officers, but was returned to duty time and time again despite being designated a danger to himself and others. In 1989 Díaz Martínez suspected that his wife, who was a fellow police officer, was cheating with a colleague. In a fit of jealous rage, he viciously beat her and then took over a police station in the town of Cataño, where he held several police officials hostage, including the acting police superintendent. After that incident, Díaz Martínez was involuntarily committed to a psychiatric hospital and diagnosed as schizophrenic. He was suspended from the force in 1990 and formally expelled in 1991. After appeals to the Police Review Board, Díaz Martínez was found "fit for duty" and reinstated to the force in 1993. It was mere months later that Díaz Martínez fatally shot José Rosario Díaz and seriously wounded María Rosario Díaz. Despite Díaz Martínez's clear instability, he remained on the force for several months *after* he shot the Rosario Díaz siblings. He retained his position until May 1994, when he brutally beat Grancid Camilo-Robles, a security guard working at the courthouse in Bayamón, after being told he could not park in a spot reserved for judges.[51]

Officer Díaz Martínez was definitely a "bad apple," but he was far from the only officer with a history of violence who interacted with civilians, particularly those in low-income areas. According to journalist Milvia Y. Archilla Rivera, writing in September 1993, "Distressingly, about 300 police officers have been reinstated to the force with diagnoses and situations similar to Díaz. This is a part of the premise of mano dura contra el crimen's policy, which mandates the reintegration of officers into the street. However, many of the officers on administrative duty were given that placement due to psychological reasons."[52] The plan to flood so-called *zonas calientes*, or crime hot spots, with police and military personnel as a way of managing crime resulted in officers with documented histories of violence or mental health issues being placed in close proximity to citizens during what were highly antagonistic and stressful situations. The presence of more officers in low-income communities exposed residents to exponentially increased verbal, psychological, and physical violence.

Perhaps one of the least examined aspects of the mano dura interventions are the instances of sexual violence and impropriety that reportedly accompanied the early-morning raids and subsequent occupation of public housing complexes. While only one accusation of rape associated with the mano dura operations was ever officially reported, a case that was eventually dismissed in court, public housing residents and individuals who worked with public housing residents say that sexual contact, both consensual and forced, was common during the operations. Criminologist Dora Nevares-Muñiz noted, "Among the problems that residents themselves mention is that most of what the officers do is chase women and intervening with drug points the least of what they do."[53] Nkechi Taifa, legislative counsel for the ACLU, drew from conversations with Hector Pérez, then copresident of the ALCU chapter in Puerto Rico, to relay to a congressional subcommittee that "flirtations with females ha[d] been a growing problem" among guardsmen and police officers stationed in Puerto Rico's public housing complexes.[54] Similarly, civil rights attorney Judith Berkan remarked that during the raids it was commonplace for guardsmen and police to "take up with women in the projects," and it was not unusual to see uniforms being hung out to dry on balconies.[55] She noted that "in the worst of lawlessness it devolves into rape and mass rape. . . . [B]ut, even in a less virulent occupation, it's pretty typical to have the military taking up with the local women and that's what we were seeing."[56]

While documented accounts of sexual contact between police and military personnel and public housing residents from the mano dura era are scant, in 2010, when Governor Luis Fortuño activated the National Guard in the face of rising crime rates and civil unrest, a number of residents came forward about the abuse they had witnessed and suffered during the 1990s, including accounts of sexual impropriety. In interviews conducted by reporters from *El Nuevo Día*, residents spoke openly about the routine sexual contact between residents and the PRPD and National Guard personnel stationed at public housing complexes. According to Orlando Rosario, a community organizer associated with the Jardines de Country Club public housing complex, "Numerous women ended up pregnant by police and National Guard soldiers. . . . That occurred in all the projects that were occupied. I was a national community leader and I had to visit projects throughout the island and I saw hundreds of women pregnant because of those men. Weren't they there to ensure people's safety? Why did women end up pregnant?"[57] Likewise, public housing resident Tomasa Rodríguez lamented, "In Monte Hatillo there are many children without last names. The women fell in love and ended up pregnant and the fathers never returned. It's terrible what happened to those women and those children."[58]

The accounts of sexual impropriety that occurred during the mano dura raids pierce the dominant notion that police violence only affects men and positions women as mere bystanders in the rollout of the punitive state. While conservative critics of public housing in Puerto Rico, as much as on the mainland United States, made much of the culture of poverty being fostered by domineering female heads of household to explain away the structural causes of inequality faced by the poor, they simultaneously effaced the presence of women as the state "got tough" on crime. With the declaration of a war on crime, public housing and other low-income communities were transformed into hypermasculine spaces of violence and illegality. The idea that dangerous Black and brown men involved with the informal drug economy dominated public housing justified the force and violence directed at public housing residents during mano dura contra el crimen. As Zaire Dinzey-Flores suggests, "Popular representations of public housing as sites of dystopia, high criminality and lawlessness that informed the creation of Mano Dura militaristic and environmental interventions have fed the perception of the racial, class, and gender composition of poor communities. The techniques, and the perceptions they posit perpetuate a stereotypical view of those who live here as being dangerous, violent, poor, young men of dark skin color."[59]

The actual demographics of public housing, however, suggest otherwise. The masculinization of public housing by political elites, law enforcement officials, and the media occurred despite the fact public housing was (and remains) largely comprised of women-headed households.[60] Dinzey-Flores notes that while politicians and law enforcement officials painted public housing as overrun by young men who had essentially formed well-armed drug militias, hell-bent on terrorizing ordinary citizens, the communities were "primarily integrated by a young population of young women that [were] not organizing militarily to fight an invasion from the government."[61]

Although women were also terrorized and maimed during mano dura raids, as illustrated by the shootings of Ada Estel Morales and María Rosario Díaz mentioned previously, the victims of police violence were mostly figured as male. There is no question that young racially and economically marginalized men had tremendous amounts of scrutiny and violence directed at them from law enforcement and their fellow citizens due to their presumed criminality. Indeed, their punishment at the hands of the state was put on display for all to see either firsthand or via media coverage. The accounts of sexual impropriety and gendered violence on the part of police and guardsmen, on the other hand, illuminate how the criminalization of public housing impacted the women who lived there in ways that often escaped recognition, let alone quantification. While women might have been less likely to be

TABLE 1 *Delitos Tipo 1* Recorded in Puerto Rico, 1990–2000

Year	Murder & Homicide	Forcible Rape	Robbery	Aggravated Assault	Burglary	Larceny-theft	Motor Vehicle Theft
1990	600	426	20,923	7,963	34,781	39,795	19,883
1991	817	424	20,003	6,901	33,649	38,916	19,021
1992	864	433	24,242	6,747	35,415	42,315	18,858
1993	954	401	18,181	6,806	33,636	43,468	17,589
1994	995	396	17,626	6,384	31,160	42,062	17,641
1995	864	324	15,753	5,509	27,689	39,960	15,989
1996	868	316	13,900	5,063	27,866	35,652	16,123
1997	724	278	13,642	4,952	26,942	32,715	15,623
1998	652	243	11,448	4,096	24,512	30,493	15,576
1999	593	223	9,827	3,563	23,033	30,206	14,435
2000	695	228	8,757	2,726	21,057	28,940	12,976

SOURCE: Junta de Planificación de Puerto Rico, "Informe social: Criminalidad en Puerto Rico años seleccionados" (Mayo 2003).

slammed to the ground, handcuffed, and thrown into the back of a police van, they nevertheless experienced insidious forms of violence and increased vulnerability at the hands of the state as a part of mano dura contra el crimen.

MAKE THE RATS SCATTER

One year after the implementation of mano dura contra el crimen, Governor Rosselló and Superintendent Toledo touted their success daily in the press, lauding their tough-on-crime approach. They boasted of decreases in the number of carjackings and assaults and assured the public that the fight against drugs and crime was being won with every public housing project occupied and every punto dismantled. Indeed, if one looks at the rates of *delitos tipo 1*, or type 1 offences, after 1992 there appears to have been a decrease in most categories, seemingly giving credence to the narrative of mano dura's incredible success (see table 1). The daily lived experiences of many Puerto Ricans, particularly those in economically and racially marginalized areas, however, reflected a very different reality.

While mano dura may have resulted in an overall decrease in many crimes, it provoked an increase in homicides. Puerto Rico's murder rate had climbed to 864 recorded murders in 1992, and the implementation of mano dura

TABLE 2 Discrepancies in the Reporting of Homicides
in Puerto Rico, 1990–2000

Year	Homicides Reported by Police (P)	Homicides Reported by Department of Health(DH)	P − DH
1990	600	583	17
1991	817	803	14
1992	864	851	13
1993	954	959	−5
1994	995	1017	−22
1995	864	929	−65
1996	868	928	−60
1997	724	881	−157
1998	652	819	−167
1999	593	705	−112
2000	695	698	−3

SOURCE: Judith Rodríguez Figueroa and Alma Irizarry Castro, *El homicidio en Puerto Rico: Características y nexos con la violencia* (San Juan: Universidad Carlos Albizu, 2003).

drove the homicide rate even higher. In 1994 police recorded 995 murders, the most in the country's history at the time, and the murder rate did not drop significantly below 1992's alarming numbers until 1997. Further, criminologists and demographers have suggested that the number of homicides during the mid- to late 1990s was actually significantly higher, but police manipulated statistics in order to support the story of mano dura's success. In their study of homicides in Puerto Rico, Judith Rodríguez and Alma Irizarry demonstrate that in the years immediately following the implementation of mano dura contra el crimen, the number of murders registered by the police was significantly lower than those documented by the Department of Health (see table 2). As Rosselló's administration and police officials celebrated the safer Puerto Rico achieved by mano dura contra el crimen, images of young men slain in turf disputes haunted the nightly news and provided stark reminders of the intense vulnerability and proximity to violence that many Puerto Ricans continued to experience.

Mano dura contra el crimen "made the streets safer" by contributing to high levels of violence in low-income and racially marginalized areas during the height of police intervention in the drug trade. Police and military intervention resulted in increased drug-related homicides and violence, especially in 1993 and 1994, as these incursions into public housing and low-income barrios with active drug trades created deadly outcomes. Police intervention and arrests resulted in abandoned puntos, which led to violent competition among dealers for these newly available spaces. As dealers were locked up or killed, the street price of narcotics increased to cover the new costs of doing business. In 1995 the constant drug raids triggered a scarcity of cocaine, driving the street price up from $10 to $30 a gram and provoking desperation on the part of both dealers and users, which in turn contributed to more violence and crime.[62] While public feelings and official discourse trafficked in the assumption that drugs and violence existed at every turn, the effects of drugs and violence in the wake of the raids remained overwhelmingly concentrated in poor and overwhelmingly Black urban areas. The movement of drug points prompted by police intervention continued to follow well-established patterns of spatial inequality and social abandonment. While a few enterprising dealers and gangs may have struck out and expanded into entirely new territory in an effort to stay ahead of the raids, most dealers moved around within already established circuits of the drug market—spaces that were becoming smaller, scarcer, and deadlier with each subsequent police intervention.[63]

This phenomenon was not unique to Puerto Rico. "Ghetto sweeps," which sought to apply increasing pressure on drug dealers and users operating within public housing and low-income, predominantly Black communities in the mainland United States, proliferated during the 1980s and 1990s. With names like Operation Hammer (Los Angeles), Operation Pressure Point (New York City), Operation Sting (Miami), Operation Snow Ball (Orange County, California), and Operation Clean Sweep (Washington, D.C.), these drug raids provoked tremendous violence with no evidence, or negligible evidence, that drug use and dealing decreased in response.[64] Puerto Rico's mano dura contra el crimen existed in relationship to a larger pattern of discriminatory and violent policing that marked the US-led global war on drugs, although it cannot merely be reduced to an importation of US punitive policy.

Police pointed to the constant movement of drug dealers from punto to punto as evidence of mano dura's success. According to police officials, one of the goals of these raids was to eliminate drug trafficking not only by disarticulating the puntos, but also by making puntos increasingly difficult for dealers to operate and maintain. A central goal of the raids was to force drug dealers to move around and engage in bloody battles over territory, as a form of deterrence. As Superintendent Pedro Toledo put it, "There could be an increase in gangland killings as *puntos* are eliminated. However, we'll continue to hit them wherever they go, keep them on the move, make it tough for them until they have to give up and go out of business."[65] Police knew that the pressure of constant raids would result in more competition between rivals and therefore more murders, but this increased violence was positioned as a necessary evil in their efforts to eradicate drug dealing and restore a sense of "peace" to the "decent" people of Puerto Rico.

The relationship between police raids and increased violence, particularly violent death, was already well known among government and law enforcement officials. For instance, Governor Hernández Colón explained and rationalized these deadly consequences of police action after police increasingly began to raid spaces associated with low-level drug dealing toward the end of his third term. In 1992, when pushed to explain a spike in homicides and violence despite increased police action and intervention, Hernández Colón said, "What is happening is that we are having more success in our strategy of penetrating the projects to eliminate the drug points, in many cases arresting those who control the drug points. This has unleashed struggles in other areas or territories or between people who work for the individual arrested to take control [of the puntos] and this is generating bloody battles between them [drug gangs] and [as a result] we are seeing many murders."[66] Hernández Colón added that while this was a lamentable outcome, the response should not be "to adopt a posture that we are going to leave them [drug dealers] with the projects and that we're not going to eliminate the drug points and bring security to the people living there."[67] In this way, the growing number of homicides related to battles over puntos became a macabre hallmark of success rather than a sign of failing police strategy. Police success *and* failure in controlling the violence generated by the puntos, then, produced even greater violence and insecurity for low-income and racially marginalized populations living in zonas calientes.

Part of mano dura contra el crimen's strategy of controlling drug trafficking and drug-related violence, then, was the tacit acceptance of continued, and indeed elevated, levels of harm and death directed at low-income and racially marginalized individuals, particularly the poor, young, Black and brown men who labored in the informal economy. Not only did state officials tolerate their deaths—or let them die in the Foucaldian sense—but their strategy of promoting and exacerbating the already tense competition over puntos created conditions that positioned violence and death as expected and acceptable outcomes of police intervention.[68] That mano dura would drive up the death toll among individuals involved with the drug economy was, for policy makers and law enforcement officials, an inescapable and justifiable fact.[69]

With mano dura contra el crimen, state officials pursued a strategy that they knew would provoke more violence and more deaths. While it might sound conspiratorial to suggest that policies were put in place with the knowledge that people involved with the informal drug economy would be harmed and killed as a result of police intervention, government and police officials regularly acknowledged this and justified it by reinforcing hierarchies that valued the lives of some Puerto Ricans over others. The deaths of individuals presumed to be part of the underground economy were naturalized as expected outcomes of police work and a necessary component of a crime prevention and deterrence strategy that would eventually result in greater public safety. While in a strict sense their deaths may not have been premeditated by the state, the state did deliberately advance informal and formal policies that "let" alleged dealers and criminals die.[70]

The responsibility for increased violence shifted away from law enforcement and onto the victims of law enforcement strategy, who were seen as "getting what they deserved" for breaking the law. Because law enforcement officials were not out in the streets executing drug dealers, the violence of the state was made invisible. The increasing drug-related murders were simply seen as "senseless" killings as a result of competition over puntos, with no mention made of the role of state policy in intensifying the violence of the drug trade. Such law enforcement prevention and deterrence efforts, which strategically utilized existing conditions of danger and harm, were, in the words of historian Kelly Lytle Hernández, "tactics that muddied the authorship of state violence."[71] Images circulated through the media of young, dark-skinned men being paraded before television cameras in handcuffs or visible only as limbs underneath a coroner's sheet positioned these young people as the perpetrators of violence and crime for many Puerto Ricans. This hyper-visibility of the policing of brown and Black youths served, for many, to eclipse the role of the state in provoking and perpetuating the violence associated with the drug economy.

Racial, spatial, and economic inequalities are among the structural forces that enabled and contributed to the discriminatory and harmful logics that drove mano dura contra el crimen. In mano dura, a history of colonial population management, intense anti-Black racism, capitalist exploitation, and urban enclosure coalesced. These processes defined the mostly young Black and brown men from public housing and barrios who labored in the drug economy as threats to el pueblo puertorriqueño that needed to be contained, if not eliminated outright. Indeed, as Ismael Betancourt Lebrón, police superintendent under Governor Hernández Colón, reportedly remarked, "The punishment of the drug dealer is that at any given moment he can get shot in the head, but that's not my problem."[72] Betancourt Lebrón's comments index a growing frustration with the informal drug economy that was unleashed in the form of violence and dehumanization against low-income Puerto Ricans, whose involvement with the drug trade was assumed. Mano dura contra el crimen seized upon and institutionalized these popular notions of "deserved" violence and proximity to death. The deaths of individuals involved with the informal drug economy were positioned as outside the purview of the police's duty to protect all citizens—*not their problem.*

As puntos moved either in anticipation of raids or in their wake, violence often followed as dealers attempted to maintain a grip on their slice of the drug trade. Captain Charles Pérez, commander of the Barrio Obrero police precinct, which had seen a rise in homicides due to displaced dealers moving into the area, said, "It's like when you move into an old house that's full of rats. What happens when you move in? The rats go running out all over the place."[73] While Capt. Pérez's metaphor attempted to capture the mercurial nature of the puntos and their mobility, he inadvertently elucidated mano dura's prevailing logic of dehumanization and disposability, which allowed and even encouraged drug dealers to eliminate each other. The idea that criminals and drug dealers were outside the bounds of normative Puerto Rican society—*rats*—guided the logic of mano dura and justified the brutal force utilized during the incursions. This logic also shaped the deliberate action and inaction on the part of law enforcement and politicians in the face of an increasingly volatile drug economy affecting some of Puerto Rico's most vulnerable communities. As Governor Rosselló regularly remarked, "habitual criminals" were nothing but "garbage," killing young people with drugs.[74] In Puerto Rico, a political and popular rhetoric that dehumanized and vilified drug dealers and users as "monsters," "animals," and "garbage" and positioned them as a threat to el pueblo puertorriqueño allowed for the creation of law enforcement policies that cultivated some lives at the expense of others. The devaluation of those lives and deaths naturalized the uneven distribution of opportunity and harm and reinforced the notion that not all lives are livable, nor are all deaths grievable.[75]

Although mano dura was constructed as an effort to "rescue" Puerto Ricans from violence, crime, and drugs, it functioned in a way that concentrated violence within racially and economically marginalized communities and exposed residents to greater harm at the hands of both police and their fellow citizens. Residents regularly pointed out the ways that mano dura had not improved their lives and, in particular, had failed to improve the lives of those young men from the barrios and public housing who spent their days and nights working at the puntos. It is this aspect of the drug economy—the labor performed and the income generated—that mano dura disrupted and sought to eliminate in low-income communities, without providing an alternative that would address the underlying structural concerns that made working at the puntos an attractive option in a post–Operation Bootstrap Puerto Rico. Six months after the National Guard and police occupied Villa España, Cruz Pizarro pointed out that the government had done nothing to address the rampant unemployment that drove many young people to look for work at the punto, nor had it provided any meaningful alternatives to drug dealing following the raids. According to Cruz Pizarro:

> When they destroyed the drug spot, they should have known there was going to be more unemployment, because like it or not, it provided jobs—seven to three, three to eleven, eleven to seven. In shifts—that's just how simple it is. And the dealers had to be on time, clean, and drug-free, just like a real job. Now I have 14 to 17 year-olds who aren't addicts who lost their jobs and want to work. But who is going to give them a job? If the governor had studied that problem then maybe this policy would have worked differently, because now we're in a crisis.[76]

One year after the raids at Villa España, Cruz Pizarro explicitly tied the government's failure to address the needs of Puerto Rican youths, particularly those from public housing, to the steady cadence of murders that the archipelago continued to experience. "That's why the murders haven't stopped," she noted. "Those unemployed kids are going to look for a dollar anywhere they can get it. . . . They [the government] haven't fulfilled their economic necessities."[77] While mano dura might have been touted as the salvation for communities in peril, it actually exacerbated the structural conditions that contributed to the explosive informal economy.

Further, residents argued for a more nuanced understanding of the drug economy that would acknowledge that the *pejes gordos*, or drug kingpins, were safe behind the gates of their urbanizaciones while the young men who worked the puntos to earn a wage shouldered all the risk of violence and arrest. Juan José Pérez of Monte Hatillo said, "It was like a war . . . but a war against the victims. The people in the projects are the victims of drug trafficking. Drugs don't leave the projects; they enter. The ones they need to look for are those who finance the drugs that enter the projects."[78] Likewise, in a letter to the editor of *El Nuevo Día*, Luz Zenaida Vélez Pérez, a resident of Manuel A. Pérez, said, "For those of us who live in the projects, we find it very difficult to understand that we are really the artery that nurtures crime in all its forms and that we control drug trafficking at all levels."[79] Public housing residents pointed out that authorities' eagerness to categorize public housing as a key site of drug distribution, and therefore a central generator of violence, obscured the fact that by and large drugs were not, and never had been, produced within public housing. And while the open-air drug markets that operated in a number of public housing complexes throughout the archipelago generated incredible profits, very little of the money made there stayed there. Public housing was simply a local site of sale—the site of low-level, hand-to-hand transactions—with the true power players of the drug game, as well as many of the consumers, typically residing outside of public housing. Public housing in Puerto Rico emerged as a node in a transnational drug network because, as a site of state abandonment, it provided a large labor force that was understood to be exploitable and expendable. In their rationale for targeting public housing, both the Hernández Colón and then Rosselló administrations failed, or refused, to grasp these complex power dynamics. The myopic focus on low-level drug dealing and trafficking taking place in public housing ignored the ways in which the real profits and players existed beyond its walls and benefited a range of interests, including Puerto Rico's powerful banking sector and burgeoning security industry.

Mano dura contra el crimen brings into sharp relief the multiple ways in which punitive policing functions under the auspices of keeping populations safe, but in fact creates only a thin veneer of security by casting certain populations as disposable and dangerous. Through both the official and unofficial methods of policing initiatives like mano dura, the state functions to further devastate already marginalized communities. The violence enacted through mano dura cannot be contained only to questions of street violence and police brutality. The police occupation of public housing complexes marked residents as "unruly subjects," which hardened existing prejudices and made it increasingly difficult for them to access a range of economic and social opportunities. Further, those involved in the drug trade who were arrested during mano dura's incursions into the puntos might have seemingly escaped harm and death on the streets at the hand of a rival or an overzealous police officer, only to encounter it in US and Puerto Rican prisons. In this way, we must consider the various forms of harm that policing does in marginalized and vulnerable communities and the ways in which it contributes to limited life chances and proximity to premature death.

TWO

Colonial Projects

ON JUNE 10, 1996, THE SUBCOMMITTEE ON NATIONAL SECURITY, International Affairs, and Criminal Justice of the United States House of Representatives met to discuss the ongoing war against drug trafficking and some recent successful measures. The hearing was convened aboard the US Coast Guard cutter *Courageous*, a vessel that had regularly participated in drug enforcement efforts in the Gulf of Mexico and Caribbean Sea since 1991.[1] The *Courageous* was auspiciously docked in San Juan, Puerto Rico, one of its regular ports of call in the Caribbean at the time. After welcoming everyone aboard, Illinois representative J. Dennis Hastert, acting chair of the subcommittee, opened the congressional hearing by praising Governor Pedro Rosselló's no-nonsense approach to drug trafficking in Puerto Rico: "Let me say that it's not by chance that we are in Puerto Rico. Governor Rosselló has shown a brand of leadership that is rarely seen. He has single-mindedly fought to turn back the rise of drugs and drug related crime in Puerto Rico. His efforts, personal conviction and perseverance have been watched by Congress, and are admired by those in both parties. Moreover, the Governor of Puerto Rico is providing a new model for effectively combating what is fast becoming a most insidious national security threat."[2] The short hearing centered, for the most part, on both the success of mano dura el crimen as a strategy for combatting drug trafficking and the extent to which its "successes" could be translated to the mainland United States. Governor Rosselló, Superintendent Toledo, and Housing Secretary Carlos Vivoni each testified about the transformation of Puerto Rico's public housing complexes from prisons of fear and despair to drug-free spaces of hope and community empowerment. They discussed how the strategy of joint police and National Guard interventions could provide a model for other large, troubled housing authorities dealing with the scourge of drug abuse and gang violence. Further, they lauded the leadership role of Puerto Rico in redefining the role of the "citizen solider" in the post–Cold War era by giving the National Guard a central role in the war on drugs.

The tenor of this congressional hearing provides familiar echoes of Puerto Rico's long history as a "laboratory" for US domestic and foreign policy.[3] Indeed, the foundation of the contemporary Puerto Rican state—the commonwealth agreement between Puerto Rico and the United States—was conceptualized, in part, as a vehicle to showcase American development strategies to the Third World during the Cold War era. As historian Laura Briggs notes, during the 1940s and 1950s, "Puerto Rico became (largely through massive federal government subsidies) a political showcase for the prosperity and democracy promised by close alliance with the United States."[4] Decades later, this hearing convened aboard a ship dedicated to drug interdiction efforts seemed to provide a glimpse at how Puerto Rico continued to operate as a colonial vitrine. In this chapter, however, I complicate this narrative by examining how the Puerto Rican government negotiated a decline in its value by attempting to reposition Puerto Rico as a model rather than a laboratory for US policy. While the semantic difference between the two might seem slight, this shift had a tremendous impact on Puerto Rico and its population at the close of the twentieth century.

During the 1990s, when increased globalization and trade liberalization caused Puerto Rico's unique political and economic relationship to the United States to gradually lose significance, the Puerto Rican government attempted to position Puerto Rico as a model in the arenas of law enforcement and public housing policy. Rather than inviting US policy makers to utilize the archipelago to test and perfect policies to be exported to the United States and Global South, Puerto Rican government officials themselves took on the task of developing "innovative" policies and practices regarding security, policing, and public housing policy as a way of demonstrating Puerto Rico's continued utility to the United States. These efforts were an attempt to reassert the importance of Puerto Rico to the United States within a newly emerging global order and to ensure the archipelago's continued incorporation within the US nation-state.

This chapter traces the ways in which the anticrime plan mano dura contra el crimen traveled both successfully and unsuccessfully between Puerto Rico and the United States and, to a lesser extent, between Puerto Rico and Latin American and Caribbean nations. Rosselló and his administration presented mano dura as a winning strategy for fighting the drug wars that could be successfully implemented in other US jurisdictions, as well as throughout the Global South. As the threat of communism was supplanted by the threat of international drug trafficking, Rosselló and technocrats within his administration touted mano dura's large-scale activation of the Puerto Rican National Guard to participate in local drug enforcement. Rosselló and his administration saw these efforts as a creative and necessary repurposing of military technology and personnel. Legislators on the mainland United States pointed to the use of the National Guard in Puerto Rico as they turned urban centers into veritable war zones in an effort to eradicate drugs and violent crime. While few mainland cities actually saw National Guard troops deployed as they were in Puerto Rico, as a vital component of antidrug policing, US policy makers celebrated the Rosselló administration's "daring innovations" at a moment when policing was becoming increasingly militarized throughout the United States.

U.S. officials looked to Puerto Rico to justify an increasingly harsh and militarized approach to law enforcement at a moment when many low-income people and people of color were already witnessing "the rise of the warrior cop" in their communities.[5] While the deployment of the National Guard was certainly central to how US policy makers understood mano dura contra el crimen, the role of drug enforcement in facilitating the transfer of public housing units from government control to private management also came to define the so-called Puerto Rican model of controlling crime and reforming public housing. Governor Rosselló, Superintendent Toledo, and Housing Secretary Vivoni presented mano dura's quelling of drug use and trafficking within public housing as a central component in the large-scale privatization of Puerto Rico's public housing authority. Rosselló and his administration seized upon US policy makers' established interest in both punitive approaches to drug enforcement and the privatization of government services, effectively twinning these two policy trends to cement Puerto Rico's value to the United States as a policy innovator.

Political elites in Puerto Rico tried to position Puerto Rico as a policy innovator in the realms of policing and privatization by alleging that mano dura contra el crimen created safe and empowered communities that were able to get by on less from the government. There was, however, an intense dissonance between the image of postintervention public housing complexes projected to policy makers in the United States and Global South and the reality experienced by many Puerto Ricans living in "rescued" public housing around the archipelago. The raids and privatization efforts aimed at public housing increased residents' vulnerability by leading to evictions, displacements, and the separation of families as a result of arrests. Mano dura and its attendant privatization efforts also did little to reduce residents' exposure to harm. Public housing residents regularly made their voices heard, using the media in an effort to disrupt the narrative of community safety and empowerment being sold in Puerto Rico, the United States, and globally by the Rosselló administration and US policy elites. No longer America's shining star in the Caribbean, Puerto Rico emerged from the dust of the Cold War as an innovator of the neoliberal carceral state *and* a glaring example of the terrible toll such policies wreaked on vulnerable communities.

NEOLIBERAL BOLIVARIANISMO

Following Pedro Rosselló's inauguration as the sixth governor of Puerto Rico in 1993, the *San Juan Star*'s managing editor, Scott Ware, published a commentary about the challenges confronting the governor. The Cold War had ended, the Soviet empire had fallen, and "old formulas that have governed the world, that have governed the United States, that have governed Puerto Rico just don't seem to be working anymore."[6] What Puerto Rico needed was new ideas, new approaches, and new modes of leadership. Ware reminded readers that it had been Puerto Ricans' openness to change and innovation that pushed the archipelago forward during the twentieth century. "Bold ideas and new thinking produced the spectacular successes of Operation Bootstrap, the 936 program, the Commonwealth Status, and a New Deal-style commitment from government to put people to work," Ware commented.[7] Those bold innovations that Ware named, however, seemed to have lost momentum by the time he penned his commentary. He asked a series of questions meant to highlight the unique challenges that Puerto Rico faced at the end of the "American Century": "Has Operation Bootstrap run out of gas? Does 936 have a place in the newly forming economic order of the Caribbean? Has Commonwealth status outlived its purpose? Can we find ways to create real jobs, and job training, in the private economy so we can reduce our bloated and inefficient government? Can we stand the plan?"[8] The questions and positions laid out by Ware in his editorial were not lost on Rosselló as he entered office, and in many ways questions like these fashioned his style of governance.

The signing of the North American Free Trade Agreement (NAFTA) by US president George H. W. Bush, Mexican president Carlos Salinas, and Canadian prime minister Brian Mulroney on December 17, 1992, sounded a death knell for Puerto Rico's special relationship with the United States and threw into question the preferred status conferred upon Puerto Rico by the commonwealth agreement. Operation Bootstrap and the commonwealth model, however, sowed the seeds for their own eventual destruction at the hands of such transnational free trade agreements. A Cold War antidote to socialist development models, Operation Bootstrap was meant to show the Third World the incredible progress that could be achieved through economic and political alignment with the United States. Predictably, as the United States promoted Puerto Rico's development model to nations throughout the Third World, its gradual widespread implementation meant the emergence of new markets and labor pools for American capital beyond Puerto Rico. As Puerto Rico's economy became more integrated into the US economy, eventually resulting in the extension of federal legal standards and practices, including the federal minimum wage, US capital left in search of cheaper labor, better corporate incentives, and less regulation. Puerto Rico's development model had provided an important reference point for the Ronald Reagan administration's Caribbean Basin Initiative and the subsequent attempts to create a hemispheric free trade zone that eventually resulted in NAFTA and the Dominican Republic-Central America-United States Free Trade Agreement (CAFTA-DR).[9]

The successful implementation of the Puerto Rican development model in other national and transnational sites around the globe would have disastrous economic consequences for Puerto Ricans in the archipelago and in the diaspora. In December 1993 the National Puerto Rican Coalition, comprised of one hundred Puerto Rican community and advocacy groups, publicly opposed the implementation of NAFTA, becoming one of the earliest Hispanic organizations to do so.[10] According to Lou Nuñez, president of the coalition, NAFTA would "make a bad economic situation even worse" for Puerto Ricans living in the archipelago and in the northeastern United States, "because Puerto Ric[ans] rely on the very jobs that would be eliminated."[11] Likewise, Rosselló acknowledged that Puerto Rico's competitive edge in relation to other Latin American and Caribbean nations was steadily eroding. Shortly after the signing of NATFA, he remarked, "What happens with NAFTA and the other treaties that will surely follow is that the advantage that Puerto Rico enjoys as a territory of the United States is no longer an exclusive advantage."[12]

Rosselló continued, "Puerto Rico can no longer compete on the basis of cheap wages. Even though salaries here are half those in the American mainland, on average they are four times Mexican wages. In any industry that depends on cheap labor, we are going to be at a disadvantage."[13]

The challenge for Rosselló and Puerto Rican elites during this period, then, was how to strengthen Puerto Rico's relationship with, and also assure continued incorporation within, the United States, when Puerto Rico's strategic and symbolic value seemed to be rapidly depreciating. While Puerto Rico's workforce could no longer be regarded as "cheap," Rosselló and his administration maintained, it *was* largely bilingual and well trained. Therefore, mediation and facilitation of US capital and interests in Latin America and the Caribbean were where Puerto Rico's comparative advantage now seemed to rest.

On February 28, 1994, Governor Rosselló met with President Salinas to discuss the role Puerto Rico could play in helping with Mexico's economic transition. Asked to elaborate about the reason for his visit, Rosselló told the press, "We came here in that spirit, a spirit of analyzing and looking at a new scenario that allows Puerto Rico to have a role of facilitator in the movement to join the greatest market in the world."[14] Rosselló presented Puerto Rico as a steady supply of highly skilled bilingual workers, well versed in American development practices and eager to assist with operations in Mexico. He announced that an office of the Puerto Rico Industrial Development Company (PRIDCO) was slated to open in Mexico City in May 1994 with the intention of providing a liaison between Mexican business elites and Puerto Rican technocrats.[15] On May 16, 1994, Rosselló met with President Bill Clinton to solidify Puerto Rico's role as the "Gateway to the Americas" in the NAFTA era. Rosselló relayed to the press that in his thirty-minute, one-on-one meeting with President Clinton, they "spoke about the role Puerto Rico could play in terms of the U.S. opening up Latin America."[16]

Puerto Rico, utilizing its experience of ongoing colonization by the United States, was to assist capital flight out of the archipelago and into more easily exploitable Latin American labor markets. "Latin America is the new frontier of Western Hemisphere commerce. And Puerto Rico is the United States' ideal gateway to that new frontier," Rosselló told a group of executives and guests of the Bank of Boston on July 15, 1994.[17] Puerto Rico, according to Rosselló, could provide the necessary human infrastructure to ensure the success of American capital and interests in the region. "Other places are now furiously launching public relations campaigns trying to pass themselves off as what Puerto Rico already IS. Other places are scrambling to project an *image*. Puerto Rico can offer a reality," Rosselló assured the group of business elites eager to jump into the Latin American market.[18] Puerto Ricans were American citizens, largely bilingual, and familiar with the ins and outs of US industry; they could provide essential services as capital relocated to other sites in the Spanish-speaking Global South.

In many ways, Rosselló's attempt to court US elites by offering a "partner in opening up these new markets" and positioning of Puerto Rico as a "conduit, through which to learn about ... and fully exploit ... that enormous potential," is hardly surprising given Puerto Rico's declining economic and political significance over the course of the 1980s and 1990s, which the implementation of NAFTA only seemed to hasten.[19] What is perhaps unexpected is the way in which Rosselló touted this colonial middleman role as a fulfillment of Puerto Rico's destiny. Puerto Rico, according to Rosselló, would be the force to finally unify the Americas. During a meeting of the American Chamber of Commerce of the Dominican Republic, Rosselló boldly stated, "Our continent can no longer look at history as a book that one reads but does not believe ... as if the Bolivarian dream was an impossibility or an idea irreconcilable with reality."[20] Rosselló celebrated free trade agreements like the General Agreement on Tariffs and Trade (GATT) and NAFTA as important and necessary steps in breaking down the national barriers that had previously prevented the unification of the Americas. He promoted a neoliberal perversion of the Bolivarian dream, arguing that Puerto Rico would have an essential role to play in making the seamless movement of US capital a reality.[21]

Rosselló sold Puerto Rico to US policy makers and business elites as the embodiment of the ideal colonial subject, enabling the metropole's smooth governance and further expansion. To his Puerto Rican audiences, he presented the idea of Puerto Rico assuming its rightful place as a bridge between the Global North and South and as necessary to repay the debt of American citizenship.[22] On July 27, 1994, shortly after his speech at the Bank of Boston, Rosselló explained to a pro-statehood crowd gathered to celebrate the birthday of José Celso Barbosa, the father of the annexationist movement, that serving as an example for Latin America was about demonstrating to the United States that Puerto Ricans are not a drain on US resources but rather valuable assets. He told the crowd:

> Little by little Puerto Rico is becoming ... an example of change in the Americas ... for our bothers in the other states. We will not just ask ... like

beggars ... with an open hand to see what we get.... We have pride ... we have history ... we have values, as a people and a society.... Therefore, we are not only the ones who ask.... Now we are also the ones who give.... And we are becoming the bridge of the Americas ... helping our fellow citizens to open and maintain a constructive dialogue ... a dialogue of the future.[23]

This approach to Puerto Ricans' citizenship as a debt to be repaid was partially a response to US conservatives' resistance to Puerto Rico's bid for statehood. Rosselló had aggressively pushed for a plebiscite, or nonbinding referendum, on Puerto Rico's status, before he even entered office. The 1993 plebiscite, although ultimately resulting in a loss for the statehood party, sparked numerous debates about incorporating Puerto Rico as the fifty-first state of the union. U.S. conservatives were concerned about fully incorporating a territory with such high levels of poverty, unemployment, welfare transfers, and crime, not to mention one marked by cultural and linguistic difference. The strategy adopted by Rosselló and his administration was therefore an attempt to bridge some of the real and perceived economic and political distinctions that were stymieing serious discussions about the possibility of Puerto Rico's full inclusion as a state, by emphasizing its value.

Rosselló's stance was in direct opposition to that of former pro-statehood governor Carlos Romero Barceló (1977–1985). Barceló is well known for his 1972 political pamphlet "Statehood is for the Poor," which attempted to rally Puerto Ricans behind the statehood party by claiming that full incorporation would increase welfare transfers to the poor. Rosselló had to convince American conservatives that continued affiliation with Puerto Rico was beneficial for the United States rather than simply the subsidization of poor islands filled with a racially and culturally distinct population.[24] At a time when Puerto Rico's utility and relevance to the United States were up for debate, and when the archipelago had become a symbol of opportunism and dependency for some US conservatives, Rosselló and his administration sought to cement Puerto Rico's importance by demonstrating that they had not only accepted the gospel of neoliberalism, but could play a key role in proselytizing to Latin America and the Caribbean. As Rosselló himself put it following his meeting with President Clinton, "We did not ask for anything. We're trying to change that image of Puerto Rico always asking. We want to show Puerto Rico as an asset to the national community."[25]

Governor Rosselló focused on issues of security in the post–Cold War period as a means of ensuring colonial capitalist development and expansion. In so doing, he worked to distance Puerto Rico from charges of a parasitic relationship and put his conservative Bolivarian rhetoric into practice. He emphasized Puerto Rico's strategic value during a time of intense transformation for Puerto Rico and the United States. Specifically, Rosselló presented mano dura contra el crimen and its "achievements" in the realms of public safety and public housing reform as a highly effective and translatable model that attended simultaneously to growing concern with the decaying physical infrastructure of public housing and the drug-fueled urban violence that public housing supposedly fostered.

MANAGING PUBLIC HOUSING

Efforts to privatize public housing in the mainland United States began in earnest in 1984, when Congress considered legislation that would allow residents to buy their units. In 1986 the House of Representatives passed a bill, sponsored by Representative Jack Kemp (R-NY), that would allow residents to purchase their homes at a price not to exceed 25 percent of their fair market value.[26] While Kemp's bill did not pass the Senate, in 1988 Congress enacted statutes designed to facilitate the transfer of the ownership of public housing units to private owners.[27] Shortly thereafter, the President's Commission on Privatization (1988) issued a series of recommendations aimed at successfully eliminating government ownership and management of public housing in the United States. Increasing voucher programs, "aggressively" selling public housing stock in good condition to residents at discounted prices, encouraging tenants to convert public housing properties to private cooperatives, and contracting out the management of large housing complexes were among the recommendations issued by the commission.[28]

The embrace of the report and its recommendations resulted in privatization becoming one of the central policy concerns of the US Department of Housing and Urban Development (HUD) at a federal level as well as within its local housing authorities. Indeed, when Kemp was later appointed secretary of HUD by George H. W. Bush, he said he would "pledge the full resources" of the federal agency to put public housing in private hands.[29] Immediately, Kemp attempted to revitalize the Housing Opportunity for People Everywhere (HOPE VI) program, which sought to transform public housing into mixed-income communities through public-private partnerships. HUD pushed these privatization programs in areas with high concentrations of "severely distressed" public housing such as New Orleans,

Chicago, and Washington, D.C. The transition to private management or the sale of units to public housing residents became a prerequisite for public housing authorities (PHAs) to get themselves off HUD's notorious "troubled housing" list or avoid hefty fines resulting from poor conditions or low rent collection rates.

Hoping to remove Puerto Rico from HUD's troubled housing list, deal with deteriorating physical conditions, and reduce the amount of drug use and trafficking that was concentrated in public housing, Governor Rafael Hernández Colón's administration signed an agreement with HUD in May 1992 to run a pilot privatization program.[30] Puerto Rico became the first large public housing authority to fully privatize the management of its entire housing stock. Although the Housing Authority of New Orleans (HANO) had signed an agreement with HUD to contract out some of the management functions of its housing authority to a private firm as early as 1988, the Puerto Rico Housing Authority (PRHA), in 1992, became the first authority to completely hand over the management of all its properties to private management firms.[31]

The contract between HUD and the Hernández Colón administration was the largest of its kind at the time and had clear implications for privatization efforts in the mainland United States. The PRHA was the second largest in the United States after New York City, providing a more appropriate model than New Orleans for reforming large, troubled housing authorities throughout the nation. Kemp explicitly stated that the pilot program could provide a model of "what could occur in urban countries or urban cities in the United States, but also in the Caribbean and Latin America."[32] Rosa C. Villalonga, manager of HUD's Caribbean Office, told *El Nuevo Día*, "We [the PRHA] are the model. . . . [W]e have the capacity to do novel things. We haven't had to look to the United States because here we have positive things that will be successful."[33] Villalonga suggested that the program would make other US jurisdictions say, "Let me look at Puerto Rico to learn something good," illustrating the extent to which this privatization program was explicitly meant to position Puerto Rico as a policy innovator.[34]

Unlike the traditional understandings of Puerto Rico as a laboratory for US practices, here we see Puerto Rican policy makers actively and strategically taking it upon themselves to model "creative" approaches to problems that the United States was grappling with as a means of cementing Puerto Rico's relevance. This is not to ignore the involvement of Puerto Ricans in earlier "modernization" efforts that occurred in the archipelago, but rather to highlight a shift in emphasis as Puerto Rican elites absorbed the responsibilities of proving Puerto Rico's utility to the United States. This effort to demonstrate the utility of Puerto Rico to the United States came at the expense of thousands of Puerto Ricans who would become ensnared in the states' iron-fisted grip as a result of increased surveillance and policing in low-income communities.

The PRHA awarded contracts to eleven private management firms to deal with the day-to-day maintenance and operation of Puerto Rico's fifty-eight thousand public housing units, affecting approximately sixty thousand families living in 332 public housing complexes. Some questioned the fairness of the competitive bidding and selection process, as a number of the contracts awarded went to firms with little to no experience in housing management. For instance, public housing management in the big island's northeast region was awarded to Rexset Enterprises Inc., a subsidiary of Rexach Construction Corp., which had been created with the sole purpose of entering the bidding process and had no experience with residential management.[35] Despite allegations of corruption and favoritism, the contracts between the PRHA and eleven selected management firms went into effect on August 1, 1992, and Villalonga supervised a shockingly fast, two-week transition from public to private management.[36]

The privatization efforts in Puerto Rico were in line with a number of the recommendations put forth by the President's Commission on Privatization. In addition to turning over the maintenance and management of all of Puerto Rico's public housing complexes to private firms, Governor Hernández Colón's administration also requested bids from contractors to make upgrades to forty thousand apartments in 184 out of 332 housing projects, which were slated to be sold to tenants under the HOPE VI federal housing program.[37] The implementation of these privatization initiatives through the hiring of housing management firms and the proposed sale of decent housing stock were all part of an effort by the Hernández Colón administration to get Puerto Rico off HUD's "troubled list," unfreeze federal housing funds and resources, and disrupt the puntos operating within public housing, which government neglect had allowed to proliferate.

The private management firms went to work modernizing the complexes immediately after the contracts went into effect, trimming grass, repainting common areas, repairing apartments, and removing debris. Some of the biggest concerns facing public housing residents, from drug dealing and abuse, to school desertion, to under/unemployment, however, proved to be much more difficult for the management companies to deal with. Indeed, the private management companies seemed ill equipped to provide the social services necessary to dramatically improve conditions for public housing residents—social services that the government had also, for the most part, failed to adequately provide. Monserate Ríos, a longtime resident of Lloréns Torres who helped organize the Lloréns Parents Recreational Council, complained that the government agencies and private management companies did not consult with residents to accurately assess the needs of the community. Ríos urged, "The community must have a say in the way of life here."[38] Without community input and collaboration, according to Ríos, any progress made would be superficial and would fail to address the particular dangers that youths in public housing faced. "Teenage boys, 15, 16, and 17 years old, are being killed off in the drug wars. Maybe one in every 100 teen-age boys in Lloréns dies in these wars," Ríos noted, enumerating the effects of government neglect and the potential for more lives to be lost if this newly imposed remedy failed. Approximately six months after the private management company took control, Pedro Berrios Martínez, an elderly resident of the Lloréns Torres complex, remarked, "I haven't seen anything new, except that the grass is trimmed and the yard is clean. They've done some repairs, but other than that nothing."[39] Thus, while the government and private management companies bragged to residents and the press about having achieved a "royal flush" on the day that the all toilets in public housing were in working condition, residents questioned the extent to which these changes to public housing's physical conditions, while necessary, would translate into truly livable conditions if the violence and drug abuse in public housing continued.

Residents were not the only ones complaining about the slow progress made following the transition to private control, particularly in the areas of drug and crime reduction. Private management firms argued that the continued presence of active open-air drug markets made it extremely difficult to live up to the image HUD expected of this pilot program. It quickly became apparent to residents, government officials, and private housing managers alike that privatization on its own was no panacea and did little to diminish drug use and dealing or improve living conditions in Puerto Rico's public housing. It was this realization that prompted the police actions in public housing that began at the tail end of Rafael Hernández Colón's third term as governor and intensified under Rosselló. Rosselló's targeting of public housing as part of mano dura contra el crimen gave these "revitalization" efforts the muscle seemingly necessary to make the pilot program a success.

"NO BETTER THAN THE UNSTABLE CAPITAL OF SOME ANARCHIST, THIRD WORLD NATION"

On the evening of February 11, 1993, televisions and radios announced that war had been declared in Puerto Rico. Rosselló, in a special address to the legislature and the people of Puerto Rico regarding the urgent crime problem, declared that the time for half measures was over; the criminals had "asked for war . . . and war they will have."[40] Rosselló would deploy the National Guard to assist police officials in drug busts and patrols. Although National Guardsmen would first be seen patrolling beaches, movie theaters, malls, and other public spaces of leisure, their presence would quickly become concentrated in public housing complexes after the first joint military and police raid at Villa España, on June 5, 1993. Rosselló's deployment of the National Guard as a central component of mano dura contra el crimen would become one of the longest "peacetime" deployments of the Guard in US history.

The unprecedented scope and duration of the National Guard's maneuvers in Puerto Rican public housing quickly caught the eye of many US policy makers. Military analysts and strategists in particular watched with curiosity as Rosselló's repurposing of the Guard seemed to respond to the challenge of what to do with surplus military technology, knowledge, and personnel following the end of the Cold War. The massive military surplus built up over the span of the Cold War years seemed to provide a ready-made solution to local and federal police agencies looking to be "tough on crime" while adhering to the neoliberal economic imperative to watch their bottom line.

Starting in the late 1980s, the US government increasingly funneled military knowledge, technology, and personnel into civilian policing efforts, particularly in the spheres of border and drug enforcement. Perceived as underutilized by some US government and military officials due to its association with infrequent occurrences such as natural disasters or civil unrest, the National Guard, in particular, found itself at the center of debates about military involvement in civilian policing. In 1989 the US Congress authorized federal funding to permit local National Guard units to support drug interdiction and other counter-drug activities, blurring the line between the rhetoric and the reality of a war on drugs.[41] States desiring to participate in the program were required to draw up plans to be evaluated and approved by the secretary of defense and the DOJ. Military grade weaponry, tanks, helicopters, and soldiers soon became regular fixtures of routine policing efforts as local governments availed themselves of federal funding and resources.[42]

On October 5, 1994, during a congressional subcommittee hearing regarding the appropriateness of using the National Guard in crime-fighting efforts, Representative Charles Schumer (D-NY) noted, "The National Guard is a powerful, ready-made fighting force. Redefining its role in the post Cold War era presents exciting possibilities in the war against crime."[43] For his part, Rosselló touted mano dura contra el crimen as an example of how to turn the "weekend warriors" of the National Guard into essential players in the US permanent war on drugs. Rosselló's testimony before Representative Schumer's subcommittee in many ways encapsulated the governor's position regarding the post–Cold War realities facing American cities, including those in the archipelago. According to Rosselló, "With the Cold War won and the Soviet Union dissolved—the time has come to direct more of our attention to internal security issues; to current dangers we face at home: drug-trafficking, and the violent crime that drug-trafficking engenders."[44] Puerto Rico, Rosselló argued, had "redefined the role of our citizen soldiers" in a way "certainly worthy of study and, and maybe emulation."[45]

City and state officials on the mainland watched Puerto Rico's deployment of the National Guard to combat crime and drugs in public housing with great interest, and it received coverage in important national news outlets such as the *New York Times*, the *Boston Globe*, the *Washington Post*, CNN and National Public Radio (NPR). American policy makers, however, struggled with how to reconcile a declared war on drugs, and the ready availability of surplus military technology and personnel, with democratic principles regarding a necessary separation between military and civilian policing. Rosselló encouraged US legislators and policy makers to dispense with needless concerns about image and confront the fact that the war on drugs was just that: a war. During an interview at the occupied San Martín housing complex, Rosselló said, "I don't care about image; I care about results. I think it would be a worse image if we just did nothing and allowed the criminals to go unchallenged. The reality is that here in Puerto Rico we're not going to tolerate this anymore. And I think other communities with high crime have a lot to learn from us."[46]

Shorty after Rosselló urged other communities to come to terms with the gravity of the situation, Washington, D.C., would become the first major US city to test the waters in trying to bring mano dura–style National Guard deployments stateside. On October 22, 1993, the mayor of Washington, Sharon Pratt Kelly, wrote to President Clinton asking him to grant her the authority to call out the National Guard to help stem the tide of drug-related violence taking place in the district. While approximately thirty-five to fifty National Guardsmen were already on the streets of the district helping police with drug interdiction efforts, Mayor Kelly asked the Clinton administration to make hundreds of troops available for up to four months to provide tactical support to police during drug enforcement efforts.[47] In a press conference detailing her request to President Clinton, Mayor Kelly declared, "We've got a war on our hands."[48] She justified the potential sight of armed soldiers on D.C.'s streets by saying, "We need the Guard's help. We've got a problem that is really of extraordinary proportions. We've got to get real and do whatever it takes to provide safety."[49] Like Rosselló, Kelly appealed to a prevailing sense of panic over "out of control" violence and crime associated with drug use and trafficking in order to rationalize such extraordinary measures.

That same day, President Clinton, speaking to the press after a meeting with members of Congress regarding the impending implementation of NAFTA, was asked about the mayor's request. Clinton acknowledged the challenges that the mayor faced, remarking, "I'm very sympathetic with the problems that the mayor has and that Washington has. There are 1,500 shootings here a year now. It's one reason—I certainly hope that we can pass this crime bill in a hurry. If we do, we'll have another 50,000 police officers on the street, and it will reduce the pressure for National Guard officers."[50] Clinton made it clear that while he supported more boots on the ground, he would prefer that those boots belonged to police officers rather than soldiers. Clinton also feared the larger implications a deployment of the National Guard would have for law enforcement around the country, noting, "It obviously is not a precedent that can easily be confined just to Washington, D.C. So there are lots of questions that have to be thought through here."[51] Four days after Kelly's inquiry, Clinton denied her request, fearing it would set "questionable precedents."[52] Clinton recommended that Kelly seek to expand the district's involvement in already established federal drug interdiction programs. One of the central reasons Clinton cited for his refusal was the fact that soldiers who serve in the Guard are not full-time military and largely serve on weekends; thus, a large-scale, extended mobilization of the Guard would disrupt the work and family lives of a large number of Americans.[53]

A memo to the president from his counsel and associate counsel urging him to deny the request, however, brought up larger concerns about committing the Guard to a mission of "uncertain scope and duration," possible violations of the *Posse Comitatus* Act, and the stress it would put on the Guard if "other crime-plagued localities (e.g. Miami, Chicago, New York, Los Angeles, and Detroit)" were to make similar requests.[54] The president's counsel also warned, "Whatever the general authority, the symbolic significance of the President calling out the military to patrol on a regular basis in the shadow of the White House and the Capitol would be enormous."[55] Harold Brazil, a member of the D.C. City Council, echoed this concern about what kind of message the military performing police duties would send to the general public. He opposed Mayor Kelly's request on the grounds that "this would show the world that America's capital is no better than the unstable capital of some anarchist, Third World nation."[56]

The conceptual and physical distancing of Puerto Rico from the mainland United States allowed for the perception that these violations of democratic principles were not already occurring under the American flag and were only possible in the supposedly retrograde space of the Third World. Indeed, Puerto Rico, because of its status as simultaneously a part of and apart, once again provided an ideal site for the limits of democracy to be tested and US state power to be consolidated. The transfer of these innovations back to the metropole, however, proved to be much more difficult than the discourse of unimpeded global flows that marked the NAFTA era would suggest. Nonetheless, technologies, practices, policy, and rhetoric *did* circulate between Puerto Rico and the United States, although often asymmetrically and incompletely.

"OWNERS OF THEIR ENVIRONMENT"

Despite Mayor Kelly's failed attempt to mirror Puerto Rico in calling out the D.C. National Guard to perform routine drug enforcement duties, US legislators and policy makers continued to consider ways to implement aspects of mano dura contra el crimen in major US urban centers. While Rosselló continued to model innovations in policing tactics to mainland legislators, US policy elites increasingly deemphasized the role of military intervention in "securing" public housing in response to pushback over the use of National Guard soldiers in street-level drug enforcement efforts. They instead focused on the ways in which "community policing" initiatives, like mano dura contra el crimen, had created safer conditions amenable to privatization efforts.

As stage one of Operation Centurion, referred to as the "Rescue" stage, grabbed headlines and the public's attention, stages two and three quietly assisted the privatization process. Stage two, "Restoration," maintained a military presence, established permanent on-site police stations, and restricted access to residents and their guests. In addition to the continued military and police presence, the Quality of Life Congress (QLC), a multiagency task force, stepped in and began to restore the physical space of the public housing complexes and set up social service programs. In the third stage, "Reempowerment," the National Guard was withdrawn, a small number of police remained, and the QLC worked to help residents "regain control" of their community.[57] However, more than merely providing social services, the QLC played an important role in smoothing out the bumps encountered when public housing management was transferred from public to private control. Rosa Villalonga, manager of HUD's Caribbean Office, went so far as to refer to the early morning sieges on public housing as providing a glimpse of "the light at the end of the tunnel" for the long-term goal of privatizing public housing.[58]

The rhetoric of "reempowerment" and "self-sufficiency" espoused by the QLC played on familiar tropes of a culture of poverty within low-income communities. Supposedly marked by a tangle of violent pathologies, public housing residents' lack of proper work ethic and values, as opposed to systemic discrimination, were to blame for the precarity that marked their lives. Public housing residents needed intensive intervention thrust upon them by the state because they were perceived to be incapable of effecting change in their own communities. Housing Secretary Vivoni spoke with great frequency about the "psychological bondage of dependency" that characterized public housing residents and identified it as the biggest impediment to improving life in public housing. According to Vivoni, the ultimate objective of the QLC was to help residents learn skills that would allow them to develop a strong will to work rather than expect government handouts.[59] "First you've got to help them regain a sense of dignity, get them away from the notion that they can't do anything unless the government comes in and does it for them. We've got to change this attitude so that they can assume control of their own destinies," Vivoni argued.[60] Such rhetoric of "reempowerment" ignores the role of structural inequality and government neglect in creating and perpetuating the precarious conditions within public housing. In addition, the push for residents to "develop a sense of independence" that would enable them to take control of their own community, as Secretary Vivoni put it, was largely about training residents to expect less and less support from the government.[61] The eventual goal of "tenant control" and "empowerment," as sociologist John Arena points out, is often structured to accommodate privatization efforts in public housing.[62]

Private housing managers understood their job as setting public housing residents on the path to home ownership and thus facilitating the complete evacuation of the state from the realm of housing. For instance, Mercedes Díaz, president of Inter-Island Rental P.R. Corp, which managed the large 2,570-unit Lloréns Torres housing complex, remarked that the work of the private managers was "to facilitate a transition, in which people who for years were neglected and forgotten and whose self-esteem was subsequently anni-hilated, could learn to stand up on their own two feet, retake control of their lives and their communities and eventually become homeowners."[63] While Díaz's comments demonstrate the ways that housing authorities partially understood their job as curing the individual and communal forms of psy-chological pathology that supposedly afflict public housing residents, her words also show that rather than simply improving the physical conditions in public housing and providing residents with necessary resources, the work of the QLC was to make sure that private managers had the resources needed to oversee this transition from public to private ownership. Vivoni stated this explicitly when he said, "We want to help the privatizers to develop and implement plans of action to attend to the communities that they serve."[64]

Government officials who backed private efforts did so to wean people off essential social services provided by the state. These officials considered com-munity empowerment and public housing completely incompatible. The deteriorating conditions that many public housing residents faced, according to many public officials, were due to the fact that residents seemingly had no proprietary claim to their communities, which contributed to their destruc-tive behaviors. As Vivoni warned following a series of mano dura raids, "If residents don't become owners of their environment, the communities will rot again."[65] It is important to keep in mind, however, as social scientists James Fraser, Deidre Oakley, and Joshua Bazuin argue in their study of the private profit motive in public housing, that privatization efforts function as a way to capitalize off surplus populations by inserting them into the housing market rather than to create lasting and sustainable community control. Fraser, Oakley, and Bazuin note that the push for resident ownership of pub-lic housing "has been an effort to move this pool of redundant laborers into the private market, which in turn has given the real-estate industry access to profit from public housing, often at the expense of the most vulnerable mem-bers of society."[66]

Further, despite a rhetoric that positioned homeownership as the ultimate goal of mano dura contra el crimen and the forms of privatization that it facilitated, few residents would actually purchase their apartment units. And many residents, in fact, did not want to. For the most part, only the management and security functions within public housing would transition from public to private control. Thus, while the state partially shifted the regulation of public housing to the private sector, the ability of public housing residents to shape conditions within their own communities remained consistently undermined. Regardless of who was running things—the state or private entities—public housing residents' visions for their community and desired solutions to many of the pressing issues they were confronted with were often ignored.

RESTORING COMMUNITIES AT GUNPOINT

Although mano dura contra el crimen explicitly sought to establish a lasting police presence in many of Puerto Rico's public housing complexes as a way of controlling drug-related crime and violence, the Rosselló administration often framed the police and military interventions in public housing as short-term efforts necessary to wrest control from the hands of drug traffickers in order to reestablish state-run social services. This approach was captured by the refrain of the Rosselló administration that *la mano amiga seguia la mano dura*, (the helping hand follows the iron fist). Alberto Goachet, Rosselló's head of communications, said that while the occupation of public housing was akin to "Arnold Schwarzenegger-Rambo," the subsequent positive invasion of the QLC was more like "Mother Teresa."[67] The false dichotomy between these two aspects of mano dura contra el crimen functioned to occlude the symbiotic and ongoing relationship between them. Rosselló and his administration maintained that, although drastic, the initial takeovers of public housing were only temporary and that the enduring outcome of mano dura would be strong, self-sustaining communities. Despite evidence to the contrary and the opposition voiced by public housing residents themselves, state officials' rhetoric of community empowerment made the interventions within public housing more palatable as a possible model for large-scale privatization efforts across the United States and Latin America. Mano dura's rebranding as "community policing" allowed Puerto Rican officials and others to downplay the extent to which public housing management in Puerto Rico had been privatized, quite literally, at gunpoint.

Under Rosselló, Puerto Rico became a pilgrimage site of sorts for US and Latin American policy experts and public officials looking to privatize public housing and "modernize" policing in urban areas. The joint military and police incursions on display were referred to as community policing initiatives despite the fact that public housing residents had little to no say in how crime was dealt with in their communities. These visits to see Puerto Rico's "revolution in public housing" were reminiscent of the trips US and Third World technocrats took during the 1950s to see the Puerto Rican "miracle"—the Operation Bootstrap development model—in action. These trips to Puerto Rico's public housing complexes, much like the ones to its factories four decades earlier, underscored the historical endurance of Puerto Rico's role as policy showcase. On July 23, 1993, Choco González Meza, deputy assistant secretary for intergovernmental relations at HUD, met with Governor Rosselló to discuss the joint police and military takeovers of public housing and the ongoing privatization efforts. González Meza left the meeting with Rosselló voicing her support for mano dura, saying, "When a model is working, you should continue investing in it."[68] Soon afterward, scores of officials visited Puerto Rico or hosted members of the Rosselló administration in order to determine the merits of investing in the model themselves. New York City mayor Mario Cuomo, US drug czar Lee P. Brown, president of Costa Rica José María Figueres, delegations of high-ranking Costa Rican and Panamanian officials, the Chicago Housing Authority, the National Center for Housing Management in Washington, D.C., and the Cuban American National Council in Miami all visited Puerto Rico or met with members of the Rosselló administration within a matter of months in 1994 to learn about the effects of mano dura.[69]

Following his tour of occupied public housing complexes on May 10, 1994, Lee Brown exalted mano dura as a model for community policing initiatives across the United States: "I certainly will share what I've seen here."[70] Brown also remarked following his visit, "I just had a very good briefing on the Quality of Life Congress, and that's an excellent example of what we mean by community policing—going into a neighborhood and taking care of the problem from a law enforcement standpoint, but then bringing in the other services of government to consolidate the gains."[71] Proponents of mano dura, however, failed to address what these gains were and whether they actually improved the conditions of livability in public housing for residents living under constant police surveillance and the ongoing threat of violence. For instance, government officials and policy makers did not respond to public housing residents' complaints that mano dura and the subsequent enclosure of their community made them feel like prisoners.[72] When government and law enforcement officials praised mano dura as a model for community policing efforts, they were celebrating not the inclusion of residents in the decision-making process regarding issues of safety and security in their communities, but rather the permanent entrenchment of technologies of surveillance, containment, and punishment in the quotidian lives of the "dangerous classes" who occupied these low-income and racially marginalized spaces. Indeed, many residents of Puerto Rico's public housing complexes and low-income neighborhoods reported not improved relations with police, but feelings of harassment, persecution, and social discrimination as a result of the raids and increased police presence.

Community policing initiatives in Puerto Rico created a bigger role for law enforcement agencies as social welfare services were eviscerated in vulnerable communities. In proposing solutions affecting vulnerable communities, community policing centered the perspectives of police and other community outsiders while marginalizing community members' experiences. Nonetheless, politicians and policy makers traveled to Puerto Rico to see mano dura contra el crimen in action and determine what they could implement within their own jurisdictions. While most visits to Puerto Rico by policy makers garnered very little attention outside of Puerto Rico and very limited political circles, a visit organized by the D.C. Department of Public and Assisted Housing in 1994 that brought public housing tenants to Puerto Rico to see the model at work focused a bright spotlight on mano dura and its attendant privatization efforts.

On July 13, 1994, the *Washington Post* ran a front-page story entitled "Housing Department Resort Trip Cost $10,800," accusing the D.C. Department of Public and Assisted Housing of sticking taxpayers with the bill for "an all-expense-paid four-night boondoggle to a beachfront resort in Puerto Rico."[73] Four staff members from that department and four tenants attended a three-day conference at the Caribe Hilton that was meant to show tenants the changes taking place in Puerto Rico's public housing and discuss ways of translating that experience to the district. The conference featured workshops on privatization, crime and drug prevention, and entrepreneurship, in addition to tours of three occupied public housing complexes.[74] According to Anne Clark, chair of the D.C. Resident Council Advisory Board, the conference was generative and informative for D.C. public housing residents: "We learned quite a bit. . . . We learned about the different ways that residents are starting their own businesses and that the National Guard carry M-16 rifles to secure public housing properties."[75] While Clark celebrated resident entrepreneurship, which was supported by private management companies and the

PRHA, her jarringly matter-of-fact description of soldiers patrolling public housing with high-power assault weapons highlights the ways in which security and profit were intertwined and seemingly dependent upon one another—a microcosm of larger logics and rhetorics at work in the post–Cold War neoliberal moment.

Jasper Burnette, acting director of the D.C. Department of Public and Assisted Housing, countered accusations of financial malfeasance by saying that the trip was far from a beach getaway and that the department had gone to Puerto Rico because it had "a large and troubled public housing agency, which [was] undergoing privatization." Burnette argued that Puerto Rico, after twenty months of experience, had unique insights to offer US cities wanting to undertake similar efforts. He stated: "Yes, it [the PRHA] is also troubled, but no other public housing authority in the country has this kind of experience on this level. If we do it, we want to do it as smoothly as possible and believe that we can learn a great deal from Puerto Rico's experience. Puerto Rico also has a unique experience with crime and the use of the National Guard to police its public housing. We wanted our residents to talk to residents there about this drastic but unique crime-prevention technique."[76] Burnett's defense of the high cost incurred by the D.C. Department of Public and Assisted Housing's attendance at the conference, based on the notion of Puerto Rico as a model, elucidates the ways in which the Puerto Rican state was actively and aggressively attempting to "sell" mano dura to US technocrats. His justification for the expenditure also illustrated the ways in which the questionable policing tactics of mano dura became strategically paired with privatization efforts in the minds of traveling officials. While officials always acknowledged the role of the police and National Guard in mano dura, they celebrated the permanent outcomes of these interventions as private, independent communities, not permanently occupied, low-income neighborhoods. This rhetorical sleight of hand on the part of policy elites denied the experiences of Puerto Rican public housing residents, who voiced concern over the failures of both privatization and militarized policing to make their communities secure in a meaningful and holistic way.

PUERTO RICO LO HACE MEJOR?/PUERTO RICO DOES IT BETTER?

On December 31, 1995, the *Boston Globe* proclaimed that the privatization of Puerto Rico's public housing management was "the most ambitious experiment going on in American public housing," characterizing it as a "quiet revolution" that "could spread to the mainland."[77] Roger Stevens, president of the National Center for Housing Management, was quoted in the *Boston Globe* article as saying, "There's a whole new attitude in Puerto Rico, a whole new approach. They were the first to take this plunge. They won't be the last."[78] On January 23, 1996, Rosselló mentioned the *Globe*'s glowing story on Puerto Rico's privatization of public housing during his annual message to the legislature and people of Puerto Rico. He positioned the *Globe*'s assessment as proof that the interventions taking place in public housing were working and that Puerto Rico was at the forefront of the fight against crime. "It should not be strange," Rosselló noted, "that the Continent looks at the actions of Puerto Rico and takes them as a model for the nation ... and that our Latin American brothers from Panama and Costa Rica, solicit our input and technological innovations for their own fight against crime."[79] Rosselló's mention of US policy makers' interest in privatization and Latin American officials' interest in crime-fighting technology in the same breath again demonstrates the extent to which crime fighting and privatization had been effectively twinned as crucial components of mano dura contra el crimen.

Rosselló boasted that he was confident that by September 1996 the Puerto Rican government would be able to convert the vast majority of public housing into private homes owned by tenants. Public housing residents, according to Rosselló, would have "a place of their own ... defensible and proudly their own ... free of drugs and crime and peaceful."[80] In less than three years, Rosselló argued, Puerto Rico had achieved something that no one dreamed possible, and for that Puerto Rico was being recognized and celebrated. The *Boston Globe* article was, according to Rossello, "another case in which inventiveness, and the desire to achieve a major change that will benefit our people, produced positive results that are seen and admired."[81] Later that year, on June 10, 1996, at the Subcommittee on National Security, International Affairs, and Criminal Justice hearing on recent successes in the war on drug crime, with which I opened this chapter, Rosselló enumerated those positive results. Rosselló announced to the US representatives present that what mano dura had "produced for [their] fellow citizens in Puerto Rico, [was] a 3-year improvement that [could] be quantified as the following: 300 fewer vehicle thefts every month; 900 fewer burglaries every month; plus a long overdue measure of blessed relief from anxiety, fear, dread and despair."[82]

Public housing residents, and even some Puerto Rican government officials, however, told another story. First, contrary to the message put forth by

Rosselló and his administration, most public housing residents did not become owners of their apartments; rather, in the vast majority of cases, the government privatized only the *management* of the complexes. On April 17, 1999, close to the end of his second term, in his weekly radio program *Rindiendo Cuentas*, Rosselló noted that while the ultimate goal was for public housing residents to become private homeowners, only a small number of public housing complexes had been sold or were slated to be sold.[83] Thus, while the narrative of promoting homeownership and self-sufficient communities was key in garnering approval for mano dura contra el crimen and the subsequent privatization of public housing, for the most part these measures only further removed community control from the hands of public housing residents.

Rather than relieving anxiety, fear, dread, and despair, the police interventions and privatization efforts in many ways exacerbated dangerous conditions and presented new challenges to which residents had to respond with fewer resources. Taking to the pages of the independently distributed 'zine *Masturbana* to disrupt the official narrative of the Rosselló administration, community activist Irmarilis González Torres noted, "This time we are the most worthy example to emulate. Now we sell ourselves internationally with [the slogan] 'Puerto Rico does it better' and the invasions that occur in our projects are being characterized as the best strategic military operations implemented in the United States in the war against crime and drug trafficking." González Torres implored her readers to question whether Puerto Rico did, in fact, do it better, and if so, what exactly Puerto Rico was doing better.[84] While Rosselló celebrated nine hundred fewer robberies every month, Puerto Rico continued to experience increases in the number of murders committed, and joint military and police raids continued to intensify battles between rivals over turf. While Rosselló celebrated three hundred fewer carjackings every month, growing arrest and incarceration rates fractured families and communities.

The number of arrests under Rosselló increased by approximately one-third over that of his predecessor, Rafael Hernández Colón. There were sixteen thousand arrests recorded in 1992, in contrast to roughly twenty-one thousand arrests each year in 1993 and 1994.[85] In addition, when President Clinton signed the federal "one strike and you're out" policy in 1996, Puerto Ricans living in public housing now faced the threat of eviction if they or a family member living with them were convicted of a drug crime. While it seems that the policy was implemented somewhat unevenly in Puerto Rico, dozens of Puerto Ricans and their families were evicted under it.[86] The constant raids in public housing as a result of mano dura contra el crimen carried not only the threat of incarceration for those swept up in the raids, but also the threat of criminalization and eviction for individuals who, for the most part, had done little but been born into a particular family.

Much like the privatization that the raids in public housing enabled, the arrests and convictions resulting from those raids created a financial bonanza for private security and prison corporations that operated in Puerto Rico. These corporations included the Corrections Corporation of America (now CoreCivic) and Wackenhut (now G4S Secure Solutions). As Manuel Calas, head of Wackenhut Puerto Rico's operations, told *El Nuevo Herald*, "That is the sad reality in which we are living. What for some is a disgrace, to us is a booming business."[87] Here, Calas referred to the incredible profits from security camera and home alarm sales that the company was experiencing during the early 1990s. Many of these private security companies were also in the private prison business, and mano dura provided them with an additional revenue stream as Puerto Rico's carceral capacity exploded.

Rates of incarceration climbed during the late 1980s and over the course of the 1990s. In 1981 the Puerto Rican prison population was 4,221; ten years later it had more than doubled, with 11,238 people behind bars.[88] When Rosselló took office in January 1993, the number of people incarcerated was approximately 14,355. The number continued to increase exponentially as mano dura wore on. Toward the end of 1993, 20,136 people were under custodial control in correctional facilities, and by 1995 that number was 24,471.[89] The numbers of people being churned through Puerto Rico's correction system were so high that the state was forced to pay tens of millions of dollars in fines as a result of dangerous and unhygienic conditions of overcrowding in its jails and prisons. These conditions, in turn, became a justification for increasing the number of correctional facilities.

In 1995 Rosselló unveiled a $400 million plan to expand Puerto Rico's carceral capacity from twelve thousand to fifteen thousand by late 1996 and then to eighteen thousand by 1999.[90] During the Rosselló administration, fourteen new correctional facilities were built, increasing the number from thirty in 1991 to forty-four in 1999.[91] Rosselló also oversaw the establishment of Puerto Rico's first private prisons, with four opened during his tenure. By the late 1990s approximately three thousand inmates were being held in private correctional facilities.[92] The number of Puerto Ricans incarcerated by the Rosselló administration in both private and state-run facilities was likely higher than during the mano dura era, but with the federalization of certain violent offenses and drug crimes, Puerto Ricans convicted of federal offenses were sometimes sent to the United States when the federal prison in Guaynabo could not accommodate them, making the actual incarceration rates for *all* Puerto Ricans more difficult to gauge.

Black-identified Puerto Ricans and individuals from low-income communities were and are overrepresented in the prison population, as are individuals with a history of substance abuse.[93] Most individuals enter the correctional system as a result of drug-related offences, with 60 percent identified as drug users.[94] The racialized and classed disparities apparent in every aspect of the Puerto Rican criminal justice system, from courtrooms to jail cells to prison blocks, speaks to how mano dura and similar crime control initiatives have criminalized both Blackness and poverty and sought the containment and incapacitation of vulnerable populations. In addition, the criminalization and demonization of drug use, and survival strategies associated with maintaining habits of addiction, led to a high proportion of active drug users winding up in Puerto Rico's jails and prisons. In private and state-run correctional facilities, drug users were given little to no access to rehabilitative tools or forms of support.

If we recognize the destruction that incarceration causes at the individual, family, and community levels, it is obvious that mano dura contra el crimen and the QLC could never produce the "reempowered" healthy and intact communities they promised. Instead they removed people from their communities and produced cash cows for the private security and housing management industries operating in Puerto Rico. Thus, whether the urban poor laid their heads down in newly privatized public housing or in one of the new privately run prisons, the Rosselló government ensured that those beds would generate enormous profits for private industry. *That is what Puerto Rico did, indeed, do better.*

"EVERYTHING IS THE SAME; NO ONE CAN FIX THIS."

A short while after the raids began, it became clear that private management companies, even with the logistical support of the PRPD, National Guard, and QLC, were largely unable to address the public safety concerns that existed in public housing. On June 17, 1993, shortly after the raids on public housing began, HUD announced that it would provide the PRHA with

$6 million for the creation of a special public housing police force and drug rehabilitation programs. According to Rosa Villalonga, manager of HUD's Caribbean Office, the lion's share of the HUD funds—$4 million—would be allocated to training 166 officers and 21 supervisors to work in thirty-one "high crime" public housing complexes.[95] In addition, the private management companies were responsible for using money from their "community initiative funds" to recruit and train residents to work as security. Police superintendent Toledo noted that, with this plan in place, the National Guard presence would be temporary, as private security, with some police assistance, would eventually take charge of law enforcement efforts in public housing.[96]

Transitioning military and police personnel out of occupied public housing complexes in a timely manner was critical due to the extremely high cost of maintaining a police and Guard presence in public housing, estimated to be as high as $1 million a month. The Rosselló administration put pressure on the private managers to build permanent controlled-access gates and hire guards so that the police and National Guard could leave.[97] Toledo noted, "Part of the second phase is for the privatization companies managing the projects to build fences and gates for the controlled access. Once they do that, we can move our personnel and they will be replaced by private security guards and by part-time police officers."[98] Despite material support from the federal and local governments, the private managers often failed to act as efficient facilitators and, ironically, often seriously frustrated the Puerto Rican state's attempts to "secure" public housing.

The failure of privatization efforts to create safer public housing communities is perhaps best illustrated by the murders that still occurred unabated. Ulises González Ortiz, a resident of the Juana Matos public housing complex and reputed *gatillero* (triggerman), was executed in broad daylight on August 11, 1995. After González Ortiz's two assailants riddled his body with twenty-three bullets, they fled on foot, unhindered by the fifteen police officers stationed at Juana Matos or the security fence surrounding the complex.[99] Less than twenty-four hours before, José Morales Pérez, another young Juana Matos resident, had died after being sprayed with thirty shots from an AR-15 assault rifle.[100] The murders of Morales Pérez and González Ortiz were the fourth and fifth to occur in Juana Matos since the police and National Guard had occupied the complex on January 21, 1994.[101]

When asked to account for how violent gangland slayings could continue apace in occupied public housing complexes, police blamed the private housing managers. A section of Juana Matos's controlled-access perimeter fence near the front entrance to the complex had been damaged during a car crash several months earlier and hadn't been repaired.[102] According to police commander Eduardo León, director of the police's Public Housing Division, Rexset Management Corp. withheld money for repairs and investment once they found out their contract would not be renewed.[103] Because their contracts were reviewed annually and could be terminated due to unsatisfactory performance, private management companies that were informed that their contracts would not be renewed for the following year had no incentive to continue providing services to public housing residents or to assist the police.

Speaking to reporters from the *San Juan Star*, José Suárez, a member of the Asociación Ñeta prison gang and a Juana Matos resident, remarked that the state and private management companies failed to provide necessary social services to public housing residents, leaving the Ñetas and other gangs to fill the void. As Suárez pointed out, "We're doing the government's job. What's the point in fixing this place up and making it look pretty if we still lack essential services?"[104] The image projected to US and Latin American legislators of mano dura's successes in the realms of security and privatization strategically omitted the reality that mano dura had profoundly failed many public housing residents.

The official narrative promoted by the Rosselló administration maintained that mano dura had seamlessly turned spaces of disorder into empowered, self-sufficient communities through intervention and privatization. Left out of this narrative was the fact that a number of public housing complexes had to be reoccupied because conditions of violence did not improve and in some cases worsened. For example, Nemesio Canales was occupied under the previous administration on February 26, 1992, one of the first public housing complexes occupied by police force.[105] On September 16, 1994, under Rosselló, the police and National Guard took over the Nemesio Canales public housing complex for a second time. This reoccupation is a glaring example of the inability of punitive force and a fresh coat of paint to meaningfully reduce violence and the drug-based informal economy that contributed to it. Police superintendent Toledo denied that Canales signaled a failure in the mano dura strategy and instead blamed the private housing managers. Toledo defended mano dura, saying, "I wouldn't say that [the takeovers are a failure]. I blame it at least in part on the privatization company assigned here and the criminal elements themselves. The fences around the project have had whole sections removed so that we cannot cover all access. No attempt has been made to repair them."[106] Toledo added, "Areas behind the buildings along the highway look like slums and jungles where dealers have wooden shacks and all kinds of hiding places for drugs."[107] The private managers, it seemed, had trouble even keeping the grass trimmed, let alone appropriately working with residents and local officials to try to create more livable conditions in public housing.

Although mano dura and the QLC promised community empowerment, private management firms rarely, if ever, solicited residents' input or opinions. For instance, when private management firms did organize programming for public housing residents, residents complained that the management companies put on programs they assumed the community needed rather than consulting with residents about their actual needs. Carlos Renta, a twenty-seven-year-old resident of Villa España, the first public housing complex to be occupied under Rosselló, complained that many of the activities were aimed at small children as a form of violence and drug prevention and largely ignored public housing youths in their teens and twenties. Renta noted, "There have been a lot of good things . . . especially around health. . . . The problem is that most of the activities they put on here are focused on children, and I understand that from a question of prevention, but we young people would like to have activities too."[108] In terms of prevention, more might have been gained by directing activities at teenagers and young adults, who were both a major concern for public housing organizers and more likely to be recruited into the drug gangs that operated in public housing. Roberto López, who ran a basketball clinic at Las Gladiolas following its occupation, complained that the private managers wouldn't even spread the word to resident youths about the activity. López said, "We tell the privatization manager and he is supposed to get the word around. But we haven't seen him or anyone else from the company. So we come and gather the kids ourselves and they call the other kids."[109] López's comment highlights the lack of support, financial and otherwise, that private management companies provided for initiatives within public housing that went beyond the edifices.

Further, when private housing managers were deemed inept and their contracts were allowed to expire, no one consulted residents about who would take over the management duties. "The *populares* [pro-commonwealth party] privatized the projects without consulting us. The *penepe* [pro-statehood party] invaded us and closed us in without our authorization, violating our human rights, injuring many people. Now, again without consulting us, they want to change the privatizers," said Juanquina Cruz, president of the

Villa España Residents Council.[110] Cruz added, "I don't defend the privatizers, they have lawyers for that; what I ask is that we, those who receive the
services, are the ones to evaluate them."[111] Cruz's comments demonstrate the
extent to which the intense interventions into public housing significantly
undermined community self-determination and ignored residents' needs.

The private management companies, government officials, police, and
soldiers that swarmed upon public housing did not make residents feel more
secure. For the most part, violence continued to proliferate within the confines of public housing. Though promised jobs and safer surroundings, residents instead encountered more of the same. Residents of Villa España
regarded the police who guarded the complex as little more than "decorative
figures," noting that when police did act it was "only to make the corner boys
run."[112] Miguel Vázquez, a resident of Villa España for three decades, noted,
"Some of the guards come to abuse and hit the [corner] boys. Everything is
the same. No one can fix this. When they [the QLC] arrived, they offered all
kinds of jobs, but nothing ever materialized. On the contrary, they gave jobs
to people from the outside."[113] Similarly, Annie Rodríguez Nazario, a member of the Lloréns Torres Residents Council, said that what residents needed
were programs that provided young people with education and employment.
As Rodríguez Nazario put it, "With the closure [of street access as a result of
the perimeter fence], everything is pretty much the same. The big problem is
the lack of employment. What they [residents] constantly ask me is, 'When
are they going to find me a job?' Stipends are needed for childcare so people
can work or study."[114] These voices run counter to the narrative put forth by
the Rosselló administration in its attempt to sell mano dura and Puerto
Rican public housing as models for the neoliberal era. What Puerto Rico had
managed to do successfully, and what other localities perhaps wished to emulate, was manage marginalized populations in such a way that enabled private
industry to capitalize off long-standing patterns of state neglect and
violence.

CARCERAL CIRCUITS

During the early 1990s the Puerto Rican state attempted to position the
archipelago as a model in the arenas of security and public housing as a way
of negotiating the commonwealth's declining significance during the neoliberal, free-trade era. As Puerto Rico lost its privileged status as a result of trade

liberalization and conservative hostility to its continued incorporation in the United States, it fashioned itself as a facilitator of US capital expansion and a model for policing and public housing policies in urban cities across the United States, as well as in Latin America and the Caribbean. What Puerto Rico perhaps best illustrated, however, was the ways in which the failures of the punitive state to create a more secure existence for the most vulnerable sectors of society created enormous profits for industries charged with keeping those populations in line.

Although some might question Puerto Rico's actual impact on US and Latin American policy regarding the policing and privatization of public housing—for example, how many localities implemented mano dura-esque models explicitly based on Puerto Rico—it is important not to lose sight of what mano dura, even in its failed attempts to jump the pond, tells us about the transforming relationship between Puerto Rico and the United States. The point of tracing these policy circuits is not to argue that Puerto Rico was "the first of its kind," or that these punitive policies and logics did not exist before their implementation in Puerto Rico. Indeed, mano dura, despite the rhetoric of innovation, was itself the progeny of already existing initiatives, policies, and rhetoric, from the broken-windows theory, to defensible space urban design, to the ghetto sweeps that had made themselves felt in low-income neighborhoods across the United States long before Rosselló ever uttered the phrase "mano dura contra el crimen." Acting as referents—"best practices"—initiatives such as mano dura, broken windows, and zero tolerance justified and drew upon one another as they traveled similar policy circuits and provided a rationale that made ravaging already vulnerable communities in order to open them up for capital extraction seem completely reasonable, necessary, and even humanitarian. Thus, although mano dura contra el crimen and the privatization that it facilitated served as policy models, they were also expressions of larger transformations that we now recognize as key components of the neoliberal common sense of our times.

With a careful mapping of the many ways in which public housing residents experienced and discussed mano dura's policing and privatization efforts, and with an attendant analysis of how Puerto Rican officials and US policy makers discussed these initiatives, it's clear that mano dura had very little to do with improving the lives of public housing residents in Puerto Rico. Instead, officials and policy makers, guided by political, social, and economic motivations, wreaked havoc on already vulnerable communities in attempts to shore up Puerto Rico's "value" to the United States as a colony.

THREE

Underground

IN EARLY DECEMBER 2011 I ATTENDED A FORUM ON CRIMINALITY and violence at the Pontificia Universidad Católica de Puerto Rico in the southern city of Ponce. It was one of dozens that took place over the course of that year as scholars, activists, and community members attempted to think through the escalating levels of violence affecting daily life in the archipelago. In the midst of the single most violent year in Puerto Rico's history, which would claim 1,136 lives by its end, the public health officials, criminologists, and legal scholars gathered that evening offered explanations for what was causing such broken social dynamics and discussed possible solutions.

One of the speakers that evening, a criminal law attorney and former police officer, caught my attention when he identified a "culture of illegality" within public housing and low-income barrios as partially to blame for rising rates of violence. He began by noting that inadequate government services and lacking infrastructure directly contributed to increased levels of violent crime by giving rise to the phenomenon of the *bichote*, or drug lord, as social provider. As the government failed to provide necessary social services to low-income Puerto Ricans, drug dealers stepped in to provide vital resources like jobs, food, clothing, and even entertainment to the residents of economically marginalized communities. This, the former police officer argued, created not only a dependence on the illegal drug economy in low-income areas, but also a troubling admiration for violent drug dealers. He supported this claim by urging us to go to public housing complexes and see who was depicted in the murals that adorned their walls. Lamentably, he said, one does not find the "great men" of Puerto Rican history like Eugenio María de Hostos, or Luis Muñoz Rivera, or José Celso Barbosa painted on project walls. Instead, one finds murals of famous drug dealers.

This admiration and respect for drug dealers, the speaker argued, bled into the culture of these communities, and nothing made this more apparent than rap and reggaeton music. Not only did song lyrics celebrate the fast, violent lifestyle of the drug trade, but rap and reggaeton themselves were supposedly integral to the drug economy because they served as laundering fronts for drug money. If we doubted this, the former police officer challenged us to explain how *reggaetoneros* and *raperos* were so wealthy when most Puerto Ricans buy pirated compact discs (CDs) or download their music for free from the Internet. Drug money was surely the source of all that bling, and young people became involved with the drug economy so that they could shine like their favorite rappers and neighborhood drug dealers.

While many elites and law enforcement officials have decried the "deficient culture" of people in public housing, this former police officer went one step further by blaming poverty, addiction, unemployment, and violence on rap and reggaeton music. As far as I could tell, no one that evening questioned the relationship between drugs and rap music that he laid out. Instead, many of the people around me—young and old—nodded and murmured in agreement with his comments. Driving back to San Juan later that night with the radio tuned to the local reggaeton station, I wondered how had it become so commonsensical to think of rap music and the lucrative drug economy that existed in low-income areas as two sides of the same coin. What ends did this connection serve?

This chapter historicizes how rap music and the drug economy in Puerto Rico's low-income areas have come to be seen and treated as mutually constitutive. There is a definite intimacy between rap music and drugs, but not necessarily in the ways outlined by that former police officer. The economic stagnation experienced by young Puerto Ricans, particularly those from economically and racially marginalized areas, caused the rap scene and the drug trade to collide in a way that indelibly marked youth culture and expression during the 1990s. The relationship, both real and imagined, between rap music and the drug trade served as a justification for the policing of low-income and Black youth, and did so through the same logics of contagion and practices of containment that propelled mano dura contra el crimen. In what follows, I mine the relationship between rap music and the informal drug-based economy for what it reveals about tensions over shifting understanding of race, class, sexuality, labor, and youth culture during the mano dura era.

Underground rap, or simply *underground* as it was known at the time, became an object of intense public scrutiny and police intervention during the mid-1990s as a result of its association with public housing and the presumed drug trade that existed therein. This concern over underground eventually culminated in a series of police actions aimed at censuring the genre, including raids against record stores, on the grounds that the music incited young people to promiscuity, violence, and drug use. The policing of underground elucidates how youth culture became a key terrain in which a range of anxieties about drugs, violence, public space, and identity played out in Puerto Rico, ultimately resulting in the surveillance and policing of young people who looked like "raperos" or like they might have lived in public housing.

The coarse, violent, and sexually suggestive lyrics of underground rap were showcased in the media to justify mano dura incursions into low-income areas as a means of establishing discipline and order. Law enforcement officials, media commentators, and more affluent members of Puerto Rican society pointed to the boasts of young men rapping about sex, drugs, and money over hip-hop and reggae beats as evidence of the immorality and criminality of public housing residents. Underground's association with urban poverty and the harsh realities of the streets led to the policing of the genre as an extension of mano dura contra el crimen's raids into public housing. The policing of underground rap, like the raids in public housing, reified and relied upon racialized and classed notions of crime, poverty, and spatial ordering, which led to further stigmatization, surveillance, and harm for the young people, particularly Black and dark-skinned men from low-income areas, who came to embody the threat of disorder during the mano dura era.

RAP INDUSTRY AND IDLENESS

The forces that contributed to the development of underground rap illuminate a series of larger transformations affecting Puerto Rican society during the 1980s. As cultural theorist Mayra Santos Febres notes, Puerto Rican rap is a musical expression of the failures of US colonialism and development. Rap music and the culture that developed around it highlight the difficult realities of circular migration and the implementation of a neoliberal economic agenda.[1] Young people from marginalized communities became key participants, both as fans and artists, in Puerto Rico's bourgeoning rap scene over the course of the 1980s and 1990s, as they were the population most likely to be exposed to neoliberal dislocations and circular migration survival strategies.

Indeed, the economic constriction, migration, growing informal economy, and enclosure of public space that marked Puerto Rico during the 1980s were as crucial to the development of underground rap as the increased accessibility of technology such as four-track recorders, turntables, mixers, and drum machines.[2] Rap was one of the cultural remittances that migrants and diasporic subjects brought to Puerto Rico. Nuyoricans in particular helped to circulate rap music as they traveled back and forth between the archipelago and New York City. Spread though informal networks rather than commercial circuits, rap became popular in working-class and low-income barrios during the early 1980s. Puerto Rican rap pioneer Vico C traces the emergence of the genre primarily to youth from the Lloréns Torres and Las Acacias public housing complexes, starting as early as 1981.[3]

As with U.S rap, public housing and low-income neighborhoods formed a key territory of Puerto Rican rap and its imaginary, with many of the genre's early artists coming from some of the archipelago's poorest communities. Puerto Rican hip-hop scholar Raquel Z. Rivera notes that rap music first became popularized in low-income barrios because these populations tended to have the most experience, either firsthand or by proximity, with migration.[4] The prevalence of migration itself speaks to a larger context of underemployment and idleness experienced by Puerto Rican youth during the l980s and 1990s. Marginalized from the formal labor market, Puerto Rican youth engaged with rap music not only as a way to pass the time or as a vehicle for venting frustrations, but also, importantly, as a possible source of economic support. As historian Robin D. G. Kelley notes in the context of US rap music, "In a postindustrial economy with fewer opportunities for wage work that might be financially or even psychologically fulfilling, art and performance—forms of labor not always seen as labor—become increasingly visible as options to joblessness and low-wage service work."[5] Rap music and culture became a vehicle for possible economic advancement at the same time that it allowed young people to surround themselves with community and pleasure in a social world increasingly marked by uncertainty, precarity, and criminalization. Underground rap emerged as another node in a vast informal economy, one that had much in common with the simultaneous rise of the drug economy, as it provided young people with an alternative path to economic and social affirmation and stability.

In their foundational work, Puerto Rican studies scholars Frank Bonilla and Ricardo Campos analyzed how the fundamental contradiction of capitalism—that is, the intimate relationship between industry and idleness—

affected Puerto Rican populations living in the archipelago and the dias-pora.[6] According to Bonilla and Campos, far from creating a workers' paradise, Operation Bootstrap and its subsequent collapse resulted in a bonanza of profits for US capital and a surplus of Puerto Rican laborers, either forced into idleness or forced out through migration. Bonilla and Campos describe the malaise of the Puerto Rican laboring classes thusly:

> In Puerto Rico, the contradictions of high-technology industrialization, led by worldwide U.S. enterprises, are acutely felt. Pressures on the work force to migrate, to accept poverty wages as the price of protecting a collective 'competitive advantage,' to experience idleness and dependency at subsist-ence levels as a 'privilege' of association with the United States—all reflect systemic changes in the way the available work force is used or not used. The same systemic changes—the relative reduction of active producers within the working class, the enlargement of the reserve labor force, the proliferation of unproductive work, the growth in government employment—have parallel effects on Puerto Rican workers in the metropolis.[7]

These failures of colonial capitalism were particularly felt by low-income and working-class youth in the archipelago and in US cities as they were con-fronted by a paucity of labor options.

Forced into idleness and underproductivity, Puerto Rican youth in the diaspora and the archipelago turned to rap music as a way to put their talents to use or at the very least kill the excess time that comes with not having to punch a clock. This is perhaps best captured through underground's lyrical obsession with *fumaera*, *gufeo*, and *jangueo*: smoking weed, playing around, and hanging out. As hip-hop scholar Raquel Z. Rivera puts it: "The absence of a work ethic defined by personal sacrifice in most rap lyrics is a response to the terrible socioeconomic prospects facing most poor youths. Personal sac-rifice seems pointless—given the high levels of unemployment, police brutal-ity, restriction of civil rights, and the lack of many government services. Many rappers . . . prefer to enjoy and to poeticize the pleasure that can be derived from idleness."[8]

The informal drug economy grew in Puerto Rico, and like the develop-ment of rap music, it took advantage of an excess of young people, particu-larly young men, who found themselves marginalized from the formal labor market. Both rap music and the drug game capitalized on the marginaliza-tion of working-class and poor youth from the formal economy. The material and structural forces that led to the concomitant rise of drugs and rap as parallel paths toward economic and social mobility tell us much about the terrain of possibility for young people in postindustrial urban contexts, in both the United States and Puerto Rico. In this sense, drugs and rap were not linked by a shared culture of violence, as some critics suggest, but by the fact that they both formed part of the vast informal economy that many Puerto Rican youths turned to in order to navigate the ruins of the commonwealth economy as well as the larger global neoliberal moment. Unsurprisingly, then, both rap and the informal drug economy existed in many of the same spaces and drew bodies from many of the same populations and, as a result, influenced and interacted with one another in a number of crucial ways. These interactions and shared historical circumstances would later be used by pundits and law enforcement officials to justify the policing of low-income and racially marginalized youth as part of mano dura contra el crimen.

SUCK IT

The intimacy of the rap scene and the drug economy manifested itself in the lyrical content of many early rap songs that discussed the realities of the punto, or drug point, and both the opportunities it provided and the destruction it caused in many low-income areas.[9] In particular, many artists recorded cautionary tales that touched upon the violence generated by the drug trade. Vico C's "La Recta Final" (1989) is perhaps the most emblematic example. In it, he raps:

Yo no planto bandera	I don't plant flags
Pues yo no soy Cristóbal Colon	Well I'm not Christopher Columbus
Yo soy de las Acacias 100 porciento de corazón	I'm from Las Acacias 100 percent from the heart
De ningún caserío yo me quiero hacer dueño	I don't want to be the boss of any projects
No soy un extranjero, soy puertorriqueño	I'm not a foreigner, I'm Puerto Rican
Los guapos se creen que son conquistadores	The tough guys think they're conquerors
Y quieren adueñarse de todos los sectores	And they want to take charge of all the areas
Ahí es que empiezan a arreglar el asunto	That's how they start to deal with the matter
Al tratar de desaparecerlos del punto	To make rivals disappear

Entonces vienen los tiros y puñaladas	Then come the shootings and stabbings from the drug spot
La vida de ese guapetón esta destrozada	The life of that tough guy is destroyed
La gente lo vio, la policía llegó	The people saw it, the police came
El asesino es bravo así que nadie hablo	The killer is bold so nobody talked
Así es la ley del asesinato aquí en Borinquén	That's the law of murder here in Puerto Rico
Dejan que todos los criminales se afincan	Let all the criminals put down roots
Si esto sigue así escucha bien mi hermano	If this continues listen well my brother
niños crecerán con un cañón en la mano	kids will grow up with a gun in their hand
Y nuestros futuros, se borraran	Our futures, they will erase
Y los tiroteos, se mantendrán	The shootings, will continue
Y los inocentes, se quejaran	The innocent, will complain
Pues no tienen la culpa de estar como están	But they're not to blame for how they are
Cerrando sus casas con mil cerraduras	Locking their houses with a thousand locks
Y así sus vidas estarán mas seguras	That way their lives will be safer
Pero para tener una vida mas pura	But to have a purer life
Creer en cristo es la mejor cura	Believing in Christ is the best cure
Yo siento pasar la balas por mi cara	I feel the bullets pass by my face
Eso para mi no es una cosa bien rara	For me that isn't a rare thing
El mundo es así y hay que aceptar	The world is like that and we have to accept
Que donde estamos viviendo es en la recta final	That we're living at the end of the line

In "La Recta Final," Vico C touches on a number of anxieties related to crime that were circulating at the close of the 1980s, such as bloody battles over puntos, the concentration of crime and violence in low-income areas, the privatization of security, and a widespread feeling of uncertainty regarding the possibility for change. Other rappers, such as Brewley MC in "La Voz del Crimen," DJ Ruben in "La Escuela," and Los Intocables in "Vive y Aprede," took a similar approach in encouraging youth to resist the lure of the streets and actively work to change the situation in Puerto Rico.

While cautionary tales still appeared on mixtapes as the genre progressed during the 1990s, lyrical content largely shifted away from critiques of violence and crime generated by the drug economy to celebrations of smoking weed and denunciations of police attempts to interfere with people working or copping at puntos. This shift in lyrical content in many ways mirrors the intensification of state repression at the tail end of Governor Rafael Hernández Colón's administration, from 1988 to 1992, and the implementation of mano dura contra el crimen under Governor Pedro Rosselló in 1993. For instance, in Master Joe and DJ Playero's "Original Si Soy Yo" from the *Playero 37* mixtape (1992), the two rap back and forth about going to the punto to buy drugs, hanging out in San Juan with their crew, and experiencing police harassment. Master Joe raps about waking up in the morning *con la gana de fumar* (with the desire to smoke weed), and the two then go back and forth discussing their plan to get high and hang out:

Master Joe: *para el punto yo corrí*	Master Joe: I ran to the drug point
Playero: *pa' poder capear*	Playero: So that I could cop
Master Joe: *par de bolsa con los socios*	Master Joe: A couple of bags with the homies
Playero: *y vernos tripear*	Playero: and watch us get crazy
Master Joe: *por la noche pa' San Juan*	Master Joe: that night we went to San Juan
Playero: *nos fuimos a janguiar*	Playero: We went to hang out

The two then describe an altercation with the police that occurs while they are hanging out with friends in San Juan. After receiving a beating, the two escape and begin to taunt the police who abused and harassed them:

Playero: *y eche a correr*	Playero: and I started to run
Master Joe: *mientras yo corría cantaba*	Master Joe: While I was running I sang
Playero: *un reggae*	Playero: a reggae
Master Joe: *que espero que todo el corillo*	Master Joe: that I hope that my whole crew
Playero: *lo cante también*	Playero: will sing too
Master Joe and Playero: *y dice prende un fili que yo quiero fumar*	Master Joe and Playero: and it says light up a philly because I want to smoke

los guardias a mi me lo pueden ma-ma-ma-ma-mar	the police can su-su-su-su-suck my dick
prende un fili que yo quiero fumar	light up a philly because I want to smoke
los guardias a mi me lo pueden ma-ma-ma-ma-mar	the police can su-su-su-su-suck my dick

Master Joe and Playero's verses are emblematic of the growing theme, featured prominently in underground rap lyrics in the 1990s, of going to the punto to buy drugs, work, or hang out; encountering police harassment; and subsequently outsmarting or mocking the police.

In another example, Las Guanabanas, in "Pa'l carajo las mente sana" on *The Noise 1* (1990), rap about encounters with the police officers who raid the puntos:

Pendiente! Pendiente!	Watch out! Watch out!
Se tira los agentes	Here come the agents
Esconda la marihuana	Hide the marijuana
Ya tu sabe, como siempre	You know, like always
Ellos se creen que nos van a voltear	They think that they're going to get the jump on us
El bicho a los otros nos van a mamar	Our dicks they're going to suck
Y seguemos y seguemos, no nos pueden parar	And we keep going and going, they can't stop us
Para llegar a la cima tú nos tienes que ganar	To reach the top you have to defeat us

Here, the raids on the puntos are portrayed as a cat-and-mouse game between dealers and police. The police mount a show of force; the dealers, anticipating this, hide their product, and this continues indefinitely. The attacks on the puntos are exposed as ineffective, and the youths who work the puntos revel in outsmarting the police and undermining their authority. We can think of this in terms of what political scientist James C. Scott has termed the "weapons of the weak," or the everyday forms of resistance, including humor and insult, that demonstrate the limits of oppressive power structures.[10]

Such lyrics make visible the cyclical nature of the drug raids and the inability of policing on its own to contain the informal drug economy. Rappers defiantly telling police to "suck it" or "fuck off" in their lyrics reflected not only a sense of youthful rebellion but also a growing sense of hostility between the young people who smoked weed recreationally or lived in communities with active drug points and the police who abused and harassed suspected drug dealers or users. Falo, in "Pal Cruce" (ca. 1994), raps about going to the punto to cop a dime bag of weed; however, at the drug point he encounters police conducting a raid. He proceeds to fantasize about teaching these officers a lesson:

Saqué una AR-15 y a todos secuestré	I took out a AR-15 and I kidnapped them all
Le amarré las manos y le amarré los pies	I tied up their hands and I tied up their feet
Le dije "hijo de puta, a tu madre me la clavé"	I told them "son of a bitch, I screwed your mother"
Los guardias se callaron, no me contestaron	The cops shut up, they didn't respond
Le boté las armas, las placas y los zapatos	I threw out their guns, badges, and shoes
Lo puse a fumar, mira, por un rato	I started smoking, look, for a while

Falo's revenge fantasy in many ways creates a mirror inverse of police violence. He takes away their weapons, badges, and police boots, stripping them of their authority, and mimics the verbal and physical abuse police often doled out during raids. Falo seeks to deeply humiliate and emasculate the officers, but unlike what youths in public housing and other low-income communities experience, Falo does not mention beating, sexually assaulting, or murdering any of the officers in order to "teach them a lesson." In addition, the fact that Falo's revenge takes the form of a kidnapping could be pointing to the well-known practice that sometimes accompanied drug raids, in which police would round up drug addicts and dealers and abandon them in remote areas outside the metropolitan area, often without their shoes.[11] Songs like "Pal Cruce" and the others cited here question the legality and efficacy of police intervention and give voice to a growing frustration with police abuse and harassment among young men from working-class and low-income areas.

Despite the clear critiques of police impunity embedded in many underground records, the sheer volume of lyrics dedicated to going to the punto to score drugs and smoke weed with friends enabled critics and police officials to use these records to demonstrate the imbrication of rap music with the drug economy and substantiate the claim that the genre served as a recruitment tool for drug dealers looking for new clientele. For instance, on February 5, 1995, Pedro Zervigón, host of the popular television show *Al Grano*, blasted Falo's "Pal Cruce" for its drug-related content and charged that "underground is *a front for the drug trade,* by stimulating the use of drugs and the creation of new clients, new addicts."[12] Eclipsed in this narrative are the ways in which these underground lyrics captured an increasing preoccupation with seemingly constant police harassment and intervention among underground fans and practitioners. Also occluded is the fact that the punto figures so prominently as a space of sociality in underground lyrics not simply because it was a point of drug distribution, but because it was also a key site in the distribution of rap mixtapes.

Reggaetoneros looking back on the days of underground rap note that the lack of access to mainstream distribution networks caused some artists and producers to turn to drug dealers for financing. Dealers not only financed recordings; they would also pay artists to perform in public housing complexes as a way of currying favor with residents. Although this history of drug dealers financing underground recordings has been downplayed and denied with the mainstreaming of reggaeton music in recent years, there is much to be gained from mining the real and imagined imbrications of underground within the drug economy, in order to understand why the threat posed by underground became so easily folded into the logics and practice of mano dura contra el crimen.

During a scene from the documentary *Straight Outta Puerto Rico: Reggaeton's Rough Road to Glory,* DJ Playero, one of the originators of the underground mixtape, takes the viewer on a tour of his old stomping grounds in the public housing complex Villa Kennedy. He shows the camera crew around his former apartment and tells them that almost any reggaeton superstar that they could name had passed through that apartment at some point to record an underground track with him. During the early days of the genre, Playero produced and manufactured mixtapes from his apartment in Villa Kennedy. Playero recalled that he would sometimes have to record the vocals for his mixtapes a cappella and later lay them over music tracks in order to accommodate the large number of people clamoring to appear on one of his tapes. "It got to the point where so many people, so many kids, appeared from I don't know where. From everywhere. Everyone wanted to record. I didn't turn anyone away," he noted.[13]

Daddy Yankee's own recollection of his first collaboration with Playero, which he described in a December 18, 2015, Instagram post, highlights the centrality of Playero's apartment in public housing to the trajectory of his career:

The year was 1991 and he arrives at building #33 of Villa Kennedy a young quiet man, a bit shy but determined to make the impression of a lifetime on this talented DJ and music producer. He is directed towards apt #501, up the stairs, he memorizes every line that he had prepared. He arrives at the living room of the apartment, where there was no studio equipment, only a concert microphone, the turntables and a small 2-channel console, where the DJ and music producer did his projects. The DJ greets him, and in less than a minute he hands him the microphone and says: "Are you ready? Remember that you can't make a mistake singing because otherwise we have to start from the beginning since we don't have professional equipment." Once again he asks—Are you ready? The young man, nervous but with no signs of nerves, responds—Yes, I'm ready. The DJ spins the vinyl, the instrumental plays, and the young man, microphone in hand spits and makes history. In PLAYERO #34 is where the word REGGAETON is born. Those young people, without knowing it, changed the course and the history of music, giving name to a movement that this day is WORLDWIDE.[14]

Daddy Yankee's description of the humble origins of reggaeton music for his millions of fans on social media, paired with Playero's tour of his old apartment for a documentary film crew, highlights that many early underground recordings were produced in public housing, featured public housing residents (such as Daddy Yankee) prominently as artists, and were purchased and distributed by public housing residents themselves.

Underground records were not financed or distributed by major record labels and were primarily small-scale, local endeavors. Initially DJs, like Playero, would produce approximately twenty copies of a mixtape; these "masters" would then be bootlegged and distributed informally around the archipelago.[15] According to rapero Master Joe, it was this lack of formal distribution networks that gave the genre its moniker; he notes, "We would record onto a cassette player then we would duplicate and duplicate and that is how we started to spread our music. That's why we called it underground because it was an underground market where we were the actual distributors, the same ones that would produce it."[16]

Without radio airplay or commercial distribution, the question of how to get people to listen to underground, let alone buy it, soon emerged. The brisk business being done at the puntos, however, seemed to provide a ready-made distribution network for the bourgeoning genre. According to Richie Villanueva of *In the House* magazine, "Many people didn't know about our music but they would go to the punto to buy drugs. So when they would go to buy their drugs we would sell them our cassettes."[17] The fact that one could buy a mixtape when scoring drugs at the local punto, combined with the lyrical content and imagery of the mixtapes themselves, helped to solidify underground's connection to the informal drug economy. This connection, however, would be magnified and distorted by the police and media in an attempt to create an equivalency between drugs and underground music.

FROM UNDERGROUND TO ABOVEGROUND

Despite the very limited informal distribution network, consisting almost entirely of hand-to-hand sales and exchanges of bootlegged cassettes, underground managed to make itself heard not only all over the archipelago, but also in the diaspora. In 1994 Wiso G's *Sin Parar* became the first underground recording to be distributed by a record label and sold in stores, followed shortly thereafter by *Playero 37* and *Playero 38*, both of which had already circulated quite a bit informally before making their debut on store shelves.[18] As the genre seemed primed to break through to the commercial mainstream, parents, politicians, and certain media outlets began to focus on the harmful influence of underground rap on Puerto Rican youth and its relationship to the growing drug use and violence that seemed to be plaguing the archipelago. This concern with the morality of underground rap and its impact on Puerto Rican youth mirrored similar attacks on arts and culture, including West Coast gangster rap and Miami bass, taking place in the United States during the early and mid-1990s.[19]

The conservative Christian watchdog group Morality in Media, led by Milton Picón, was at the forefront of the offensive against underground. Picón, a former officer of the San Juan Vice Squad turned evangelical pastor, alerted the police about underground and its role in the drug economy. According to Picón, it was entirely hypocritical for the state to say that it is committed to the war on drugs if rappers were allowed to promote the use of controlled substances through their lyrics. He said, "It would be totally contradictory for the government, private companies, advertising agencies and other community organizations to conduct a campaign against drug use at the same time you hear songs from groups that capture the attention of our youth and prompt them to do the opposite, to experiment with all kinds of controlled substances."[20] Picón urged law enforcement, parents, teachers, small business owners, and the media to come together to "halt the dissemination of this harmful material to our children and youth."[21] For Picón, it would take a concerted effort by various sectors of society—public and private—to keep young people safe from the evils promoted by underground rap music.

Particularly distressing for Picón was the fact that this music was *not* underground at all, but could be heard in all corners of the archipelago, particularly in schools. Indeed, by the time underground music appeared on Morality in Media's radar, the genre could be heard across Puerto Rico and, especially troubling for many, across social classes. As Vico C rhymes on his 1993 hit "Xplosión": "Yo no soy de alta posición social, pero su hijo mi cassette se lo quiere comprar" (I'm not from the upper class, but your kid wants to buy my cassette). While the lyrical content and the way in which underground cassettes circulated led to the widespread notion that rap functioned as a front for the drug trade, the highly racialized and classed nature of mano dura contra el crimen helped to conflate rappers with drug dealers in the minds of many members of the public as well as police.

As policing and "crime fighting" became increasingly concentrated in low-income and predominantly Black spaces during mano dura, young men, particularly those with darker skin, from the barrios and *residenciales* came to embody the threat of crime and violence in the minds of many Puerto Ricans watching the war on drugs and crime unfold daily on their televisions, radios, and newspapers. Since so much underground music was made in public housing, featured young people from public housing and other low-income communities as artists, and sometimes circulated alongside illicit drugs, law enforcement and others increasingly constructed the genre and the youth who produced it as dangerous and contaminating. The justifications summoned by critics for criminalizing underground music closely mirrored the rationale put forth by the state for the necessity of mano dura contral el crimen. Underground music was suddenly a public safety issue and central to Puerto Rico's hard-line approach to drug enforcement. Soon the policing of underground music was nearly indistinguishable from the police interventions in public housing.

Under growing pressure from Morality in Media, during the first week of February 1995 Puerto Rico's Drugs and Vice Control Bureau conducted raids on six high-profile San Juan record stores, confiscating 401 underground cassettes and CDs and issuing citations to six store employees.[22] According to Jesús García, director of the Drugs and Vice Control Bureau, these recordings were confiscated because their lyrics violated local obscenity laws under article 113 of the Penal Code. In addition, police officials, drawing on popular opinion, told the public that underground music promoted drug use, violence, and promiscuity among Puerto Rican youth. Unfortunately for the police, morality, as had become evident in earlier cases against British punk rockers The Sex Pistols and the Miami rap group 2 Live Crew, was not enough of a legal justification for seizing the underground recordings.[23] The police action was ruled unconstitutional, and on February 17, 1995, the Superior Court of San Juan dismissed the charges against the music stores and their employees.[24] Despite the case's dismissal, the struggle against underground was far from over. As police superintendent Pedro Toledo told *El Nuevo Día*, "We will see where we failed. We will continue our struggle. . . . If the courts want to allow the sale of this kind of pornographic material, then we have to find ways to challenge the law and prevent these cases from failing."[25]

Following the court dismissal, and without legal recourse, efforts to police underground became increasingly informal. In the fight against underground, police employed tactics of race- and class-based surveillance and spatial control similar to those that had become central to mano dura contra el crimen. These new measures took advantage of the dispersed nature of underground's distribution circuits to justify closely monitoring young people who fit the rapero stereotype, in essence profiling poor and working-class racialized youth. According to rapero Mexicano, "If you were in the car listening to this kind of music and a cop would catch you, they would stop you and confiscate your tape."[26] Mexicano's experience echoes that of many underground fans and practitioners at the time and highlights the diffusion of sites of police power into more public and quotidian locations.

When police were prevented from raiding record stores, they turned to policing youths in schools, much as they harassed rap fans on the streets and in their cars. Schools became a key site at which police informally controlled the influence and spread of underground music. Elementary and high schools were another central point for the exchange and purchase of underground. According to DJ Playero, the first thirty-six volumes of his mixtape series were largely sold in schools until *Playero 37* was distributed in stores.[27] Because underground albums were easily dubbed from cassette to cassette, students would sell or give bootlegged mixtapes to their friends at school. Students who attended public schools were perhaps the most important distributors of underground music during its early days. Young people were in many respects the motor driving the underground movement both in terms of practitioners and consumers. Because police could not legally halt the sale of underground mixtapes in the formal sphere, for example by confiscating albums from record stores, law enforcement took advantage of their growing presence in public schools to limit the circulation of underground cassettes and CDs.

On August 23, 1994, Governor Rosselló signed an executive order to create Zonas Escolar Libre de Drogas y Armas (School Zones Free of Drugs and Firearms), or ZELDAs, at 328 intermediate and high schools around Puerto Rico.[28] The goal of the program, based on the federal model, was to eliminate drug use and violence in schools through the implementation of a permanent police presence, antidrug programming, "voluntary" body searches, and the cultivation of student informants.[29] On the first day of classes, September 6, 1994, students attending 428 of the archipelago's high schools were asked to submit to body searches as they entered the school. Although it is illegal to conduct body searches on minors, Education Secretary Victor Fajardo argued that students could decline to be frisked, and therefore the practice was within the bounds of the law.[30] It is questionable whether students entering school on their first day were aware of the laws protecting minors from body searches. As a result, the practice of frisking students and searching their belongings became quite common at public schools. An expansion of the ZELDA program in 1995 increased the number of schools with a permanent police presence to 611, over a third of the archipelago's 1,575 schools.[31]

It is within this context that, in 1995, along with patting down students in search of drugs or weapons, officials added underground mixtapes to the list of contraband. Following the police raids of record stores, the Department of Education banned "obscene music" on school grounds, specifically targeting underground music.[32] In March 15, 1995, a little over a month after the record store raids, El Nuevo Día reported that police officials had conducted searches at schools in Arecibo, Humacao, Loíza, Caguas, San Juan, and Luquillo in search of drugs and weapons. The newspaper noted that among the contraband seized from students were "marijuana, syringes and envelopes with suspected drugs, bottles of alcohol, underground music, beepers and cell phones."[33] As Petra R. Rivera-Rideau notes, these search-and-seizure operations at Puerto Rican public schools demonstrate the ways that "the popular association between drug use, crime, and underground persisted even through a judge had dismissed the charges against the owners of stores targeted by the raids."[34] In addition, in 1998, further cementing the policing of students fitting the rapero stereotype and underground in general as part of the war on drugs, Puerto Rico's public schools also banned baggy pants worn below waist level.[35]

Empowered explicitly by the Department of Education and tacitly by Superintendent Toledo's calls to do whatever it took to stop underground from corrupting Puerto Rican youth, police began harassing students who looked like raperos or were caught listening to underground on school grounds. David Lizardi, a professor at University of Puerto Rico–Cayey, recalled, "It was zero tolerance. Even kids, their bags were searched [and] if they had tapes they were confiscated."[36] Underground rap playing in students' Walkmans was a source of great concern for parents and police alike because of the commonly understood relationship between drugs and underground music. Young people were perceived as particularly susceptible to the lure of drugs and street life promoted by underground, which allowed police and media outlets to scrutinize and attack the genre in much the same way they would the drug trade. This focus on youth, however, reinforced notions about what kind of young people were in need of saving and what kind were already understood as a threat. These police interventions specifically targeted low-income and racially marginalized youth in public schools. Underground music's move aboveground spawned a multitude of racialized and classed anxieties that justified the policing of marginalized young people as part of mano dura contra el crimen. Young people in the underground scene were treated like vectors of contagion, exposing their peers not only to a life of drugs and crime but also, and perhaps most alarmingly, a life of promiscuity and sexual perversion.

SEXUAL DEVIANCE

While race and class structured and justified the surveillance and harassment of young people, especially young men, from low-income and predominantly Black neighborhoods, gender and sexuality were also front and center in the debates about underground as they increasingly came under the purview of mano dura policing efforts. Police officials, religious figures, and school administrators targeted underground because of its barrio-centric content, its real and imagined relationship with the informal economy, and the ways that it embodied Blackness. However, the genre's in-your-face, aggressive sexuality and emphasis on nonprocreative sexual relations also played a significant role in bringing it to the attention of the public and police. Although mano dura contra el crimen is most closely associated with the targeting of public housing residents, it also sought to squash explicit sexuality in the public sphere by raiding strip clubs for minor offenses, arresting sex workers, and harassing the LGBTQ population.

A little over a week after the vice squad raided San Juan record stores and pulled rap records off the shelves, Cups, a lesbian bar in San Juan, was also raided on the grounds of obscenity. Police raided the bar at 1:30 a.m. on February 18, 1995, when it was filled with members of the Gay Officers Action League (GOAL), a US-based gay and lesbian police officers' association that was in town for a convention. Tellingly, the raid occurred soon after Superintendent Toledo, when asked about GOAL's upcoming visit to Puerto Rico, reportedly suggested that police officers cannot enforce mano dura with a limp wrist.[37]

The raid at Cups was part of a larger pattern of police discrimination and harassment against LGBTQ populations in Puerto Rico. As Georgie Irizarry Vizcarrondo of the Puerto Rican Lesbian and Gay Coalition of the Human Rights Project wrote in a letter to the editor of the *San Juan Star*, there existed a long-standing pattern of police intimidation and harassment against LGBTQ people that had nothing to do with fighting crime. Irizarry Vizcarrondo noted, "[Police brass] have initiated open season on lesbians and gays. And the police force has followed through raiding a lesbian-owned business and harassing gays and lesbians in the streets, telling them in what direction to walk and how."[38] Transgender women who engaged in sex work in Santurce and Condado were regularly targeted for arrest and harassment during this period, and businesses that catered to nonprocreative and non-normative sexualities also felt the squeeze of the police's mano dura. For instance, police raided Condomanía, a popular adult novelty shop, along with other stores that sold sex toys, pornography, and sexual education materials, during this time. Scholars Rafael Bernabe and Nancy Herzig suggested, "To appear that they are doing something for the island, [police] launch raids against record stores, places where young people or gays and lesbians hang out, and against (the few) stores that sell materials with explicit sexual content."[39] Journalist John Marino similarly remarked, "With AIDS, murder, and drug-related crime on the rise, people are feeling under attack and are looking for easy answers. And blaming art that reflects these problems seems like good one."[40] It is in the figure of the rapero that seemingly disparate threads of policing came together; often racialized as Black, poor, young, and sexually provocative, the rapero seemed to encapsulate the sum fears of a Puerto Rican society facing significant social transformation and a crisis of authority.

Further, this emphasis on the aberrant sexual practices supposedly promoted by underground rap music played on racist and classist assumptions about poor and Black people's sexuality and supposed perversity, assumptions that gained new cultural traction during the mano dura era. Low-income and racially marginalized youths, almost always understood as male, were positioned as not only sexually promiscuous but also sexually hostile. Critics strategically deployed the casual sexism and homophobia that peppered underground lyrics in order to demonstrate that low-income youths were enmeshed within a degenerate culture, which threatened to spread if left unchecked.

No group came under as much scrutiny during the maelstrom over underground as Las Guanabanas. Two of the group's songs, "Maldita Puta" and "Un Día Con Carlitos," which appeared on *The Noise 1* (1990) five years before the record store raids, reemerged and came to represent everything wrong with underground and the youth who participated in the scene. The obscenity-laden track "Maldita Puta" opens with the following lines:

Maldita putas	Damn whores
Maldita bellacas	Damn horny bitches
Se pasa toda la vida saboreando matraca	They spend all their life sucking dicks
Chingan en los paris	They fuck in the parties
Chingan en los montes	They fuck in the hills
Chingan en tu carro y donde quiera que se monten	They fuck in your car and wherever else they go
Méale la chocha, escúpele la cara	Piss on her pussy, spit in her face
A esa jodía perra que no vale nada	'Cause that fucking bitch isn't worth shit

In "Un Día Con Carlitos," which followed "Madita Puta" on the mixtape, Georgie of Las Guanabanas tells an alarming tale of trans/homophobic panic and violence:

Un día con Carlitos fui para San Juan	One day with Carlitos I went to San Juan
Estábamos bellacos, queríamos chingar	We were horny, we wanted to fuck
De momento yo vi dos tremendas gatas	All of a sudden I saw two sexy chicks
Fuimos donde ellas a tirarle la labia	We went up to them to spit some game
Por supuesto ellas cayeron	Of course they fell for it
Con nosotros ellas se fueron	With us they went
Y rápidamente llegamos al apartamento	And we arrived at the apartment right away
Desespera'o estaba yo	I was impatient

Le baje el pantalón	I took down her pants
Le pregunto su nombre y me dice "Ramón"	I asked her name and she told me "Ramón"
Oh shit, la noche se jodio	Oh shit, the night is fucked
Por estar bellaco mira lo que me paso	Look what happened to me because I was horny
"Oye, mira Georgie, pero tu no hiciste na'?"	"Hey, look Georgie, but you didn't do anything?"
Espérate, Carlitos, déjame terminar	Wait, Carlitos, let me finish
Del carro lo amarre	I tied him to the car
Pa' Villa lo lleve	I took him to Villa
El no se imaginaba lo que yo le iba hacer	He couldn't imagine what I was going to do
Del carro lo solté	I let him out of the car
Corriendo el se fue	He went running
Saque mi .9mm y par de tiros le pegue	I took out my .9mm and I hit him with a few shots

These violently transphobic, homophobic, and misogynistic lyrics came to epitomize an entire genre, rather than this particular group, in the eyes of many critics. Furthermore, critics alleged that such lyrics provided a window onto the increasingly violent, irrational, and antisocial behavior of young people from economically disenfranchised areas who had too much time on their hands. As renowned Puerto Rican poet Edwin Reyes put it in a searing critique of the genre: "The problem is that rap, as a massive commercial phenomenon, is an expression that tends to promote these anti-social and perverse attitudes that come from the world of '*la jodedera*' [screwing around]."[41]

Critics of the genre and proponents of its censorship posited a causal relationship between the violent attitudes toward women and queer people expressed in underground songs and the *ola criminal* (crime wave) gripping the archipelago. This process of scapegoating functioned to ignore and mask the structural causes of violence as well as the entrenched sexism promoted by the media and conservative segments of Puerto Rican society. Underground was positioned as particularly retrograde and exceptional in its heterosexism, when in fact it very much reflected conservative ideas about women's roles and sexuality that widely circulated within the public sphere. For instance, critics took to the pages of local newspapers to slam underground rappers for reducing women to sexual objects in their songs and videos but did not bat an eye at the bikini-clad woman who sometimes graced front pages as the *bombón*, or eye candy, of the week. Similarly, conservative Christians lambasted rap music for its moral degeneracy and disrespect of women at the same time that pastors called on men to shepherd their families and on women to act as dutiful servants. I point to these examples not to excuse the heterosexism and misogyny of underground music, but rather to note that underground was in many ways positioned as particularly sexist and dangerous. The critiques of underground dovetailed with stereotypes that cast poor men and Black men as inherently and irrevocably sexist. The attack on underground meshed with the resurgence of culture of poverty myths that justified the interventions into low-income and racially marginalized communities as part of mano dura contra el crimen.

Further, the concern that government officials, religious figures, and pundits professed over how women and queer people were represented in rap music was often in stark contrast to their support of policies that harmed women and queer people or their own radically misogynistic and trans/homophobic attitudes. Claiming to speak on behalf of aggrieved women and queer people who needed to be protected from the violence of rap music, conservatives were able to conveniently mask their reactionary censorship efforts behind a façade of progressive and inclusive politics. These conservative forces were not, for instance, asking that young people be given a feminist and sex-positive education that would challenge the heteropatriarchal structure of Puerto Rican society; rather, they simply wanted the racialized and classed subculture associated with rap music to be contained and eliminated, and attacking the genre's sexism provided them a means to do so.

Songs like those of the rap duo Las Guanabanas were taken as accurate indicators of the advanced levels of depravity and irrationality among youth involved with underground as either fans or artists. This positioning of poor Black and brown youth as depraved fed the idea of a culture of poverty among barrio and public housing residents that circulated in the popular imaginary and provided a justification for mano dura measures in low-income areas. Raperos, just like public housing residents, were figured as unable or unwilling to govern themselves due to a deficient morality/culture and were therefore in need of state intervention. In this way, the policing of underground illuminates the ways in which a general concern with policing bodily comportment, particularly displays of nonnormative sexuality in the public sphere, played an important, although analytically neglected, role in designating certain populations for surveillance and control as part of mano dura's fight against crime.

¡DILE NO AL ABUSO OFICIAL!/SAY NO TO POLICE ABUSE!

Underground ignited a culture war in Puerto Rican popular media during the mid-1990s, with misconceptions about rap music and calls for its eradication taking up a great deal of media and popular attention. At the same time, underground fans and practitioners defended the genre and pointed out the racism and classism driving attempts to censure it. In their defense of underground, fans and practitioners linked the censorship efforts launched at it to the mano dura interventions in urban space. Supporters pointed out that the commonwealth government was using underground as a scapegoat to explain the sudden spike in violence and crime that occurred in the first part of the 1990s. As rap producer Karl William Morales noted at the time: "'Underground' is the music of the barrio and, as a result, not commercial. It is a form of protest and an artistic expression of the environment surrounding us in public housing. It's the image of a governor who 'goes hard against crime' and a year that ends with an increase in murders perhaps because people are 'listening to too much underground.' Rappers are going to have to form a union so we can defend our freedom of expression."[42] Here we see Morales pointing to the failure of mano dura contra el crimen to stem the rising number of homicides. It is no coincidence that in 1995, when police were raiding record stores, clubs, and spaces where marginalized communities gathered, Rosselló and Toledo were coming under fire for the fact that homicides had not decreased, as promised, but had *increased* (see chapter 1). Supporters of underground saw the attacks on the genre as little more than a political shell game; as the government maintained that it was effectively combating crime through mano dura, officials accused underground of undermining and complicating their successful efforts by promoting deviance, drug use, and violence among Puerto Rican youth. Indeed, raperos and fans alike provided nuanced analyses of the situation, pointing out that the focus on underground as a primary catalyst for crime, drug use, and violence obscured the failure of the state to provide security and financial stability to all of its citizens, a failure that was the root cause of the growing sense of anxiety and precarity that many Puerto Ricans experienced.

In addition, the attempt to cast raperos, and by extension youths involved in the informal economy, as delinquents hell-bent on terrorizing the hard-working people of Puerto Rico obscured the ways in which many low-income youths had been rendered redundant by colonial capitalism. In an incisive critique that appeared in the pro-independence student newspaper *Poder Estudiantil*, Karen Entrialgo noted that the policing of underground put on full display the failures of the state:

> Given the government's inability to offer real alternatives to social problems, it has chosen to reduce the problem of growth in the populations getting into the drug business to one that can be articulated in the following way: "The reason why more and more young people are consuming drugs is that a group of young people are making an open call, through an already popular music that incites it." This represents a discursive strategy that seeks, on the one hand, to divert attention from the real causes of drug trafficking and its social complexity and, on the other hand, to make it appear as though there is a clear commitment to solve the problem.[43]

The policing of underground, as part of the larger mano dura initiative, criminalized youth not only for their economic decisions in a context of dwindling opportunity but also for having the gall to openly discuss this reality through their lyrics. The celebrations of smoking weed, hanging out, trying to get laid, and trying to get paid that structured the genre's lyrical content rendered visible a reality of idleness and informality experienced by many young Puerto Ricans *trying to live* in the midst of an ongoing crisis of colonial capitalism.

Youths who fit the rapero stereotype experienced heightened levels of harassment and discrimination in stores, clubs, and on the streets, hardening preexisting prejudices about race, class, and youth. In an interview with the *San Juan Star* following the police raids, members of the rap group Nizzie complained about the way that raperos were constructed as little more than ignorant and dangerous delinquents. Discussing how critics of the genre often overlooked the level of skill involved in rapping, Pita Boom, a member of the group, explained, "It's like poetry but really very loose, without grammar rules and using the language of the streets, with similes, metaphors, or personification," slyly adding, "I may be a rapper, but I'm not ignorant."[44] Indeed, the members of Nizzie disrupted many of the preconceptions about raperos that circulated in the media. Starfleet attended college in New York, Pita Boom and Mr. G were both students at the UPR, and Dickie, who had left school, would be going back as one of the stipulations of a recording contract that the group had signed.[45] Rappers sought to draw attention to the ways in which the efforts to censure underground reified preconceived ideas about the inherent ignorance, violence, and deviance of low-income Black and brown youth, painting them as a "criminal class" and positioning them as a foil to students who attended university.

Further, the rappers of Nizzie denounced the hypocritical rhetoric and actions of groups like Morality in Media, which proclaimed a desire to save youth from drugs and violence but made no effort to work with young people in the barrios and residenciales, who were the most likely to experience drug-related violence and crime. Starfleet indignantly stated, "I just love it how people who would never be caught dead in a *barrio* are always ready with opinions. . . . These Morality in Media people don't come to the *barrios*, and if they drive by it's with the windows up and the doors locked. They're hypocrites."[46] The campaign against underground succeeded in further marginalizing youth who lived in some of the most economically marginalized areas and reinforced the idea that barrios were dangerous places that produced dangerous subjects, implicitly justifying increasing police intervention in these areas. The youth who experienced the brunt of these interventions, however, made it clear that they were not blind to how a discourse of protecting young people from drugs and violence was not directed toward them because their class, race, and spatial location already constructed them as threats to normative Puerto Rican values and culture.

While raperos and fans outspokenly defended the genre in the media, artists also penned songs and lyrics that critiqued not only the censorship of it but also growing police violence and impunity in economically and racially marginalized areas as a result of mano dura contra el crimen. Ivy Queen, one of the few women in the underground scene, rapped on DJ Joe's *Underground Masters*, vol. 2 (1995):

A los raperos nos critican	They critique us rappers
también nos metan presos	they also want to stick us in jail
solo por eso	just for that
solo por eso	just for that

For his part, Daddy Yankee denounced the police practice of fabricating cases in order to make drug arrests in "Abuso Oficial," which appeared on *Playero 39* (1995). In the song, Yankee raps that his barrio is on high alert because there is a corrupt officer on the loose planting evidence in cars and harassing innocent people. He implores everyone to call out this practice for what it is: police abuse. Yankee tells his audience:

Y si ellos buscan la manera de estar fabricando casos	And if they're looking for a way to fabricate cases
Tú le dices es abuso oficial	You tell them that is police abuse

Si lo sabes tú mi gente de quién te estoy hablando	My people you know who I'm talking about
De la uniformada, también de la estatal	The local uniformed cops, as well as the state cops

Yankee calls on the police to stop this corruption ("¡Por favor para el abuso!") and suggests that communities suffering the effects of police discrimination and abuse expose these practices. Further, picking up on a long-standing tradition in underground, while critiquing the injustice he sees in his community, Daddy Yankee still manages to tease corrupt police officials by suggesting that the reason they harass rappers is that they're jealous of their money and fame.

Perhaps the most emblematic and, indeed, successful instances of a rapper speaking back against the increased surveillance and police intervention thrust upon both the genre and young people who fit the rapero stereotype were the single and video for Eddie Dee's "Señor Oficial," released in 1997. The twenty-one year-old rapper had written the track a year and a half earlier based on his experiences with the police and the experiences of his friends.[47] The video for the song begins with the young rapper stepping out of his SUV to greet his friends, who are standing in front of a *colmado* (convenience store). Almost instantly, undercover officers jump out of a car with guns drawn, pointing them at Eddie Dee and his friends. Eddie Dee is then shown lying flat on the ground while police handcuff him and check his pockets for drugs and weapons. The camera cuts from a scene of Eddie Dee being arrested and taken away by the police to the rapper standing against a stark black background, singing:

Señor oficial	Mister Officer
déjeme cantar mi canción	let me sing my song
señor oficial	Mister Officer
déjeme ser como yo soy	let me be how I am
señor oficial	Mister Officer
comprenda que usted hizo hace tiempo	understand that you once did
las cosas que yo hago hoy	the things that I do today
señor oficial	Mister Officer
no diga que soy un ladrón	don't say that I'm a thief
señor oficial	Mister Officer
tampoco que soy un matón	or that I'm a killer
señor oficial	Mister Officer
mejor diga que soy un cantante	better yet say that I'm a singer
que lo hace de corazón	who does it from the heart

After the chorus, we see Eddie Dee handcuffed and being led into the police station, where the police are examining surveillance footage from a robbery. The camera cuts again to show Eddie holding a number in front of him and stepping into a lineup with other young men of similar appearance. A police photographer snaps pictures of each man—locked hair, Black skin, and baggy clothes—each of whom fits not only the rapero stereotype but also notions of who commits robberies in the minds of many Puerto Ricans. As the lineup is taking place, Eddie Dee asks the officer to explain "porqué personas juzgan a los otros sin razón" (why people judge others without reason). Pushing him further, Eddie Dee raps:

Por que los suyos persiguen	Why do your officers pursue
a los raperos que en tarima se exhiben	the rappers that get up on stage to perform
estamos en el party y nos mandan a apagar	we're at a party and you send them to shut it down
sin saber que estoy cantando para mi madre ayudar	without knowing that I sing to help my mom
y porque...	and why...
porque si voy para la esquina me quieren voltear	why if I go to the corner you want to search me
si voy al caserío creen que voy a comprar	if I go to the projects you think I went to buy
si salgo en el carro usted me manda parar	if I go out in my car you tell them to stop me
porque prendo el equipo o me ve con celular	when I turn on my sound system or you see me with a cellphone
me juzgan como si algo malo hice	they judge me like I did something bad
yo solo canto rap, pues fui lo que quise	I only rap, it's just what I wanted to do

In the next scene Eddie Dee takes to a podium, posing as a politician in a suit and tie. He chides people for saying that rap is responsible for the crime and violence in Puerto Rico and talks about how he is discriminated against because of how he looks:

No se como personas hoy siguen pensando igual	I don't know how people today still think the same
Dicen que mi recorte y mi pantallas estan mal	They say that my haircut and my earrings are bad

si visto con mi estilo al pub no me dejan entrar	if I dress my style they don't let me in the pub
y cuando entro a una tienda se creen que voy a asaltar	and if I go into a store they think I'm going to rob it
los padres a sus hijos no los dejan escuchar	parents don't let their kids listen
El underground pues piensan que ellos se van a dañar	They think that underground will ruin them
pero ellos solo se quieren expresar	but they just want to express themselves
como el eddie que ahora va a cantar	like Eddie who's now going to sing

Afterward, Eddie is shown once again getting out of his SUV, but this time he isn't jumped by police. Instead, he is shown entering a bar, where he is meeting the officer who arrested him to explain to him the error of his ways. As he gets out of the car and walks to the restaurant to sit down with the officer, we hear him rapidly spitting:

Estoy molesto por todas las cosas que estoy viendo	I am bothered by all the things that I see
como la droga y la gente ya esta muriendo	like drugs and the people that are dying
pero también me enfada oír gente diciendo	but I also get upset hearing people say
que es culpa de nosotros lo que esta sucediendo	that everything that's happening is our fault

The video ends with Eddie Dee sitting across from the officer, explaining that all the terms that the officer thought were criminal code were just slang, similar to things the officer said when he was young. Eddie Dee then stands up, puts money on the table for his drink, and leaves. As Eddie leaves the bar, we see the officer put his head in his hands, realizing the error of his ways. While naively idealistic, the video and song highlight both the ways in which the police, public, and media conflated rap and criminality and how young people were affected by such misconceptions. The video also demonstrates the ways in which criminality was sutured to the phenotypical and aesthetic markers of Blackness, highlighting the ways in which race, alongside class, overly determined police intervention during the mano dura era.

"Señor Oficial" garnered a lot of attention within and outside of the underground scene. The song's success in many ways marked the tail end of the crusade against underground rap. The state, media, and members of the public had seriously attempted to silence the voices of marginalized youth in the public sphere. Underground rap would soon give way to the reggaeton explosion of the 2000s. Still, despite international success and the best efforts of raperos to illuminate both the complexities of the informal economy in Puerto Rico and the violence of the mano dura era, the idea that underground was little more than a front for the drug trade persists in the minds of many, and does so with very serious consequences.

LIVE AND DIRECT FROM THE CEMETERY OF THE LIVING

As evidenced by the remarks that opened this chapter, there remains in the minds of many Puerto Ricans a stubborn understanding of rap and reggaeton music as an expression of violent cultural pathology that doubles as a laundering operation for the drug trade. This vision of rap and reggaeton as pathologically criminal obfuscates the glimpse rap and reggaeton music provide of the realities and aspirations of low-income Puerto Rican youths, who are largely shut out of mainstream public discourse. But this begs the question: So what? Why does it matter that some members of the Puerto Rican public view rap and reggaeton music in this way? As I have shown, this simplistic understanding of the relationship between the rap industry and the drug trade deeply impacted the lives of many young people in Puerto Rico during the 1990s. These youths were inserted into the war on drugs because of the music in their cassette players and the way they wore their jeans below their waists. These associations not only conflate comportment and style with criminality; they also foreclose analyses of the political economy in Puerto Rico and questions regarding the relationship among idleness, colonial capitalism, and underground. At the same time, these associations preclude the kind of incisive analyses, made by fans and raperos themselves, of the racialized police violence that animated mano dura policing. In other words, these associations have dire consequences that exposed, and continue to expose, young people to the violence of punitive governance.

The case of Puerto Rican rapper Tempo perhaps best illustrates how the association between drugs and rap music that solidified during the mano dura era maintained the potential to derail lives and entomb people within the carceral system even after the genre had "crossed over" into mainstream success during the 2000s. On October 15, 2002, the Drug Enforcement Agency announced the conclusion of Operation SOS II, an initiative targeting drug trafficking in Ponce and the big island's southern coast. The DEA was specifically interested in drug trafficking organizations operating out of a number of low-income barrios and public housing complexes.[48] As part of the operation, seventy-five indictments for conspiracy to distribute heroin, cocaine, and other controlled substances were handed down, and eighty-seven arrest warrants pursuant to the indictments were issued.[49] One of the arrest warrants was for David Sánchez Badillo, who was wanted for possessing more than thirty kilos of heroin with the intent to distribute. Operation SOS II would have occurred with little fanfare were it not for the fact that Sánchez Badillo was the government name of the well-known and respected Puerto Rican rapper Tempo. Federal authorities arrested Tempo on October 18, 2002, at the San Juan courthouse when he appeared for a preliminary hearing on unrelated gun charges.[50]

According to federal authorities, the rapper controlled the lucrative drug trade operating out of Residencial Los Lirios del Sur in Ponce and was responsible for numerous acts of drug-related violence. Despite an overwhelming lack of evidence, authorities maintained that Tempo was a violent drug trafficker. Without physical evidence connecting Tempo to the crimes he was accused of committing, the prosecution largely relied on hearsay to build its case against him. During the trial the prosecution introduced Tempo's song "Narcohampon" as evidence that the rapper was indeed a drug kingpin in control of the big island's southern coast. In "Narcohampon," Tempo raps about involvement with the drug trade, committing murder, and bribing law enforcement officials. He opens by rapping:

Soy un Narcohampón	I'm a drug kingpin
tengo el control del área sur	I have control of the whole south
traficante	trafficker
de kilates	of kilos
pero cantante	but a singer
tú? no!, solo eres mula!	You? No! You're just a mule!
ya lo supe	I already knew
yo voy hacer que de ti se ocupen	I'm going to make them worry about you
aquí yo soy el que suple	Here I'm the supplier
no hagas que me pare	don't make me get up
a corta distancia y te dispare	I'll shoot from close range
con mi pistola plástica	with my plastic gun
y mi lengua elástica	and my elastic tongue

In addition to rapping about how he is "the star of the crime scene," Tempo goads the authorities, saying that he'd love to come face to face with Superintendent Toledo, and that if he ever ends up in court for all he's done, he'll tell the judge what he can do with his zipper. The prosecution, judge, and jury took "Narcohampon" as an admission of guilt rather than an artistic production, and Tempo was sentenced to twenty-four years in a federal facility for trafficking in heroin and marijuana.[51] Daniel Domínguez, the presiding judge, after sentencing the rapper said, "You are a prominent musician, but also a terrible example for the youth."[52]

In 2006 Tempo gave an interview to the television news program *Al Rojo Vivo* from inside the Coleman Federal Prison in Florida, which he referred to as "the cemetery of the living." In the interview, Tempo maintained his innocence and described the way that he was held responsible for the deeds of his artistic persona. According to Tempo, he never actually sold drugs, which is why there was no physical evidence of his illicit activities. However, he regularly discussed the glamour and violent power struggles of the streets in his lyrics. He discussed the use of his song "Narcohampon" as evidence against him in this way: "I have a song that was really *real* . . . and in this song I talked in the third person. They used it as evidence to be able to say that I was a danger to society. In the song I say 'I'm a drug kingpin / I have control of the whole south / trafficker / of kilos / but a singer' and they put together those elements and said, 'that's for real, that's him.' You know? It's like a soap opera."[53] Almost a decade after underground music became a target of mano dura policing, the use of Tempo's song "Narcohampon" as evidence against him demonstrates how rap music remains unquestionably hitched to the informal drug economy and its participants are figured as dangers to Puerto Rican society.

Eventually Tempo's lawyer was able to argue for a reduction in the original sentence, and he returned to Puerto Rico on October 9, 2013, to serve out the remaining six months of his sentence in a halfway house.[54] When Tempo was arrested, he was about to sign with US-based rapper Fat Joe's Terror Squad Records and was primed to become a major crossover artist in the hip-hop scene. Tempo's incarceration derailed those plans as he joined the other Puerto Ricans exiled in US federal facilities for drug-related charges. While Tempo's case is perhaps one of the most extreme examples of the dangerous repercussions of policing of rap music in Puerto Rico, he is far from unique, in the sense that rap music continues to be treated as probable cause when it comes to drug enforcement in the archipelago.

In 2015, in some ways mirroring Tempo's case, reggaetonero Neftalí "Pacho" Álvarez Núñez received a severe sentence for the illegal possession of a firearm and prescription drugs after a federal judge reviewed the content of his lyrics and music videos. In March 2015 Álvarez Núñez, a member of the group Pacho y Cirilo, was arrested for possession of a firearm that had been illegally modified to make it automatic and Percocet tablets without a prescription.[55] Álvarez Núñez took a plea deal, but in the recommendation for sentencing, the prosecution pointed to song lyrics and videos created by Pacho y Cirilo in order to paint Álvarez Núñez as dangerous. Because Álvarez Núñez pled guilty to the charges he was accused of and because he had no previous record, the prosecutor recommended a sentence of twenty-four to thirty months. Federal judge José A. Fusté, after listening to Pancho y Cirilo's lyrics and viewing the accompanying videos, disregarded the prosecutor's recommendation and sentenced Álvarez Núñez to ninety-six months in prison, triple the prosecutor's suggestion.[56] In particular, the video for "Como Grita el Palo," referring to the sound that a long, automatic rifle makes, which was filmed in the Juana Matos public housing complex in Cataño and features young Black and dark-skinned men holding various assault style automatic weapons and mugging for the camera, was a source of concern for the judge. Judge Fusté imposed the lengthy sentence because the songs and videos supposedly proved that Álvarez Núñez had "an inclination toward violence" and that his artistic expression revealed his criminal state of mind. Eventually an appellate court reversed the excessive sentence, noting that musical content could not be factored in as "objective evidence" during sentencing without corroboration. Nonetheless, rap and reggaeton music continue to be seen as indicators of criminality.

The Puerto Rican state "rolled out" schemes of punitive control during the 1990s, at precisely the moment when the colonial benefactor state was being "rolled back." These schemes, such as mano dura contra el crimen, fell squarely on marginalized youth because of the racial, spatial, and classed formations that structured their positionality within Puerto Rican society. The associations that sutured rap to criminality under the guise of mano dura persist today as Black and brown youth in Puerto Rico continue to be profiled, surveilled, and targeted by police and fellow citizens because of their style. As Raquel Rivera has rightly noted, "Censoring a music genre is, of course, a much more manageable task than reducing unemployment, improving the quality of public education, providing healthcare, or lowering the murder rate."[57] Analyzing the censorship of underground rap in tandem with mano dura policing, and the ways in which its effects remain with us, reveals how the Puerto Rican state tried to use marginalized young people and their cultural expressions as scapegoats instead of confronting the root causes of societal insecurity at the close of the twentieth century.

FOUR

The Continued Promise of Punishment

IN THE SUMMER OF 1999 PEDRO ROSSELLÓ ANNOUNCED that he would not be seeking reelection as governor of Puerto Rico. At the time his administration was deeply mired in a series of corruption and ethics scandals. When the dust settled, Rosselló's administration would go down as one of the most corrupt in Puerto Rico's modern history, with twenty-five government officials ultimately being convicted of a range of offenses ranging from money laundering to extortion to witness tampering.[1] Despite widespread accusations, and in some cases evidence, of corruption, Rosselló left office with a surprisingly high degree of public support. The former pediatric surgeon endeared himself to many Puerto Ricans with his reform of the public health system, which extended health insurance coverage to some of Puerto Rico's most impoverished populations. Rosselló also inaugurated a number of large-scale infrastructural projects that transformed the landscape during his time as governor, including the *tren urbano* rail system, expanded highway construction throughout the archipelago, the construction of a new aqueduct system for the metropolitan area, and the creation of a central conventions district, to name a few of his accomplishments. Rosselló is also credited with beginning the process that resulted in the eventual ouster of the US Navy from the island municipality of Vieques following the death of Puerto Rican civilian David Sanes at a bombing range in 1999. The candidates who threw their hats in the ring during the 2000 gubernatorial race had to contend with the shadow cast by Rosselló's carefully crafted image of a no-nonsense politician willing to do what it took to *echar pa'lante*, or bring Puerto Rico into the future.

One of the ways that the governors who entered La Fortaleza after Rosselló tried to distinguish themselves was by criticizing mano dura contra el crimen, questioning whether his administration's tough-on-crime approach had actually increased public safety, and if so, at what cost. This was especially true for the two PPD governors who succeeded Rosselló, Sila María Calderón (2001–2004) and Aníbal Acevedo Vilá (2005–2008). Both Calderón and Acevedo Vilá rejected the overly militaristic and punitive style of mano dura contra el crimen. They argued that mano dura's predawn raids were ineffective publicity stunts that further isolated and stigmatized the poor. During their electoral campaigns, they both vowed to focus on rehabilitation, education, economic development, and community empowerment as opposed to punitive policing measures as a solution to the insecurity facing many Puerto Ricans. It seemed that politicians were finally listening to what public housing residents and community activists had been saying for years: mano dura contra el crimen was a dangerous failure that did little but criminalize poverty.

Yet once Calderón and Acevedo Vilá entered office, both of their administrations approached issues of public safety and security in ways that were remarkably similar to that of Rosselló. This chapter examines how the policing and crime reduction measures of the Calderón and Acevedo Vilá administrations reinforced a central assumption of mano dura policing, namely that poor and working-class people were the key generators of violence and crime and that their communities needed constant surveillance and intervention. This continued reliance on the strategies associated with mano dura occurred despite a rhetorical shift that sought to mark a break with mano dura contra el crimen and its patterns of discriminatory policing. Tellingly, both governors, but in particular Calderón, recast and justified their turn to punitive policing as a form of "community policing," framing a permanent police presence as well as regular intervention in low-income communities as crucial steps in reestablishing the trust between law enforcement officials and the public that mano dura had eroded.

The administration of Sila María Calderón promoted what it called *la mano firme*, or the firm-handed, approach to dealing with crime, which would aggressively prosecute government corruption and high-level drug trafficking while emphasizing rehabilitation and prevention as solutions to low-level offenses. Calderón's mano firme, however, became nearly indistinguishable from Rossello's mano dura when crime rates surged during her term. Calderón's administration encouraged police to engage in targeted hot-spot policing in an attempt to disrupt the drug trade, which produced deadly consequences in vulnerable communities just as it had under Rosselló. Calderón also ordered police to raid and occupy public housing and other low-income communities, eventually activating the National Guard to participate in policing efforts. Aníbal Acevedo Vilá, who succeeded Calderón as governor, in response to criticism of the PPD for being soft on crime took a more hard-line approach, instituting his crime plan, known as *castigo seguro*, or certain punishment, which relied on hot-spot policing in low-income communities, increased surveillance of public housing residents with the installation of security cameras, and the reappointment of Pedro Toledo as police superin-tendent. Though critical of Rosselló's mano dura contra el crimen, Calderón and Acevedo Vilá relied on many of the same logics and practices. In addition, both Calderón and Acevedo Vilá deepened the reach of the state's security apparatus in public housing and other low-income communities.

This chapter traces how politicians and law enforcement officials institu-tionalized and normalized the practices and logics associated with mano dura contra el crimen, despite publicly dismissing and distancing themselves from the controversial anticrime plan. This chapter also focuses on the administra-tions of two governors associated with Puerto Rico's pro-commonwealth political party, which is often perceived as being more liberal than the pro-statehood party, in order to ask how exclusionary and harmful tough-on-crime policies and logics have become a wholly bipartisan affair. By focus-ing on Calderón's and Acevedo Vilá's approaches to questions of security and public safety, I challenge the prevalent assumption that punitive and discrimi-natory policing are the exclusive province of conservative politicians. Their administrations demonstrate how liberal politicians in Puerto Rico have contributed to, rather than reduced, the oppressive presence of law enforce-ment in racially and economically marginalized communities.

THE PENNINGTON PLAN COMES TO PUERTO RICO

Sila María Calderón, then mayor of San Juan, ran on a platform promising the complete opposite of Rosselló. She vowed to tackle the corruption and abuse that Rosselló and the Partido Nuevo Progresista (PNP) had turned a blind eye to, and in some cases encouraged, over the past eight years. Calderón pledged that her administration would restore the people's faith in their elected offi-cials by aggressively prosecuting government corruption. She vowed to address income inequality and work with poor and working class populations to reha-bilitate the housing and infrastructure in their communities. Committed to the betterment and empowerment of Puerto Rico's economically marginalized communities, Calderón assured the voting public that she would make Puerto Rico safer, but without the criminalization of poverty that marked mano dura contra el crimen. In the platform document for her candidacy, she made this explicit:

> I am not the first to say that the current administration claims that there has been a marked reduction in the incidence of crime, but the perception of the citizens is that it has been steadily increasing. The population notes that there is little reality behind the signs of Drug Free Schools, the futility of "occupying" public housing residences following the initial publicity, the weakness of the so-called raids where massive numbers of arrest orders are carried out without getting near those that control the large scale trafficking of drugs. In short, "Mano Dura" has not worked.[2]

Calderón said that her administration would focus on preventing crime and drug abuse through a series of programs that aimed to address not only crime but also its root causes through an emphasis on education, economic development, and community empowerment.[3]

Calderón defeated PNP candidate Carlos Pesquera and Partido Independentista Puertorriqueño (PIP) candidate Rubén Berríos in the general election, becoming the first woman to ascend to the governorship. Her election seemed to signal a shift away from the tough-on-crime policies and exclusionary rhetoric that marked Rosselló's time in office. And indeed, internal documents generated during her first two years in office suggest that her administration was eager to make a break with the past. Key to Calderón's efforts would be a complete overhaul of the PRPD. After being elected, Calderón appointed the respected judge Pierre Vivoni del Valle to replace Pedro Toledo as police superintendent. Vivoni had no experience with the police rank and file or leadership structure prior to his appointment, which Calderón possibly felt contributed a fresh perspective on the myriad problems confronting the force. Together, the two aimed to develop a plan to reform the police in a way that decentralized command, refocused attention on investigative work, and improved community-police relations through ongoing training initiatives. The model that provided the basis for the PRPD's reform, however, recycled many of the same ideas about "hot-spot" policing in economically and racially marginalized communities that had dominated law enforcement strategy in many US jurisdictions during the 1990s, including Puerto Rico.

New Orleans emerged as a model for the Calderón administration as it weighed different approaches to increasing public trust in the PRPD and lowering rates of violent crime. New Orleans, like other large urban police departments in the United States during the 1990s, had undergone a series of reforms aimed at addressing rising crime rates. In 1994 the newly elected mayor of New Orleans, Marc H. Morial, appointed Richard J. Pennington as superintendent of the New Orleans Police Department (NOPD). Pennington, a career law enforcement officer, had risen through the ranks of the Metropolitan Police Department of the District of Columbia, eventually becoming assistant chief of police. Upon taking the reins at the NOPD, Pennington starting putting together a plan of action to drastically overhaul the police force.

Released on January 11, 1995, the "Pennington Plan" put forward a series of action points aimed at decreasing violent crime, especially homicide rates; raising morale within the ranks; and increasing public trust and confidence in law enforcement.[4] These action points included replacing Internal Affairs with a "Public Integrity Division" to investigate police involvement in criminal activities; establishing a police early warning system to identify and monitor police conduct based on civilian complaints; implementing an intensive community policing strategy in areas designated as high crime; creating more training opportunities for all police personnel; and improving police pay and benefits to boost morale.[5] When announcing the plan, Pennington stated that "a battle for the soul of our City starts with the implantation of Police Department reform and reorganization," before adding: "This effort is a major step towards curtailing our crime epidemic, restoring public confidence and bringing dignity, respect, and integrity back to the NOPD."[6]

While boosting both police morale and civilian trust were central to the Pennington Plan, much of what the plan outlined was the implementation of an aggressive "quality of life" and community policing strategy in New Orleans's low-income, predominantly Black communities. Pennington suggested that in New Orleans violent crime, particularly homicide, was uniquely concentrated in the city's public housing developments, something that would eventually resonate with Puerto Rican officials. According to police data, 26 percent of all homicides occurred in three of the city's ten public housing complexes.[7] The Pennington Plan concentrated police attention on these crime "hot spots" through traditional mechanisms such as increased patrols and targeted raids, as well as through the implementation of a wide range of community policing initiatives.

The turn toward community policing was positioned as responding to the needs of communities that had been ignored or disappointed by the NOPD in the past. As internal planning documents from the Morial transition team noted, "The idea of relationships is very important here. Without a sincere effort made by the NOPD to get back into the community and form relationships with the people, little progress will be made in our war on crime. [...] The families of New Orleans must be safe in their neighborhoods. We believe they want a partnership with the New Orleans Police Department."[8] The centering of community policing in New Orleans sought to weaponize the frustrations of residents and make them foot soldiers in the city's escalating war on crime. As cultural geographer Lydia Pelot-Hobbs notes, under Pennington, the NOPD provided hundreds of residents with "crime-fighting training" through the NOPD Citizens Academy and encouraged the formation of neighborhood watch groups throughout the city.[9]

As evidenced in the Pennington Plan, community policing in designated high-crime areas sought to accomplish two interrelated goals. First, it aimed to reduce rates of crime by building trust between law enforcement officials and the public in the hopes that increased trust and confidence in the police would induce civilians to collaborate with police in identifying and solving crimes. Second, community policing aimed to reduce crime by saturating designated crime hot spots with an elevated and constant police presence. While police presence in the community was not to appear adversarial, as it would during raids or vehicular patrols, the presence of so-called officer friendlies who *could* function as warrior cops should the need arise would be constant. Community policing was never imagined as a mythical return to Mayberry, but rather a turn toward human-terrain counterinsurgency in American inner cities. A draft of a City of New Orleans crime abatement and prevention plan, which foreshadowed the logics of the Pennington Plan, stated the goal plainly: "This plan is designed to treat the crime issue as a war. All city and community resources shall be mobilized to win this war, including, other supportive community services, non-profit agencies, and businesses already fighting crime on a fragmented bases [sic]. This plan will encourage an integrated effort and commitment to total anti-crime system as described in this plan."[10] The Pennington Plan therefore mandated the deployment of Community Oriented Police Squad (COPS) officers to three public housing complexes—Desire, Florida, and B. W. Cooper—and the creation of a police substation in the city's historically Black Ninth Ward to accelerate and deepen the war on crime, not as a shift toward something radically different.[11]

While the first phrase of the Pennington Plan's implementation emphasized the rollout of "quality of life" and community policing measures throughout the city, but particularly in New Orleans's poor and working-class Black communities, the second phase focused on the professionalization of the police force.[12] Under Pennington, the NOPD adopted CompStat, a computerized data system popularized by William J. Bratton during his time as police commissioner under New York City mayor Rudolph Giuliani. CompStat tracks crime patterns as well as police activity in order to identify crime hot spots where police need to be more effectively deployed to address and prevent criminal activity. The CompStat program also involves notorious weekly meetings at which police district and unit commanders are forced to publicly account for failing to reach particular rates of arrest and/or crime reduction goals. In addition to adopting CompStat, the NOPD itself was radically reorganized under Pennington. The chain of command was decentralized, giving district commanders greater discretion and power. Further, the ranks of the NOPD swelled, as Pennington announced that he would be increasing recruitment efforts to expand the force by 30 percent.[13] The second phase of the Pennington Plan meant more cops in communities under more pressure than ever to produce "results" to be presented at weekly CompStat meetings, which only led to more arrests in New Orleans's economically and racially marginalized communities.

When Calderón and Vivoni were contemplating how to approach the reforms to the PRPD that would be "necessary" to recover from the damage done to public trust as a result of mano dura contra el crimen, the Pennington Plan seemed to address many of the problems that the PRPD was facing at the time. After being declared the "Murder Capital of America," under Morial and Pennington homicide rates and crime overall in New Orleans had fallen dramatically. Pennington had received praise from law enforcement officials and politicians across the United States for cracking down on police corruption and restoring the public's faith in the capabilities of the NOPD. For instance, in 1998 *Governing*, a magazine for state and local officials, recognized Pennington as its public official of the year, noting, "He had managed to turn himself into perhaps the most popular public official in the city, as well as one of hottest properties in American policing."[14] The write-up on Pennington went on to declare: "He did this by leading the transformation of the New Orleans police department from an object of outright derision into a force that chiefs in other cities look to these days for inspiration. When Pennington took over, crime in New Orleans was skyrocketing, morale on the force was nearing rock-bottom, and corruption on the force was endemic."[15] To interested observers, Pennington had seemingly transformed the NOPD from a bushel of "bad apples" into a well-trained and equipped, professionalized force that could marshal the trust and confidence of residents. For Calderón and Vivoni, this was precisely the kind of transformation that the PRPD desperately needed.

During its first year in office, the Calderón administration contracted NOPD major Felix Loicano, who had helped to oversee the introduction of the Pennington Plan in New Orleans, as a consultant to advise them on how to approach reorganizing and reforming the troubled PRPD. For months Loicano was in communication with the Calderón administration and even traveled to Puerto Rico to meet with government officials and high-ranking PRPD officials to assess the situation within the police department. Loicano made a series of recommendations aimed at helping the PRPD to successfully implement the Pennington Plan. Key for Loicano was changing the public perception of the PRPD as ineffective and corrupt. In order to increase the PRPD's credibility, Loicano recommended hiring skilled media and public relations consultants, improving ethics training for police officers, investing in more advanced and publicly accessible statistical information technologies that would appear to make manipulation more difficult, and increasing police interaction with the public through community policing initiatives.[16]

Loicano also encouraged the Calderón administration and PRPD officials to begin shifting their language away from "zero tolerance or *mano dura*" during press briefings or communication with the public, encouraging them instead to emphasize "quality of life issues."[17] Many of Loicano's recommendations revolved around changing the public's *perception* of the PRPD rather than addressing public demands to meaningfully transform the PRPD's structure and practice. As an annotated agenda for a meeting of the Governor's Security Council put it, Superintendent Vivoni and other top police officials needed to establish uniform procedures for dealing with abuse and corruption and effectively communicate them to the public in order to "gain credibility, change the image of the police and reduce the number [of] complaints that are filed against the agents."[18] Through a series of strategic reforms and public relations efforts, the PRPD could appear to address long-standing public concerns regarding performance without fundamentally altering existing patterns of policing.

Although a number of Loicano's recommendations were superficial and didn't meaningfully tackle public concerns regarding police practice, particularly entrenched violence and corruption, he did recommend a radical restructuring of the PRPD's command structure, similar to that of the NOPD. District commanders would be given greater discretion to direct the officers in their district and shape localized responses to crime. Perhaps the greatest restructuring of the force that Loicano discussed with the Calderón administration was related to the overall number of police officers on the force. A fax to Superintendent Vivoni from José R. Negrón Fernández, the governor's adviser, noted Loicano's shock at the size of the PRPD. According to Negrón Fernández, "Loicano was surprised by the high number of uniformed officers in the Puerto Rico Police. He understands it to be one of the largest police forces in the United States. For this reason, he invited us to analyze if we want to continue recruiting new cadets or if, on the contrary, we must direct our resources to re-training the police, offering better salaries and obtaining new and modern technology."[19] While substantially growing the NOPD was a major component of the Pennington Plan's implementation in New Orleans, Loicano advised the Calderón administration to consider pumping the brakes on recruitment efforts and to allow for a reduction in the total number of PRPD officers through attrition. According to Loicano, maintaining such a high number of officers on the force, let alone trying to increase those numbers, was untenable if the Calderón administration was serious about modernizing the police and increasing salary and benefits as a way to boost morale.

Following Loicano's recommendation to interrogate whether maintaining the current size of the force would impede reforming the PRPD, the Calderón administration began to seriously discuss shrinking the force. Annotated agendas from meetings of the Governor's Security Council point to ongoing discussions about redirecting resources away from recruitment toward better training, new technology and equipment, and salary increases.[20] Tellingly, these discussions did not suggest redirecting the money saved by reducing the total number of PRPD officers toward nonpunitive crime reduction efforts or community investment initiatives. Nonetheless, these discussions seemed to be a step in the right direction, since as activists had long pointed out, increasing the number of police in Puerto Rico had not contributed to less crime but had contributed to increased tensions between police and the public. The Calderón administration's new crime plan would implement many aspects of the Pennington Plan, making nominal gestures toward addressing community demands while shoring up a carceral apparatus experiencing a deep legitimacy crisis.

In November 2001, as the Calderón administration was in the midst of discussing Loicano's recommendations and what the reform of the PRPD might look like, Superintendent Vivoni stepped down to take a judgeship in the Appeals Court. Following Vivoni's resignation, Calderón appointed Miguel Pereira, a career civil servant and attorney, as police superintendent. Pereira, like Vivoni, did not come to the position of superintendent by rising through the ranks of the police force or through experience with federal law enforcement, which caused concern about his ability to effectively handle the proposed restructuring and reform of the PRPD while addressing increased public concern with crime. Vivoni's sudden departure, Pereira's appointment, and the fact that the Calderón administration had not released a substantive anticrime plan almost a year after taking office began to erode public confidence in how the administration was handling crime and insecurity. A scorecard generated by *El Nuevo Día* based on public surveys gave Calderón a C in her overall performance, but came down especially hard on her handling of the crime problem.[21] Calderón's mediocre grade showcased a growing dissatisfaction with what many Puerto Ricans perceived as inaction and a lack of leadership.

Calderón and Pereira finally unveiled the administration's anticrime plan on May 9, 2002. The administration's security plan, which it named Operación Fuerza Contra el Crimen, or Operation Force Against Crime, integrated many components of the Pennington Plan, including more power for district commanders, increasing the number of cleared cases, implementing better mechanisms for tracking crime statistics, and an emphasis on restoring community trust and fostering civilian collaboration with law enforcement. Above all, Calderón and Pereira stressed in their comments to the press that the administration's anticrime plan would emphasize prevention and community policing in order to meaningfully reduce crime. Calderón asserted, "The Security Plan is an integrated and strategic effort involving several state and federal agencies. And it depends largely on the participation of citizens."[22] She continued, "I believe in creating spaces for citizen participation. Each Puerto Rican must be a social actor with an effective voice in identifying problems and searching for solutions."[23]

One way that Operación Fuerza Contra el Crimen aimed to increase civilian participation was by expanding the "Koban" program. In Japan, Kobans are small neighborhood police stations with a small staff of officers who interact with citizens on a regular basis. When the idea of community policing started to gain traction during the 1990s, the Japanese Koban model circulated as a best practice and model.[24] During the 1990s, with the financial backing of the Milton S. Eisenhower Foundation, "safe haven mini-stations" explicitly modeled on Kobans were established in Chicago, Boston, Baltimore, Philadelphia, and San Juan.[25] The San Juan Koban was established in the Caimito sector of San Juan and was run by the nonprofit organization Centro Sor Isolina Ferre. Criminologist Elliott Currie describes the Caimito Koban program in his book *Crime and Punishment in America*:

> Each site mixed community policing with a variety of youth development initiatives. The San Juan program, for example, operated in Caimito, an extremely poor neighborhood with high unemployment and school dropout rates. A well-established Puerto Rican nonprofit organization, Centro Sister Isolina Ferre, established a "campus" in Caimito that joined a neighborhood police koban with classrooms, small businesses, and recreation facilities. There were computer and office skills training classes, day care, alternative schools for dropouts, health screenings and immunization for neighborhood children, and an after-school "safe haven" program for six-to-twelve-year-olds.
>
> Centro also hired "streetwise" young people to work as youth advocates (or "intercesores"), mediating among neighborhood youth, the schools, and the justice system. These advocates worked closely with the koban-based police, who would contact them when local youths were detained. In pursuit of what the [Eisenhower] foundation calls "community equity policing," the youth advocates and neighborhood residents worked as genuine partners with the police; community leaders even helped to select and train the koban-based officers. Estimating the impact of local programs like these on crime rates in intrinsically difficult, but a careful evaluation found that serious crimes fell significantly over 4 years of the program in Centro's target neighborhood—considerably more so than in the city as a whole.[26]

The Caimito Koban was widely accepted as a successful example of community policing, and the Calderón administration sought to replicate the model in other neighborhoods. The administration wanted to create Kobans in the Manuel A. Pérez public housing complex in the Hato Rey section of San Juan and the Villa Esperanza public housing complex in Cupey, just south of Río Piedras.[27] The expansion of Kobans into public housing was intended to complement the other proposals in the security plan, which included increased coordination between the Department of Housing and the PRPD to have police officers offer sports activities, as well as technology, art, and music classes for young people in public housing.[28] In addition, the

Puerto Rican National Guard would be enlisted to help combat school desertion among young people in public housing.[29]

The Calderón administration's new anticrime plan seemed to continue the previous administration's focus on public housing and low-income communities as areas that needed constant police intervention and attention. While the police would not be systematically raiding poor communities in search of drugs in the wee hours of the morning, they would be engaging in a "soft" occupation of public housing and other low-income communities as a crime abatement strategy. Nonetheless, Calderón repeatedly emphasized to the press and the public that her administration's security plan was a departure from mano dura contra el crimen. According to Calderón, any action that the police took would be done with respect for civilians. Trying to point to the differences between her security plan and Rosselló's, Calderón repeatedly came back to the idea of respect: "What we are presenting today is different because it is an effort open to the Puerto Rican people, measurable, based not on the iron first, but rather in the firm but respectful hand."[30] Seemingly exasperated with reporters' attempts to conflate her crime plan with that of the previous administration, Calderón stated, "People are used to hearing catchphrases, emblems, and slogans such as 'mano dura contra el crimen,' they are accustomed to having tanks and machine guns put into public housing where poor people live and poor people are not necessarily criminals."[31] Calderón emphasized that she felt criminalizing the poor and holding them responsible for all the crime that occurred was wrong and that her administration would not engage in such practices. "I was ashamed when they filled public housing with tanks and machine guns," the governor told the press, while stressing her administration would focus on prevention.[32]

Almost a week after Calderón and Pereira unveiled the new anticrime plan, the administration announced the first security measure to be implemented: the enclosure of a large number of public housing residences through the installation of police-manned guard shacks at the entrances. The governor announced that her administration would spend an estimated $24 million to fully gate and create controlled-access entrances at seventy-eight public housing complexes.[33] Of those seventy-eight, twenty-nine complexes, which were designated as high-crime areas, would also be subjected to around-the-clock police patrols.[34] According to police superintendent Pereira, the police presence as a result of these patrols would be constant, but not necessarily permanent.[35] Along with the installation of controlled access and the implementation of round-the-clock preventative patrols for designated complexes, the administration announced that it would also be doubling the number of police officers exclusively assigned to work in public housing to one thousand.[36] Approximately twenty-five thousand residents living in seventy-eight complexes could now expect increased surveillance of their daily lives and greater interaction with police.[37]

Following the Calderón administration's announcement about increasing controlled access in public housing, criticism emerged from public housing residents, activists, journalists, politicians, and other members of the public, questioning the governor's commitment to reducing the criminalization of the poor as well as the efficacy of the measure. Veteran crime beat journalist Carmen Edith Torres noted the incongruence between the governor's statements at the press conference announcing the new security plan that the poor must not be criminalized and stigmatized and the announcement a week later that the administration would be beefing up controlled access and preventative patrols only at public housing complexes.[38] Torres also noted that in expanding controlled access in public housing, Calderón was merely building on efforts that had begun under Governor Hernández Colón and intensified during Rosselló's administration.[39] Public housing residents interviewed by the media about the controlled-access plan were for the most part unimpressed or skeptical. Some residents pointed out that the previously constructed *casetas*, or entrance guard shacks, were badly placed or that the police officers manning the entrance did nothing all day. Carmen Rivera of the Los Alamos public housing complex in Guaynabo was in favor of increasing funds for security-related efforts in public housing because, as she pointed out, the previous controlled-access measures were *porquería*, or trash.[40] Felix Machuca, a community leader at the Villa España public housing complex, said he hoped that the administration would consult with residents before taking any actions because "if the community doesn't want it, that won't work."[41]

In the press, police superintendent Pereira responded directly to the criticism of the plan to install controlled access in public housing by calling out what he saw as a class bias against poor people's desire for safety. According to Pereira it was wrong that poor people were denied housing with the controlled-access gating that people like him enjoyed, simply because they lacked economic means. "We do not want to confine [public housing] residents. We want residents to share with their more affluent Puerto Rican brothers and sisters a sense of what it is to be safe in their immediate community," Pereira explained.[42] Striking at the morality of his critics, Pereira stated, "The question is what price do we place on the security of the poor, and the way I understand it our security should not be measured in money."[43] In addition, Pereira criticized mano dura, not because of how it criminalized poverty, as Calderón charged, but because it was ill-conceived and poorly implemented. When asked by a reporter where Rosselló's crime plan had failed, Pereira responded, "in everything."[44] For Pereira, the "military occupation of Puerto Rico's public housing failed because it was a completely unsustainable idea" that lacked a real vision for how that occupation would be maintained.[45] With the new security plan being implemented by the Calderón administration, the question of how to maintain a permanent police presence in low-income communities, and in public housing specifically, without massive government spending and alienating public opinion seemed to have been addressed through the "soft" but ongoing occupation enabled by community policing and enclosure.

Following the Calderón administration's announcement of its anticrime plan, PNP political figures repeatedly criticized it, not based on its proposed actions but rather on its unoriginality. The mayor of San Juan, Jorge Santini, said, "I read the alleged content of this anti-crime plan and there is nothing new."[46] The secretary general of the PNP, Angel Cintrón, expanded on this sentiment: "Even worse in the budget that is being discussed, there is not a single penny of allocated for the Puerto Rico Police, not for equipment nor for a salary increase. And the operations [in the Calderón plan] are ideas that Pedro Rosselló had already implemented since 1993."[47] Although these PNP officials were merely trying to undercut the Calderón administration's crime plan, their comments highlighted an important truth that beyond rhetoric and theatrics there was little difference between Rosselló's mano dura and Calderón's mano firme. Both administrations saw Puerto Rico's poor as dangerous and in need of intervention.

While a number of strategies and tactics put forth by Calderón seemed to draw heavily from Rosselló's mano dura, one key difference was the Calderón administration's continued discussions about dramatically shrinking the size of the police force. In the months after the anticrime plan was released, the administration continued to discuss reducing the total number of PRPD officers, with the explicit involvement and support of Superintendent Pereira. Narrative budget documents as well as annotated agendas from the Governor's Security Council meetings note that although Calderón initially promised to increase the size of the force by four thousand new officers while she was on the campaign trail, the administration should aim to reduce the number of police by more than that.[48] Responding to the budget associated with Calderón's Puerto Rican Project for the Twenty-First Century, Superintendent Pereira noted, "The statistics demonstrate that there is no correlation between a bigger police force and a reduction in the rates of criminality."[49] He recommended cutting the current force from approximately 18,500 to 12,000 in order to be able to implement the anticrime measure's focus on better training and equipping police officers. "As I understand it, it is not necessary to recruit more police, but rather to better train them and adequately equip them and this is only possible if we aspire to reduce the total number of police to 12,000," Pereira suggested.

The members of the Security Council discussed Pereira's suggestion to dramatically reduce the size of the force and were for the most part in agreement with his conclusions, but they were concerned with how such a move would be interpreted by the public. José R. Negrón Fernández, the governor's adviser, noted that as crime in Puerto Rico had steadily increased since the 1970s, so too had the number of police officers, illustrating that having more police does not equal having less crime.[50] For Negrón Fernández, if the goal of the anticrime plan was a police force that was well prepared, trained, and equipped, "then increasing the number of police under a limited budget" would result in many police who would be "poorly prepared, poorly trained, and poorly equipped, which means a force that [would be] incompetent and unmotivated."[51] While the Security Council was generally in agreement with Pereira's assessment of the situation and what needed to be done, there was concern that the decision to halt recruitment efforts and reduce the force through attrition could be badly perceived by the public, since "the public perception [was] that the greater the number of police, the more security and therefore less crime."[52] The Security Council recommended informing people of the logic behind the effort to reduce the police force as well as explaining that this reduction would occur without firing current officers. A spike in violent crime, however, put an end to efforts to reduce the size of the police force and pushed the administration toward the explicitly hardhanded policing tactics from which it had tried to distance itself.

SUSPENDED DISBELIEF

On October 21, 2002, the PRPD, in coordination with a number of federal law enforcement agencies including the Federal Bureau of Investigation,

Bureau of Alcohol, Tobacco, and Firearms, and US Marshals Service, raided three public housing complexes in the Río Piedras area of San Juan: Monte Park, Monte Hatillo, and El Flamboyán.[53] The federal law enforcement agencies planned to serve a number of arrest warrants, while the PRPD used the opportunity to search for drugs and weapons. The police confiscated a small number of illegal arms and narcotics and made a couple of arrests as a result of the raids.[54] Although the police raids at all three complexes barely produced enough contraband for a good "drugs on the table" photo op, Superintendent Pereira still ordered police to stay behind at Monte Hatillo and El Flamboyán to reestablish order. According to Pereira, between thirty-five and forty officers would temporarily occupy Monte Hatillo, while between twenty and twenty-five would stay in El Flamboyán. He explained, "We will stay here a couple of days. The good neighbors of the area have requested this action and we are responding."[55]

For residents of the three public housing complexes raided and occupied by police officials, there was little difference among Calderón's mano firme, *pero respetuosa*, and Rosselló's mano dura. All three complexes had been raided and occupied during the Rosselló administration, and mano dura now emerged for residents as an immediate frame of reference to understand what they were (again) experiencing in their communities. Just like during the previous administration, residents saw helicopters flying overhead and hundreds of armed police officers and federal agents stationed around complexes knocking on and kicking down doors. While some residents defended the law enforcement operation, particularly those in Monte Park, where shootouts were occurring on a nearly daily basis, many residents who spoke to the press following the raids expressed skepticism and frustration. "Let[']s see how long it lasts this time. . . . [Let's] see if what they did yesterday is another show," remarked a resident of Monte Hatillo following the operation.[56] A number of residents complained that police stationed at the complexes following the raids "did nothing but sitting around when not giving parking tickets" to residents and visitors when they entered and exited.[57] According to some residents, police issued so many moving violations and spent so much time hassling residents who were not carrying identification that people had trouble leaving and getting to work on time following the raids.[58] María Rodríguez, a resident of Monte Park, told reporters, "I don't feel safe," while Lourdes Castillo of El Framboyán pointed out, "Sometimes, in places where the police get involved things get worse."[59] Castillo also complained that despite Calderón's rhetoric of respectful actions in public housing, the police were rude and unapologetic when they mistakenly entered people's apartments.[60]

While residents could not only see but also *feel* the similarities between mano dura contra el crimen and mano firme, police and government officials repeatedly tried to draw distinctions in ways that strained credulity. Calderón's chief of staff, César Miranda, said that what had occurred at the three public housing complexes in Río Piedras was "dramatically different" from mano dura because the police now acted with the "utmost respect and ... aimed first at the safety and dignity of the people."[61] The PPD senator Cirilo Tirado, for her part, said, "Mano Dura was a different vision and philosophy that consisted in enclosing the problem in a community. It was the era of the famous gates with police stationed 24 hours a day, because it was a government that criminalized the community."[62] Tirado did not mention that Calderón had approved measures to expand controlled-access enclosures in public housing and that police would indeed be surveilling some public housing complexes 24/7. Meanwhile, the spokesperson for the PPD in the House of Representatives, Roberto "Junior" Maldonado, without a hint of irony, said that these operations didn't stigmatize public housing residents because police were also targeting low-income *barriadas* like La Perla, which police had occupied about a month earlier. According to Maldonado, "This is not about a witch hunt like in the past administration."[63] For PPD officials, the shift away from a macho, tough-on-crime rhetoric masked the striking parallels between mano dura contra el crimen and Calderón's "firm, but respectful" approach to law enforcement.

Like members of her administration and other PPD officials, Calderón repeatedly stressed to the public, through the media, that these recent police operations were not a return to mano dura. Calderón noted, "What was called '*mano dura*' was an occupation of all public housing complexes and of all the places where there were communities experiencing economic hardship, something that was, for me, the criminalization of poverty."[64] The recently ordered operations in Río Piedras, by contrast, were "specific operations in places where there was a need for intervention and where police had to intervene for the security of those communities and the communities nearby."[65] For Calderón, intention, in a sense, seemed to trump action. Her administration did not intend to criminalize the poor; in fact, her administration was vehemently opposed to criminalizing the poor and felt that it was not only unfair but also posed a danger to democratic principles. This intention allowed her to dismiss the very real ways in which residents and observers drew connections between mano dura contra el crimen and this shift in the Calderón administration's anticrime efforts. If public housing residents expressed frustration and concern about these measures, they *misunderstood* the intentions of the administration and needed to trust that they were not actually being criminalized through such policing efforts.

Days after the police operation in Río Piedras, police launched a series of raids on public housing complexes in Cataño, just south of San Juan. On Saturday, October 26, police raided the Las Palmas public housing complex in search of drugs. When officers tried to arrest four residents on suspicion of drug possession, neighbors tried to physically stop the police carrying out the arrests. Residents hurled insults at the police and put their bodies between the police and their neighbors. As Superintendent Pereira described the incident, "Various neighbors, including teenagers with months old babies in their arms, intervened to stop the arrests. We had to send for reinforcements and finally were able to realize the arrests."[66] Residents of Las Palmas, including young mothers, rallied to protect each other from these unjustified arrests and the targeted harassment of their community. While Pereira criticized these young women as careless with their children, implicitly suggesting that their age made them ignorant and impulsive, their actions speak to a rejection of the ways that police action and arrest fracture communities and families. Such efforts by residents to sabotage police operations flew in the face of the Calderón administration's suggestions that the majority of residents had requested and desired these interventions.

The next day, at four in the morning, police raided the Juana Matos public housing complex in an operation that one reporter said was "comparable to scenes from a war movie."[67] Approximately two hundred officers were mobilized to serve eleven arrest warrants related to weapons possession. A helicopter hovered above the complex, casting a harsh spotlight, while dozens of officers clad all in black with their faces covered and carrying high-powered assault weapons took up strategic positions around various buildings. Police found small quantities of drugs and arrested a number of residents, but the large stash of illegal weapons they expected to find in the residents' apartments never materialized. In their search for a large cache of weapons, police broke down the doors of an apartment in building 14 that functioned as the complex administrator's office, leaving the space in complete disarray. "They looked where they didn't need to look," a resident complained.[68] Following the raid, Pereira said the police would not occupy the complex long term because there was already a minicuartel on the property that just needed to be shored up, highlighting that the infrastructure of minicuartels established under mano dura contra el crimen supplanted the need for long-term police occupations while still achieving the goal of constant police presence in public housing. The Calderón administration took up and expanded this infrastructural integration of permanent policing in low-income communities, which had begun under Rosselló, particularly as it embarked on a campaign of direct intervention in public housing complexes.

In addition to expanding the Koban program into public housing, the Calderón administration launched an initiative called Policía y Comunidad, which would install greater numbers of community police officers in public housing complexes. Superintendent Pereira announced the Policía y Comunidad program immediately following the raids in Cataño. The inspiration for the program was the Arístides Chavier public housing complex in the southern city of Ponce.[69] Following the occupation of Arístides Chavier as part of mano dura contra el crimen in February 1998, the Rosselló administration, as it had done in numerous other complexes, established a permanent police presence by creating a minicuartel or assigning officers to round-the-clock preventative patrols. According to Pereira, Arístides Chavier was a model for how to increase civilian and police interaction in a way that produces a favorable reduction in crime and feelings of insecurity. Pereira, however, did not share this evidence with the press or public, noting only that residents wanted a change and partnership with the police had a positive impact on public safety.[70] Pereira and the rest of the Calderón administration continued to distance themselves from mano dura and its criminalization of the economically vulnerable at the same time that they drew constant inspiration from mano dura's successful saturation of low-income communities with a "soft" law enforcement presence. While loudly criticizing mano dura in the press, the Calderón administration recuperated the controversial policing strategy and further entrenched it in low-income communities by recasting these measures as preventative, community-focused policing. Under Calderón, as with Rosselló, residents still had no input into how to address issues that affected their communities.

Even as the Calderón administration worked with the PRPD to saturate low-income communities and public spaces with a constant police presence, crime continued to climb. Raids and patrols in public housing, more police officers in schools, and greater police surveillance of pubs and discos where young people hung out all seemed to address "quality of life" concerns while having little discernible impact on the crime rate. During this uptick, the command structure at the PRPD experienced yet another shake-up when Superintendent Pereira stepped down to run the Puerto Rico Department of Corrections in December 2002. Pereira swapped positions with Víctor Rivera González, who went from being the secretary of corrections to police superintendent, taking over for Pereira at the PRPD. Like the two previous superintendents appointed by Calderón, Rivera González was not a career cop. Calderón was now on her third police superintendent in just two years.

The game of musical chairs between Pereira and Rivera González occurred at a moment when crime rates seemed to be increasing, which provoked concern about the governor's lack of control over the police as well as her failure to adequately address issues of public safety. Although Calderón attempted to assuage public concern over the increased rate of crime by suggesting that numbers were going up because the previous administration had manipulated the statistics, many continued to see her administration as woefully inept in responding to the crime problem.[71] Continued criticism of her administration's handling of the crime problem and the return of a familiar figure to the political stage would result in Calderón's embracing the tough-on-crime practices and rhetoric of mano dura contra el crimen as the PPD sought to shore up its authority and retain political power in the upcoming gubernatorial race.

THE RETURN OF MANO DURA

Shocking many, in May 2003 Calderón announced that she would complete her term but would not be seeking reelection as the governor of Puerto Rico. She told the public that her decision had to do with the fact that by the end of her term she would have already spent eight consecutive years in office, first as the mayor of San Juan and then as governor. She wanted to continue her public service out of the spotlight and spend more time with her family. Rumors immediately started to circulate that Calderón might have been pressured by the PPD not to seek reelection, while others suggested that the governor was battling serious health issues. Whatever the reason behind Calderón's decision not to run as an incumbent, her impending departure from La Fortaleza created challenges and opportunities for Puerto Rico's two main political parties. For both parties, punitive solutions became a central axis for establishing political credibility in opposition to Calderón's weak (read: feminine) response to crime and violence. During the run-up to the

2004 election, both parties advanced rhetoric and proposed solutions that returned to macho, tough talk and strategies. And in response, Calderón herself turned to explicitly militarized and punitive responses to crime toward the end of her time as governor despite her previous attempts to emphasize prevention and rehabilitation, at least on a rhetorical level.

Following her announcement, Calderón threw her support behind Aníbal Acevedo Vilá, the PPD candidate for governor. Acevedo Vilá, who had made a name for himself by advocating for an "enhanced" Commonwealth status during his time as Puerto Rico's resident commissioner in Congress, was billed as the fresh, new face of the PPD. Soon, however, a much more recognizable face reemerged to challenge Acevedo Vilá. After spending the past three years teaching and speaking at prestigious US universities, Pedro Rosselló announced that he would return to Puerto Rico to run as the PNP candidate for governor. Rosselló's latest bid for the governorship emphasized many familiar policy planks, including strengthening Puerto Rico's faltering economy and aggressively pushing for statehood, but a return to the sense of safety and security supposedly provided by mano dura became his signature rallying cry on the campaign trail. Rosselló pointed to the troubled socioeconomic landscape that had taken root since he left office as proof that Calderón's way of governing did not work. He positioned rising crime rates as the ultimate signifier of her and the PPD's failures.

Calderón pushed back on the allegation that crime was out of control and that she didn't have a handle on the situation. Yes, rates were going up, but that was because for the first time, the PRPD was using reliable metrics for recording crime and not manipulating the data, so the numbers only *appeared* higher, she repeatedly suggested. Challenging the idea that she was "soft" on crime, Calderón completely reversed course on reducing the size of the PRPD. Although she had been following the suggestions of the NOPD's Felix Loicano to reduce the size of the force early on during her term, facing mounting criticism, she went back to her initial campaign promise to increase the number of PRPD officers to twenty-five thousand, despite extensive evidence that such a move would likely result in a police force lacking in training, resources, and morale. Calderón increased recruitment efforts and gave the go-ahead to fast-track cadets in the academy to get them on the streets sooner.[72] Police superintendent Víctor Rivera González supported increasing the force to twenty-five thousand and alleged that the root of the crime problem was insufficient police staffing.[73] Rivera González remarked to *New York Times* reporter Abby Goodnough that he envied the NYPD's force of forty thousand officers, ignoring the fact that the NYPD and PRPD had the same ratio of officers to residents. With this comment, Rivera González equated recruiting more and more police—doubling the force—to fixing the crime problem in Puerto Rico.

Speeding up the initial training time in the academy for cadets and increasing recruiting efforts was part of a major plan to saturate drug points with police and raid *hospitalillos*, or "shooting galleries" where intravenous drug users gathered, in order to cause major disruptions to the drug economy. For instance, a report prepared by the PRPD for the governor noted that the agency's goal for December 2003 was to "eliminate 350 drug points in addition to the 500 already eliminated, for a total of 850 to eliminate or impact 1600 identified drug points" and "eliminate 12 *hospitalillos*."[74] This report noted that crime had been decreasing in many major categories, but that homicides showed a steady upward trajectory. As had been the case under mano dura contra el crimen, hot-spot policing did not seem to have a positive impact on rates of homicide and likely drove numbers up by causing massive disruptions to the drug economy and provoking desperation on the streets as a result of drug scarcity. Nonetheless, the PRPD and Calderón administration stubbornly clung to such tactics, and indeed intensified them over the course of Calderón's last year in office. While the Calderón administration never intimated as much, it seemed that Rosselló's attacks on the governor's approach to crime fighting from the campaign trail seemed to push the administration toward harsher and more visible forms of policing in order to demonstrate that she had not lost control of the situation.

After Rivera González announced that he was stepping down as police superintendent just a year after his appointment, however, it didn't matter how many police were on the streets raiding puntos and *hospitalillos*, because it seemed that the PRPD was in disarray and Calderón had lost control of the department. In January 2004, her last year in office, Calderón appointed her fourth police superintendent, Agustín Cartagena Díaz. Cartagena Díaz was a departure from Calderón's previous picks in that he had been working closely with the PRPD for over three decades, joining the PRPD's Education and Training Division in 1970 and rising through the ranks. At the time of his appointment, he had been working as the chief of Puerto Rico's Fire Department. Cartagena Díaz's appointment had the unanimous support of Puerto Rico's three police unions, and police leadership saw it as a long-delayed step in the right direction for the embattled governor in her fight against crime. José Taboada de Jesús, president of the Asociación de

Miembros de la Policía, echoed a number of police officials when he said, "We hope that with the experience of the colonel, friend and compatriot Cartagena [Díaz] the police will get a breather, and, in the short time that is left in the governor's term, he can formulate a concrete plan to combat the criminality that surrounds the island."[75]

Cartagena Díaz spent his year as top cop addressing rising crime rates and feelings of public insecurity by redoubling police efforts in public housing and intensifying the frequency with which police intervened with drug dealers and users. He launched a series of "mega operations" around the archipelago to arrest large numbers of "criminals," in order to reduce the murder rate. During these mega operations, police targeted people for arrest, generally from poor communities, who had committed a wide range of criminalized activities, ranging from trivial to more serious offenses, most of which, however, were in no way connected to open murder cases. In conjunction with these mega operations, police also instituted an even more aggressive posture toward drug points, attempting to disarticulate five hundred puntos over the course of several months. Knowing that puntos move following police action, police planned to "give chase to disarticulated *puntos*, to prevent them from being reestablished. Every precinct and every district in all police areas [would] form a group to give chase made up of at least five agents."[76] Thus, police intended to cause massive and constant disruptions to the drug market through constant pressure tactics, without a plan for dealing with the violence that was sure to follow.

What's more, these police efforts were overwhelmingly concentrated in low-income areas, meaning that Puerto Rico's most vulnerable populations would not be experiencing the respite from criminalization and police violence originally promised by the Calderón administration, but rather an intensification that would produce deadly consequences. Of the twenty communities initially identified by Cartagena Díaz to be rescued by police, thirteen were public housing complexes and four were identified as low-income *barriadas*.[77] This overwhelming focus on public housing persisted even though of the 528 puntos identified by police, which they planned to raid and dismantle over the course of the next six months, only 151 were in public housing.[78] The myopic focus on public housing, therefore, had no empirical basis in reality, but rather drew on a classed and racialized understanding of crime and danger that had only became more solidified through policing over the course of the 1990s.

In early July 2004, as crime rates stubbornly refused to stop their upward climb, Superintendent Cartagena Díaz began discussing with Calderón the possibility of activating the Puerto Rican National Guard to assist in breaking up puntos. National Guard soldiers were already deployed throughout a number of low-income communities to assist with community policing initiatives aimed at preventing school desertions. Cartagena Díaz proposed moving them out of this "community policing"–oriented role into an explicitly law enforcement capacity similar to that during mano dura operations. During these initial conversations about reintegrating the National Guard into the war on drugs, the Calderón administration tried to downplay this militarized escalation by suggesting that the National Guard would only be accompanying PRPD officers in a supporting role and that they wouldn't be carrying their normal long-range, assault-style rifles, and might not even be armed at all. Chief of Staff Miranda told the press, "If the National Guard was to be used it would not be used to stigmatize the poor people of Puerto Rico. It would be used in places where it is indispensable to ensure the safety of the people. Their job wouldn't involve the use of weapons."[79] This statement drew the attention of former police superintendent Toledo, who had overseen the joint National Guard and PRPD raids into public housing under Rosselló, and he mocked this plan in a radio interview shortly after it was announced. According to Toledo, "Drug dealers are powerfully equipped and they can't be confronted with short ammunition. The police has to be well equipped, it can't go in with water pistols."[80] Toledo defended mano dura and its militarized response to crime and challenged the Calderón administration to step up to the plate and do whatever it took to reduce crime.

On July 18, 2004, Calderón activated the National Guard to assist with crime reduction efforts.[81] She positioned the need for greater police and military presence in the streets as a response to a spate of deadly drug-related turf wars.[82] Like the previous administration, Calderón positioned the rising murder rate as a result of police *success* in attacking drug trafficking and putting pressure on low-level players in the drug economy. This initial deployment mobilized 500 National Guard soldiers to accompany 1,947 PRPD officers on preventative patrols in San Juan, Bayamón, Carolina, and Ponce.[83] Brigadier General Francisco Márquez, commander of the National Guard, said the soldiers would mostly be helping the police patrol public spaces and events where large groups of people gathered, such as festivals and malls, which would free police up to respond to issues in high-crime areas.[84] If crime rates did not decrease, National Guard soldiers would be ordered to patrol "housing projects and other high-crime areas" and, as a last resort, could be stationed there long term.[85] The PRPD's security plan for July to October, however, shows that those five hundred National Guard soldiers would from the very beginning be part of preventative patrols in public housing and other low-income communities.[86]

By the end of her term, unable to assuage public concerns over rising crime rates, Calderón welcomed the familiar embrace of the punitive strategies that she had seemingly been trying to outrun her entire term. For public housing residents, this move was familiar and caused significant apprehension. Following the governor and superintendent's announcement, community leaders and residents from public housing complexes in the San Juan area met with their elected officials to voice their concerns and propose measures that they would like to see instituted in their communities to reduce crime. Residents met with Senator José Ortiz Dalliot and Representative José Luis Colón to voice their opposition to the administration's decision to activate the National Guard and to register their rejection of this militarized presence in their communities.[87] They noted that a lack of trust in law enforcement made them feel less likely to cooperate when crime and violence did occur within their communities, and they castigated the media for portraying public housing as the only place where crime and violence occurred.[88] In addition, residents demanded greater communication with government officials and a bigger say in what happened in their communities and requested more activities and resources geared toward young people in public housing as a crime prevention strategy.[89] Public housing residents knew what they needed to feel safe in their own communities; however, their voices were seldom included during discussions about how to reduce crime and respond to rising feelings of personal insecurity among Puerto Ricans. This disregard for the needs and opinions of low-income people as they articulated them in relation to policing and violence prevention was perhaps one of the clearest threads connecting the Rosselló and Calderón administrations.

Predictably, the continued targeting of low-income communities through hot-spot policing and the activation of the National Guard to fight crime alongside police did little to abate crime, and likely contributed to worsening conditions of vulnerability and violence in communities with active drug markets. On the campaign trail, Rosselló pointed to rising crime rates over the course of Calderón's time in office to argue that the PPD had no plan to deal with crime and suggested that Acevedo Vilá would only continue Puerto Rico's supposed downward spiral into unchecked criminality and delinquency. Rosselló reminded Puerto Ricans of the declining rates of crime witnessed during his two terms and promised them a return to the security offered by mano dura contra el crimen. Rosselló claimed, "We've succeeded in the past. We've also learned from other people's mistakes. I come to guarantee the peace and safety that you want and deserve. I come to recover the route to progress filled with opportunities and achievable goals."[90] Correcting past mistakes, this time mano dura would include more prevention-oriented programming and elicit greater community participation. The great irony of Rosselló's statement was that by this time Rosselló's and Calderón's crime-fighting strategies had become virtually indistinguishable in their logics and practice. For overpoliced and criminalized communities, Calderón offered little beyond a seemingly "softer" version of mano dura contra el crimen, and the results it produced were just as exclusionary and violent.

MORE COPS, MORE CAMERAS, MORE PUNISHMENT, LESS CERTAINTY

The 2004 election season undoubtedly hardened political rhetoric regarding crime and witnessed the incumbent governor institute explicitly punitive and exclusionary policing measures throughout the archipelago, but particularly in the metropolitan areas of San Juan and Ponce. Even though Calderón had decided not to seek reelection, stepping aside to let Aníbal Acevedo Vilá, a rising figure in the PPD, make a run for the governorship, she and Rosselló frequently overshadowed Acevedo Vilá. Calderón and Rosselló were constantly trading jabs at each other in the public arena, forcing Acevedo Vilá to vie for media coverage and public attention. Rising crime was the ammunition that Rosselló used to snipe at both Calderón and Acevedo Vilá, forcing both PPD politicians to push their rhetoric and practice to more punitive extremes to combat Rosselló and the PNP's accusations that the PPD was soft on crime and lacked a plan to effectively deal with the fear and insecurity being experienced by many Puerto Ricans.

In early May, Acevedo Vilá unveiled his anticrime plan, *Puerto Rico sin miedo* (Puerto Rico without fear). The cornerstone of this plan was the installation of an expansive network of surveillance cameras to augment preventative patrols and aid in criminal investigations. Acevedo Vilá stated, "We're going to give certain punishment to the criminal, the narcotrafficker, and the corrupt official with better investigative capacity and more rigor in the courts."[91] The idea of castigo seguro (certain punishment) would become central to Acevedo Vilá's approach to crime, emphasizing constant surveillance as a deterrent to crime and assuring lawbreakers that they would be caught, tried, and punished to the fullest extent of the law. Acevedo Vilá tried to distinguish himself from Calderón by adopting a tougher rhetoric around criminality and emphasizing increased technological support and innovation for existing police efforts. In contrast to Calderón's strained relationship with the PRPD, Acevedo Vilá promised to reinforce police efforts and provide them with greater funding and resources. In essence, Acevedo Vilá tried to communicate to the public that unlike Calderón he would have a good working relationship with the force that would allow him to effectively combat crime. There would be no shake-ups at the PRPD if he was elected, and he sought to prove that he could be just as much a friend to the force as Rosselló had been.

After a contentious election requiring a two-month recount, Acevedo Vilá beat out Rosselló for the governorship by a razor-thin margin. Taking a page from Rosselló's book, Acevedo Vilá appointed Pedro Toledo as police superintendent. Toledo had served as head of the PRPD for eight years under Rosselló and had overseen the mano dura operations. His reappointment signaled a return to expanded police power, limited civilian accountability, and explicitly tough-on-crime, punitive approaches. Although Toledo was closely aligned with the PNP, his appointment as superintendent demonstrated the extent to which tough-on-crime rhetoric and policies had become a completely bipartisan affair, openly embraced by both parties. Speaking to this in his 2006 State of the Nation address, Acevedo Vilá remarked, "The superintendent and I are an example of an alliance between two people with different ideologies, who have overcome their differences in order to work together for the good of the country."[92] He continued, "But the main reason we are working for success is because we are on track to give the criminal certain punishment [castigo seguro]."[93] Conservative or liberal, pro-statehood or pro-commonwealth, political orientations seemingly dissipated in the face of the surging crime rate. Punitive governance effectively twinned Puerto Rico's two main political parties. Thus, it mattered little to people in criminalized communities whether the PNP or PPD were in power; the outcomes were likely to mirror each other in terms of the policing of their everyday lives and the intensification of their vulnerability to violence.

Acevedo Vilá's promise to do whatever it took to inflict castigo seguro on criminals created an environment ripe for police corruption and abuse. The Civil Rights Division of the DOJ conducted an extensive investigation of the

PRPD between 2004 and 2008, spanning nearly all of Acevedo Vilá's time in office, which was published in 2011. The investigation found the force to be one of the most violent and corrupt in the United States, declaring it "broken in a number of critical and fundamental respects."[94] The DOJ claimed that during the period under investigation, the PRPD regularly used excessive, sometimes deadly, physical force during the course of arresting or detaining individuals who either posed little to no threat or offered minimal resistance. The investigation cited the murder of Miguel Cáceres as one particular example that exposed the larger flaws of the PRPD.

On August 11, 2007, Cáceres, a forty-three-year-old father of three, was directing traffic as part of a motorcade for a *quinceañero* celebration in the eastern coastal town of Humacao. Officers Javier Pagán, Carlos Sustache, and Zulma Díaz de León drove by Cáceres to tell him to keep traffic moving. The officers stopped their vehicles after hearing a perceived insult from Cáceres. Officer Pagán, a member of the Tactical Operations Unit, known locally as the Fuerza de Choque (Shock Force), approached Cáceres and got into a verbal exchange with the civilian as his fellow officers looked on. The altercation turned physical when Pagán told Cáceres he was under arrest and wrestled him to the ground. During the course of the struggle, Pagán accidentally discharged his firearm, shooting himself in the leg. Officer Pagán then unholstered his gun and shot Cáceres multiple times at close range as he lay facedown on the ground. After the shooting, officers Sustache and Díaz de León drove Pagán to the hospital without notifying central command that anyone else at the scene had been wounded.

The initial police report indicated that Pagán had acted in self-defense, alleging that Cáceres had actively resisted arrest and tried to grab the officer's gun. Shortly afterward, however, a video taken by a witness on a cell phone surfaced on YouTube and the local media. There was no way to spin what had occurred. The video clearly showed that Cáceres had neither resisted arrest nor posed any threat to the officers when Officer Pagán killed him. Even Superintendent Toledo had to admit that what the Puerto Rican public had witnessed on the nightly news was an execution. The murder of Miguel Cáceres Cruz, according to the investigation, served as an "illustrative example" of the PRPD's institutional dysfunction: officers engaging in verbal confrontations with civilians; frivolous arrests; excessive use of force; a lack of meaningful supervision and accountability structures; and the failure of internal affairs to investigate matters in an objective and timely manner, if at all. During the course of the DOJ investigation of the PRPD, over fifteen hundred complaints were filed against officers for unjustified or excessive force and assault. We cannot separate this culture of impunity outlined by the DOJ from Acevedo Vilá and his administration's promise of castigo seguro.

Castigo seguro remained overwhelmingly directed at low-income and racially marginalized communities and deepened the state's surveillance and reach in these communities. In addition to enduring controlled-access gates, minicuartels, and around-the-clock preventative patrols, public housing residents and residents of low-income barrios now had hundreds of surveillance cameras pointed at them. Castigo seguro attempted to create near-total panoptic conditions in vulnerable communities. According to Acevedo Vilá, "The cameras have been proven to reduce incidents of criminality and it lets the criminals know that we will be watching. That is real change."[95] Police data, however, showed only a small drop in crime in public housing complexes and other areas where security cameras had been installed.[96] Although the government spent an estimated $13.2 million to create a national surveillance system, an investigation by the Centro de Periodismo Investigativo showed that the vast majority of the cameras installed had been vandalized or had fallen into disrepair just a few years later.[97] Whether they were effective or not, the message of these cameras was the same: public housing residents and other poor people needed to be under constant surveillance in order to keep the country safe. In this way, during his time in office Acevedo Vilá followed the well-worn path set before him by two decades of politicians from both political parties who had criminalized the poor and positioned them as a threat to the safety of "the public."

TWO WINGS OF THE SAME BIRD

When I was in Puerto Rico conducting the research for this book, a common refrain I heard from my interlocutors was that the PPD and PNP were "the same shit." Echoing familiar complaints about the two-party system, the Puerto Ricans I spoke to pointed out that beyond their stance on Puerto Rico's political status, the differences between the two main political parties were minor and mostly a matter of rhetoric. Both parties favored continued incorporation into the US nation-state; promoted neoliberal economic policies; and positioned crime and disorder as one of the most significant problems, if not the most significant one, facing contemporary Puerto Rican society. According to one activist whom I interviewed, the only difference between the two parties was that the PPD was "more subtle in their politics."[98] In this sense, the PPD and the PNP functioned not so much as political foes or opposites, but rather as two wings on the same bird. The work of both sides keeps the current political arrangement based in colonial capitalism moving forward.

The association of mano dura and other tough-on-crime politics as the sole province of conservative politicians inures the public to the ways in which seemingly liberal politicians often expand the reach of the carceral state. As political scientist Naomi Murakawa has shown, both liberals and conservatives promise their constituents a "right to safety" and freedom from fear, which has resulted in the criminalization of race and poverty by *both* parties. As Murakawa points out, "With eyes fixed on the incendiary sins of conservative law-and-order, liberal agendas become contrast background, glossed quickly and presumed virtuous."[99] As the examples of Sila María Calerón and Aníbal Acevedo Vilá demonstrate, liberals "shaped, complicated, and ultimately accelerated carceral state development."[100] One could argue that the shadow cast by Rosselló and his reappearance on the political stage pushed Calderón and Acevedo Vilá toward more explicitly punitive rhetoric and practice. However, that fails to explain why they constantly promoted increased police presence and surveillance in poor and Black communities as a "reform" and central component of "community policing" that was at odds with mano dura contra el crimen and somehow a solution to its overreach. Indeed, what the examples of Calderón and Acevedo Vilá show us are the "subtleties" of punitive governance and the ways that liberals have recoded increased police power as reforms aimed at restoring civilian confidence in law enforcement and guaranteeing safety and freedom to "decent, hardworking Puerto Ricans." The eight years of the PPD rule in between two PNP governors was not a respite or a rupture, but more of the same operating under different names. And as we shall see in the following chapter, for young people struggling against neoliberal disinvestment and political repression, mano dura was not a distant relic of their childhoods; it formed the very terrain within which they operated.

FIVE

Policing Solidarity

ON FEBRUARY 9, 2011, IN THE MIDST OF AN ongoing student-led strike against state and university officials' efforts to shrink and privatize the UPR system, students at the university's flagship campus in Río Piedras (UPR-RP) organized a *pintata*, or paint-in, as an artistic protest against administrators' attempts to silence them with police intervention. An event in which students planned to spend the afternoon painting messages of resistance on the street in front of the university library ended unexpectedly as one of the most violent moments of the strike.

With the pintata under way, students became outraged when they spotted a police officer videotaping the activity. A group of students approached the officer and asked why they were being recorded when they were not doing anything wrong and demanded to know what the police planned to do with the video.[1] Almost immediately the situation grew tense, as the students insisted on answers and more police arrived on the scene. Eventually one of the students attempted to take the camera from the officer, and the situation turned violent. Metal-tipped batons, boots, and fists rained down upon the protesters, some of whom responded by throwing paint at the police, turning their dark blue riot gear white. As students ran to try to escape the violence, police officers tore through campus trying to catch them, swinging their batons wildly and hitting anyone in their path. That afternoon, both blood and paint stained the pavement in front of the university library. Video and photographic footage shows police officers using excessive force, deploying pepper spray and other chemical irritants, unrelentingly beating students with batons, and applying illegal chokeholds and pressure techniques on students.[2]

Images of the police violence that students endured during the pintata flashed across television and computer screens all over Puerto Rico as a shocking spectacle. By the time of the pintata, there was already a pervasive sense that many Puerto Ricans had grown tired of the violence that seemed to be steadily engulfing the campus since the police had been stationed there in early December. After the violence of the pintata, the police presence on campus became dangerous and unacceptable. For instance, an editorial that appeared in the *Puerto Rico Daily Sun*, the local English-language newspaper, the following day compared the police attack on students to "the acts of the dictatorships we all denounce and reject."[3] The editorial asked readers, "Is this to be the new institutional order? Police every 100 feet? The right to free speech reduced to the 100 square feet between police officers? Has the UPR become the testing grounds for a new institutional order?"[4]

The pintata and the other moments of state violence that punctuated the two student strikes at the UPR—which occurred respectively from April 21, 2010, to June 21, 2010, and from December 7, 2010, to March 7, 2011—were certainly worthy of outrage and condemnation. The violence unleashed on students did not, however, evidence new contours of policing and state repression, as the editorial team at the *Puerto Rico Daily Sun* and others suggested. Instead, both the violence of the state during the UPR strikes and the range of reactions that it provoked revealed much about where, under what circumstances, and against whom violence had been rendered acceptable within contemporary Puerto Rican society. What happened during the UPR strikes provided many relatively racially and economically privileged Puerto Ricans a glimpse into forms of state violence that had become routine in the archipelago's predominantly Black, low-income, and Dominican im/migrant communities over the course of the 1990s and early 2000s. In this way, observers perceived patterns of police brutality, harassment, and surveillance as "new" when enacted against UPR students, particularly those at the Río Piedras campus, who are more likely to come from the middle and upper classes. Yet these practices had been a central part of policing low-income communities since at least the era of mano dura contra el crimen. This unwillingness to see an expansive trajectory of violent policing in Puerto Rico demonstrates the extent to which much of the public had normalized police violence against racially and economically marginalized Puerto Ricans.

The strikes at the UPR put on full display forms of police repression and violence that had been long tested, deployed, and confined within public housing and other low-income areas around Puerto Rico during mano dura and its aftermath. As Xiomara Caro, a UPR law student and spokesperson for the strikers, put it, "Now it's the only strategy. I would say it's not *mano dura contra el crimen, es mano dura contra todo el mundo* [it's not iron fist against crime, it's iron fist against everyone]."[5] This chapter explores how police violence against student protesters and their supporters drew upon strategies of containment solidified, in part, through the policing of racially and economically marginalized populations during the mano dura era. This chapter also carefully charts how UPR students' exposure to state violence and repression created moments of solidarity with racially and economically marginalized communities who had been criminalized. At the same time, I detail moments when students sought to leverage their privileged positions to assert they were "students not criminals" and thus *undeserving* of state violence. Students responded to their own experiences of brutality and repression by either undermining or reifying the structures of anti-Black racism, segregation, and classism that had animated policing throughout the archipelago. The strikes at the UPR illuminate how punitive policing, and mano dura contra el crimen in particular, have created a complicated legacy that young Puerto Ricans are forced to negotiate as they weigh the benefits of forging solidarity across race and class differences or adhering to hierarchies of belonging and exclusion that mark criminalized populations as disposable.

THE RADICAL OPPOSITION FROM THE STREETS

The battle for accessible and affordable public education that occurred at the UPR in 2010 and 2011 emerged within a context of intense neoliberal reform, marked by the dismantling of the public employment sector, the privatization of public resources, protracted economic recession, and a seemingly hard right turn in Puerto Rican politics. In the spring of 2009, Wall Street credit houses such as Moody's and Standard & Poor's threatened to demote Puerto Rico's credit rating to junk status. Against this backdrop, on March 9, 2009, Puerto Rico's republican and pro-statehood governor, Luis Fortuño, introduced Ley 7, or Public Law 7, a "special law declaring a state of emergency and establishing a plan for fiscal stabilization to save the credit of Puerto Rico."[6] Scholars Yarimar Bonilla and Rafael Boglio Martínez note that Ley 7 enabled Fortuño to "'restructure' public employment in ways that would otherwise be illegal: unilaterally suspending union contracts, overriding labor laws in order to dismiss public-service workers, and denying those who remain employed the job protections guaranteed in their union contracts."[7] This law was particularly devastating in its targeting of the public sector, which had emerged as the largest employer in Puerto Rico following the collapse of the industrial economy during the 1970s.

In early September 2009 the Fortuño administration announced that it would be laying off more than 17,000 public sector workers in an attempt to stabilize the economy. Puerto Ricans took to the streets throughout the month of September to protest the decision. On October 15, 2009, an estimated 200,000 demonstrators flooded the streets of San Juan as part of a one-day general strike protesting the economic and political agenda of the Fortuño administration. The one-day Paro Nacional del Pueblo (People's National Stoppage) was a manifestation of the widespread discontent with Fortuño's so-called economic recovery plan and the annexationist governor's attempts to further integrate Puerto Rico into the US economy despite clear negative consequences for the working class.

University students were very active in mobilizations protesting Ley 7 and the Fortuño administration. In fact, students were perceived by state officials as such a galvanizing force that the administration closed ten out of eleven UPR campuses in the week leading up to the Paro Nacional in an attempt stop protesters from using the campuses as rallying points.[8] Students mobilized against Ley 7 not only in solidarity with public sector laborers but also because the law slashed university funding. The government used Ley 7 to alter the formula used to allocate funds to the university, with UPR's percentage of the state budget dropping from 9.6 percent to approximately 8.1 percent. To make up for the shortfall in funding, university administrators announced that they would be increasing tuition, decreasing scholastic and athletic scholarships, and doing away with fee exemptions for university employees and their families.[9] Students argued that these actions by university administrators would make it significantly harder for many low-income and working-class families, who were already underrepresented in the student body, to send their children to study at the UPR. For student activists, Ley 7 and the budgetary cuts at the UPR were asking the poor and working classes to disproportionately shoulder the costs of the economic crisis at the same time that engines of upward social mobility, such as public sector employment and public education, were being destroyed.

After the Paro Nacional, students, especially those who would become active participants in the UPR strikes, lamented the lack of sustained action and coordination on the part of the labor unions that had helped organize the massive one-day stoppage. According to student activist Abner Y. Dennis

Zayas, "After the *Paro Nacional* the labor movement threw in the towel. . . . [T]hey did absolutely nothing. That, of course, has a series of explanations, but, in that sense, the radical opposition from the streets against the policies of the government fell to the student movement."[10] Student activist Roberto José Thomas Ramírez used similar terms. After the Paro Nacional, he explained, "We were already conscious that we had become the only real opposition to the government. The only sector of society that was standing up to the government saying, 'what you are doing is unjust, and we are not going to permit you to do this.' And in that sense, a debate emerged about what we were planning, because this was a historic moment where the student movement could assume a greater responsibility, and we couldn't get locked into discussing issues that only affected the university."[11] A number of student activists understood the university to be a potential catalyst for a renewed, broad-based social movement against the neoliberal agenda of the state. Ricardo Olivero Lora, a UPR law student, summed up this perspective during the first transmission of Radio Huelga, or Strike Radio, a student-run radio broadcast. He said, "These times are crucial for society because the current government, in an abusive manner, has launched an offensive against the working class, to the point that many are in a state of hopelessness. We want to make this a place where we can return that hope."[12] Understanding and positioning themselves as a vanguard, students felt that the struggle at the UPR had the potential to spark larger mobilizations against the agenda of the Fortuño administration across Puerto Rican society.[13]

In addition, for student activists the university seemed to be an ideal site to discuss how the crises affecting Puerto Rico hit youth especially hard. Lourdes C. Santiago Negrón, a student activist and reporter for Radio Huelga, recalled that the strike began in part as a way to make the university more accessible in order to combat economic stagnation. She noted, "The job market is very small and studying is a way for people to survive and have something to aspire to. That is the main concern for us who are students in the struggle—for future generations to have a possibility. That's under attack and we're struggling against it."[14] The selective admission process at the UPR, especially the Río Piedras campus, combined with the common perception that UPR students were more engaged in disruptive protests than they were in their studies, had funneled many students, especially low-income students, into private educational institutions. More than half of all Puerto Ricans at colleges and universities in the archipelago were enrolled at private institutions.[15] Nonetheless, many Puerto Ricans have historically understood and celebrated the UPR as an important path to social mobility and inclusion for the poor and working classes. Recognizing this history and perhaps acting as beneficiaries of it themselves, student activists at the UPR hoped that they could help respond to the challenges Puerto Rican youth faced as they navigated Puerto Rico's anemic economy: limited upward mobility, rising personal indebtedness, and a continued reliance on outward migration for decent employment options. In this vein, the student movement posited a reinvigorated public university as a possible path toward personal and community empowerment. However, contradictions would emerge over the course of the strikes as it became apparent that a more affordable UPR would not necessarily correspond to an accessible and welcoming public university system for racially and economically marginalized youth.

THE THREAT OF CONFRONTATION

Months of organizing preceding and following the Paro Nacional eventually culminated in students at UPR-RP calling a forty-eight-hour strike on April 21, 2010. Students asked the administration to stop tuition hikes, reinstate fee waivers, and guarantee that none of the UPR campuses would be privatized. The students told administrators that if university officials failed to meet their demands, they would go on indefinite strike. The administration failed to take the students' demands seriously, and as a result, students at the UPR-RP announced an indefinite strike on April 23 to force the administration into negotiations. The Association of Puerto Rican University Professors and the Brotherhood of Non-Teaching Employees of the University of Puerto Rico both urged their members to respect the picket line. By May 4, ten out of eleven campuses, which are spread out across the big island, had joined the indefinite strike. Only the Recinto de Ciencias Medicas, the University of Puerto Rico's medical school, did not join the indefinite strike, which was due to the time-sensitive nature of its scientific investigations and its work with patients. The medical school did, however, hold a brief work stoppage in solidarity with the other campuses on strike.

The Fortuño administration stationed police on the perimeter of the UPR-RP campus immediately following the announcement of an indefinite strike. The police remained at the perimeter and did not enter the campus due to the política de no confrontación, or nonconfrontation policy, an informal agreement between university administrators and the PRPD that prohibited police from intervening in campus affairs. The nonconfrontation policy had emerged from a long history of state violence and repression directed at the student movement. As Abner Dennis Zayas told me, "There is a history of bloodshed here," because the UPR, especially its Río Piedras campus, has long served as a site of pro-independence and leftist organizing.[16]

The UPR, since its founding in 1903, has played a central role in the US colonization of the archipelago. As a result, bitter debates and physical battles over the future of Puerto Rico and its people have often played out on the UPR's campuses. The UPR was initially established with the goal of training public school teachers to aid in the Americanization of Puerto Rican children.[17] During the university's first two decades of existence, and as a result of its mission to advance American colonial rule and capitalist interests, students mostly came from the landowning and professional classes.[18] By the 1930s, mirroring larger political and cultural shifts in Puerto Rico at the time, the UPR, while still bound up with American colonial rule, emerged as a "house of learning" dedicated to studying pressing issues within Puerto Rican society. From the 1930s to the 1980s, the university, and in particular the UPR-RP campus, not only played host to debates about Puerto Rico's status in relationship to the United States, but also emerged as a site of violent confrontation between independentistas, annexationists, and police.

One of the first major instances of state repression and violence on a UPR campus occurred in 1935, in what became known as the Río Piedras massacre, when Nationalist Party leader Pedro Albizu Campos was barred from campus and an altercation between Nationalist students and police left four students dead. Over the course of the 1940s and 1950s, the UPR remained a site where ideological battles raged over Puerto Rico's status, particularly when the archipelago was incorporated as a commonwealth in 1952, although in the wake of the Río Piedras massacre, these battles rarely escalated into full-blown physical violence. The relative calm of the 1950s gave way to more than two decades of turmoil and violence as students targeted the university's Reserve Officers' Training Corps (ROTC) program to express their rejection of US militarism and colonial rule and police cracked down on protesters. In 1964, for instance, when pro-independence students tried to march from the plaza in downtown Río Piedras to the campus, they were met by pro-annexationist students and police, who blocked their entrance. Skirmishes between students eventually prompted police to intervene by assaulting students, deploying tear gas, and discharging their firearms in an attempt to disperse the protesters.[19]

Clashes over the presence of the ROTC on campus, the draft, and US aggression in Southeast Asia continued during the remainder of the decade and into the next. On March 4, 1970, following a confrontation between ROTC cadets and independentistas, the Fuerza de Choque (police antiriot squad) entered the UPR-RP campus and began violently beating students in an attempt to subdue the protests. The event left more than one hundred injured, and police shot and killed one student, Antonia Martínez.[20] In 1971, another clash between ROTC cadets and independentistas resulted in the Fuerza de Choque once again entering the UPR-RP campus. After the Fuerza de Choque came onto the campus, a melee ensued that resulted in widespread police brutality, mass arrests, businesses in Río Piedras engulfed in flames, and three dead.[21] The 1970s ended with the police entrapping and executing two pro-independence students at Cerro Maravilla on July 25, 1978, which had a chilling effect on pro-independence organizing. As scholar Alessandra Rosa notes, during the 1970s student activists attempted to *"puertorriqueñizar la Universidad,"* or challenge the idea that the university was merely a site for the transmission of American ideologies or a military training site.[22] For much of the decade, students' refusal to comply with the colonial relationship between the United States and Puerto Rico put student activists into direct and often violent confrontation with the state.

In September 1981 students went on strike to protest tuition increases and demand greater autonomy for the university. On November 25, Governor Carlos Romero Barceló ordered police to "clean up" the university; over the course of an hour, police used guns, batons, fists, and boots to remove student protesters from the UPR-RP campus and the surrounding neighborhood of Santa Rita. More than twenty people were injured during the ensuing chaos, including both students and police.[23] The scenes of violence not only shocked observers, but also prompted the question: What kind of learning environment is this? An editorial by *El Nuevo Día*, following the events on November 25, asserted that the UPR not only had to put an end to the violent confrontations between protesters and police but also had to reestablish the university as a place where students could learn in peace.[24]

Following the culmination of the strike, which lasted an unprecedented five months, the university instituted a series of changes in how it would handle student protests on campus, which became known as the nonconfrontation policy. With this policy, the university administration leveraged its institutional power within Puerto Rican society to prevent the very visible clashes between students and law enforcement that regularly marked student protests. This move not only aimed to prevent violence on campus but also sought to improve the reputation of the university by assuring parents and students that the police would no longer be seen on campus *repartiendo palos*, or giving out clubbings. The nonconfrontation policy rehabilitated the image of university administrators, who had been seen as so intransigent in the face of student demands that they were willing to allow the UPR to descend into violence in order to avoid meeting students at the negotiating table. The policy promised students, as well as members of the public, that rather than calling the police, administrators would move forward with a willingness to "maintain an academic atmosphere open to dialogue, respect, and negotiation."[25]

Although it was only an informal agreement between university administrators and police, the nonconfrontation policy's implementation led to an immediate decrease in instances of political violence on the university campus. While students would still experience violence during their participation in larger public protests that occurred off campus, police violence against the student movement dissipated a great deal. It is important to note, therefore, that the implementation of the policy strengthened the privileged position of UPR students in relation to other Puerto Ricans who did not or could not attend the university. Students' status as UPR enrollees provided them an assurance that they would be shielded from the kind of violence regularly visited upon racially and economically marginalized Puerto Ricans, who were unable to say no to police intervention and did not have one of the most important institutions in Puerto Rico advocating on their behalf. In many ways, the nonconfrontation policy was part of the constellation of formal and informal policies devised by elite segments of Puerto Rican society during the late twentieth century that further concentrated police violence in economically and racially marginalized spaces.

Although the nonconfrontation policy was firmly in place during the 2010 strike, the threat of police brutality and harassment remained real in the minds of many students and their supporters. Immediately after the strike was announced on April 23, 2010, heavily armed riot police became regular fixtures outside the campus's perimeter gates. Police officers looked on as UPR-RP students created encampments at each of the seven *portones*, or entrance gates, controlling access to the university campus. University administrators, meanwhile, called in additional private security guards to monitor and control the protesters. Then, on May 13, 2010, during a campus assembly, students voted to continue the strike. With the strike's ratification, state officials and university administrators grew increasingly concerned, and police became more aggressive in their approach to the strikers and their supporters.

Although the police could not enter the university, they tried to prevent necessary provisions from reaching students. The Fuerza de Choque attempted to prevent parents and supporters from giving food, water, or medicine to the students on strike inside the campus. On the morning of May 14, police officers beat and arrested a father who was attempting to bring food to his son on the inside. Onlookers caught the violence on their camera phones, and images and videos of this police brutality quickly circulated on social media and in the mainstream press. According to student activist Waldemiro Vélez Soto, "With that, by midday we had dozens and hundreds of people bringing us food at all the different portones."[26] Laughing, Vélez Soto continued, "We never had as much food as we did after the police tried to prevent it from reaching us. People identified with the father or mother trying to get water to their child at the same time that all the laid-off workers identified with the students."[27] Vélez Soto's account of solidarity highlights how student activists were able to effectively mobilize Puerto Ricans sympathetic to their cause to act as a protective force against police violence and provide material support to students in order to keep their strike going. While a powerful display of support and solidarity, the outpouring of support that Vélez Soto described also speaks to how willing some sectors of Puerto Rican society were to take a stand against police violence when it affected students and their supporters, who were perceived as undeserving of brutality and repression, in comparison with the silence that often met victims of police brutality in low-income neighborhoods.

On May 20, 2010, students took their demands beyond the portones and joined union leaders, public employees, and others in protesting a political fund-raiser at the Sheraton Hotel that Governor Fortuño was attending. As the students had moved beyond the campus grounds, they were beyond the reach of the nonconfrontation policy. When students and labor activists attempted to disrupt the fund-raiser, police responded by unleashing tremendous violence upon the protesters. Images and videos from the Sheraton showed police punching, kicking, clubbing, and applying illegal chokeholds to students and other protesters. A particularly shocking image showed the PRPD's second in command, José A. Rosa Carrasquillo, kicking UPR student José "Osito" Pérez Reisler in the genitals as he lay restrained and defenseless on the floor.[28]

Following the incident at the Sheraton, instead of condemning police violence against peaceful protesters, conservative politicians attempted to paint students as dangerous instigators determined to plunge Puerto Rico into anarchy. Jennifer González, president of the Puerto Rican Senate at the time, said that "a group of radicals" had provoked the police violence at the Sheraton in an attempt to "destroy democracy through violence."[29] Governor Fortuño similarly denied police culpability for the violence that took place at the Sheraton by characterizing activists' attempts to disrupt the fundraiser as "an act of violence and intolerance" that deserved "everyone's condemnation."[30]

Status updates from PRPD officers' own Facebook pages, however, seemed to confirm that the police went to the Sheraton looking to harm protesters in general, and UPR students specifically. Facebook user Alexander Luina, who identified himself as a member of the PRPD, wrote, "Finally, after 12 days I can use my baton in this damn strike."[31] Perhaps most disturbing, Facebook user William Concepcion, who identified himself as a member of the Fuerza de Choque, wrote, "I finally clubbed somebody today. Fuck, I hope things get crazy so I can empty out this rifle."[32] After a variety of Puerto Rican news outlets publicized the Facebook accounts and posts, police superintendent José Figueroa Sancha ordered an investigation to determine the legitimacy of the cited Facebook accounts and status updates. He stood by the actions of the police at the Sheraton, calling the police "heroes" and denouncing the students for provoking them.[33]

While university and government officials attempted to paint the student movement as violent and dangerous following the incident at the Sheraton, the violent words and deeds of the police led a growing number of Puerto Ricans to come out to the portones in support and protection. The scores of people joining the strikers in solidarity with their demands forced university administrators to meet students at the negotiating table. After two months of protests and with ten of the UPR's eleven campuses shut down, the strike came to an end on June 21, 2010. Administrators met many of the students' basic demands, including reinstating canceled tuition wavers, delaying the imposition of tuition hikes and fees, and protecting student leaders from reprisals.[34] The student movement, and much of the public, regarded the agreement between strikers and the university as a historic victory for the student movement and a serious blow to the Fortuño administration's neoliberal agenda. The victory, however, was short-lived, as state and university officials quickly began to reverse the hard-won achievements of the student movement.

In the aftermath of the successful strike, state officials and administrators quickly took steps to reverse the gains of the movement. The legislature added four new appointees to the UPR's board of trustees in an attempt to stack the board in favor of the then current administration and neutralize opposition.[35] The new board of trustees lost no time imposing an $800 student fee, which would go into effect in January 2011. The university administration also made substantive cuts to faculty benefits and eliminated or put on "pause" a number of academic programs across the university system. Students responded to the university and state officials' duplicity with threats that they would once again paralyze the university system with a strike.

Students at the URP-RP began a forty-eight-hour stoppage on December 7, 2010, demanding that the administration overturn the imposition of the new student fee. If the administration did not comply with the students' demand to repeal the $800 fee, they vowed to once again go on indefinite strike. In response to the stoppage and a looming second, indefinite strike, university administrators contracted the private security firm Capitol Security for approximately $1.5 million.[36] On the evening before the forty-eight-hour stoppage, the firm, on orders from university administrators, demolished the iconic entrance gates to the Río Piedras campus in an attempt to prevent student strikers from once again shutting down the university. According to student activist Xiomara Caro, "When the *portones* were taken down... that was the moment when we knew this is war. Capitol Security was, for sure, the first time that we knew *esto va a ser una huelga de mano dura* [there is going to be an iron fisted response to the strike]."[37]

While students did not anticipate the removal of the gates, they were even more surprised by the individuals who showed up wearing T-shirts with the word "SECURITY" emblazoned in yellow letters on the front. Capitol Security had hired young, inexperienced men and women from Villa Cañona in Loíza, a predominantly Black and low-income barrio in a predominantly Black and low-income municipality, to tear down the portones and act as security personnel during the stoppage and potential strike. According to some of the youth recruited to work security at the university, a municipal employee approached local young people, offering them $10 an hour to "work" at the UPR.[38] "They told us: 'get in the van, we have work for you.' No one trained us for that," remarked a twenty-five-year-old from Villa Cañona who worked security during the stoppage.[39] On an archipelago with official unemployment statistics hovering above 16 percent and where the federal minimum wage was $7.25 an hour, it is not surprising that youths from one of the poorest municipalities in Puerto Rico jumped at the opportunity Capitol Security presented.[40] The encounters between student activists and the mostly low-income, young, Black men from Loíza would illustrate how policing manifested itself through and further entrenched extant inequalities operating within Puerto Rico society. Further, the encounters would show how the state sometimes conscripts victims of its violence to enact violence against other populations marked as dangerous and threatening to the imperatives of the state.

Youths from Loíza, untrained and without much information about what exactly they would be doing on the university campus, were brought in, in lieu of police, to subdue the students. The youths from Loíza represented a way around the university's nonconfrontation policy that would allow state and university officials to violently repress the student movement and reestablish control without formal police intervention. Although Capitol did not provide the youths with any form of training for the situation they were about to encounter at the university, some reported being explicitly told to use violence against the protesters to maintain order.[41] Shortly after the destruction of the portones, the youths contracted by Capitol Security were seen "patrolling" the campus, some armed with wooden two-by-fours, metal pipes, and knives, and getting into verbal and physical confrontations with protesters. A video of one of the confrontations that went viral on social media outlets showed a young man contracted by Capitol Security threatening a female student and telling her to "eat shit" when she asked him about his qualifications, while other guards in the video referred to student protesters as "idiots with their faces covered" and "cocksuckers."[42] The rapid circulation of this video and others like it worked to reinscribe the youths working for Capitol Security as alien and threatening to the UPR community. These videos often circulated on social media with a narrative that a gang of violent thugs hired by the university was threatening students, which played into a history of racialized and classed representational practice directed at low-income youths, particularly those from spaces like Loíza.

A news segment that aired on WAPA-TV's news program *Telenoticias* on the evening of December 7 further cemented the notion that the youths contracted by Capitol were particularly dangerous because of where they came from and what they looked like. In the segment, correspondent José Esteves approached a number of Black and brown young men contracted by

Capitol to ask them about their qualifications. At one point, he approached two guards sitting in a parked car and asked, "What kind of experience do you have?," to which one of the guards responded, "We're from Loíza. We do this almost every day." "You do what every day?" asked Esteves. The young guard then responded, "Kicking, punching." When Esteves asked why, the guard coolly replied, "There [Loíza] because it's fun, here [UPR] because they pay us." Esteves asked another guard what he thought about the work he was doing, to which the guard replied that he liked it so far because he liked to hit people: "me gusta dar cantazo."[43] The circulation of this news segment, along with other videos capturing hostilities and altercations between students and the youths working for Capitol, confirmed for many people their already held racist and classist notions about the inherent violence and criminality of economically and racially marginalized Puerto Ricans generally, and *loiceños* (residents of Loíza) specifically.

Some students understood the young men in the clip as merely performing toughness for the camera; other students and members of the public, however, saw their performance as a very real indicator of the kind of violent pathology allegedly endemic to spaces like Loíza. These assumptions about poor Black and dark-skinned youths had been historically solidified through the spectacle of almost two decades of intensified, targeted police raids in public housing complexes and low-income barrios such as Villa Cañona. The enclosure and militarized policing of economically and racially marginalized communities marked these spaces as hot zones of violence, or zonas calientes, characterized by deviance and immorality, which needed to be controlled and contained through state intervention.

The sight of low-income, Black, and dark-skinned youths on the grounds of the UPR campus prompted journalist Benjamín Torres Gotay to note in his blog for *El Nuevo Día*'s online portal that those contracted by Capitol Security "look more like thugs from the corner than security guards."[44] Student activist Giovanni Roberto, himself a young Black man from a low-income family, heard fellow students using similarly racist and classist language to describe the youths from Capitol. According to Roberto, "In the Fine Arts *porton* the interaction between the students and the people contracted by Capitol Security began to turn increasingly tense. There were people who wanted to prevent them from removing the *portones*, and with much indignation they shouted; they shouted at 'those people.' That same night I started to hear one or another racist or classist comment. 'Where did they find these murderers?' or more blatantly 'What slum or project did they get them from?'"[45] The violent antagonism that emerged between the student protesters and the youths from Loíza unleashed responses that played upon prejudices about Loíza, Blackness, and poverty that had long been a feature of the Puerto Rican popular imagination.

Such responses reproduced the state's justification for disproportionate police intervention, like mano dura, in low-income and predominantly Black areas, which rendered these areas and populations as dangerous and threatening with a natural propensity toward, and even enjoyment of, violence. According to Roberto José Thomas Ramírez, the administration tried to create an "an animosity" among UPR students and "the expectation that they [the youth contracted by Capitol] came to kill."[46] Thomas explained that this narrative would in turn make the student movement act aggressively toward these low-income youths in a way that would undercut the movement's claim of inclusivity and solidarity with the poor and working classes. The university administration, acting on behalf of the state, exploited existing prejudices against these young people from Loíza, based on their racial, spatial, and economic background, and pitted them against university students in the hopes of frustrating any form of alliance or solidarity between them.

Students' and their supporters' race- and class-based prejudices toward the young people contracted by Capitol allowed the machinations of the state and its security apparatus to remain hidden. The racist and classist interpretations of these tensions functioned to occlude the ways in which the state was enacting, or at least attempting to enact, violence by proxy. As the state could not send the police into the university without violating the nonconfrontation policy and threatening its legitimacy, it instead subcontracted security functions to young people from Loíza, many of whom were themselves intimately familiar with state violence. It is no mistake that the state conscripted the youths of Villa Cañona and expected them to mimic the routine violence that they had experienced or witnessed during police raids in their communities. In 2007 police had occupied Villa Cañona under the auspices of dismantling the drug points that operated there. Rather than reducing drug dealing and drug-related violence, the police occupation of Villa Cañona resulted in dozens of reports of police brutality and misconduct, prompting investigations from the Puerto Rican Civil Rights Commission and the local branch of the ACLU.[47]

Disturbingly, Benjamin Rodríguez, a supervisor at Capitol Security who helped to recruit the youths from Villa Cañona as guards during the UPR stoppage, had played a central part in the occupation and raids that occurred in Villa Cañona as the PRPD's then assistant superintendent of field operations. According to Villa Cañona community leader Maricruz Rivera Clemente, Rodríguez "takes the Black people of Loíza like all they're good for is to beat people up and they don't recruit us for other work."[48] Rivera Clemente added, "They take them to give the students at the university a beating. Instead of giving them scholarships so they can be students, they want them to reproduce the suffering of their communities of origin."[49] Through their recruitment by Capitol Security on behalf of the state, these youths from Villa Cañona were in some respects made victims of police violence twice over: first by witnessing and experiencing rampant police brutality in their community, and second through the dehumanizing expectation that they would enact a similar violence against others as police proxies.

Furthermore, these youths were subjected to the psychologically violent realization that the only way they would be allowed to set foot on the UPR campus was as violence workers.[50] Many of the young loiceños reported that the first time they had visited the Río Piedras campus was when they showed up to take down the portones. This narrative of the foreclosed space of the university speaks to the incredible inaccessibility of UPR-RP to many racially and economically marginalized young people.[51] This reality is something that some students were acutely aware of when the young guards showed up on campus. Student activist and Radio Huelga reporter Lourdes Negrón Santiago put it this way:

> You have a university that proclaims an open campus policy, but what does open campus mean? Is it for the people? Like, common, everyday people? Is it open for private interests? What is the relationship with communities that the university has? So this "open campus policy" you see it, for example, with how they removed the gates. The University contracted people from the Black, poor communities to come and work as security here in the campus. And it was like, really? The people that don't get any chance to attend UPR? It was their first time seeing the university and they're going to be security for the university? It was really sad, you know? It was a really sad thing for us.[52]

State and university officials relied on the disenfranchisement and marginalization of low-income, racially marginalized youth from Loíza to manage and discipline student protesters in exchange for wages.

University officials sought to exploit the marginalization of populations long excluded from the university in order to enforce an agenda that would further deepen their separation from the UPR by making the university more costly and inhospitable for racially and economically marginalized young people. At the same time, university officials hoped to appeal to students' sense of privilege to foster conflict between the students and guards, which would allow the administration to step in and prevent the impending indefinite strike in the name of public safety. As a result, student activists struggled to reconcile an expressed desire to make the UPR more accessible to all Puerto Ricans with the racist and classist attitudes that existed within the student movement, which were brought to the surface with the presence of young loiceños brought in to police the protesters.

Leaders within the student movement struggled with how to respond to the young guards recruited by Capitol and the racist and classist responses that their presence on campus generated among some students. Student leader Giovanni Roberto was incredibly troubled by the racist and classist sentiments he heard within the student movement. At the same time, he was disgusted by what he saw as an overt attempt on the part of the administration to play on racial, spatial, and class cleavages to prevent solidarity between young people who were experiencing different manifestations of Puerto Rico's ongoing economic and social crisis. One moment in particular crystallized for Roberto the need for the student movement to reach out to the young people from Loíza in a sincere and earnest way. On the evening of December 7, at the end of the first day of the forty-eight-hour *paro*, or stoppage, while watching coverage of the paro on the local news Roberto spotted a former student of his from when he worked as a teacher in Loíza in 2008. "One of the students from that school was there, on the other side, on behalf of the administration and the government. I was disheartened seeing him on the television. I felt rage and sadness, but I confess that I had no idea how to deal with the situation," he recalled.[53]

Later that night, troubled by what he had seen, Roberto had a long conversation with fellow student activist Xiomara Caro about how to respond to the situation. According to Roberto, he and Caro debated whether one had to be full of "hate—*desprecio*—toward the system, towards capitalism, towards what capitalism is, what capitalist systems do all the time to people" in order to be an activist and effect change or if a movement needed "a feeling of love, to be united, to have human connection" to be successful.[54] Roberto notes that in his conversation with Caro they came to an understanding that a hatred of capitalism and inequality alone cannot fuel social transformation; rather, social movements must be driven by solidarity and connection with others feeling the effects of an oppressive system.[55]

This recognition of the importance of love and solidarity in social movements informed Roberto's subsequent approach to the youths contracted by

Capitol Security. Roberto added that the racial composition of the student movement also made him conscious of the need to respond to the situation with love and understanding for the young people from Loíza rather than with the class and racial hostilities that university and state officials hoped to exploit. According to Roberto, "the fact that part of the movement were white boys" who hadn't "lived the life that young Black, mostly male, people live" created an inability for many within the student movement to identify with the young guards and caused them to instead react with contempt.[56] He continued, "So when they saw Black people, the way they were dressing, the way they were acting and talking, I felt that a lot of people were rejecting them in a negative way. I heard comments and I felt bad. I felt angry. I'm part of a movement that does not understand this situation. The situation that causes those young people to be scapegoats, in a way. Or be divided against other young people."[57]

Recognizing his commitment to the student movement and simultaneously having an intimate understanding of its blind spots regarding race and class, Roberto worked to conceive of ways to connect both groups of youths subjected, albeit in radically different ways, to the violence of the state. At 7:45 a.m. on the morning of December 8, after a night of altercations and vandalism on campus, Roberto addressed the young people contracted by Capitol in front of students, supporters, and the press. He began his address to the guards by letting them know that he and the student movement did not consider them enemies. He said he wanted to clarify for the guards what exactly the student movement was struggling for and against. Roberto related to the guards, saying, "Part of my personal story, and what explains why I am so convinced of what were are doing here, is that I am also from a poor *barrio* and I am also Black just like you all. When I was young, my parents couldn't find work, just like you all who don't find work now. And I lived for many years on *cupones* [federal assistance]. I lived until I was sixteen years old on *cupones*. Until I was sixteen. Almost my whole life."[58] Roberto explained that he was on strike in part because ever since he was a small child his mother had taught him that everyone has a right and should aspire to be equal. Continuing, he asked the guards:

> But what's wrong? In this world we are not all equal. Why is Loíza *un pueblo de negros* [a Black town]? Why is Carolina *un pueblo de negros*? Why are Dorado and Condado considered *pueblos de blanquitos* [towns full of rich whites]? It's called racism. It's called institutionalized racism. It's been called racism for many years. Decades. They don't want us to leave. Those born in

Loíza stay in Loíza. Those born in Carolina stay in Carolina. When we come here to fight everyday, it's so that all of you also have an opportunity to break that cycle.[59]

Roberto urged the young guards to leave their posts and join the students in struggling for a more accessible educational system, and by extension a more equitable society. Students had in fact taken up a collection offering to pay the youths from Loíza their day's wages if they left their security posts and joined them in protest. "I think that all of you, who today are standing on that side, tomorrow should be on this side. *On this side.* Know that what we want is for you all to have an opportunity to study here. That is what we are fighting for," he said before extending his hand to one of the young security guards.[60] When the young guard refused to shake Roberto's hand, another guard approached him to shake his hand and then hugged him. After a night of violence between students and guards, Roberto's speech to the guards ended with a remarkable sight: students and guards shaking hands and hugging one another.

The embraces and words exchanged between the guards and students represented a utopian moment in which the student movement challenged the racism and classism within its ranks and constructed connections with youths whom both the university administration and its students often excluded from the elite space of the UPR-RP campus. It also represented a moment when young people who were being pitted against each other could come together, if only for a brief moment, and if only symbolically, and express solidarity with one another. This was all the more impressive when the segregation that structured these young people's lives had typically made that incredibly difficult. The UPR reproduces hierarchies of power and privilege within Puerto Rican society and as a result places limits on meaningful connections across race and class differences both on campus and beyond. The segregation perpetuated by the university, as well as that which marks Puerto Rican society more generally, makes this display of solidarity between students and the young loiceños important. On the morning of December 8, Giovanni Roberto succeeded in cogently outlining for both students in the movement and the young guards the ways in which the state benefited from the antagonism between them. Simultaneously, Roberto challenged UPR students to confront their own racism and classism, which caused them to lash out against the youths contracted by Capitol. For Roberto, the student movement needed to shift in order to make itself relevant in the lives of the economically and racially marginalized youths who had often been excluded from spaces of privilege such as the UPR.

When I asked student activists about this moment and the decision to reach out to the young people working for Capitol, they noted that it was in large part Roberto who pushed the need for the student movement to express solidarity with young people from Loíza and consider what it would mean to bring their concerns into the student struggle. Many of these same students also noted that that moment was *only* possible because of Roberto's own embodiment and experience. A few times, I heard some version of the remark, "Well, it *had* to be Giovanni who spoke to the young people working for Capitol." Such comments highlight the burden placed on Roberto to act as a liaison between the student movement and the youth working for Capitol. Roberto was expected to act as a "bridge leader" because so few self-identified Black and low-income students were involved in the student movement as leaders.[61] The general makeup of both the student body and the student movement at the UPR, especially the UPR-RP campus, helps to explain why student activists may have had difficulty recognizing their own racial and class privileges and biases as they interacted with the young people working for Capitol. Roberto's leadership during this moment, and his willingness to act as a bridge between these two groups of young people, challenged the student movement to consider the gulf between its rhetoric of inclusivity and its actual exclusivity when confronted with race and class differences.

Roberto's utopian gesture of solidarity, however, was short-lived. Capitol's management personnel replaced the young guards he had addressed a short while later with a group of older guards in the hopes of short-circuiting any potential identification or solidarity with the student movement. According to an executive from Capitol Security, the company replaced the guards "because they suffered from Stockholm Syndrome," implying that the students were somehow the guards' captors.[62] State and university officials immediately prepared to implement a new security regime on campus. For the first time in the thirty years since the implementation of the nonconfrontation policy, police could officially enter the Río Piedras campus to "reestablish order." The violence experienced by students following the installation of the police on campus, and the circulation of images of that violence via both traditional and social media, provided for many Puerto Ricans a glimpse of police power and practice that had long occurred, largely out of public sight, in low-income barrios and public housing residenciales.

University administrators and government officials positioned the conflicts between students and guards and acts of vandalism that occurred on the evening of December 7 as evidence of the need for police to enter the UPR-RP campus. According to Governor Fortuño, the police would provide necessary protection for the faculty and students being threatened by a small, radical fringe terrorizing the campus. In a press conference announcing the installation of police personnel on campus, Fortuño said, "The acts of violence and vandalism that all of us witnessed early on Tuesday were the last straw. The people of Puerto Rico have been more than patient and university officials more than lenient during this conflict. Enough is enough."[63] Attempting to minimize the support that the student movement had garnered within and outside of the university, Fortuño added, "The instances of terrorism perpetrated over the past 48 hours have clearly shown that the violent actions of a small minority of individuals claiming to represent students are promoting an agenda that really is alien to the vast majority of students at the UPR and has nothing to do with the issue of the *cuota* [$800 fee], which they are using as an excuse."[64]

Fortuño's lambasting of the student movement came after Roberto's speech went viral in the archipelago and diaspora and after it became clear that some of the youths from Loíza were unwilling to carry out the violent will of the state. The student movement felt that the police presence on the interior of the campus, in lieu of the guards from Loíza, was meant to frustrate this nascent sense of solidarity. Suddenly, the police officers in riot gear who had been outside the portones during the first strike and the forty-eight-hour stoppage were inside the gates to ensure "order." As has often been the case in Puerto Rico when police forces occupied a space under the auspices of guaranteeing public safety, their presence generated greater fear and violence. Police officers harassed, abused, and arrested students participating in strike-related activities. The administration placed a ban on political protest on campus immediately following the stoppage, and as a result, police were able to arrest students for small acts of resistance such as handing out pro-strike pamphlets on campus.

While government and university officials justified police intervention by equating protesters with terrorists and extremists, police command also tried to make a case that rampant drug dealing on campus necessitated their presence. Police superintendent Figueroa Sancha announced his desire to eventually see a minicuartel installed at the university. Similar to the ones installed in public housing residences during mano dura, a minicuartel on campus would ensure constant police surveillance and disciplining. Figueroa Sancha told the press, "The idea is that the police are here to stay in the university. Not only in Río Piedras, all the campuses should have some police presence. I would like to see a police station in the Río Piedras campus in the near future."[65] He alleged that a police station at the UPR-RP campus would allow police to attack the puntos that had been allowed to proliferate in the university system because of the nonconfrontation policy. "They sell everything there: heroin, cocaine, Percocet. In the university you can buy anything," the superintendent claimed."[66]

The police used this familiar strategy of criminalizing an area and population by associating it with drug use and trafficking to justify increased police presence and intervention. The UPR was now not just a site of protest, but yet another one of the police department's zonas calientes. Recalling this moment, Abner Dennis Zayas called out the administration and state's pretenses of drug dealing and terrorism as little more than a smokescreen that would allow them to use the police force to squash radical resistance on campus while opening up the UPR to private interests. Indeed, the pattern and practice of police installation and intervention in the university resemble the occupations under mano dura that sought to silence political unrest and facilitate privatization efforts. According to Dennis Zayas, "For a long time the police superintendents have been crazy to enter the university. They couldn't enter because it has a very high political cost. For the governor of Puerto Rico to order the police to enter the University of Puerto Rico, you already know that what is going to take place is pure violence. And that's what happened."[67]

On December 10, 2010, a group of community leaders representing a number of barrios and public housing complexes issued a statement denouncing the police presence on the UPR campus. These community leaders, who were active in a number of residents' councils and community organizations in low-income communities around the big island, called for an end to police aggression and announced their solidarity with the student movement and its goals.[68] The statement read, in part: "They've cornered them, they imposed a fee that they can't pay, they prevent them from protesting anywhere, they surveil them, they deny them dialogue and solutions. The police and University administration treat our young people like animals, like lesser humans, without rights. These students are our children, our grandchildren, neighbors in our community; they are people who do not have the money to pay this fee and are seeking a decent public education for all Puerto Ricans. We're going to support them, there is no doubt."[69] In the statement, organizers linked the brutality experienced by the student movement to the police repression of their communities, creating connections and solidarity between their two struggles. They highlighted the ways in which violent and discriminatory policing, which had been perfected in low-income communities, was now on full display at the university, noting, "Our communities are familiar with police brutality. We have experienced in the flesh the discrimination and violation of the rights of our residents on multiple occasions. In a country where the state disproportionately abuses its power, there is no choice but to mobilize, university and community, to address these abuses that are now daily."[70] This expression of solidarity not only condemned the state's violence against student protesters but also reminded a public that may have been sympathetic to the plight of UPR students that such rampant abuse was quotidian in low-income and racially marginalized communities. In this way, their expression of solidarity both supported the student movement and called for an end to police violence on campus, while also drawing attention to the routine violence experienced in marginalized communities that often garnered little outrage or solidarity.

For their part, student activists attempted to draw attention to the state's use of police violence as a blunt instrument of repression at the UPR and in public housing in order to connect struggles that were often viewed in isolation from one another. For instance, following attempts by university and government officials to paint students and protesters as responsible for the violence taking place on campus, José García, a student and spokesperson for the Organización Socialista Internacional (International Socialist Organization), issued the following call for solidarity to public housing residents: "You know who the violent ones are who come to club people. You know it's the police. We must remind the country who the violent ones are."[71] Though students at times glossed over the differences in power and privilege between themselves and the residents of marginalized communities, their attempts at solidarity revealed important parallels, with the potential to result in coalitions against state abuse. Students also looked to the long-standing resistance against the repressive agenda of the state in public housing and low-income barrios as a source of inspiration and strength in their own organizing. As Xiomara Caro put it, "Resistance, where you see it most, is in the *caseríos* [public housing] . . . and what we did in *la iupi* [UPR] was a resistance. . . . [S]o there's a parallel there because we're both, in a way, trying to resist what the system is trying to turn us into."[72]

As students and activists from low-income communities were working to challenge state repression, government and university officials were working equally hard to frustrate any kind of alliance between the two. In addition to installing the police on campus, on December 20, 2010, the university administration announced that it would be summarily suspending Giovanni Roberto. Some within the student movement felt that his suspension was politically motivated and had to do in part with his success in building bridges between the student movement and low-income communities. Caro noted of his suspension, "He, at various moments, has discussed how he arrived at the university in a way that is emblematic of the students that we're fighting for; students who, thanks to scholarships and other opportunities could study at the university."[73] Caro added, "It is evident that this is a political suspension, attempting to decapitate the movement. . . . [T]hey don't understand the logic of how the student movement works. You can't decapitate the movement because there is no head, so we will continue."[74] Roberto's suspension, along with the suspension of other students who had been highly visible during the strikes, demonstrated the extent to which state and university officials tried to destabilize the movement. Roberto's suspension in particular, however, also suggests an active effort by the UPR administration to prevent the student movement from mobilizing alongside racially and economically marginalized communities in the struggle to demand greater accessibility and accountability in state-run public resources.

As the second strike progressed, state and university officials attempted to deepen racial and economic animosities and prevent cross-coalitional organizing. To do so, they employed the physical infrastructure the state had created while policing public housing communities. Following the administration's ban on on-campus protests, police took students arrested for violating the ban to minicuarteles in nearby public housing complexes. One of the lasting features of mano dura contra el crimen is an archipelago of mini-police stations and holding cells built in public housing complexes. As noted in the first chapter, these minicuartels were built, much like the perimeter fences around public housing complexes, to discourage drug trafficking and ensure a permanent police presence within public housing. During the second strike, police arrested students, separated them by gender, and took the men to the station in the Monte Hatillo public housing complex and the women to the station in the Manuel A. Pérez public housing complex.

The sheer number of arrests taking place at the UPR-RP campus as a result of the protest ban ensured a steady stream of police, students, and supporters entering and disrupting the lives of these public housing communities. Pedro Lugo, a student activist and reporter for Radio Huelga, suggested that the police brought arrested students to Monte Hatillo and Manuel A. Pérez to create conflict and resentment between students and residents. Lugo recalled, "The police took them to the project jails because they thought that the community would reject the solidarity of the supporters that would show up to support the jailed students."[75] The presence of community outsiders entering public housing to support arrested students, along with the increased police presence, resulted in tensions among students, their supporters, and community residents. According to Lugo, at one point some residents threw rocks at students and their supporters to express their resentment against the growing police presence in their community. Following the incident, student activists approached residents and discussed the ways in which police forces were trying to create conflict between them and asked for their support. "Some people talked to them and they understood the problem. A couple of days passed without any incidents with the community, so the police decided not to take them [there] anymore. The police said that they moved them [to new locations] because those headquarters have the biggest cells."[76]

The communities of Monte Hatillo and Manuel A. Pérez had been subject to ongoing raids by police forces since the early 1990s; it is no surprise, therefore, that a sudden influx of increased police forces in addition to community outsiders would lead to tensions and resentment. Knowing this, it does not take much of a stretch of the imagination to see this as a deliberate tactic on the part of the police to create conflict between UPR students and public housing residents. Did police hope that this tactic of placing university students in holding cells in public housing complexes would make arrested students feel even more isolated, under the assumption that these two populations were disconnected from and even hostile toward one another? Did police purposefully attempt to disrupt the lives of public housing residents by bringing arrested students, and subsequently their supporters, to Monte Hatillo and Manuel A. Pérez in order to breed resentment between these groups? The fact that the police stopped bringing arrested students to Monte Hatillo and Manuel A. Pérez once residents, students, and activists were able to reach an agreement with one another suggests that the state had a vested interest in exploiting and exacerbating racial and class cleavages in order to once again prevent solidarity between low-income communities and the student movement. The use of public housing minicuarteles, alongside the employment of young men and women from Loíza to act as police proxies, highlights the vulgar and intentional ways in which the state has attempted to manage populations through difference.

"¡FUERA, FUERA, FUERA POLICÍA!"

While state and university officials attempted to use heavily racialized and classed police violence to prevent cross-coalitional solidarity with the student movement and its demands, the state's violence against the student movement eventually moved thousands of Puerto Ricans to align themselves with the students and demand an end to the police occupation of the university. Interactions between students and police at the university became increasingly violent and frequent as the strike went on. These incidents of regular police brutality, harassment, and arrest crescendoed with the pintata on February 9, 2011, that began this chapter. The pintata seemed to signal a tipping point on a variety of levels. First, the extreme brutality of the police during that moment signaled to many Puerto Ricans that there was no possible justification for the violence that was occurring. Xiomara Caro narrated the mayhem in this way: "When we got to *sociales* [the social science building] we started knocking on teacher's doors and being like, 'people need to get out of the university NOW.' *Porque* [Because] we suddenly realized that there was no formation, *venia guardia de todos lados con macana* [police were coming from everywhere with their batons], individually, which means they can do whatever they want because they're not following an order."[77] Once a critical mass of students had reached *sociales*, they began to march across campus in the hope of picking up people along the way in order to protect them from being brutalized by police.

Caro noted that for many students, even those who were not active participants in the strike, the events of the day generated feelings of complete frustration and hostility toward the police stationed on campus. This resentment speaks to the privilege long accorded to UPR students that allowed them to protest on campus without fear of police violence—a privilege they lost when the administration and state decided to cast aside the nonconfrontation policy at the outset of the second strike. According to Caro, "It created a climate that had nothing to do with the strike. It's that people were not used to it, they didn't like it, and people were ready to fight. I'm talking about girls in flip-flops throwing stones!"[78] Images surfaced in the press of students throwing stones at the police and police retreating and hiding in bushes or, in some cases, throwing stones back.

This literal blow to the authority of the police, alongside the growing public outrage over what was transpiring on campus, played a role in the decision to eventually remove police forces from campus. Caro noted, "And at that point, I think the government said we can't risk people losing all respect for the police because no one is going to be able to establish order. Right now that's what's happening a lot in the *caseríos*. Guards are getting beat up, police officers don't want to go to work, don't want to deal with this, and the government is starting to lose . . . *esa mano dura* is losing . . . people are getting tired of it."[79] Caro's comments, on the one hand, draw from narratives circulating within Puerto Rican society that public housing complexes are spaces of lawlessness that even police are scared to enter. On the other hand, however, her comments signal a respect for public housing residents' strategies of self-defense and physical resistance against relentless police harassment and brutality. Though Caro attempted to draw parallels between public housing residents and students who were fighting against police violence, her comment doesn't touch on the asymmetrical responses of the state to articulations of resistance by each group. Unlike public housing residents, who often experienced greater police repression in response to displays of physical resistance, at the UPR the state was forced to reconsider its strategy given the serious political costs of images circulating in the media that showed police abusing university students and university students refusing to back down.

Immediately following the pintata, professors and employees of the UPR announced a twenty-four-hour work stoppage in solidarity with the students in light of recent events.[80] Then, on February 12, 2011, approximately ten thousand Puerto Ricans marched through the streets of Río Piedras in solidarity with the students, calling for a complete withdrawal of the police from campus. The march, *Yo amo la UPR* (I love the UPR), was filled with people from various sectors of Puerto Rican society, including many parents of current UPR students and alumni. For instance, Beatriz Miranda, the mother of a student at UPR-RP, said she participated in the march, "to make the government understand that these kids aren't alone. What they're doing to the students is an outrage."[81] A constant refrain shouted throughout the march was ¡*Fuera policía, fuera!* (Get out police, get out!) and ¡*Fuera, fuera, fuera, policía!* (Out, out, out, police!). On February 14, heeding these calls, the Fortuño administration called for the police to be removed from campus.

At a press conference following the massive march in support of the students, Governor Fortuño said that he would be withdrawing police from the Río Piedras campus. Fortuño admitted that the events of the pintata weighed heavily in his decision to remove the police from campus. He added, "The police should not be inside the university; they need to be in the streets."[82] The message was clear to the thousands of Puerto Ricans who marched under the banner *Yo amo la UPR* that their dissent had helped to halt the violent repression of the student movement. While this display of solidarity culminated, swiftly, with the ejection of the police from campus, it simultaneously shifted focus away from the initial demands of the student movement and instead toward calls for an end to police brutality.

Although the second strike did not officially end until March, many Puerto Ricans outside the student movement understood the removal of the police from campus to be the effective end of the strike at the UPR.[83] Though the police were no longer on campus attempting to disrupt the student movement, state violence continued to contribute to the premature end of the student agitation for a more accessible and equitable university system. The events that unfolded at UPR-RP during the second strike demonstrate how police violence neutralizes political dissent in ways that are more complex than they initially appear. The violence experienced by students and their supporters did more than just instill fear or discourage people from protesting. It also diverted attention from the original demands of the student movement in a way that benefited a state unwilling to halt the UPR's march toward an increasingly exclusionary public educational system. Rather than struggling to make the university more accessible and accountable, students were instead forced to mobilize against police violence. As students and their supporters worked to force the government and university to reinstate the nonconfrontation policy and get the police to leave campus, the student movement suddenly became reduced to a movement against police brutality. In this way, victory for the student movement, in the eyes of many supporters, became contingent upon the removal of police from campus rather than the protection of the university against privatization or the cultivation of efforts to create a public education system accessible to all Puerto Ricans.

For some student activists, the focus on removing the police from campus, while necessary, inadvertently resulted in their larger questions of economic and social justice losing urgency in the face of immediate bodily danger and harm. Thus, when the police left campus, the strike was considered over despite the fact that students found themselves, in many ways, in a similar position to the one they had been in when the strike began. This outcome was central, and not incidental, to the state's utilization of police violence to respond to popular protest. Police violence functioned to divide the movement by forcing it to shift attention away from the initial demands of the students and toward responses to police brutality. As students were compelled to focus on an end to police brutality as a demand of the student strike, tensions grew among various factions of the student movement and between student activists and their supporters. These tensions demonstrated the difficulties of building and maintaining solidarity under a repressive state.

Reflecting on how the second strike ended, Xiomara Caro noted, "In retrospect, one of the criticisms . . . at least internally, is that it became an issue of police brutality. We sold out to everyone else."[84] According to Waldemiro Vélez Soto, this shift in attention fragmented the student movement and confused the public about the demands of the strike. He stated, "It was a mistake. For example, if the demands were accessibility, a university open to the people, the poor, workers, etcetera. . . then victimizing ourselves because of police abuse is moving us onto another issue. It gives emphasis or impetus to that issue when that was never the primary issue when we started this struggle. You confuse the people because suddenly it becomes a principle demand. Then, when the police leave then the strike is considered over, no?"[85] Giovanni Roberto made a similar point: "I think one of the problems was [that] one of the main goals was to get the police out of campus, which was never the main goal for us [in the student movement]. But for the people who supported us, in some way, they established that as the main topic. And that was a mistake in my opinion."[86] According to Roberto, the shifted focus onto police violence allowed for the subjects of the student movement's initial concern—a shrinking and increasingly inaccessible public university system—to continue unaddressed as long as overt physical violence ceased. "We should reject the whole politic that the administration was doing in the university. If we [just] concentrate on the security policy, the whole thing is going to continue," he noted.[87]

In this way, while police brutality became a rallying point of solidarity for Puerto Ricans in the archipelago and diaspora, some students within the movement saw this emphasis on ending police brutality as foreclosing or displacing what they understood as more important conversations about austerity, public resources, and social access. That police violence was perceived as a distraction from the "real" issues of the student movement highlights the difficulty that students had at times decentering narrow student concerns in favor of broader issues affecting nonstudent populations, especially those living in racially and economically marginalized communities. For Puerto Ricans who found themselves under assault almost daily by police repression, standing up against the violence aimed at UPR students could have represented a point of connection and solidarity, even if they might not have identified with issues such as halting tuition and fee hikes. Including an end to police brutality and repression as a central plank of the second student strike, especially given the students' expressed desire to build a more expansive and inclusive student movement following the interactions with the young guards working for Capitol, could have had the potential to bring el barrio and *la iupi* together across racial, spatial, and classed divides to challenge the agenda of the state.

Violent criminalization by the state represented a point of commonality between UPR students and Puerto Ricans who lived in so-called zonas calientes. However, at times students attempted to challenge their criminalization without also challenging the underlying logics of criminalization that ensnared so many beyond the university's gates. Perhaps one of the most common refrains heard during protests and seen written on signs was *Somos estudiantes, no somos criminales* (We are students, we are not criminals). Another common slogan was, *Luchar por una educación pública de excelencia no es un delito* (Fighting for a quality public education is not a crime). While these slogans rejected the state and university administration's attempts to criminalize protest and dissent, they also reinforced the idea that students, unlike "real" criminals, are undeserving of violence at the hands of the state. In formulations like these, students were undeserving of violence *because* they were students and not common criminals, which implicitly sanctioned state violence against those involved, either by choice or by lack of choices, in the informal economy.

Appealing to hierarchal notions of belonging and worth within Puerto Rican society, students missed opportunities to make connections with other populations experiencing criminalization and challenge the implicit understanding that people who are designated criminal are violable and expendable. As Latina scholar Martha Escobar points out in another context, such "decriminalizing motions turn into violent acts themselves" as the innocence of some is secured at the expense of others.[88] In other words, appeals to tropes of innocence and merit reinforce the idea that there are real criminals who are deserving of the violence visited upon them at the hands of the state and their fellow citizens.[89] By dismissing the centrality of challenging police violence to the student movement and appealing to privileged notions of students' inherent "goodness," student activists missed an important opportunity to build a coalition around mutual experiences of criminalization. This kind of coalition building might have allowed the student movement to make stronger and more lasting connections to racially and economically marginalized communities.

BUILDING COALITIONS IN THE SHADOW OF THE STATE

Although students struggled with how to express and forge solidarity across difference, the strikes of 2010 and 2011 nonetheless facilitated necessary connections between the student movement and residents of economically and racially marginalized communities, who are often excluded from the UPR. Reflecting on the strike, and in particular on the incidents that occurred between the students and the Loíza youths contracted by Capitol Securities, Giovanni Roberto suggested that the experience with Capitol showed the student movement how the state uses racial and class tension to consolidate power and protect capitalist interests. Roberto noted, "The incident with the Capitol guards was important and positive, in my opinion, because it allowed us to target the capitalist system, the exclusions that exist and hide behind the university's title of public, the racial composition that no one speaks about, and the necessity of solidarity from below, from a class perspective."[90] He also noted that the incident with the youths contracted by Capitol prompted the student movement to be more explicit in including marginalized communities in the struggle for accessible education and helped to establish connections between university students and the barrio. "Some of the strikers made contacts in *barrios* and communities and managed to meet and interact with some of the young people recruited during those days. We broke the tactics of repression and we opened up a space for unity," he concluded.[91]

During my discussions with a number of the individuals who had participated in the 2010 and 2011 student strikes, many of them expressed a genuine desire for the UPR to become a more inclusive and accessible space that did not reproduce the pernicious forms of segregation that mark Puerto Rican society more generally. This was particularly true for those students who themselves hailed from low-income and lower-middle-income neighborhoods.

The elite status ascribed to the UPR, as well as students' own desires for economic security through upward mobility, sometimes made meaningful and lasting coalitions with the communities who regularly experienced police violence difficult. And sometimes these displays of solidarity on the part of students did not resonate with racially and economically marginalized communities, nor were they always reciprocated. Nonetheless, the fleeting displays and expressions of solidarity between students and low-income communities that occurred during the strikes had lasting transformational effects on many of the individuals involved and challenged the scope of the student movement and its demands. These moments of tension and solidarity, although fraught, illuminated a common struggle against the various spatial, racial, economic, and political inequalities endemic to state violence and the state-sanctioned use of policing as a solution to crisis.

SIX

————

#ImperfectVictims

CULTURAL THEORIST CARLOS PABÓN SUGGESTS THAT Puerto Rico has been in the midst of "an (in)visible social war" since the 1990s, if not longer. He notes, "During the previous decades, there has been a remarkable increase in homicides, particularly among young people. However, this phenomenon of social violence has failed to be articulated as a political problem. On the contrary, it appears to have been naturalized and invisibilized."[1] In the various chapters of this book I have endeavored to explain how violence can on the one hand be an intense source of concern for many Puerto Ricans and on the other hand fail to generate widespread alarm or demands for change when the archipelago's most vulnerable populations are those most affected. As I have shown in the preceding pages, policing has played a large role in propagating and normalizing notions about who must be protected from violence and who is allowed to suffer harm and death as a routine part of life in Puerto Rico. Race, space, gender, sexuality, class, and citizenship inform the hierarchies of human value that in many ways dictate popular and state-sanctioned understandings about who *deserves* to experience violence and when and where violence can be *allowed* to proliferate.

In this context, antiviolence activists in Puerto Rico have worked to challenge popular ideas about victimhood, violence, and criminality that discriminatory and harmful forms of policing such as mano dura contra el crimen have normalized for more than two decades. Increasingly, many recent antiviolence grassroots and pedagogical campaigns have taken place on or are mediated through social media. Digital platforms like Facebook, Twitter, Instagram, and YouTube have become venues for publicizing information that often fails to make headlines, informing the public about particular social and political issues and demanding societal transformation. Although social media can provide some Puerto Ricans with a space to reckon with the devastating effects of structural and interpersonal violence in the hopes of effecting change, popular social media discussions about violence also demonstrate how exclusionary logics can seep into antiviolence organizing in a range of unexpected ways.

This chapter examines the complex and sometimes contradictory responses to violence and death that have emerged on Puerto Rican social media in recent years. In many ways, sites like Twitter and Facebook function as quotidian spaces in which Puerto Ricans engage with one another to make sense of everyday life. This can happen through simple verbal exchanges, by sharing and "liking" articles, or by skewering the absurdities of contemporary life in Puerto Rico through the creation and circulation of memes. As might be expected, the entrenchment of violence and the fear of violence in the everyday lives of many Puerto Ricans off-line often show up online. Social media, then, can become a space in which Puerto Ricans work to understand violence by expressing emotional exhaustion, frustration, anger, and a desire for things to be different. Antiviolence activists strategically use social media to challenge punitive and exclusionary logics circulating in Puerto Rican society; they use digital campaigns aimed not only at changing people's attitudes and behaviors, but often also at changing existing public policy.

It is not surprising that antiviolence activists have turned to social media platforms to amplify their message, given how central digital communication is to contemporary social life, especially for many young people. According to data compiled by the World Bank, in 2014 approximately 76.1 percent of Puerto Ricans had regular access to the Internet via computers or mobile devices. Puerto Rico also has one of the highest rates of Internet usage in Latin America and the Caribbean.[2] In addition, those Puerto Ricans with web access are spending considerable amounts of time on social media sites. A survey by the Interactive Advertising Bureau estimates that 88.1 percent of Puerto Ricans connect to social media sites such as Facebook, Twitter, Tumblr, and Instagram at least once a day, with approximately 50 percent connecting for more than three hours a day.[3] The significant presence of the digital sphere in the lives of many Puerto Ricans has allowed social media to become a potent site of political discussion and activist organizing.

Despite their limitations, social media platforms have provided an important space for many Puerto Ricans, particularly those from marginalized sectors of the population, to contest dominant understandings of violence and victimhood that circulate through the mainstream media and state and popular discourses.[4] By using the "virality" of social media to their advantage, "hashtag activists" are able to quickly and effectively create, spread, and amplify counter-narratives that disrupt the exclusionary logics pervading understandings of violence in Puerto Rico.[5] Social media not only fill in the gaps when mainstream media are silent on issues affecting marginalized populations, but also provide a space for users to "call out" or reject dominant discourses and representations that are exclusionary and promote an uneven distribution of harm.

Further, as anthropologists Yarimar Bonilla and Jonathan Rosa point out in their analysis of the social media activism around the police killing of Black youth Michael Brown, although social media sites like Twitter are "fleeting by nature," they are also "inherently aggregative."[6] In other words, the outrage and demands for action that often appear on social media can be "fueled by accumulated frustrations over previous mediatized moments of injustice and guided by previous digital campaigns."[7] Drawing from his research on Spain's *indignado* movement, anthropologist John Postill similarly notes, "The nanos-tories being shared about specific protests or power abuses may be short-lived, but over time they add up to a powerful sense of common purpose amongst hundreds of thousands of people. Together, they form a grand narrative of popular struggle against a corrupt political and economic order."[8]

Social media campaigns and hashtag activism rarely occur in isolation. Instead, they seek to make connections to long-standing practices of dis-crimination, exclusion, and brutality directed at marginalized groups in order to mobilize a sense of collective outrage that hopefully will form a cata-lyst for broad political and social transformation. Far from being a wholly liberatory space, however, the digital sphere is plagued by many of the very same hierarchies and forms of prejudice that structure Puerto Rican society "in real life." As a result, social media campaigns can sometimes reify puni-tive logics and understandings, reflecting the difficulties of escaping the exclusions and hierarchies that structure daily life in Puerto Rico.

In what follows, I discuss two examples of recent social media campaigns in Puerto Rico and its diaspora in order to explore the potential as well as the limitations of social media as a tool to challenge punitive logics and under-standings of violence. I begin by looking at social media mobilizations sparked by the carjacking, beating, and immolation of José Enrique Gómez Saladín in November 2012. Following the discovery of Gómez Saladín's body and revelations about the brutal way in which he was murdered, Puerto Ricans took to social media using the hashtag #TodosSomosJoseEnrique (#WeAreAllJoseEnrique) to speak out about the violence that they felt was consuming the archipelago. I follow conversations related to Gómez Saladín's murder that took place online for what they reveal about popular perceptions of violence, crime, and victimhood. In particular, I focus on how rumors regarding Gómez Saladín's sexuality and involvement with illicit economies forced antiviolence organizers to confront the ways in which some deaths are normalized and rendered permissible. These rumors were eventually broadcast on the popular gossip entertainment show *SuperXclusivo*, on which La Comay (The Godmother), the larger-than-life marionette that hosted the show, insinuated that Gómez Saladín got what he deserved for being a sexual deviant. Using the hashtag #BoicotLaComay (#BoycottLaComay), activists demanded the cancellation of *SuperXclusivo* for promoting the idea that death is an acceptable outcome for nonnormative behaviors.

I then examine the social media response to the death of Puerto Rican folk singer Ivania Zayas Ortiz in February 2015. Zayas Ortiz was walking back to her apartment in Río Piedras after a night out when she was struck by a car, whose driver fled the scene and left her to die. Soon after the discovery of her body, during a press conference, Félix J. Bauzó Carrasquillo, director of the Homicide Investigation Division in San Juan, suggested that Zayas Ortiz had been responsible for her own death by asking what a respectable young woman was doing walking the streets alone at night. Feminists immediately took to Twitter with the hashtag #AndandoLaCalleSola (#WalkingTheStreetAlone), first, to interrupt the notion that women who fail to live up to normative gender expectations deserve to experience harm, and second, to argue for gender-inclusive education in Puerto Rican schools and government agencies.

Using these examples, I show how antiviolence activists in Puerto Rico have used social media to challenge entrenched ideas about death and violence as acceptable consequences for social transgression. I also explore moments when these social media campaigns inadvertently reified exclusionary understandings of violence and victimhood. In doing so, I highlight the ways in which punitive logics can impact the terrain of antiviolence and transformative social efforts. In this way, social media provide us with a unique glimpse into the various ways that Puerto Ricans experience, understand, negotiate, and contest violence.

WE ARE ALL . . .

On the evening of November 29, 2012, thirty-two-year-old publicist José Enrique Gómez Saladín called his wife to let her know that he was leaving a party at La Concha, an upscale hotel in the Condado area of San Juan. He told her he was going to stop to get something to eat and would be home soon. Miles away, and short on rent money, Edwin Torres Osorio and his friends Lenisse Aponte, Alejandra Berrios Cotto, and Ruben Delgado Ortiz set out to find somebody to rob. The five encountered each other a little before midnight in Caugas. According to reports, Torres, Aponte, Barrios, and Delgado carjacked Gómez Saladín and forced him to withdraw $500 from a nearby ATM. They then drove Gómez Saladín to a Shell gas station, where they filled up an empty gas canister they found in the car. They pulled Gómez Saladín out of the car in a desolate area of Cayey. The four assailants forced Gómez Saladín to his knees, and as he begged for his life, beat him with metal pipes, doused him with gasoline, set him ablaze, and left him to die. Gómez Saladín's body was found four days later near an abandoned prison.

The murder of José Enrique Gómez Saladín followed on the heels of several high-profile murders and seemed to signal a tipping point for many Puerto Ricans. Following Gómez Saladín's murder, Puerto Ricans took to social media to express their concern, fear, and outrage over the violence occurring in Puerto Rico. Within twenty-four hours of the discovery of Gómez Saladín's body, hundreds of Puerto Ricans in the archipelago and the diaspora began posting pictures of themselves on Instagram, Twitter, and Facebook holding signs that read "*Todos Somos José Enrique* (We Are All José Enrique). Celebrities such as salsa singer Victor Manuelle, boxer Orlando Cruz, and pop star Ricky Martin posted "selfies" proclaiming that they too were José Enrique.

Puerto Ricans, including those scattered throughout the diaspora, took to social media to think through how violence was affecting Puerto Rico and to show solidarity with one another during what they understood as a moment of intense insecurity. Social media users appended other hashtags such as #BastaYa (#EnoughAlready) and #LosBuenosSomosMas (#ThereAreMore OfUsWhoAreGood) to the end of tweets, status updates, and alongside photos in reference to Gómez Saladín's murder. Media outlets such as Fox News Latino and Al Jazeera picked up the story and dubbed the resultant social media outpouring the "Boricua Winter," referencing the massive uprisings of the Arab Spring. Commentators optimistically speculated that this social media movement had the potential to bring attention to and perhaps halt the escalating levels of violent crime. While the Boricua Winter did not decrease levels of violent crime in Puerto Rico, it did showcase competing understandings of violence and the extent to which the fear of violence seemed to structure life for many Puerto Ricans.

A number of tweets and Facebook status updates that circulated in response to Gómez Saladín's murder lamented the rampant violence occurring in the archipelago and the extent to which it had disrupted the lives of many Puerto Ricans. One example of many is a December 4 tweet by a user named Ana Marie (@Anamarierr), which read: "This can't stay like this now I get scared even leaving to go to work #WeAreAllJoseEnrique."[9] Through such comments, social media exposed an extant discussion about expanding geographies of insecurity, violence, and fear that formed an undercurrent of daily interaction in Puerto Rico.

A number of the people whom I spoke with while I was doing research in Puerto Rico from 2011 to 2012, one of the bloodiest moments in the archipelago's history, reflected sentiments like the one above. During many of the regular conversations that punctuated my time in Puerto Rico, people would often describe how fear of crime and violence had caused them to restructure their days and the ways in which they moved in public space. When news of another drive-by shooting on the nearby expressway flashed across the television in the convenience store where I bought my newspaper every day, the owner remarked that Puerto Rico was a place where we were not even safe in our cars. Exchanging routine pleasantries while buying coffee in Old San Juan would sometimes suddenly morph into a conversation with the baristas and other patrons about how "things keep getting worse," even in well-off areas of the city. When I asked the young queer man who cut my hair about the hip places to party in the metropolitan area, he told me he wasn't a good source of information since he had stopped going to the gay clubs in the Santurce district of San Juan for fear that he might be robbed or worse. For many Puerto Ricans, concern and fear over violence structured contemporary life. Embedded in the phrase "Todos Somos José Enrique" was an understanding that violence could occur at any moment and that anyone could be a victim. With the social media mobilization around the death of Gómez Saladín, we see concern about the ubiquity of violence in Puerto Rico, as well as the degree to which a rhetoric of "citizen-as-victim," to borrow from legal scholar Jonathan Simon, had become accepted as common sense.

Social media also illuminated how violence had come to shape the Puerto Rican diaspora. In response to Gómez Saladín's murder and the subsequent social media outpouring, filmmakers Carlitos Ruiz and Mariem Pérez, along with actress Laura Alemán, created the virtual event "Un Abrazo Para Puerto

Rico" (A Hug for Puerto Rico), which sought to commemorate not only Gómez Saladín's life but also all the lives lost to street violence. On December 8, 2013, individuals gathered in cities across the United States and around the world to observe a moment of silence for Gómez Saladín and stand in solidarity with Puerto Ricans in the archipelago. Shortly after 5:30 p.m. eastern standard time, coordinated pictures of candlelight vigils, both small and large, from the United States, Latin America, Europe, and Africa began to appear on social media with the hashtag #UnAbrazoParaPR.[10] These selfies and images from around the globe represented an act of solidarity meant to bring attention to the alarming rates of crime and violence in Puerto Rico. Describing the impetus behind "Un Abrazo Para Puerto Rico," Carlitos Ruiz, one of the organizers, explained, "We want every Puerto Rican to hug Puerto Rico before it breaks. This first event is to unite people and to unite all the minds in order to show that all of us want change."[11]

Ruiz was one of the hundreds of thousands of Puerto Ricans who had moved to the United States, fearing that he might get caught in the debris of a broken homeland. Over the course of the twenty-first century's first decade, the Puerto Rican diaspora has grown by approximately 35 percent.[12] In 2003 the numbers of Puerto Ricans living in the archipelago and in the diaspora were in equal proportion, approximately 3.8 million each.[13] According to 2012 Census Bureau data, however, 4.97 million people who identified as Puerto Rican lived on the US mainland, while the number of Puerto Ricans in the archipelago had decreased to 3.51 million.[14] Crime, in addition to Puerto Rico's failing economy, has been blamed for what is the largest exodus of Puerto Ricans since the Great Migration of the Operation Bootstrap era. #UnAbrazosParaPR provided a space for those in the diaspora to show solidarity with those in the archipelago, while also highlighting how violence was effectively forcing people out of Puerto Rico.[15]

The social media mobilization around Gómez Saladín's death also illuminated the implicit and explicit frictions between those Puerto Ricans who felt that they had been forced to become diasporic subjects and those in the archipelago who felt that they had been left behind to deal with the dangerous and deteriorating situation. In fact, the image of a Puerto Rico that had become, by chance or by design, a nearly deserted island overrun by criminals appeared in a number of tweets. For example, on December 4, 2013, Emanuel R., using the Twitter handle @emarosario, tweeted a screenshot of a Facebook note about Gómez Saladín's murder, which read:

It's fucked, and excuse the word but it's the only one that makes sense, the things we see in our island. Professional man, classmate of my sister for more than 10 years. It's disgusting to see how criminals here do what ever they want with people's lives for a measly $500. . . . Sometimes for less they take the lives of people who are trying to do something positive for 100x35 [referring to the big island of Puerto Rico] which has become a jungle of survivors succumbing to fear, oppression, and the bullshit of those who think they can lack respect for human life. They say the best justice is divine justice. . . . I hope that that is the case. It really disgusts me to see what happens in our island every day. . . . We cannot leave the island to the criminals and lock ourselves away.[16]

Emanuel's description of Puerto Rico as "a jungle of survivors" tacitly criticizes the thousands of Puerto Ricans who have fled the archipelago in recent years for abandoning those left behind. At the same time, Emanuel cautions fellow Puerto Ricans against locking themselves away and allowing the "criminals" to have free rein. Meanwhile, Twitter user @noralissoe attached the hashtag #TodosSomosJoseEnrique to a tweet from December 4 that suggested robbers, murderers, rapists, and drunk drivers should be left alone on the big island in the hopes that they would eventually kill each other off.

The ubiquity of this image of Puerto Rico as a deserted island revealed not only a widely shared frustration with seemingly out-of-control levels of crime but also a feeling of abandonment on the part of some Puerto Ricans living in the archipelago. Tweets addressing this theme reveal a tension among Puerto Ricans around the question of whether to stay and try to improve things or flee what many saw as an increasingly intolerable and insecure existence. Fear of violence therefore formed a unifying theme in the archipelago, as well as between the archipelago and diaspora, while also illustrating tensions and competing responses to violence between them.

TO LIVE AND DIE IN PUERTO RICO

Mobilization around the idea that "we are all José Enrique"—that we can all become victims of violent crime at a moment's notice—worked to bring together Puerto Ricans in the archipelago and the diaspora who at one point or another felt besieged by criminality and violence. This emphasis on a shared familiarity with fear occluded the ways in which distinct sectors of the population experienced violence and fear differently. Despite a general feeling that harm could be lurking just around the corner, the overwhelming majority of violent crimes committed in Puerto Rico continued to disproportionately affect economically and racially marginalized communities. In many ways, Gómez Saladín's death stirred such deep affective resonance among so many Puerto Ricans precisely because it *did not* fit the dominant trend of who is murdered in Puerto Rico. Most homicide victims receive scant attention beyond their mere impact on the homicide statistics. It is telling that of the 1,136 homicides in 2011 and the 1,004 in 2012, only a select few were seen as worthy of public outrage and sustained media coverage. To put it in starker terms, between 1990 and 2009, approximately 15,717 people were killed in Puerto Rico.[17] Why, then, did it take the death of José Enrique Gómez Saladín to finally say #BastaYa?

As the drug wars of the late 1980s and 1990s raged into the new millennium, a populist discourse and common sense understanding of violence and victimization cohered, which constructed homicide as an outcome of criminality. In particular, this populist discourse associated the drug trade, and its victims, as deserving of violence and death. Police and government officials during the 1990s, and continuing into the present, have occluded the complex and multifarious causes of violence and homicide in Puerto Rico by maintaining that drug trafficking alone has been responsible for the overwhelming majority of the murders that have occurred. This has provided an easy explanation for a complex social problem, ignoring the extent to which social inequality, economic collapse, and the failure of the state to provide for its citizens have fueled violence and crime.

During the mano dura era, politicians and police attempted to assuage public concern over an alarming increase in the rate of homicide by suggesting that the killings were a result of police pressure on the drug points. They insinuated that the only individuals being murdered were active participants in drug trafficking. Homicide thus became the punishment of the guilty: an informal death penalty imposed on an archipelago where the practice had been abolished since 1929. In addition, as many homicide victims tended to be young men from economically and racially marginalized areas, who were already perceived as active in criminal enterprises, segments of the public and the media rationalized and normalized these deaths. Regardless of whether these individuals were in fact active within the drug economy, during the 1990s many Puerto Ricans tacitly accepted death as a form of public safety. The conceptualization of certain populations as deserving of death continues to structure conversations about violence and crime in Puerto Rico. As a result of conservative political discourse and police strategy, death and violence have become, in the minds of many Puerto Ricans, the exclusive province of the illegal drug economy—although many still live in fear of the moments when it spills beyond its original, and acceptable, confines.

The social media mobilization around Gómez Saladín's death attempted to posit an understanding of violence as touching the lives of *all* Puerto Ricans. Yet it is the exceptionality of Gómez Saladín's death—the fact that he was *not* assumed to be involved with the drug trade and that he embodied a white, professional-class masculinity—that made him an icon for *la gente decente*, who felt that they were under attack. For Puerto Ricans who feared that the violence that had long been allowed to proliferate in low-income and predominantly Black neighborhoods could at any moment "accidentally" claim their lives, his death symbolized a manifestation of their worst nightmares. It was the fact that Gómez Saladín was seemingly *innocent* and *didn't deserve* to come to such a violent end that became grounds for mobilization and contributed to the sense that "enough was enough" among Puerto Ricans in the archipelago and in the diaspora. The rallying cry "Todos Somos José Enrique" obscured the ways in which empathy and recognition were for the most part foreclosed to many homicide victims in Puerto Rico because of their presumed involvement with criminality, particularly drug use or trafficking.

The collective claim "Todos Somos José Enrique" flattened out the uneven geography of violence and crime and ignored the concentration of state-sanctioned violence in marginalized communities. Further, because economically and racially marginalized communities were perceived as the generators of violence and crime in Puerto Rico, excessively punitive forms of policing, such as mano dura contra el crimen during the 1990s or castigo seguro in the 2000s, exposed them to greater harm than the general population. The Boricua Winter's narrative of out-of-control street violence in some ways subsumed a nuanced acknowledgment of the incredibly varied ways that violence *already* operated in Puerto Rico along lines of racial, socioeconomic, spatial, sexual, and gendered difference.

José Enrique Gómez Saladín came to represent the scores of "innocent" victims of seemingly random acts of violence in Puerto Rico. In addition to the shockingly brutal nature of his murder, the fact that Gómez Saladín seemed to be a "good guy"—*un tipo bueno*—was part of what prompted such widespread outrage. Unlike the thousands of Puerto Ricans who lost their lives in the drug wars, Gómez Saladín, the outrage emphasized, *didn't deserve to die*. His position as an exceptional victim of violence allowed for collective outrage by individuals who felt that violence was steadily reaching beyond its typical spatial and social boundaries and affecting more and more *gente decente*. The ability to identify with Gómez Saladín as an innocent victim, however, was quickly shattered upon the apprehension of the individuals suspected of his murder.

"HE WAS LOOKING TO GET KILLED"

For thirteen years, millions of Puerto Ricans tuned into WAPA-TV at 6:00 p.m. on weeknights to watch Puerto Rico's highest-rated television show, *SuperXclusivo*. *SuperXclusivo* was an entertainment news program hosted by La Comay, a giant matronly puppet, and her sidekick Héctor Travieso. Comedian Antulio "Kobbo" Santarrosa created, voiced, and puppeteered La Comay, which translates to the Godmother. Although *SuperXclusivo* was primarily a gossip show, with La Comay and Travieso divulging scandalous details about the personal lives of celebrities and political figures, the show often offered commentary on a variety of sociopolitical issues affecting Puerto Ricans. On December 4, 2012, La Comay promised to reveal shocking details about the murder of José Enrique Gómez Saladín.

The four individuals suspected in the Gómez Saladín case were taken into police custody a couple of days after the murder and immediately questioned. Information from some of their confessions began to trickle out to the media by the afternoon of December 4, and that evening *SuperXclusivo* featured a segment on the murder. La Comay reported that on the evening of November 29, the four assailants set out for Calle Padial in Caguas, an area known for sex work, in order to rob a john. Although one of the women in the group reportedly told both her father and the police that Gómez Saladín attempted to solicit her and the other woman for sex, La Comay told her audience a different story.[18] According to La Comay, Gómez Saladín attempted to solicit one of the men and one of the women from the group for a sexual encounter, and things may have taken a bad turn during a dispute over money.

Prefacing her statements with the phrase "apparently and allegedly," La Comay pointed out that Gómez Saladín was on Calle Padial, "a center of male and female prostitution." "What is a gentleman doing, calling his wife and saying that he's leaving Condado, and, apparently and allegedly, he's on Calle Padial? What is he looking for on Calle Padial? There's nothing good worth looking for there. I repeat, male prostitution and female prostitution. Homosexuality is what there is," La Comay asserted.[19] She continued by asking whether Gómez Saladín might have known these individuals, whether this was a sexual encounter gone awry, or possibly retribution for payment owed. Finally, La Comay drove home her accusations: "People of Puerto Rico, I ask, what was José Enrique doing on Calle Padial in Caugus, which is a center of homosexuality, prostitution, and who knows what else? . . . I say all these things because all of Puerto Rico and everyone watching on WAPA America is alarmed and everyone here is alarmed, [saying], 'Listen, you can't even go to the ATM,' etcetera, etcetera, but the question is, *was he looking for this?*"[20] La Comay emphasized that despite the fact that Gómez Saladín might have contributed to his own death, there was no need for the accused to murder him in such a "savage way." She concluded the segment on Gómez Saladín's murder by advocating for the reinstatement of the death penalty to reduce the levels of violent crime. "People don't want to pay attention to me. I repeat, ladies and gentlemen, here in Puerto Rico we have to reinstate the death penalty. . . . Puerto Rico is getting very bad. It's getting to the point where you have to take the Jet Blue *avioncito* [little plane] and flee to whatever part of the United States because it is really violent here, people of Puerto Rico," La Comay lamented.[21]

Although La Comay was primarily known as "La Reina de la Bochinche" (the queen of gossip), in the years leading up to the segment on Gómez Saladín, *SuperXclusivo* began to dedicate more and more airtime to some of Puerto Rico's most high-profile unsolved crimes. As journalist Ed Morales noted, "Comay/Santarrosa's focus on unsolved crimes [has] struck a deep chord among Puerto Ricans, who are suffering one of the worst surges in violent crime ever experienced."[22] With deep pockets and a cultivated team of reporters and informants, *SuperXclusivo* staff would often receive critical information on high-profile cases before the police did, and many Puerto Ricans were aware of this, which contributed to the feeling of trust in the show's reporting. Once, when I walked into the home of a family member a little past 6:00 p.m. and caught her watching *SuperXclusivo*, I teased her for getting her news from a puppet. Unfazed and adamant, she shot back, "Well, she has information that the other news channels don't have because she has the money to pay for it. Even the government and police pay attention to what she says." And she was right; over the preceding years La Comay had hosted a number of local politicians on her show, including former governors Luis Fortuño and Aníbal Acevedo Vilá, in what was often cast as an attempt to keep elected officials honest and accountable to el pueblo puertorriqueño.

According to Kobbo Santarrosa, the creator and puppeteer behind La Comay, while La Comay was an embodiment of the town gossip, she also served the public and its political needs.[23] Television and media scholar Melissa Camacho notes, "*SuperXclusivo* serves this function by investigating claims of corruption and other misdeeds going on in Puerto Rican society. La Comay not only acts as the show's representative in these instances, but also uses these opportunities to remind public figures that they are accountable to the Puerto Rican public."[24] La Comay was therefore positioned not only as a key provider of information but also as a kind of moral figure fighting for the people.

La Comay's brand of populist outrage mixed with sensationalism often mirrors what are among the most socially conservative and retrograde attitudes in Puerto Rican society. Communications scholar Manuel G. Avilés-Santiago notes that La Comay cast herself as the voice of Puerto Rico's more rural, and therefore more socially "pure," sectors. In order to appeal to this base and speak for *real* Puerto Ricans, she frequently articulated racist attitudes toward Black people, intense xenophobia and animus toward Dominicans, and open homophobia.[25] According to Avilés-Santiago: "Magali Febles, a Black Dominican-born celebrity hairstylist and former owner of the Miss Puerto Rico pageant was often referred [to] as 'mona' (in Spanish female monkey) by the puppet. Similarly, broadcast journalist and TV presenter Belen Martínez-Cabello was labeled a 'black whale' in obvious reference to her weight and skin color. In 2012, La Comay dedicated a whole segment of the show to 'outing' local celebrities and politicians, using the slang term, pato [literally duck, but colloquially a derisive epithet for gay men]."[26] As a voice that reflected Puerto Rico's socially conservative sectors, La Comay's decision to lend credence to rumors surrounding Gómez Saladín's sexuality carried much weight. Her remarks echoed the prevailing assumption that some populations were deserving of death and violence because they posed a threat to "real" Puerto Ricans, who were *gente buena*.

Indeed, the segment on Gómez Saladín was not the first time La Comay appealed to homophobia to justify a ghastly murder. In 2009, during a segment on the brutal killing of nineteen-year-old gay youth Jorge Steven López Mercado, whose body was found decapitated, dismembered, and partially burned on November 13, 2009, in Cayey, La Comay suggested that López Mercado had been looking to get killed because he was in drag the night he was murdered.[27] Her remarks echoed those of the police investigator handling the case, Ángel Rodríguez, who implied that López Mercado deserved what he got because of his "lifestyle." During a televised press conference Rodríguez said, "When these type of people get into this and go out into the streets like this, they know this can happen to them."[28]

The homophobia of La Comay's comments about queer people, their lives, and their deaths reflects a widespread pattern of disregard for queer life among conservative sectors of the Puerto Rican public. Her comments also bolster the pervasive notion that death is a deserved consequence for behavior that is perceived as risky or unsavory. At least eighteen members of Puerto Rico's LGBTQ community were murdered between 2009 and 2011, the period immediately before Gómez Saladín's killing. Police have for the most part failed to properly investigate those cases or have made public statements blaming the victims for their own demise.[29] La Comay's comments about the circumstances surrounding the deaths of both Jorge Steven López Mercado and José Enrique Gómez Saladín demonstrate the ways in which their queerness, presumed and otherwise, became a justification for the violence inflicted upon their bodies as well as a warning to others (perceived to be) engaging in similar behaviors.

After La Comay suggested that perhaps Gómez Saladín got what he deserved, some Puerto Ricans on social media responded to this new information about his death with direct and surging vitriol. Users on Twitter started to use the hashtag #YoNoSoyJoseEnrique (#IamNotJoseEnrique) or appended a question mark to the statement "Todos Somos José Enrique," in order to show that Gómez Saladín was a sexual deviant who got what he deserved. Twitter user @colongil tweeted on December 4: "Jose Enrique was the typical lying macho boricua that cuckolded his wife with whores and faggots in the street. #TodosSomosJoseEnrique."[30] Similarly, on December 8, Joshua Rivera, using the Twitter handle @Im_Freshh, tweeted: "#TodosSomosJoseEnrique You all want to be a guy who cheated on his wife and fucked faggots mmmm?? I am not him, you all go ahead."[31] Blogger El Vlade, on December 4, told his Twitter followers, "That guy looked for death because he was a PIG. #YoNoSoyJoseEnrique."[32] Like La Comay's comments on *SuperXclusivo*, a parallel narrative began to emerge on social media that because Gómez Saladín might have been soliciting sex work or looking for gay sex, he, like the other "criminals" and "deviants" of Puerto Rican society, was deserving of death. In this formulation, Gómez Saladín is just as, if not more, responsible for his death than the four individuals who actually murdered him. The comments by La Comay and hostility directed at Gómez Saladín on social media following the news that he had encountered his attackers on Calle Padial expose the ways in which Gómez Saladín's supposed proclivities—both criminal and queer—allowed for him to be constructed as a subject deserving of violence and death: *killable*.

#BOICOTLACOMAY

Although some on social media echoed La Comay's sentiments and claims that Gómez Saladín no longer fit the bill of "innocent" victim deserving of public outrage, others took to social media to express their own outrage with La Comay's suggestion that Gómez Saladín had brought his death upon himself. Rather than attempting either to recuperate José Enrique as an exceptional/innocent figure or position him as deserving of death because of his involvement with criminalized behaviors, activists instead argued, first, that no Puerto Rican deserves to experience violence, and second, that the work of creating a more just and secure Puerto Rico must extend to *all* sectors of Puerto Rican society. Prominent LGBT activist Pedro Julio Serrano, for example, took to Facebook and Twitter to challenge the irresponsible assertions made by La Comay, saying, "If you think people will stop being indignant about the vile murder of José Enrique because you want to criminalize homosexuality in the same way that sex work is unfairly criminalized, you are wrong."[33] He continued, "No one deserves, nor seeks, to be killed, NO ONE. Violence is perpetuated by attitudes such as this that blame the victim. You are as responsible for the violence, intolerance, and hatred that eat away at our country because, with your program, you perpetuate prejudices and discrimination that do not correspond to who we are as a people."[34]

Carlos Rivera, an IT specialist living in New York, created a Facebook page calling for a boycott of *SuperXclusivo* by advertisers and viewers. The expressed goal of the Facebook group Boicot La Comay (Boycott La Comay) was to challenge the hatred and discriminatory rhetoric exemplified by *SuperXclusivo* in an effort to change the discourse around violence in Puerto Rico. According to an open letter from the group, "It is time for WAPA-TV to cancel *SuperXclusivo* and remove La Comay—and in its place put programming that does not sow hate or the desire for vengeance in our people."[35] The message seemed to resonate, as Puerto Ricans in the archipelago and the diaspora quickly joined the group and spread the message about a boycott of *SuperXclusivo* on various social media sites. By the end of the day on December 4, the group had five hundred members, the next day the group had thirty thousand members, and within a few days the group would count more than seventy thousand members among its ranks.

While it is easy to dismiss this as mere "Facebook activism," little more than clicking "Like" or posting a status update, the Boicot La Comay campaign succeeded in challenging the dominant discourse around violence and death in Puerto Rico, in addition to creating financial and public relations consequences for public figures who espouse such harmful rhetoric. On December 5, 2012, one day after the boycott of *SuperXclusivo* was announced via social media, a number of companies, including Chevrolet, Triple-S, Claro Cellular, Borden Dairy, ATH (an ATM network in Puerto Rico), Gillette, Welch's, and Corona Extra, withdrew advertisements and/or product placements from the show. *SuperXclusivo* was WAPA-TV's most expensive hour of programming in terms of the cost of advertising during the 6:00 p.m. to 7:00 p.m. time slot. Business analyst Michelle Kantrow notes, "According to the local station's most recent and current advertising rate card, a 30-second spot during 'SuperXclusivo's' 6 p.m. to 7 p.m. time slot costs about $6,000 from Monday through Friday. To that, WAPA adds another $7,500 or so for product placements during the show, which could average between two and three per episode," meaning that, according to Kantrow, a successful boycott of the show would cost WAPA-TV close to $1.3 million a week.[36]

The boycott continued to gain momentum as a number of high-profile public figures voiced their support and large corporate sponsors continued to drop the show. On December 6 came one of the boycott's largest successes: multinational conglomerate Walmart announced that it would cancel its advertisements on *SuperXclusivo*, citing the boycott as the impetus. The company made this announcement via a status update on its Facebook page. The status read, "Walmart is committed to improving the quality of life of the people of Puerto Rico. Following the controversy surrounding the program *SuperXclusivo*, we have made the decision to cancel our advertising on that program. We reiterate our commitment to Puerto Rico and the communities we serve."[37] Notwithstanding the inherent irony of Walmart voicing its commitment to Puerto Ricans' quality of life even as it pushed small local shops out of business, the conglomerate's support of the boycott was crucial to legitimizing the protesters' position and getting *SuperXclusivo* off the air. Within days other large companies, such as AT&T, S.C. Johnson, Coca-Cola, Ford, Goodyear, and DISH network, also withdrew their advertising from the show.

On January 7, 2013, just moments before the broadcast, and following the loss of over forty-five advertisers, an announcement from the head of the station that the show would be prerecorded, and continued pressure from individuals and organizations in the archipelago and the diaspora, Kobbo Santarrosa announced that he was quitting. On January 9, WAPA confirmed that Santarrosa had left the network and that it would no longer air *SuperXclusivo*. That same day, as many awaited confirmation of Santarrosa's departure from WAPA, a video was released featuring Puerto Rican artists and political figures who sought to challenge traditional conceptualizations of violence and situate the boycott against *SuperXclusivo* as part of a larger organizing effort against violence. The video, *Nuevas Voces diciendo "NO a la Comay"* (New voices saying "NO to la Comay"), starts with the words "Porque no apoyo la Comay" (Why I don't support la Comay) superimposed against a black background, referencing an earlier video of the same name. One by one, each person in the video explains why he or she does not support La Comay:

Because making fun of someone is violence.
Because homophobia is violence.
Because intimidation is violence.
Because discrimination is violence.
Because defamation is violence.
Because bullying is violence.
Because racism is violence.
Because intolerance is violence.
Because indifference is violence.
Because insult is violence.
Because oppression is violence.
Because xenophobia is violence.
Because prejudice is violence.
Because sensationalism is violence.
Because I do not support violence . . .
. . . I say no to La Comay.
Don't support violence.
Say no to La Comay.[38]

This video, which began to circulate just as news of the cancellation of *SuperXclusivo* was being confirmed, gestured toward the broader potential of the so-called Boricua Winter to change the conversation about violence in Puerto Rico. What would it mean to move beyond highly individualized narratives of violence that have dominated Puerto Rican society since the onset of the drug wars to acknowledge the interlocking and varied forms of psychic, social, and physical harm that affect marginalized communities and populations?

Nuevas Voces diciendo "NO a la comay" pushed viewers to consider violence as a constellation rather than a singular exceptional act or event that affects a single individual. As anthropologist Nancy Scheper-Hughes points out, violence occurs on a continuum, which is "socially incremental and often experienced by perpetrators, collaborators, bystanders—and even the victims themselves—as expected, routine, and even justified."[39] This continuum of violence expresses itself through often naturalized forms of oppression that enact psychic and physical violence on populations marked as inferior. The boycott of *SuperXclusivo* urged Puerto Ricans to recognize that the routine violence of discrimination, intimidation, intolerance, and indifference is central to the violence of killing and letting die. The video asks viewers to consider the ways in which discrimination, oppression, and the sensationalization of "street violence" constitute violence in and of themselves and contribute to an intensification of physical violence directed at marginalized populations.

While activists mobilized around José Enrique Gómez Saladín to challenge the idea that some Puerto Ricans are deserving of harm and death because of who they are or what they do, the success of the campaign to get La Comay and *SuperXclusivo* off the air in some ways illuminated once again the limits of empathy and recognition within Puerto Rican society. Gómez Saladín's professional class status and whiteness allowed for him to be recuperated by antiviolence activists despite his assumed queerness or association with illicit sex, which rendered him killable in the eyes of others. Without minimizing the important challenge that the boycott of La Comay posed to entrenched hierarchies of belonging and the violence those hierarchies produce in Puerto Rico, it is worth considering why a massive boycott against La Comay was not called after any of the many incidents in which she used virulent anti-Black, xenophobic, sexist, and homophobic language on prime-time television. Gómez Saladín's presumed queerness may have temporarily undermined his innocent victimhood, but ultimately his whiteness and class position—the fact that he wasn't a young Black or dark-skinned man from a low-income barrio or public housing community—enabled antiviolence activists to ask Puerto Ricans to recognize that he didn't deserve to die. In other words, Gómez Saladín's whiteness helped to render his premature death as unfair and undeserved.

The Boricua Winter that the media celebrated, while short-lived, show-cased a growing disillusionment with revanchist solutions to feelings of insecurity while also creating a space for new understandings of violence and justice to emerge. Three years later, when a young woman, Ivania Zayas Ortiz, was killed during a hit-and-run, Puerto Ricans again utilized social media to challenge dominant narratives around gender and respectability that contin-ued to frame understandings of victimhood and violence. In particular, feminists used the circumstances and responses to Zayas Ortiz's death to push for gender-inclusive curriculum in public schools as a way of reducing and preventing the myriad forms of violence women regularly experience in Puerto Rico.

#ANDANDOLACALLESOLA

On February 8, 2015, Ivania Zayas Ortiz, a thirty-eight-year-old local folk singer, was on her way home after a night out when she was hit by a blue GNC Envoy as she attempted to cross road PR-181 where it intersects with Avenida 65 de Infantería in Río Piedras. Tyrone Rohena Vélez ran his SUV into Zayas Ortiz at 12:34 a.m. and did not stop to check if she was hurt, nor did he call emergency services. Zayas Ortiz died almost immediately from the impact. Rohena Vélez kept driving until he reached Villas de Lomas Verdes, a public housing complex in the nearby town of Cupey, where he abandoned his vehicle.[40] While the circumstances of Zayas Ortiz's death were certainly tragic—a talented singer cut down in her prime by a driver who could not be bothered to call 911—it was how the police framed her death that sparked mobilizations on and off social media that called out patriarchal sexism in Puerto Rico.

Lieutenant Félix J. Bauzó Carrasquillo, director of the Homicide Investigation Division in San Juan, broke the news to the public that Ivania Zayas Ortiz had been killed in a hit-and-run. During the press conference, Bauzó Carrasquillo shared the little information that police had on the case and said that they were working diligently to find out more. Apparently one of the things that the police had to investigate was *why* Zayas Ortiz was walk-ing alone at that time of night. According to Bauzó Carrasquillo, "It is unu-sual for a lady, close to 1:00 in the morning, to be crossing the [Avenida] 65 de Infantería and that's why we have to investigate whether she was alone or accompanied. If she was alone, well, it is worrying, and if it was accompanied, well, look, it would be interesting to know where they were coming from, what they were doing, those kinds of details."[41]

The lieutenant's comments immediately sparked outrage over what many perceived to be a macho and patronizing attitude toward Zayas Ortiz's death. Implicit in Bauzó Carrasquillo's comments were ideas about when, where, and with whom it was appropriate for women to walk the streets and occupy public space. By stating that it was "unusual for a lady"—*una dama*—to be walking around that area at that time of night, Bauzó Carrasquillo marked Zayas Ortiz as transgressing the boundaries of respectable womanhood and suggested that this transgression played a role in her untimely death. Further, his comment that if Zayas Ortiz was indeed alone, it was "worrying" illuminated the ways in which patriarchal ideas of chaperonage were still very much entrenched within Puerto Rican society. Bauzó Carrasquillo's comments hinted that only *mujeres malas* (bad women)—fast women, sex workers, addicts, and queers—roam the streets unaccompanied late at night, and everyone knows that bad things happen to bad women.

Given the Lieutenant's comments, a number of Puerto Rican women were concerned that the police would not take seriously or properly investigate Zayas Ortiz's death because she was seen as somehow bringing her fate upon herself—something that has happened time and time again in cases where men abused or killed women. Social media became a platform for these women and their allies to voice their frustration with the sexist and patriarchal ideas that not only frame Puerto Rican society generally but also specifically shape how the police approach incidents of violence against women. Women on social media worked to hold Bauzó Carrasquillo personally accountable for his comments by demanding a formal apology. They also made structural critiques by challenging the dominant ideas about respectable gender roles that his comments represented, reiterating that regardless of perceived transgressions, no one deserves to experience violence. Last, building on existing queer and feminist organizing efforts, women on social media advocated for *la perspectiva de genero*, or antisexist, gender-inclusive education, in public schools and governmental agencies. Organizers hoped that the inclusion of antisexist education in schools would halt the reproduction of the heteropatriarchal attitudes that rationalized the death of a young woman because she was walking alone at night.

Immediately following Bauzó Carrasquillo's press conference, three independent journalists—Ana Teresa Toro, Luara Candelas, and Mari Mari Narváez—created the hashtag #AndandoLaCalleSola (#Walking

TheStreetAlone). They encouraged women to take photos of themselves walking in the streets in order to push against restrictive notions of respectable femininity in the public sphere and discuss the need for la perspectiva de genero. According to Ana Teresa Toro, "The problem is not that Ivania was walking the streets by herself. The problem is that it is a problem for a woman to be walking the streets by herself. #AndandoLaCalleSola is an invitation for women to be aware that we should be able to walk down the street by ourselves and demonstrate through an affirming gesture that the streets are ours."[42] Luara Candelas added that Bauzó Carrasquillo's comments demonstrated the incredible need for la perspectiva de genero in Puerto Rico's schools and government agencies, including the police academy. "I don't know what the problem is with accepting that we are equal. If it was a man that was run over, they would not have mentioned the hour, or the location, or if he was by himself or not," noted Candelas.[43]

Toro, Candelas, and Narváez aimed to create a virtual space to voice frustration and anger with what many Puerto Rican women understood as a harmful and dangerous double standard directed at women who experienced violence. This double standard not only excused heterosexist and patriarchal violence but also functioned to discipline women through fear. In this way, comments like Bauzó Carrasquillo's reminded many women that if they became victims of violence, they would likely be held responsible and asked what they had done to deserve what happened to them.[44] As human rights advocate and attorney Amárilis Pagán put it, "The thing is, in Puerto Rico, women are murdered and it's their fault; they are sexually assaulted and it's their fault; and now, they are run over and it's their fault. In the Puerto Rican Police, moral judgment seeps in when the victims are women."[45] Women and their allies took to social media in the days following Zayas Ortiz's death to assert their right to public space and lambast what they saw as troubling attitudes about gender and bodily comportment.

Following the launch of the #AndandoLaCalleSola hashtag, thousands of status updates, pictures, and tweets inundated social media. Some women posted photos of themselves walking in the streets with messages affirming their right to move around in public space without fear that they will experience violence at the hands of a man. These photos also included Puerto Rican women in the diaspora and other women around the world who had heard about Zayas Ortiz's death and wanted to show solidarity. Men also used the hashtag and photos to show solidarity with Puerto Rican women. Writer Max Chárriez, for instance, posted a photo of himself on Facebook standing on the street outside a train station in Santurce with a caption that read, "Here I am walking the streets alone. Since I am a gay man I guess if I am run over it's because I was up to something at that hour in the street and I was looking for it #walkingthestreetsalone #weneedgendereducation."[46] As we saw with the case of José Enrique Gomez Saladín, men who are queer or engaged in illicit sexual behaviors, or whom others simply perceive to be so, are often blamed for the heterosexist violence they experience. Chárriez, as a gay man, used social media to, show solidarity with Puerto Rican women who also experience the violent policing of their gender and sexuality in a society that devalues their lives and exposes them to violence.

As we saw with some of the social media mobilization around Gomez Saladín's murder, many of the social media responses to Zayas Ortiz's death also stressed the idea that no one deserves to experience violence. Using social media, Puerto Rican women and their allies rejected the understanding that they are somehow responsible for the harm that befalls them, which excuses the structures and popular attitudes that perpetuate violence against women. On February 9, 2015, Twitter user @sharonclaudia tweeted a drawing of a nude woman in the middle of a road carrying a banner with the hashtag #andandolacallesola. The text of the tweet accompanying the drawing read, "#walkingthestreetsalone naked, with clothes, however I feel like!"[47] With this tweet, @sharonclaudia challenged the sexist trope that women's wardrobe choices are to blame for the violence they may encounter on the street, such as harassment, rape, and murder. The drawing and the accompanying tweet challenged the normalization and justification of sexualized violence against women and asserted a woman's right to occupy public space without being harmed.

Other women also tweeted challenges to positions that normalized the violability of women's bodies.[48] Twitter user @Alexandrita_03 tweeted, "#walkingthestreetsalone and that doesn't mean that I deserve to be a victim of any kind of violence #Equality #Woman."[49] Similarly, @_rubimarie said, "I spend all day #walkingthestreetsalone and that doesn't mean that someone has to assault me or run me over. #equality."[50] Others made this point painfully clear using biting humor and sarcasm. Adriana Cuevas, using the Twitter handle @lagitanita17, wrote, "I'm at fault, irresponsible, inept... I take the bus and the train alone... and I cross various streets everyday! #walkingthestreetsalone."[51] Blanca Rodríguez, using the Twitter handle @bandarrita, explicitly linked the rhetoric surrounding Zayas Ortiz's death to the rhetoric that excuses the sexual violence committed against women when she darkly remarked, "From the creators of the smash hit 'If you're raped its your fault,' now comes 'If you're run down you were looking for it.' #walkingthestreetsalone."[52]

In addition to providing a virtual space to challenge dominant discourses and perspectives regarding violence against women, #AndandoLaCalleSola played a crucial role in propelling questions of machismo and gender difference into the mainstream. The women and men who came together under the hashtag exposed a broad cross-section of Puerto Rican society to questions of gender inequality and the violence it produces and sustains. Further, they used their vigorous digital activism to implement meaningful change off-line by demanding the implementation of la perspectiva de genero in schools and government agencies. While #AndandoLaCalleSola worked to challenge dominant and harmful gender norms, it also helped make the case for gender-inclusive education in Puerto Rican public schools, which had been blocked by a small but powerful group of fundamentalist Christian conservatives who perceived it as part of a "gay agenda" to corrupt Puerto Rican children and youth.

Social media users explicitly tied the sexism and ignorance of Lieutenant Bauzó Carrasquillo's remarks to the importance of teaching young people to respect and value gender and sexual difference. On February 10 Twitter user @marilola wrote, "Reason #1,000,000 to defend education with #genderperspective: Walking the streets alone at night without us being questioned. #walkingthestreetsalone."[53] Similarly, on Instagram, user alejandrat67 posted a photo of herself and two friends with a caption that read, "#WalkingtheStreetsAlone Because I am free to walk with who I want at the time I want without being seen as something perverted and NOBODY has to question me about it much less do I have to subject myself to public scrutiny if my actions don't affect others. Another of the many reasons why we need to understand #GenderPerspective."[54] Even former Puerto Rican governor Aníbal Acevedo Vilá came out in support of la perspectiva de género, tweeting on February 9, "We must combat ignorance with education. We cannot postpone any longer. A woman should never again be judged for #walkingthestreetsalone."[55]

Tweets such as these spurred renewed activist efforts around gender equality in Puerto Rico and assisted in amplifying a conversation about gender-inclusive education that had long been silenced by religious fundamentalist groups. For instance, the group Movimiento Amplio de Mujeres de Puerto Rico, which had been tirelessly advocating for la perspectiva de genero for years, used the renewed attention and interest generated to intensify its activism. Further, the group now also had a concrete example of how sexism and gender inequality literally harms and kills women. In a statement, Nirvana González Rosa of the group stated, "This is a clear example of how gender inclusive education is necessary in all spaces, in government institutions, in the police, and in schools."[56] On February 25, 2015, roughly two weeks after Zayas Ortiz's death, and after the attention and political pressure generated by the social media campaign, the Department of Education signed an order approving gender-inclusive education in Puerto Rican public schools.[57] The synergy between #AndandoLaCalleSola and the struggle to introduce la perspectiva de genero in schools and government agencies demonstrates how online activism can impact and work in conjunction with activist efforts "in real life." Alongside the social media uproar that resulted in the cancellation of *SuperXclusivo*, it is difficult, if not impossible, to discount the significance of digital activism in affecting cultural politics and even legislative policy.

The general tenor of the social media circulating around Ivania Zayas Ortiz's death was one of frustration, anger, and exhaustion. These affective responses, first, highlight the prevalence of such instances of violence and victim blaming in Puerto Rico. Second, these negative affects were a catalyst for imagining and demanding something different. George Rivera penned a column for the Puerto Rican "geek" digital magazine *QiiBo* about Zayas Ortiz's death that asked readers "¿No les cansa?" (Doesn't it tire you?). After noting that Bauzó Carrasquillo demonstrated the deep-seated machismo of a Puerto Rican society in desperate need of gender-inclusive education, Rivera stated, "Either way, it doesn't matter if she was in the street just walking or hanging out. What the hell is the problem? What difference does that make? Moreover, you know what, if she was selling drugs, buying them, or if she was a prostitute, what does that matter? Then she wasn't a lady? Then she deserved to be run over and abandoned like nothing?"[58] Rivera's post captured the sense of exhaustion with the police and segments of the public using victim blaming to account for an inability to keep Puerto Rican women specifically, and other marginalized Puerto Ricans more generally, free from violence. In many ways, social media activists' rejection of the sexist narratives surrounding Zayas Ortiz's death indicated the limits of punitive logic in Puerto Rico. While punitive governance sought to limit the state's responsibility for protecting its citizens by normalizing and justifying the deaths of particular populations that fall outside of the boundaries of respectable citizenship, the social media activism around Zayas Ortiz's death rejected the notion that certain groups and individuals were to blame for their own deaths and rejected the claim, either implicit or explicit, that society did not owe them the opportunity to *live* a full life.

Months after Zayas Ortiz's death, police and the attorneys for Tyrone Rohena Vélez, the man who ran her down, attempted once again to blame her for her death when they released a toxicology report that showed Zayas Ortiz had been drinking the evening she was killed.[59] Puerto Ricans, especially women, on social media once again responded by rejecting the notion that Zayas Ortiz was to blame for dying in a hit-and-run because she had been out drinking with friends beforehand. It was clear that the fact Zayas Ortiz had been drinking was given extra scrutiny because she was a young single woman. Again, the question arose: If the victim had been a man, would it matter that he had had a couple of drinks out with friends on a weekend before he was run down? Shifting the responsibility back to where it belonged, social media users pointed out that Rohena Vélez was driving with a suspended license at the time, he had more than sixty outstanding traffic tickets, he did not call emergency services, and he had fled the scene. Further, police were unable to determine if Rohena Vélez was driving under the influence due to the fact that he fled the scene and was not apprehended until much later, when a blood-alcohol test could no longer be administered.

Although Rohena Vélez pled guilty to killing Zayas Ortiz, the blame police and others directed at Zayas Ortiz let him escape stiffer punishment. He was allowed to plead down to reduced charges of negligent homicide, fleeing the scene of a crime, and driving without a license. Judge Gisela Alfonso Fernández only sentenced Rohena Vélez to complete three years and six months of house arrest so as to not disrupt the stability of his "nuclear family."[60] Without advocating for punitive punishment and incarceration, it is important to note that the rationale for sentencing—to keep a heterosexual nuclear family together—is indicative of the kinds of heterosexist and patriarchal logic in Puerto Rican society that influenced responses to Zayas Ortiz's death from the beginning. The light sentence given to Rohena Vélez also speaks to the gendered and sexual violence imbedded within the legal system, from police investigations to judicial discretion. #AndandoLaCalleSola and the social media mobilization around Zayas Ortiz's death indicted the ways in which the criminal justice system has not only condoned gendered and sexual violence but also has been an active perpetrator in direct and indirect ways.

The #AndandoLaCalleSola social media campaign highlighted a number of key realities about gender and violence in contemporary Puerto Rico. It provided a crucial space for Puerto Rican women to not only interrupt heterosexist and patriarchal rhetoric but also illustrate how such rhetoric normalized, promoted, and was itself a form of gendered and sexual violence. The hashtag activism around Zayas Ortiz's death also allowed feminists to advocate for la perspectiva de genero as a first step toward reducing violence against women. #AndandoLaCalleSola demonstrates how social media activism has not necessarily supplanted "traditional" modes of political organizing and activism, but rather exists alongside them while simultaneously amplifying issues that the mainstream media too often neglect.

BEYOND DESERVING

The social media campaigns that emerged in response to the deaths of José Enrique Gómez Saladín and Ivania Zayas Ortiz provide an alternative archive with which to chart the ways that Puerto Ricans understand crime, violence, and victimhood. While social media campaigns can reproduce dangerous and pervasive ideas about deserved and undeserved violence, they can also function as a space to challenge such logics and imagine alternative ways of organizing society. Hashtag activists used social media to not only challenge victim-blaming ideology and rhetoric but also achieve concrete gains with significant potential to reduce harm, upending the claim that what occurs on social media has little effect or meaning "in the real world." In the case of José Enrique Gómez Saladín, social media provided a space to challenge suggestions that Gómez Saladín got what he deserved because of potentially illicit behavior, which resulted in the removal of La Comay's hateful and punitive rhetoric from the airwaves. In the case of Ivania Zayas Ortiz, feminists on social media not only challenged the way in which women are often held responsible for the violence they experience but also successfully advocated for the implementation of gender-inclusive and responsive education in Puerto Rico's public schools. These two discrete but related case studies point to the ways in which some Puerto Ricans are rejecting the punitive common sense promoted by the police and mainstream media and naming the logics and structures that actually perpetuate harm and violence; they are indicting not only those who leave their victims to die in the street but also those who condone their behavior by suggesting the victims got what they deserved. As is evident from this chapter, as well as the next, Puerto Ricans are using a variety of tools and strategies to think beyond *la politica de mano dura*.

SEVEN

Security from Below

IN JUNE 2012 THE ACLU PUBLISHED A report that outlined the corruption, violence, and abuse of power that permeate the PRPD. The report, entitled *Island of Impunity: Puerto Rico's Outlaw Police Force*, found that "police brutality [was] pervasive and systemic, island-wide and ongoing" and went on to suggest that the PRPD was "steeped in a culture of unrestrained abuse and near-total impunity."[1] While it was clear the PRPD's interactions with a wide range of citizens were marked by repressive behavior, there was no doubt, according to the report, that low-income populations, as well as Black Puerto Ricans and Dominican im/migrants, received the harshest treatment at the hands of law enforcement officers. The report noted, "PRPD officers routinely use aggressive tactics that disproportionately target racial minorities and the poor. Young men who live in predominantly low-income, Black or Dominican communities reported to the ACLU that PRPD officers subject them to constant harassment and intimidation."[2] Unsurprisingly, Loíza, which is synonymous with Blackness for many Puerto Ricans, was one of the communities identified by the ACLU in which police harassment and violence were especially widespread.

Drawing from interviews with community members, the ACLU presented disturbing evidence of rampant police brutality and racism directed at residents of Loíza. Evelyn Rivera, a resident of the Villa Cañona sector of Loíza, told the ACLU that her son, Edgar Pizarro Rivera, a cognitively disabled adult, had been beaten and pepper-sprayed by police numerous times while out riding his bicycle around the neighborhood. Rivera noted that as a result of this ongoing abuse and harassment by police, Edgar had become frightened of playing outside. Rivera witnessed one of the attacks on her son and said that the attack was racially motivated, at least in part, because she heard police officials call him *negro sucio*, or filthy Black.[3] For Rivera, what happened to her son was far from an isolated occurrence. She suggested, instead, that the police frequently displayed racially inflected hostility in their encounters with loiceños. Rivera told investigators that the experiences of her family and neighbors with the police had weakened her belief that the police could have a positive impact in the community, saying, "I have never had confidence in the police, and every day I trust them even less."[4]

Luis Ayala Rivera, a young Black man also from Villa Cañona, described for the ACLU the night that he saw officers from the Fuerza de Choque shoot his bother, José Amaury Ayala Rivera, in the head. On a Saturday evening in September 2010, the two men were on their way home from a party when the police approached them. Frightened, José Amaury Ayala Rivera ran. According to Luis Ayala Rivera, "I saw it all. They told him to stop and he began to run, and they shot at him. The officer fired two shots. The first missed its mark and the second struck my brother in the head. Then the officers made a barrier and would not let anyone pass to get to my brother and help him."[5] The police bullet that wounded José Amaury Ayala Rivera left him paraplegic and permanently confined to a wheelchair. For Luis Ayala Rivera, what happened to his brother was part of the constant police harassment suffered by the low-income and mostly Black residents of Loíza's barrios. He explained, "Racism is very, very, very bad against our community."[6] He added that police were seemingly always present in the community and often resorted to violence at the slightest provocation. "If people are gathered at a business or a party in our neighborhood, everyone minding their own business and not breaking the law, the police will come and injure people without any reason," Luis Ayala Rivera remarked.

Ayala Rivera's comments allude to the "Loizazo," one of the most well-known instances of recent police violence in Loíza. On June 17, 2001, friends and family gathered at the events hall at the Centro Vocacional de la Unión Independiente Autentica to celebrate the first birthday of Joredimar Rivera Vázquez. There were approximately fifty people there, having a good time, when a skirmish broke out among some of the partygoers. An employee of the Centro Vocacional called the police to break up the fight. By the time the police arrived, the altercation had subsided; nonetheless, Fuerza de Choque officers entered the space aggressively. One of the partygoers recording the festivities captured numerous instances of police brutality on video.

The video shows the police officers enter the hall and immediately, and without provocation, start shoving and hitting men, women, and children with their batons.[7] Police backed a number of partygoers against a wall and started relentlessly beating them with batons. Some tried to run and escape the scene of violence but were stopped by the force of police batons against their bodies. Police then started to flip tables and kick chairs in what appear to be fits of uncontrollable rage, actions that further terrorized the friends and family who had gathered to celebrate a year in the life of a little girl. The naked aggression and violence of the Loizazo shocked many Puerto Ricans, while also confirming a pattern of racialized police abuse well known to many Puerto Ricans who live in predominantly Black communities like Loíza.

Despite the outrage prompted by the public release of footage from this birthday party gone horribly awry, many police officials stood by the individual officers responsible for the violence and justified their actions. The president of the Frente Unido de Policías Organizados (FUPO), the local police union, José Taboada de Jesús, for instance, defended the officers' brutality by showing photos of drugs supposedly taken from partygoers.[8] Eventually, six Fuerza de Choque officers were found guilty of using excessive force. Still, as the testimony gathered by the ACLU demonstrates, police officers in Loíza continue to display race- and class-based contempt for residents, which far too often results in bruises, broken bones, bullets tearing through flesh, and less visible forms of trauma.

The police are ineffective at reducing violence in communities like Loíza because police power plays a central role in maintaining racial, capitalist, and colonial order in Puerto Rico. Their role in maintaining exploitative social structures within Puerto Rican society often pits the police against racially and economically marginalized populations or politically dissident groups. Despite a near-constant police presence in Loíza, residents note that police do little to address the territorial gang violence claiming the lives of the area's young people. And police are themselves key instigators and perpetrators of violence against loiceños. In other words, there is a sense that police can and often do make things worse and that involving them in community affairs may increase the probability of physical and psychological harm.

What, then, might attempts to address violence and create a safer community look like for Loíza without the involvement of the police or privatized security forces? What alternative understandings of security and accountability might be possible if punitive police power were decentered as the primary response to crime and violence? To answer these questions, I examine the work of Taller Salud, a feminist public health organization that has been based in Loíza since 1979. I trace the emergence of its violence reduction and prevention program, Acuerdo de Paz (Ceasefire), which operated at full capacity from 2012 to 2016. Acuerdo de Paz based its organization on and affiliated with Cure Violence, an organization that utilizes public health approaches to decrease gun violence and deaths. Acuerdo de Paz, like other Cure Violence affiliates, employed community members with "street credibility" to work with individuals at "high risk" of experiencing or enacting violence, to mediate situations with the potential to end in violence, and to denormalize violence as a solution to conflict.

Gary Slutkin, a white physician and epidemiologist, developed the Cure Violence (formerly known as CeaseFire) model in 1995 based on fifteen years' experience treating infectious diseases such as tuberculosis, cholera, and HIV/AIDS in various countries throughout the African continent.[9] When Slutkin returned to his hometown of Chicago, he began to "make connections" between, for instance, the spread of cholera in Somalia and the gun violence affecting young people in Chicago's Black and Latinx neighborhoods. Slutkin teamed up with Tio Hardiman, an African American West Side community activist, to help develop and implement the CeaseFire model in Chicago. At Hardiman's urging, Slutkin hired men and women with strong ties to the community who had been formerly incarcerated and/ or involved with gang violence and as a result of their own experiences were interested in reducing gun violence.[10] Slutkin and Hardiman directed these new recruits, dubbed "violence interrupters," to focus on deescalating conflict through direct mediation. These conflicts ranged from acts of retribution to squabbles resulting from a minor slight. The violence interrupters would also work alongside the traditional outreach workers to help vulnerable individuals access critical social services.

Cure Violence and its founder, however, have not been without criticism. Some criminologists and public health officials have questioned the program's strategy and results, suggesting that the very metrics of "success" that provide the basis for Cure Violence's wide-reaching application are less impressive than they appear.[11] Other critics are troubled by the logics of disease and contagion that drive the Cure Violence model. Ethnic studies scholar John D. Márquez, for instance, challenges what he sees as an overreliance on scientific discourse, which ignores how structures of oppression drive violence in low-income communities and communities of color and harkens back to an earlier era of racialized phrenology and scientific inquiry aimed at understanding the so-called criminal mind.[12]

Rather than focusing on whether Acuerdo de Paz is a successful or faithful adaptation of Cure Violence's model of "violence interruption" or the Cure Violence model is itself the "best practice" for reducing gun-related violence in Puerto Rico, I instead explore how and why such a model may have been attractive to activists and community members in Loíza. I argue that Taller Salud carefully adapted the Cure Violence model to Loíza in a rejection of prevailing punitive policing practices and logics. I demonstrate how Taller Salud sought ways to respond to high levels of intracommunity violence while recognizing that the dogma of mano dura had not made the community safer and had, in fact, contributed to experiences of greater harm.

In what follows, I trace the circumstances and events that led to the creation of Taller Salud's Acuerdo de Paz violence prevention and reduction program. As a part of the Loíza community, members of Taller Salud felt that they needed to do something about the gun-related violence, primarily fueled by territorial gang disputes, that claimed the lives of young men in the community and contributed to a general sense of insecurity for a wide range of loiceños. Taller Salud reached out to Cure Violence to bring its nonpunitive, public health approach to violence to Loíza. I discuss how Taller Salud adapted the Cure Violence model to the local context in Loíza, as well as the points at which Acuerdo de Paz and Cure Violence diverged. There is significant evidence to suggest that Acuerdo de Paz assisted in reducing rates of violence, in particular homicide, in Loíza, demonstrating the importance of efforts that respond to crime and violence in nonpunitive ways.

Acuerdo de Paz also challenged the police's assumptions about what was causing violence in Loíza, which failed to account for the complex social contexts that generate and perpetuate violence. Specifically, Acuerdo de Paz challenged law enforcement's myopic claim that drug use and trafficking were responsible for the overwhelming majority of violence occurring in Puerto Rico, an assessment that became cemented as common sense during the mano dura era of the 1990s. According to Acuerdo de Paz, the war waged on racially and economically marginalized communities in the name of eradicating drug trafficking ignored how the territorial gang conflict they were seeing often had little to do with the drug market. Acuerdo de Paz rejected the dominant misconception that positioned drug trafficking as responsible for the violence affecting Loíza and instead worked with local *corillos*, or gangs, to understand and attempt to address some of the factors that push young people onto the streets and toward violence as a preferred method for resolving conflict. Acuerdo de Paz equipped young people with skills to resolve conflict through nonviolent means, worked to reintegrate individuals who had committed violence or experienced violence into the community, and discussed with young men how gendered expectations can create volatile situations with the potential to end in violence.

Acuerdo de Paz is just one example of how Puerto Ricans have challenged the punitive policies and logics that have dominated understandings of security in recent decades. Beginning from the simple notion that "to live in peace in Loíza is possible," Acuerdo de Paz worked to dismantle the politics of disposability shaping life and death in Puerto Rico. It also attempted to shift attention away from overzealous drug enforcement and toward identifying the structural forces that contribute most to conditions of insecurity in Loíza. Initiatives like Acuerdo de Paz thus provide a glimpse of alternative, nonpunitive practices and imaginaries that speak to the desire to look beyond policing as a solution to crisis and insecurity in contemporary Puerto Rico.

EL CEMENTERIO DE LOS JÓVENES/THE CEMETERY OF THE YOUNG

Although Acuerdo de Paz did not officially launch until early 2012, the program had its roots in an event that shook Loíza in the fall of 2009. On the afternoon of September 30, 2009, in the midst of a basketball clinic at El Ceiba's basketball court in the Villa Cristiana area of Loíza, individuals armed with assault rifles opened fire in the direction of the court. The triggermen shot seventeen-year-old Luis O'Neill Carrasquillo Cirino, who died immediately at the scene, and mortally wounded Luis Joel López Meléndez and Jonathan Carrasquillo Carrasquillo, both fifteen years old. All three of the young men who lost their lives hailed from Sector Las Carreras in Loíza, where area gangs had been involved in a long-standing territorial battle with gangs from Sector Melilla.[13]

It was clear to community members as well as the authorities that these young men were likely killed because of this territorial dispute, whether or not they were members of any gang. The deaths of young people in Loíza as a result of these territorial conflicts had become so pervasive that locals dubbed the new municipal cemetery *el cementerio de los jóvenes*, or the cemetery of the young. Although such shootings had become expected, in a sense, the shooting at El Ceiba's basketball court utterly shocked many in Loíza. The shooting broke with the established patterns of violence that had emerged in relation to the gangs; for instance, it occurred in broad daylight during a basketball clinic. In addition, it took place in an area that was largely considered "neutral" territory, where young people could hang out and play ball without fear of catching a beating or a bullet. The shooting signaled a tipping point for community leaders, who felt that little was being done to stop the killings claiming the lives of young loiceños. Zinnia Alejandro, coordinator for the Acuerdo de Paz program, recalled, "That was the event that made the community leaders in Loíza wake up and say, we need to do something to minimize this, to deal with this."[14]

As the nature of the shooting shocked community leaders into action, Taller Salud also took note of the fear that it generated among the young people with whom the group worked. According to Alana Feldman Soler, general coordinator for Taller Salud:

> We had to deal with the trauma and the after effect of that shooting on our kids. It was very hard. It was really hard, not just because they were devastated, but because they were there—they saw their friends get shot. They ran and left anything behind and trampled whatever was in their way. It was a very strong emotional experience, to say the least. We could tell that they were traumatized. They stopped coming to group for months. We had to go to their homes to go find them and talk to them. . . . Moms would tell us that they wouldn't leave their rooms; they wouldn't come out from under their beds, wouldn't go to the bakery—things like that.[15]

In talking to young people and their families, it was clear to Feldman Soler and other Taller Salud staff members that while they might not be able to immediately eliminate the conditions that made these young people feel unsafe in their community, Taller Salud could at least play a role in helping them process what had occurred. However, it quickly became apparent that there were few resources available to do so. "We weren't able to find any support resources at all in Loíza. We were looking for resources outside of Loíza and most people don't want to go to Loíza to do anything because Loíza has a bad reputation," noted Feldman Soler.[16] Staff at Taller Salud were eventually able to locate some support services (e.g., a group of psychology graduate students from the UPR came to work with some of the young people in the community following the shooting), but such efforts tended to be unreliable and short term. Recalling that time, Feldman Soler noted, "It was kind of a shock for us to realize that we needed to do something to provide access and support to, at the very least, the kids we were working with, and we weren't able to provide what they needed. Much less to the greater community."[17]

With this realization in mind, Taller Salud staff participated in a series of meetings with community members to discuss what could be done to not only reduce gang violence in the area but also address some of its long-term effects.

While there was much debate about what exactly was to be done, many people were in agreement that reducing violence in the community should not be entrusted solely to the police because they were embarking on a campaign of punitive intimidation in Loíza.[18] Following the triple homicide at the basketball clinic, police launched an operation targeting drug puntos, which they argued had motivated the recent battles between the area gangs.[19] On the morning of December 10, 2009, police raided homes and drug points in the Melilla, Villa Santos, Las Carreras, and Medianía Alta sectors, arresting twelve people, including three individuals suspected of involvement with the triple homicide at the basketball clinic.[20] Following the early morning raids, police superintendent José Figueroa Sancha told the press: "This is not an operation for one single community; this is an operation taking place throughout the municipality to restore the quality of life of Loíza's residents."[21] The superintendent pulled officers from other parts of the big island and stationed them throughout the municipality. Hundreds of officers patrolled Loíza in twelve-hour shifts in patrol cars, on foot, on horseback, and on bicycles. The high concentration of police officers in Loíza made some residents feel under siege and fearful of police brutality and harassment. Feldman Soler recalled, "There were so many cop cars that they would block each other along the way on the road. You know, cops standing with weapons on the corners. Some people felt like it was about time—a 'this is what they needed to do from the beginning' kind of thing. But a lot of us who are a lot more wary of security were like, 'wait, I don't want to live in a military zone.'"[22]

Some residents and activists, concerned by the police's record of racist and classist aggression toward residents in the past, worried that an increased police presence would only contribute to more violence in the community. Only two years earlier, for example, police had occupied the community of Villa Cañona in Loíza in order to dismantle the drug points that operated there. Rather than reducing drug dealing or gang violence, police terrorized residents with threats and acts of brutality, which were sometimes accompanied by racial slurs. The reports of police brutality were so widespread that the Puerto Rican Civil Rights Commission and the local branch of the ACLU launched separate investigations in response. The memory of recent police violence in their community remained fresh in the minds of residents and activists as they saw Loíza once again occupied by police and contemplated how best to respond to the violence claiming the lives of local youth.

Ironically, neoliberal ideas about privatization and Puerto Rico's deepening financial crisis opened up space for community activists in Loíza to experiment with nonpunitive solutions to violence. In the weeks and months following the shooting at El Ceiba, residents and community activists continued to meet regularly to come up with a plan to respond to gang violence. During one of those meetings, representatives from the governor's office showed up along with representatives from the PRPD. They informed the residents and activists gathered there that maintaining the constant police presence in the area was draining their capacity and that they would soon start returning officers to their normal posts. Government officials said that although they were withdrawing the police, they did not want to leave a security vacuum in their absence; they explained that they were willing to fund a community-based violence reduction program if community members came up with a proposal.[23] Devolution and the withdrawal of the state from its security functions in Loíza created an alternative terrain of possibility for activists and community members in Loíza to think beyond the narrow strictures of safety represented by the police. Community activists began researching different violence reduction models in order to submit a proposal to the governor's office. This research eventually led Taller Salud to the Cure Violence model.

BEYOND POLICING

In the wake of the shooting at the basketball clinic, Feldman Soler contacted the main Cure Violence office in Chicago for more information. After reviewing the Cure Violence website, the informational materials the organization sent, and existing evaluations of the model, Feldman Soler presented the model at a community meeting. Following her presentation, she explained, "Everyone agreed that the model seemed to respond to the kind of violence that we were seeing—territorial, apparently drug related but in reality really not, and long lasting, coming from so far behind that people can't even remember where the feud started."[24] After community members expressed interest in piloting the Cure Violence model in Loíza, Taller Salud stepped forward to develop and run what would eventually become the

Acuerdo de Paz program. As Feldman Soler explains, "It was contracted out to Taller Salud because there weren't really any other organizations in the group [that] were interested in being the host. It required a certain structure and it required a certain commitment to community organizing and community work in general. There are not a lot of organizations in Loíza and most of them have very specific goals. [. . .] Taller Salud stepped up and said we're willing to do it if you all will back us up on it and the community said that they were willing to do that."[25]

The Cure Violence model allowed for Taller Salud to address the territorial gang violence that was robbing Loíza of its youth by providing a framework for addressing violence that did not rely on the police or punitive force. Cure Violence not only provided a relatively flexible model for Taller Salud to follow, but also made Taller Salud palatable to the local Puerto Rican government through its international cachet. The first Cure Violence site, launched in 2000 in the West Garfield Park area of Chicago, was immediately hailed as innovative and successful. According to founder Gary Slutkin, funders asked him and his colleagues to "do it again."[26] The program received praise far and wide—from local politicians, the Department of Justice, and even First Lady Laura Bush. By 2005 the Cure Violence model had expanded to twelve sites around Chicago, and the accolades continued to pour in.[27] In 2008 famous journalist Alex Kotolwitz profiled Slutkin and Cure Violence in the *New York Times Magazine*, and in 2011 the program was the subject of the critically acclaimed documentary *The Interrupters*, which premiered at Sundance. The positive attention directed at the program, and the funding that often accompanied it, allowed for the Cure Violence model to be replicated quickly and widely. This international acclaim validated the Cure Violence model for Puerto Rican government officials. This was especially important given that the local Puerto Rican government historically had a poor record of meaningfully supporting community-based organizations around the archipelago. Affiliating Acuerdo de Paz with Cure Violence therefore provided Taller Salud with tangible and intangible benefits while simultaneously enabling it to create the space necessary to address the needs and concerns of loiceños in a holistic way.

Further, because Cure Violence had expanded to sites around the world (more than fifty sites throughout the United States and eight sites internationally), its capacity for oversight was become somewhat limited. Taller Salud thus had a high degree of autonomy in terms of how it ran Acuerdo de Paz, allowing it to respond to the specific needs of Loíza and its residents and address the structural causes of violence. As Feldman Soler explains, "We have complete freedom. No one from Chicago is here checking out what we do or how we do it. The only thing that is required of the program is that your staff members have credibility in the community and have the experience with violence that is required to have credibility with the highest risk people. [. . .] But what we do and how is really up to us."[28] Emphasizing the autonomy that Acuerdo de Paz had in relation to the central Cure Violence office, Feldman Soler stressed the ways in which this program, in contrast to programs run out of other Cure Violence sites, was an explicitly feminist one. She explained, "And us being a feminist organization we have done a lot of gender training with our staff as far as how gender norms of masculinity promote violence."[29] Pointing to Acuerdo de Paz's autonomy is not to suggest that it had no relationship with Cure Violence in Chicago or any of its other affiliates. According to Zinnia Alejandro, "They come to visit every six months to do a training or to see how things are going—the successes that we've had. . . . The reality is that they have a lot of interest in whether the program works or not."[30] Indeed, prior to our interview, Alejandro had just returned from a trip to El Salvador, where she discussed the experience of implementing the Cure Violence model in Loíza with antiviolence organizers there. Acuerdo de Paz figured into Cure Violence's efforts to expand into Latin America and the Caribbean, at the same time that it benefited from a largely decentralized organizational structure that allowed it to create highly localized responses to violence in Loíza.

After Taller Salud received community approval to move forward with the Cure Violence model, it approached representatives from the governor's administration to secure the funding that had been promised when the police were withdrawn from the area. Taller Salud was guaranteed $800,000 to fund a three-year pilot program. The disbursement of the funds, however, posed an early threat to Taller Salud's desire to develop responses to violence in Loíza that decentered the role of the police. Initially, state officials wanted to route Taller Salud's funding for the Acuerdo de Paz program through the PRPD. This upset community members, who viewed this as an attempt by state officials to keep police involved in violence reduction efforts in Loíza.[31] Personnel from Taller Salud as well as other community activists demanded that the government use another agency to disburse the funds, arguing that even the appearance of police oversight or involvement would undermine the goals of the Acuerdo de Paz program. "Part of the reason we decided this model was something that could adapt to our reality is that it doesn't work with the police, so why would I be sending in reports to the police? What are they going to do with that?" Feldman Soler asked.[32]

According to Zinnia Alejandro, from the outset Acuerdo de Paz emerged from a desire to try something "different from the work that the police were already doing, which is punitive, which is about punishment."[33] She elaborated:

> It's a desire to try something new, and, the way I understand it, the desire to do it that way is because *la mano dura* that the police say will resolve the situation has not produced results. We have seen situations where the police have abused people. So, if that happened, then we understand that that [mano dura] is not the way. The police should do their jobs; let them do their jobs. I'm not against the police doing their job, but we have discovered a more humane and more sensible way to deal with violence that is able to reach the hearts and minds of people and change attitudes. The other way you don't change attitudes—you only force people.[34]

As Alejandro's comments illustrate, community members and local activists had seen the harm that *la politica de mano dura* had done in Loíza and were open to experimenting with new approaches to security. The abuse that police had doled out in Loíza and other low-income communities around the archipelago solidified, for community members, the understanding that punitive policing was "not the way" to create safety.

Though advocates of mano dura contra el crimen argued that it had dramatically reduced instances of crime and violence, for residents of Loíza, punitive policing had not translated into safer everyday conditions. There was therefore an agreement among many activists and community members that the police should not be involved, in any capacity, in the oversight or evaluation of the Acuerdo de Paz program. After a series of back-and-forth discussions, government officials finally agreed to disburse the funds for the program through the Department of Housing. The first funds were released to Taller Salud in September 2011, allowing it to start building up capacity for the Acuerdo de Paz program.

In October 2011 Feldman Soler traveled to Chicago to meet with Cure Violence personnel to discuss how to go about implementing the model in Loíza. Upon returning from Chicago, Feldman Soler and others from Taller Salud met with community organizers to establish the structure of the program and write job descriptions for Acuerdo de Paz's program coordinator, outreach workers, and violence interrupters. In November 2011 Taller Salud hired Zinnia Alejandro to serve as Acuerdo de Paz's program coordinator.

Alejandro, a lifelong resident of the Miñi Miñi sector of Loíza, was immediately tasked with staffing the Acuerdo de Paz program.

In contrast to many community-based violence prevention programs in Puerto Rico or the United States, and even in contrast to most other Cure Violence affiliates, Acuerdo de Paz paid its staff a full-time living wage and provided fringe benefits. This decision to hire full-time, salaried employees reveals much about how Taller Salud understood the importance of the labor performed by the Acuerdo de Paz staff, at the same time that it indexes a rejection of both punitive and short-term responses to violence in Loíza. First, it recognizes that violence in Loíza is a problem that requires long-term efforts and the work of committed community members in order to effect any lasting change. Rather than having students or activists from outside of Loíza "parachute in," impose a plan of action on the local community, and quickly leave, Acuerdo de Paz employed community members to assess and address their own needs. Relatedly, this means that Acuerdo de Paz focused on the knowledge and expertise of those in the community who had committed violence and/or experienced violence in order to reduce conflict and harm in Loíza. Upending the dominant society's devaluation of individuals who have engaged in acts of violence or been incarcerated, Acuerdo de Paz did not reject or support the exile of these individuals from the community; instead, it saw them as essential members of the community and asked them to contribute to the work of creating a safer Loíza. Acuerdo de Paz understood that in order to create a sense of peace and safety in Loíza, *all* members of the community had to feel that they were included and valued. Finally, Acuerdo de Paz's decision to hire full-time employees recognized the value and inherent risks of the labor performed by its staffers. Given that a number of Acuerdo de Paz employees, particularly the violence interrupters, were at some point in their lives gang affiliated, Taller Salud was concerned that their outreach efforts could expose them to retaliatory acts of violence. For both Feldman Soler and Alejandro, it was crucial that Acuerdo de Paz staff received salaries and benefits that appropriately compensated them for the potential dangers of their work and allowed them to work in the community without having to worry about providing for themselves and their families.

Despite Acuerdo de Paz's commitment to providing its staff with a living wage and access to health benefits, the organizers encountered some initial difficulty in staffing the program, as some felt that this kind of direct-outreach violence prevention work was simply too dangerous an undertaking. Alejando notes that she approached a number of individuals about working for Acuerdo de Paz, and although they were interested in the model promoted by the program, they declined to become involved because they were worried about the violence they might encounter in the field. For instance, as Alejandro recalled, one individual whom she approached to become a violence interrupter was already very involved in the community and was interested in reducing violence, but he ultimately felt that getting in the middle of the territorial disputes between the gangs could cost him his life or put his loved ones in danger. "He was perfect, and people respected him, but in his mind he understood that it was too dangerous," Alejandro lamented.[35]

As much as Acuerdo de Paz required its staff to have knowledge about the community and respect on the streets, it soon became clear that a willingness to confront personal fears and to risk encountering violence would also be necessary qualifications. Not only were potential staffers expected to frequently immerse themselves in potentially dangerous situations; they were also expected to come to terms with and regularly draw upon their own past experiences of violence. Alejandro pointed out, "We're talking about people who have lived through violence that we know carry a trauma inside of them that they are dealing with. In that way, they are brave people who confront their fears everyday."[36] After identifying a number of individuals in the community interested in working for Acuerdo de Paz, Alejandro helped to set up a series of community panels that would further vet potential staffers.

It was crucial to the mission and success of Acuerdo de Paz that various community constituents be involved throughout the process of staffing the program. Looking back on the hiring process, Alejandro noted that she consulted with a range of community members in addition to drawing upon her own knowledge of the community and the people in it:

> It was a completely community based process. Number one, I had to do the work—I was the first person they hired, so I had to do the work of finding people. I had to walk the community a lot. Ask questions. Moreover, with the experience I had in the community—I've lived here since I was a little girl—well, I know the people in my neighborhood. I know the people that, at a certain time, were committing violence and then they got out of it. Little by little, I looked around and I asked people if they would be interested in working with a program like this.[37]

For Alejandro, staffing the program depended on and drew from the intimate familiarity and trust between people in the community. Acuerdo de Paz set up community panels to vet potential hires as opportunities, in

Alejandro's words, for members of the community to voice their support or concerns regarding whether a potential staffer was "more or less able to do this work."[38] The panels played a key role in mobilizing the knowledge of longtime community members to build an effective and trusted staff. At the same time, the panels gave community members a voice in the development of the program, which helped to create a sense of commitment and investment in its success. Typically, Feldman Soler and/or Alejandro would sit on the panel and be accompanied by four to five other individuals with roots in Loíza. The panelists could be small business owners or church leaders, or they could simply be people who lived in the same neighborhood as the potential staffer. The police were also invited to send a representative to participate on the community panels in order to verify that the potential staffer under consideration was not, unbeknownst to community members, engaging in illegal activities or acts of violence, but police officials seldom participated.[39]

During the meetings of these community panels, the panelists acted as interviewers, asking each potential staffer a series of questions in order to determine the candidate's readiness to undertake the kind of emotionally intensive and risky work that the Acuerdo de Paz program entailed. According to Alejandro, the panelists were clear that people's past behaviors were not to be held against them as long as they had taken steps to change their lives and expressed a desire to help reduce violence in the community. The panelists were expected to take seriously the idea that people could and do change and that individuals who had been marked as "criminals" or "violent" were not to be discarded or shamed, but rather brought into the fold and centralized in the work of creating community safety. Alejandro noted:

> I think people were clear about the program. For example, in the community panel, we were clear about what we were looking for and there wasn't resistance. There *was* resistance if the person we were interviewing hadn't yet completely left that situation. The panel would say, "well, they're not quite ready because they're still getting together with their corillo and making things difficult within the community." They weren't yet ready and we were clear about what we were looking for, so we wouldn't select that person. But those that did arrive and they had undergone a process of transformation were accepted by the panel because we were clear about what we were looking for—people with credibility within the community who had testified that their lives had changed and who desired that the lives of other at-risk young people also change.[40]

Following an initial series of community panels held between December 2011 and January 2012, Acuerdo de Paz hired three staff members. That number would eventually grow to eight by 2015.[41]

VIVIR EN PAZ EN LOÍZA ES POSIBLE/TO LIVE IN PEACE IN LOÍZA IS POSSIBLE

With the pilot program under way, Acuerdo de Paz staffers set out to challenge the notion that violence is an expected and everyday part of life in Loíza. Many Puerto Ricans outside of the municipality justified the violence occurring in Loíza through racist and classist assumptions. Many saw violence in Loíza as stemming from a deficient and destructive culture endemic to both poverty and Blackness. While those outside of Loíza problematically normalized the violence that occurred there, Acuerdo de Paz staffers felt that some community members had also internalized the notion that Loíza was inherently violent. Acuerdo de Paz thus undertook a range of efforts aimed at denormalizing violence in Loíza by promoting the idea it was possible to live in peace there. Acuerdo de Paz strategically occupied public spaces, ranging from street corners to the sides of public buses, billboards, banners, and other paraphernalia, in order to send the message that life was valuable in Loíza and to create a strong sense of community accountability. Through its direct outreach and grassroots pedagogical campaigns, Acuerdo de Paz sought to provide community members with an alternative understanding of what it meant to *live* in Loíza. At the same time, Acuerdo de Paz served as a resource to help loiceños imagine and work toward a goal of community safety that did not rely on carceral systems such as police or prisons.

In February 2012, people might not have known what Acuerdo de Paz was or what it was trying to do, but that soon changed as its name and logo, often accompanied by phrases such as *Zona de Paz* (Peace Zone) and *Vivir en paz en Loíza es posible* (To live in peace in Loíza is possible) started popping up all over the municipality. Acuerdo de Paz's logo could be seen anywhere and everywhere over the course of its three-year pilot program: on posters in store windows, bumper stickers, and T-shirts; on the plastic liquor cups and napkins used at the *chinchorros* in Piñones; on cards found underneath people's windshield wipers after a day at the beach; and on the sides of public buses that drove throughout the metropolitan area. The goal was to bombard loiceños with Acuerdo de Paz signs and paraphernalia so that at a very basic level people knew about the program and had its contact information. Every item that had an Acuerdo de Paz logo on it also had a number to call for more information about the program or to call in case people found themselves in a situation with the potential to escalate into violence. According to Feldman Soler, "It's hard to find someone in Loíza that does not know about the existence of the program. It's just everywhere. We give out t-shirts that say 'Zona de Paz,' we give out stickers, we have posters in the businesses. So, it's really hard to find someone that doesn't know."[42]

In response to an uptick in violence in the tourist area of Piñones in 2013, Acuerdo de Paz not only dispatched violence interrupters to work with "high-risk kids" in the area but also made a deliberate effort to educate the public about its role in helping to decrease violence without having to call the cops. Acuerdo de Paz staffers ran training sessions with local business owners to help them identify potentially violent conflicts and determine which situations they might be able to mediate and which required them to call Acuerdo de Paz to dispatch someone to try to de-escalate things. Feldman Soler explained:

> We worked with the businesses, and the other thing we did was we were working with the visitors. For about 4 or 5 weeks we stood on the corner giving out cards and putting stickers in people cars and putting notes on people's windshield wipers that had just general [info] about how to get along peacefully at the beach—instructions. Here's our phone number, call us if it gets out of hand. But how about you try talking? How about you try getting a third person involved with the situation? It's not working? Here's our cell phones, call us.[43]

Through campaigns such as these, Acuerdo de Paz attempted to educate the public about alternatives to violence as a solution to conflict and alternatives to punitive policing. This effort was crucial in providing loiceños with a concrete alternative to calling the police during moments of conflict or potential violence. Acuerdo de Paz also allowed community members to take a proactive, but nonpunitive, approach to safety that focused on eliminating violence through de-escalation as opposed to the reactive approach of law enforcement, which focused on incapacitation after harm had already occurred.

Through its public education campaigns, Acuerdo de Paz attempted to foster a sense of community accountability that hinged on a desire to keep everyone free from harm and violence, whether they were longtime residents of Loíza or just stopping by to have a beer and salted cod fritter in Piñones.

The group explicitly articulated this notion of accountability through a public project it initiated early on during the pilot program that documented the number of days that had elapsed without a murder in Loíza. Reminiscent of the occupational safety signs that sometimes hang in factories alerting staff and visitors to the number of days without injury, Acuerdo de Paz hung a large banner in a central location in Loíza that read "[blank] días sin muertes," with the phrase "vivir en paz en Loíza es posible" printed below. According to Feldman Soler, one central goal of the banner was to shock people into awareness when lives were lost in Loíza. As she put it, "We wanted people to be aware that somebody died. We wanted to not be able to say, 'Oh, so there's another dead person . . . back to my kitchen, I'm just going to turn on a movie, not pay it much attention."[44] With the banner, Acuerdo de Paz fought against the desensitization of many Puerto Ricans to violent and premature death in racially and economically marginalized communities like Loíza, where state officials constructed harm as deserved punishment for assumed involvement with illicit activities. Further, the group hoped that the banner would push against the feelings of resignation and acceptance that some loiceños felt about the seemingly regular—in fact weekly—pace at which someone in their community was murdered.

The banner became in some ways an indication of the success Acuerdo de Paz was having with its community outreach and violence interruption efforts. As staffers walked the barrios and spoke to the young men involved in local corillos to help them figure out how to avoid instances of violence between the various neighborhood gangs, staffers were able to put more and more days up on the banner: 5 días sin muertes, 10 días sin muertes, 30 días sin muertes, and so on, until Loíza experienced 114 days without a murder.

According to Alejandro, Acuerdo de Paz initiated its work during a moment when there was a tremendous sense of exhaustion with the ubiquity of violence in Loíza. In particular, young men involved in gangs experienced fatigue with quotidian forms of violence they experienced, which helped bring the community together to achieve more than three months without a single murder. As Alejandro put it, "We went *barrio* to *barrio* talking about what we wanted. And in the town there was a really intense sense of exhaustion. You know? The people were exhausted by so much death. It seems to me that there was so much exhaustion in town—the young men on the streets were exhausted—and a new voice came along and said we can fix this by doing something new. And we had one hundred days without a murder, when in Loíza there was at least one murder every week."[45] On September 16, 2012, two weeks after Acuerdo de Paz marked one hundred days without a murder in Loíza, a multiple homicide took place in the municipality. The next day, the banner once again read "o días sin muertes." Acuerdo de Paz never got to celebrate that many days without a violent death again, but it was able to mark significant periods of time without anyone being killed in the community. "We haven't been able to have those hundred days again, but I want them! We haven't had those hundred days again, but we've have thirty days without a murder, fifteen days without a murder. We don't have that feeling of having to deal with that difficult news [of someone being killed] every week," Alejandro noted.[46]

Acuerdo de Paz eventually retired the banner after a disagreement with Mayor Eddie Manso over the message that the banner was sending to both loiceños and visitors to the area. One day Acuerdo de Paz staffers were told by community members that officials from the mayor's office had taken down the banner and hidden it in the public works department. When Acuerdo de Paz staffers approached Mayor Manso about his having removed the banner without their permission, he justified his behavior by suggesting that a sign reading "o días sin muertes" reinforced the idea of Loíza as dangerous and violent. Acuerdo de Paz fought the mayor and his office about the banner for months, even going so far as to get the local ACLU involved on the basis of free speech suppression, but ultimately the group decided that the fight over the banner was an unnecessary distraction from its work.[47]

The banner provided a glimpse into the substantial reduction in violence and murder that Loíza witnessed during the Acuerdo de Paz pilot program period. In 2011 Loíza recorded forty-three murders, making the municipality one of the most deadly in Puerto Rico. In 2012, the first year of the pilot program, homicides in Loíza decreased by 53 percent, with twenty murders registered. Though 2012 saw an archipelago-wide decrease in violent crime, including homicides, it would still be difficult to argue that Acuerdo de Paz's numerous trainings, public education programs, and thirty to forty monthly mediations had no bearing on the dramatic decrease seen in Loíza. Acuerdo de Paz staffers were careful not to claim sole responsibility for the decrease, noting that a range of factors and social actors helped to achieve that reduction in violence in Loíza, but they did feel incredibly proud that they were a part of it.

Bringing together various sectors of Loíza's community in an effort to reduce violence and build new forms of safety and accountability, particularly through the mobilization around the banner, is one of Acuerdo de Paz's most visible and celebrated successes. However, Acuerdo de Paz was involved in efforts to reduce violence that were far less visible and much more difficult to quantify. The group crafted a constellation of other strategies that attempted to challenge social norms and illuminate the ways in which structural inequality fuels violence in Loíza. In particular, Acuerdo de Paz sought to counter law enforcement's erroneous construction of violence in Loíza as a mere symptom of the drug trade by focusing on the ways in which power dynamics and inequalities around gender, race, and class play a central role in prematurely sending young people to the municipal cemetery.

"DRUG TRAFFICKING IS THE CONTEXT, BUT IT'S NOT THE ROOT"

In a short segment recorded for a promotional Cure Violence video, Hazael Pérez, a violence interrupter with Acuerdo de Paz, informs the viewer, "Drug-related violence is almost non-existent here. People who aren't from here say, 'That's really strange, because most gang wars are drug-related.' But here, it's mostly about revenge."[48] And indeed, Perez's comments are likely to elicit disbelief from many experts familiar with patterns of violence in contemporary Puerto Rico and with how violence operates in a range of urban contexts in the United States and throughout the world. Many scholars and policy analysts rightly note that structural inequality plays a role in producing the volatility of the drug trade as it tears through communities that have experienced social abandonment, political disenfranchisement, and economic disinvestment. However, drug use and drug trafficking are nonetheless too often (mis)understood as the wellspring from which the vast majority of violence, crime, and harm flows. That widely accepted and perpetuated notion is what has fueled decades of punitive drug wars that lead the public to believe that eradicating drugs will alleviate the insecurity they experience. This misconception is also what makes nonpunitive pedagogical efforts aimed at reducing violence in vulnerable communities so underfunded and difficult to implement.

Acuerdo de Paz's efforts did not try to reduce drug use or drug trafficking in Loíza because, as Feldman Soler noted, "Drug trafficking is the context, but it's not the root."[49] Like Feldman Soler, Alejandro suggested that the reality of the way that violence operates in Loíza is subsumed by the dominant narrative that all violence stems from drug-fueled disputes or battles over puntos. "Here, people think that it's because of drugs, because they think: well, in Puerto Rico, everything is because of drugs," Alejandro stated.[50] Both Felman Soler and Alejandro suggested that in Loíza, the drug trade does not generate enough income for it to provoke the kinds of intense bloodshed seen in other areas of the archipelago. They both maintained that a number of the young men involved with corillos might also be active in the drug economy, but that jockeying for profits is seldom at the root of the violence in Loíza because the money simply isn't there. "Here, the one who sells drugs isn't driving around in a luxury car; the one selling drugs is riding around on a bicycle," Alejandro explained.

Felman Soler acknowledged that the territorial battles between the gangs resemble the battles over drugs affecting other parts of the archipelago, but these conflicts have a range of complex underlying social causes that go beyond the drug trade. She said:

> People outside of Loíza feel that the violence in Loíza is drug related. They think that it's people fighting over a *punto de drogas* and it's not. The *puntos de drogas* in Loíza don't sell much, so there's not much to fight over. People don't have money so they're not selling very much. But they are territorial, so, 'this is my sphere of influence and this is my group of people who support me'— because that's kind of what they are, they're a support network. If you didn't have the teachers, the parents, the professors, the employer, the church, whatever it is that you believe in that you want to listen to, you look to your peers. So, we have these *corillos* and they are territorial because they feel like this is my identity, I identify with this one community and these people who are here.[51]

Recognizing that these territorial disputes between Loíza's different corillos are not reducible to the volatility of drug trade and often, in fact, have absolutely nothing to do with the local drug trade, Acuerdo de Paz worked to recognize and, when possible, address the root causes of conflict and violence in Loíza. These root causes, in Acuerdo de Paz's estimation, stem from dynamics of oppression and power that exceed the scope of drug trafficking that policing initiatives often focus on.

Acuerdo de Paz named as one of the central contributors to the rise of the corillos and the violence associated with them the social inequality that results from many Puerto Ricans' racist and classist attitudes about Loíza and the people who live there. Young loiceños, especially young men, see the corillos as a coping mechanism to negotiate the social discrimination and exclusion that they experience outside of their barrios. Acuerdo de Paz and its staffers were careful not to reinforce a rhetoric that constructs the corillos as a violent and pathological subculture arising from poverty and racism. Rather, the corillos emerged as a way for some young men to try to create a sense of respect, dignity, and community in a societal context in which they were systematically disempowered because of where they came from, how much money they had, and the color of their skin. Alejandro saw discrimination against loiceños and the lack of resources that it produces as *pushing* young men into corillos. "They are really discriminating against the town [Loíza] and against public housing. As if the people who live there aren't human beings. And in Loíza there is violence, but, if you talk to the young men who are at high risk, you notice that, at some moment, they lacked mentorship and possibilities because they [employers outside Loíza] close off possibilities to them," she asserted before clapping her hands together for emphasis.[52] She continued, "And with a lack of possibilities they don't have much else to do than what they're doing. They are full of frustration and they are full of rage because the reality is there aren't many possibilities for them. Those young men, unfortunately, are prisoners in their communities. That hurts a person."[53]

Like other racially and economically marginalized youth, young people in Loíza find that when they try to leave the area to obtain work or vocational training opportunities, they encounter intense stigma and discrimination. Echoing a well-known form of discrimination directed at public housing residents, Alejandro relayed how young loiceños complained that if they filled out applications with an address in Loíza they would rarely receive a call back, but if they told potential employers that they lived in the neighboring areas of Río Grande or Canóvanas they would receive more serious consideration. Such experiences of discrimination, or the fear of encountering such discrimination, makes the acceptance and support that the corillos provide particularly appealing.

While young men from Loíza experience discrimination outside of their barrios, Alejandro pointed out that municipal officials also treat them as a problem population to be managed through policing or simply just ignored, and fail to provide them with necessary resources or viable alternatives to the corillos:

> As I understand it, the municipal government can do more.... They can bring in services or some kind of help for the young men at high-risk, but they forget about them. They forget about them. It's something that is normalized because they are showing them that they don't matter and, if they don't matter, then it's best that the police take them away. You understand?

And, in a way, I blame the municipal government. If they looked at the boys and paid attention and supported them and covered their needs, this could change, because this is a question of covering necessities with a good job or a job with dignity.[54]

Here, Alejandro highlighted how many young men in Loíza have been rendered disposable by political forces within and outside of the municipality. Rather than countering dominant perceptions about the young men, particularly young men of color, who reside in Loíza, municipal officials reproduce and reinforce the notion that their lives are insignificant, or that Loíza and Puerto Rico would somehow be better off without them. Thus, local political officials' refusal to recognize the value of these young men, or even on a basic level their humanity, contributes to the central role that the corillos play in the psychic and social lives of young loiceños.

The corillos provide many young men in Loíza with a space where they can feel respected and empowered; however, those feelings of respect and empowerment must be vigorously defended, which is what Acuerdo de Paz staffers felt motivates the territorial violence between the gangs. In staffers' conversations with the young men in corillos, the youths often expressed feelings of having to fight for recognition and respect from those around them. "You've got to defend it [your sense of dignity and respect] with violence because you don't have the money to assert your power. Or you're not white enough to be recognized as deserving of power. You know, things like that. You can see those dynamics, and they're not explicit, but you can see it in the fabric of the conversation" Feldman Soler noted.[55]

Of course the intimate relationship among power, respect, and violence is related to hypermasculine logics, performances, and embodiments—a relationship that Acuerdo de Paz staffers labored to help the young men with whom they worked understand. As a project administered by Taller Salud, an explicitly feminist organization, Acuerdo de Paz tried to help young men identify how toxic hypermasculinity and sexism influence the violent conflicts between the corillos. Although the vast majority of individuals who experience harm and death at the hands of gang-affiliated youth are other young men, Acuerdo de Paz sought to illuminate the ways in which this violence is, in part, *gender violence*. As feminist legal scholar Angela P. Harris notes, gender violence does not produce only female victims; rather, men often enact violence against other men as a way of solidifying their own gender positioning and claiming the respect and recognition that being a "real man" accords.[56] Harris explains that although the unequal power relations expressed through gender violence make themselves most apparent in cases when men harm women, we should not be blind to the ways in which "hierarchies of race, class, sexual orientation, and *gender itself* also mark out men as vulnerable to the violence of other men."[57] For Acuerdo de Paz, recognizing the role that gender plays in acts of community violence and working to shift norms around gender, power, and sexuality are crucial to the amelioration of violence in Loíza.

The willingness to resort to violence in order to protect one's turf, one's community, one's corillo, and/or one's self-worth is not a sign of pathological behavior stemming from a deficient culture born and bred in Loíza. Rather, it is a hallmark of masculinity and its reliance on violence to access and consolidate power. For young men in Loíza, like many young men around the world, violence becomes a mechanism for overcoming perceived inadequacies, whether they are internally validated or externally imposed (or both). As Michael S. Kimmel and Matthew Mahler put it, "Shame, inadequacy, vulnerability—all threaten the self; violence, meanwhile, is restorative, compensatory."[58] In a context in which the state and dominant society implicitly and explicitly create barriers to inclusion and acceptance, young men in Loíza create support networks (corillos) that provide them with the kinds of validation that they are often denied. The validation offered by the corillos hinges on proving oneself to be a real man: a man who defends his family, his barrio, his corillo, and himself from degradation and disrespect.

The sense of value derived from performances of appropriate masculinity can bring young men into deadly conflicts with their peers over slight provocations, which are interpreted as attacks on one's manhood and one's sense of worth. Remarking on the kinds of conflicts that Acuerdo de Paz mediated, Alejandro mentioned to me that a few days before our meeting, two young men from the community got into an argument resulting from a simple misunderstanding, and the situation escalated until two people were dead from gunshot wounds. "In that way, here in Loíza people aren't killed because of drugs; people are killed because there is little tolerance. There is no dialogue. There isn't a culture [among the young men] of resolving things with communication. Everything is solved *a lo macho* and cowboy style," Alejandro told me.[59] In another example, Alejandro reiterated that much of the violence between the young men in corillos was about an unwillingness to tolerate perceived slights because it imperiled the sense of dignity and control they derived through the masculine performance demanded by the streets. "Unfortunately," Alejandro said, "if you're in a *barrio* and they find out you're from another *bando*, then that is sufficient [for a rival corillo to kill you]. If they decide to give you a break and let you be there, then you know if you mess up they can kill you."[60]

The streets of Loíza's barrios, then, function for many young men as a space where they develop and exhibit their manhood and seek positive affirmation. At the same time, the streets are a proverbial gauntlet where young men are exposed to victimization if they fail to prove their masculinity sufficiently. As sociologist Victor Ríos notes in his study of criminalized young men in Oakland, "The young men in this study faced constant interrogation about their manhood on the streets. Questions such as 'Is he really a homey?' and 'Is he really a man?' if answered in the negative, typically resulted in stigmatization or victimization. At the core of growing up in their community, the boys felt a constant necessity to prove their manhood."[61] Young men in Loíza face a similar pressure to assert their manhood—often through displays of violence against other young men—or risk experiencing violence and exclusion.

Acuerdo de Paz worked to manage the gender anxieties that young men experienced and tried to challenge how they would conflate violence and force with masculinity. Staffers knew that this would be a laborious and incredibly slow-moving process, but they recognized that little by little they would change the attitudes and norms around masculinity that contribute to violence in the community. As Feldman Soler told me about her and other staffers' interactions with the young men with whom Acuerdo de Paz worked, "It's interesting to see them now—one, two, three years down the road—because they can identify patterns that are, you know, of that construction of masculinity. How you've got to be the man so you've got to shoot this guy. Or how something completely stupid, like somebody stole some idiot, little thing from me and I just can't let that happen because everybody else is saying, 'what are you going to do about it.' So they can now relate that to the construction of gender and I think that's really cool!"[62] Feldman Soler's excitement that the discussions that had been taking place for days, months, and even years were eventually bearing fruit in small and unexpected ways demonstrates Acuerdo de Paz's commitment to the slow and ongoing work that social transformation requires. Rather than the "easy" and "quick" solutions to violence promised by punitive measures, Acuerdo de Paz emphasized the deliberate and incremental transformation of social norms as one of the most important ways to create meaningful and lasting community safety.

Related to its work around masculinity, Acuerdo de Paz also sought to explicitly change young men's attitudes toward women, which also play a large role in the conflicts between local corillos. According to Acuerdo de Paz staffers, so-called *líos de faldas*, or girl troubles, often formed an undercurrent to the violence between the young men with whom they worked. Early on during the pilot, Acuerdo de Paz ran a focus group with local youth to try to figure out what they felt was triggering the violence in their community. According to the young people who participated in the focus group, "girl trouble" triggered a startling number of the altercations between young men that ended in murder.[63]

These líos de faldas involved women in a range of ways, from fights that erupted because one young man hit on a young woman who "belonged" to another, to insults or other forms of disrespect directed at the women in a young man's family, to information provided by young women who collaborated with the corillos as *chotas*, or snitches. According to both Feldman Soler and Alejandro, líos de faldas index a set of attitudes held by the young men that understand women as property or inherently (sexually and emotionally) duplicitous. As Feldman Solder noted, these attitudes also derive from the young men's understanding of masculinity. "You know," she explained, "that thing of 'I'm the protector of my mother and sister, but the partner is mine—she is my property. So, you can't look at her, you can't tell her she's pretty, you can't comment on her clothing, you certainly cannot steal her from me.' Those kinds of things will lead to violence."[64] The parents of the young people in the community also identified this relationship between sexist and hypermasculine attitudes toward women and incidents of violence between young men. When Acuerdo de Paz staffers spoke to parents about what factors they felt were driving violence in Loíza, a number of them mentioned that they started to fear for their sons' lives when they were old enough to start dating.[65] Parents reported feeling anxiety that their sons might accidently become involved with "another's girl" and end up paying for that perceived disrespect with their lives.

Having conversations with the young men in corillos that encouraged them to develop different views of the women in their lives and in their community thus became another central component of Acuerdo de Paz's violence reduction strategy. As Alejandro explained:

> This means that we can say that we are creating peace for a whole community at the same time that we're constructing a new way for the young men to think. They don't own women like property. Because sometimes when a couple has been broken up for a while, if this girl has another partner, they

[the young men] think that she still belongs to them. So, when we work with them we also tell them that women aren't belongings; rather, the reality is that we make decisions and they have to respect those decisions and respect women as people.[66]

In these moments, although Acuerdo de Paz was engaging almost exclusively with young men in the community, it was also working to foster attitudes that would reduce harm and discrimination against women in Loíza. Alejandro asserted that while the main demographic that Acuerdo de Paz worked with was young men, the group was employing a feminist understanding of community and accountability that was not reducible to or synonymous with working only with women. She stated, "This goes further than just that we're working with men. Within what we're doing, we're creating peace and a safe environment for the community, an environment that benefits mothers, that benefits every women who will ever walk around Loíza. A safe environment benefits the women of our community. Taller Salud is dedicated to working for the health of women. Indirectly, we are working for women's health and safety."[67] For emphasis, Alejandro added, " In that way, we deal with violence, but we're working towards an environment of peace in that impacts everyone, not just our young men. Our work impacts the whole community—women, everyone."[68]

Alejandro's comments illuminate the contours of Acuerdo de Paz's feminist commitments and praxis. Acuerdo de Paz worked to address the full scope of gender violence in Loíza; its labor asks us to think in more nuanced ways about what feminist violence prevention and reduction looks like. In many ways, Alejandro's words and, by extension, Acuerdo de Paz's work, echo the vision of safe and empowered communities put forth by women of color and Third World feminist writers and activists in the early 1980s. As Cherríe Moraga famously posited in the preface to *This Bridge Called My Back*, what would it mean for radical feminists to fight to keep young Black boys from getting shot in the head by police with the same ferocity those feminists direct at ending patriarchal violence against women?[69] To see their struggles as intrinsically linked? What does it mean to embrace an intersectional feminist position that eschews single-issue politics and instead strives for safe and empowered communities where everyone is free from harm? Acuerdo de Paz and Taller Salud did not ignore the ways in which gendered violence specifically affects young girls and women in Loíza; rather, they recognized that Loíza will never be at peace and women will never feel safe if the territorial battles between young men in the community are allowed to continue claiming lives. Acuerdo de

Paz and Taller Salud enacted a radically intersectional praxis by situating the struggle against state and community violence, racial segregation, and economic disinvestment as essential components of their feminist vision and practice.

THE CHALLENGES OF RESTORATION IN THE
NEOLIBERAL PUNITIVE STATE

The interviews that I conducted with Alana Feldman Soler and Zinnia Alejandro, which form much of the basis of this chapter, occurred during the summer of 2015. In those interviews I was immediately stuck by the sense of pride and hope they both expressed as they told me about Acuerdo de Paz and the successes of the program in helping to reduce violence in Loíza. Their exuberance, however, was tempered by an uncertainty about the program's future. The grant to run a three-year pilot program had ended, and a justice assistance grant that they had received from the Justice Department to keep the program running while they tried to secure more long-term funding was about to run out. Staffers were struggling to apply for funding opportunities to keep financing the program's various outreach initiatives, especially the violence interrupters. As Alejandro told me during our meeting, "Our funding expires the 30th of this month [June]. And the reality is that we have to pay our employees because this is a very dangerous job that involves a lot of conversation with the community and a lot of hours. We clock seven and a half hours, but the reality is that it's much more than seven and a half hours. [. . .] The central government supported us for three years; I'd like if they supported us for ten more years."[70]

Acuerdo de Paz's affiliation with the internationally celebrated Cure Violence organization did not protect it from being underresourced and underfunded, much like affiliates on the mainland. And although the commonwealth and municipal governments celebrated the significant decrease in violence in Loíza and credited Acuerdo de Paz with playing a role in the reduction of violence and murder in the municipality, they still would not guarantee Taller Salud a steady source of funding. On July 6, 2015, Acuerdo de Paz posted a status update on its Facebook page that read: "The funds allocated for the development of the Acuerdo de Paz program in Loíza expired on June 30. We still have not received a response to our requests for continuing funds. If you think Acuerdo de Paz has been beneficial in reducing violence in Loíza and it is important to keep up the community mediation efforts that have been started, express your opinion to cesarmiranda@justicia .pr.gov and alastra@vivienda.pr.gov."

Taller Salud was forced to terminate its Acuerdo de Paz program less than one year later, in May 2016, due to a lack of funding.[71] Taller Salud has since revived but has been unable to fund Acuerdo de Paz at full capacity and therefore has a much more limited scope. A large part of why Acuerdo de Paz could not secure continued funding from the government is that the expiration of its existing funding coincided with the deepening of Puerto Rico's financial crisis. With the local government largely unable to fund essential and emergency services by the time that Acuerdo de Paz's funding ran out, there simply didn't seem to be money in the government budget for small-scale, community-based initiatives like Acuerdo de Paz. I also argue that the program's emphasis on transformative and restorative justice efforts that decentered the role of policing in vulnerable communities like Loíza made it illegible to the government as an "essential service" working toward a safer, more secure community. For government technocrats struggling to allocate funding and resources in the midst of the worst economic downturn in Puerto Rico's modern history, and when millions of dollars were already going toward "keeping the streets safe" through policing and incarceration, justifying hundreds of thousands more for an additional few years of funding for Acuerdo de Paz made little sense. And indeed, as policing has long served as a form of crisis management for political elites, it was unlikely that funding would have shifted from militarized police units like the Fuerza de Choque to community-based initiatives that seek to provide concrete alternatives to punitive and carceral policies.

Acuerdo de Paz provided loiceños and other Puerto Ricans with an alternative vision of justice, safety, and community that decentered punitive policing and sought to restore a community dealing with the effects of race-, class-, and gender-based violence. By challenging the presupposition that drugs are the biggest contributor to violence in Loíza, Acuerdo de Paz was able to identify the intimate relationships between masculinity and violence; between state neglect and a politics of disposability; and among racism, sexism, classism, and community insecurity. Moving beyond the logics of punitive policing and the war on drugs, Acuerdo de Paz worked with young men in the community to advance a holistic, feminist vision of safety and accountability in Loíza. Acuerdo de Paz illuminated alternative strategies to remediate territorial gang violence that sought to restore community relationships rather than fracture them through punitive policies. As opposed to law enforcement's emphasis on quick and quantifiable change that functions through the removal of "dangerous" individuals from their communities, Acuerdo de Paz undertook the often slow and difficult work of changing social relations in the hope of creating a meaningful and lasting sense of safety and peace in Loíza. At the same time, Acuerdo de Paz provided us with an example of intersectional feminist politics in action: a feminism that seeks to ameliorate gender violence as well as the violence of racism, poverty, and spatial segregation.

Postscript

BROKEN WINDOWS AND FUTURE HORIZONS
AFTER THE STORM

BEFORE FALL 2017, THERE WERE MANY WAYS I imagined I would end this story. I wanted to talk about how, as Puerto Rico's so-called debt crisis worsened, its colonial relationship became harder and harder to deny. In June 2016 US president Barack Obama signed the Puerto Rico Oversight, Management, and Economic Stability Act (PROMESA) into law.[1] It was particularly poignant that the bill was named *promesa*, which means promise in Spanish, since it brought to the fore the question of what exactly continued incorporation into the United States and American citizenship promised for the future of Puerto Rico and Puerto Ricans. The PROMESA bill created a Federal Control Board to oversee the archipelago's finances. The Federal Control Board, or *la junta* as locals refer to it, consists of seven members appointed by the president with congressional approval. With virtually no local input, la junta has the power to override the commonwealth government and implement austerity measures in order to service the debt. The commonwealth government, whether PNP or PPD, has forced austerity and privatization schemes on the Puerto Rican people since the 1990s, and the results of this disinvestment have been disastrous for many Puerto Ricans, but particularly the most economically vulnerable populations. PROMESA is only different in terms of degree and severity.

PROMESA and the imposition of la junta have exacerbated the situation in the archipelago, making the possibility of growing up in Puerto Rico and staying there increasingly untenable for growing numbers of Puerto Rican youths. As Puerto Rican anthropologist Hilda Lloréns has noted, there is a sense that the only bodies that remain in some rural communities are those of the elderly and the dead.[2] When I was in Puerto Rico conducting the bulk of the on-the-ground research for this book in 2011 and 2012, a number of the young people I spoke to lamented that they felt staying in Puerto Rico meant confining themselves to a lifetime of economic struggle or outright poverty, given the cuts to the public good that were announced nearly daily. In my return trips since then, this feeling has only grown more pronounced. More and more young people feel that in order to have a "good life," one marked by a modicum of financial opportunity and security, they have to leave their home. With the imposition of PROMESA and the deepening of the debt crisis, the sense of frustration and desperation is palpably evidenced by the massive migration of Puerto Ricans to the continental United States. Indeed, Puerto Ricans are migrating to the United States in numbers not seen since the "Great Migration" of the 1950s and 1960s, and now more Puerto Ricans live in the continental United States than in the archipelago. Just as in the mid-twentieth century, today's migration has everything to do with the deleterious effects of colonial capitalism on Puerto Ricans.

I wanted to write about the collusion of the commonwealth and federal governments to ram austerity down the throats of the people. When the people refused to swallow the lies they were being fed, they took to the streets in protest, where they were met with excessive punishment and brutality at the hands of the state's repressive apparatus. I wanted to talk about the seven UPR students facing federal charges and months in prison for interrupting a board of trustees meeting on April 27, 2017, at which the board was discussing proposed cuts to the UPR system to the tune of hundreds of millions of dollars.[3] I wanted to talk about the case of Nina Droz Franco, a young woman who, despite scant evidence, was arrested and eventually sentenced to three years in prison for supposedly attempting to set a fire at the Banco Popular Center building in the heart of San Juan's financial district during a 2017 May Day protest.[4] During her time in federal custody she has been subjected to intense surveillance and harassment.[5] I wanted to talk about Alejandro Medina Colón, who was run over by a police vehicle during a protest in front of the offices of the Fiscal Control Board organized by the activist group Se Acbaron las PROMESAS (The PROMISES Are Over) on February 20, 2018. I wanted to talk about how Scott Barbés and Damián Hernández Marrero were arrested for trying to help their comrade following the impact.[6]

I wanted to talk about how even in the diaspora, Puerto Ricans protesting PROMESA and la junta experience state violence and harassment. On February 1, 2018, the Fiscal Control Board held a "listening session" at the Alexander Hamilton Building in lower Manhattan. Hundreds of people converged on the federal building to protest and disrupt the junta's meeting. The New York Police Department deployed a heavy police presence to the area to confront protesters. NYPD officers, along with agents with the Department of Homeland Security and personnel from the private security firm ESC, which was charged with security for the Fiscal Control Board members, corralled protesters into the designated protest area and barred entry to the meeting. Officers from Homeland Security got rough with protesters and were captured on video shoving them without provocation.[7] A Puerto Rican photojournalist was prevented from entering the building to cover the event even after producing the necessary press credentials because he was deemed a threat to the security of the Fiscal Control Board.[8]

I wanted to talk about how the commonwealth government has doubled down on dirty economies in response to the fiscal crisis, creating "sacrifice zones" in low-income, racially marginalized areas in the big island's southeastern region.[9] In 2014 the private energy company AES, which owns a 454-megawatt coal-fired electric power plant in the town of Guayama, announced that it would be dumping the coal ash generated by the plant in local dumps. When AES finally revealed that it would be dumping this deadly waste in the small southern town of Peñuelas, Puerto Ricans responded by putting their bodies on the line to physically stop dozens of trucks from transporting the coal ash from Guayama to Peñuelas. The commonwealth government responded to these protests by mobilizing hundreds of police officers to act as armed escorts for the trucks carrying coal ash. In addition to facilitating toxic dumping, police used extreme force against protesters attempting to stop the trucks carrying ash from entering Peñuelas. I wanted to talk about how this highlights the various kinds of harm policing enacts in low-income and racially marginalized communities. I wanted to write about how the "slow violence" of environmental toxicity is just one facet of the various forms of violence that policing produces in already vulnerable communities.[10]

I wanted to talk about all of this. I wanted to spend the pages of this conclusion tying these stories to the larger story I tell about punitive governance and its impact on how life and death are experienced in Puerto Rico. I wanted to craft a conclusion not to neatly tie this story together, but to gesture toward the sometimes difficult-to-discern ways in which punitive governance, environmental degradation, and colonial violence are linked. But then Hurricane María happened.

．．．

On September 20, 2017, Hurricane María battered the archipelago in ways that no one was prepared for. Puerto Ricans had dealt with the effects of Hurricane Irma only two weeks before, which had caused damage around the archipelago and had hit vulnerable communities, like Loíza, particularly hard. Everyone knew María was going to be different; it was going to be much worse. I spoke to my father the day before the storm to check in. I knew my family would weather the storm well. My family is middle class and lives in the town of San Sebastían in the western interior of the big island. They have a cement house, two portable generators, large tanks of water reserves, and the money to stock up on necessary supplies. My father is a roofing contractor, and he knew how to prepare the house for the storm. When we spoke the day before the storm was supposed to hit, he told me that my brother and sister and stepmother were all home and ready; they would all hunker down together. I was relieved to hear this since my sister, at the time a student at UPR–Aguadilla, lived in a small apartment in a flood zone close to the beach with three other young women. My father told me he had checked on my grandmother and grandfather in their homes and made sure they were ready. He told me that my stepmother, who worked for the power authority, said the storm was going to be really bad and would likely knock out electricity for a while. None of us had any idea just how long it would be out.

Like millions of other people with familial ties to Puerto Rico, I watched with horror as the scope of the devastation revealed itself. The storm knocked out communication, and I was unable to reach my family. I imagined the worst even though I knew my family was economically privileged and therefore likely had been spared the deadly effects of the storm. For days I called nonstop, trying to reach my family members. My uncle, growing increasingly concerned and impatient with the situation, bought a plane ticket and traveled to Puerto Rico with cash and a satellite phone, determined to verify the family's well-being. Ten days after the storm, I spoke to my father on my uncle's satellite phone as he choked back tears and told me everyone was okay. This was a privilege. My family would have power and communication restored a couple of weeks later. Others were not so lucky.

Life and death in Puerto Rico are unevenly distributed along lines of race, class, region, sexuality, gender, and citizenship status. Natural disasters, such as Hurricane María, function to bring the divisions that structure society into sharper relief. While my family was undoubtedly affected by Hurricane

María, they were able to weather the storm well in comparison to other Puerto Ricans, not only because of their geographic location (i.e., far from where María made landfall) but also because they were middle class, they were not undocumented, and they did not live in a racially marginalized community. Those Puerto Ricans who, unlike my family, could not afford to make up for the government's disinvestment in their communities and infrastructure, were fully exposed to the deadly effects of the storm. In the aftermath of the storm, recovery efforts have similarly been unevenly distributed along racial, economic, and spatial hierarchies already at work in Puerto Rico. The most vulnerable within Puerto Rican society bore the brunt of the storm's effects and now are essentially being told to brace for more and more austerity or get out. Indeed, la junta has not slowed down its efforts to service Puerto Rico's debt in the face of the disaster and the humanitarian catastrophe it has caused. And the federal government is applying pressure on the Fiscal Control Board to speed up asset recovery for Puerto Rico's creditors.

Hurricane María brought to light not only the hierarchies that exist within Puerto Rican society but also the ways that colonial development schemes have consistently failed Puerto Ricans. Colonialism is an inherently extractive enterprise; it steals the bodies and resources of the colonized. Hurricane María revealed what colonial development and its ideological apparatus attempt to mask: that the current political arrangement works to make it impossible for Puerto Ricans to dictate the terms of their own future. Colonialism attempts to steal the future of the colonized, to make them believe there is no other way. Following Hurricane María, it was clear the federal and commonwealth governments were set on *rebuilding* Puerto Rico, or getting Puerto Rico back to the baseline "normal" needed for colonial capitalism to function efficiently, while many people increasingly asked what it would mean to *transform* Puerto Rican society.[11] Nothing demonstrates this juxtaposition more clearly than the commonwealth government's attempts to revive zombie policies that don't work but refuse to die, such as broken windows policing, in the aftermath of the storm against the responses of everyday Puerto Ricans to work toward new ways of living in Puerto Rico based on principles of solidarity and mutual aid.

After the New Year and about three months after María struck Puerto Rico, the US attorney in Puerto Rico, secretary of the Puerto Rico Department of Public Security, and Puerto Rico's secretary of justice all held a press conference and announced that they would be implementing broken-windows-style policing in response to a surge in murders. This news was already misleading, as it positioned broken windows as something new to Puerto Rico. Puerto Rico's secretary of justice, Wanda Vázquez, told those gathered, "We are a nation of law and order, and that's the way we're going to behave."[12] The officials said that they would be mobilizing local and federal resources to go after drivers with expired tags, with illegally tinted windows, or who run red lights. The logic was that people who commit these traffic violations are "the same people who commit murders," according to Vázquez.[13] This, again, was misleading, as anyone who has spent a significant amount of time in Puerto Rico could attest, because *comerse la luz*, literally "to eat the light," meaning to run a red light, particularly after midnight, is a practice that has been widely tolerated by law enforcement in order to prevent carjackings since at least the early 1990s. So, yes, people who commit murders are probably running red lights, but in the early morning hours, so are a whole lot of Puerto Ricans just trying to get home from work or a night out. Despite the fact that broken windows was not new and that it would be targeting a widely tolerated illegality, law enforcement officials promised the public that this aggressive policing would alleviate the feelings of insecurity that many felt following María. As this book has shown with example after example, this is a false promise.

Here, in the aftermath of the storm, we see again the ways in which punitive governance deploys simplistic responses to complex social problems. It is true that Puerto Rico saw a spike in homicides following the storm, but broken-windows targeting of low-level traffic violations would never come close to addressing their causes or reducing their occurrence. For instance, broken-windows policing would not have stopped someone from being killed in the process of trying to steal a neighbor's generator because they could not face another day *sin luz*. Broken windows would not have protected the women and children experiencing domestic violence who, following the storm, found themselves with few alternative housing options and stuck in volatile situations with the potential to turn deadly.[14] Broken windows didn't address the fact that Puerto Rico was essentially cash only before power was restored and that some people turned to robbery and theft in order to secure food and other basic necessities. Broken-windows policing would not change the fact that the drug economy, just like every other business in Puerto Rico, was upended by the storm. Gangs fought to retain or expand their territory, and addicted individuals encountered increasing difficulty in accessing the criminalized drugs they depend on, which undoubtedly contributed to increased rates of violence. And broken windows certainly wouldn't have decreased the alarmingly high numbers of Puerto Ricans killing themselves in the wake of the storm because a future in the archipelago seems utterly impossible for more and more people with few resources.[15]

In many ways, these are problems that the commonwealth government is ill equipped or unable to deal with because of the constraints of colonialism in Puerto Rico. These are also complex forms of violence that can't be dealt with by simply trying to arrest, detain, and incapacitate vulnerable and traumatized populations. But of course that doesn't mean the state won't try to do just that. Dealing with these complex problems and preventing their harmful outcomes in the future means a fundamental transformation in the current sociopolitical and economic systems, one that political elites in Puerto Rico and the United States are unwilling to entertain. As a result, the local and federal governments have joined together to react to, as opposed to prevent, violence by implementing punitive measures that are meant to communicate that *something* is being done, all while maintaining the existing social order based in extraction and exploitation of the land and people.

The revival of useless political strategies—broken-windows policing and the expanded efforts to court foreign investors to Puerto Rico with significant tax breaks at the expense of the local population—and the failure to provide Puerto Ricans with adequate and necessary disaster relief following Hurricane Maria have reaffirmed for many that the state will not provide for them. After the storm, the notion that only the people will save the people— *que es el pueblo que va salvar el pueblo*—gained traction and expanded on grassroots networks that were initially created before the storm to deal with the effects of the mounting debt crisis on the everyday lives of Puerto Ricans. The groups and collectives that distributed necessities, cleared debris from the roads, set up drinking water oases, tarped roofs, and made sure that people had nutritious food to eat saved lives and ensured people's survival in those days and weeks immediately following the storm. Importantly, as the immediate effects of the storm have dissipated, these groups continue their work trying to repair not only what María ravaged but also what Puerto Rico's prolonged fiscal crisis had already threatened. These survival programs work to model an alternative Puerto Rican society, one based in the principle of *autogestión*, or self-management. *Autogestión* proceeds from the idea that the communities themselves are best able to assess and address their own needs. In other words, if given the space and resources, communities can solve the issues that confront them through solidarity and mutual support.

Unsurprisingly, Taller Salud has emerged as a key player in the Red de Apoyo Mutuo Autogestionada, or Self-Managed Mutual Aid Network, that expanded following the storm. Taller Salud, along with other groups such as Brigada Solidaria del Oeste, IDEBAJO/Coqui Solar, El Hormiguero, Comedores Sociales, and dozens of Centros de Apoyo Mutuo (mutual aid centers) around the archipelago are engaged in revolutionary praxis aimed at responding to the crises provoked by colonialism while working with community members to cultivate empowerment and a sustainable future for *all* Puerto Ricans. Perhaps also unsurprisingly, many of these groups count alumni of the 2010 and 2011 UPR *huelga* among their ranks, as the fight to protect public education stoked a desire to work toward a different future for many of these student movement *veteranxs*. These groups subvert the circuits of colonial capitalism at work in Puerto Rico by promoting solidarity as the way forward. They draw on political traditions and ideologies ranging from anarchism to abolition to radical feminism, refusing to allow colonial capitalism to shape their vision of Puerto Rico's future. While the collision of colonial capitalism and environmental catastrophe has left a trail of physical destruction and physic trauma in its wake that will likely impact Puerto Rico and Puerto Ricans for years to come, there are Puerto Ricans on the ground working toward a future grounded in notions of justice and freedom with the potential to dismantle the systems of inequality maintained by punitive governance.

NOTES

INTRODUCTION

1. Giovanni Roberto, interview by the author, Río Piedras, Puerto Rico, January 31, 2012.

2. Roberto interview, January 31, 2012.

3. United States Department of Justice, Civil Rights Division, "Investigation of the Puerto Rico Police Department," September 5, 2011, 5, www.justice.gov/sites /default/files/crt/legacy/2011/09/08/prpd_letter.pdf. For more on the DOJ's investigation of the PRPD, see Marisol LeBrón, "Neocolonial Policing in Puerto Rico," *NACLA Report on the Americas* 45, no. 1 (2011): 12–16.

4. USDOJ, "Investigation of the Puerto Rico Police Department," 44–45.

5. Policía de Puerto Rico, "Reglas para el uso de la fuerza por miembros de la Policía de Puerto Rico" (OG-2012-601), January 31, 2012. Translation by author.

6. "Peligrosa arma en la Policía," *El Nuevo Día*, January 30, 2012, www.elnuevodia .com/noticias/locales/nota/peligrosaarmaenlapolicia-1177902. Translation by author.

7. Much like the terms *zero tolerance* and *broken windows*, in recent years *mano dura* has become shorthand for punitive police practices broadly, particularly those targeting low-income communities in Puerto Rico or those marked by brutality. In this way, mano dura is not solely confined to the 1990s for most Puerto Ricans; rather, it is understood by many Puerto Ricans as informing policing in the present day.

I use the term *archipelago* to refer to Puerto Rico throughout this book as opposed to the more common designation "the island." Puerto Rico consists of a big island as well as two small island municipalities, Vieques and Culebra. The island municipalities are often rendered invisible through the designation of Puerto Rico as simply "the island." In addition, we can conceptualize Puerto Rico as an archipelago not only in terms of its geography but also in terms of its patterns of diasporic settlement. Thus, *archipelago* is a more inclusive and accurate term that acknowledges the geographic and historical realities of contemporary Puerto Ricans.

8. Roberto interview, January 31, 2012.

9. Throughout this book I use the phrases "the state" and "the Puerto Rican state" to refer to the Puerto Rican government and its agents. I realize, of course, that within the context of continued US colonial control, making claims about the will or agenda of the Puerto Rican state can be difficult; still, I employ this phrasing while recognizing the way in which US imperatives can influence the actions of the Puerto Rican government and its agents.

10. Anthropologist Roger Lancaster defines punitive governance as the erosion of liberal notions of burden of proof, which result in a presumption of guilt and a predisposition to crime on the part of offenders. This inversion of a common law concept—being innocent until proven guilty—results in "more stringent laws and disciplinary measures" aimed at incapacitating threats. He notes: "In practice no parsing of the offense ever seems sufficiently through, no punishment is ever quite enough, and no monitoring regime ever proves sufficiently vigilant. Punitive governance is punitive justice codified, writ large, and suffused throughout a wider body of practices." My understanding of punitive governance builds upon Lancaster's; however, I depart from his analysis in that I don't view punitive governance as a break from legal norms but rather as an extension of the entrenched, legal hierarchies of freedom and unfreedom that structure so-called liberal democracies based in colonial and capitalist exploitation. For more see Roger Lancaster, *Sex Panic and the Punitive State* (Berkeley: University of California Press, 2011).

11. Activist groups, in addition to mainstream legal and civil rights organizations, have noted patterns of targeted harassment and harm directed at non-Puerto Ricans residing in the archipelago. Dominicans, Haitians, and other Caribbean im/migrants, particularly those who are Black, have experienced tremendous police violence and repression in Puerto Rico. I do not engage extensively with the policing of Caribbean im/migrants and their decedents living in Puerto Rico, although it does enter into the narrative at select moments I hope this book can be useful to future researchers exploring how punitive governance is exercised against Black Caribbean im/migrants living in Puerto Rico.

12. Lisa Marie Cacho, *Social Death: Racialized Rightlessness and the Criminalization of the Unprotected* (New York: New York University Press, 2012), 4–5.

13. Cacho, *Social Death*, 4–5.

14. Ruth Wilson Gilmore, *Golden Gulag: Prisons, Surplus, Crisis, and Opposition in Globalizing California* (Berkeley: University of California Press, 2007), 26.

15. Déborah Berman Santana, *Kicking Off the Bootstraps: Environment, Development, and Community Power in Puerto Rico* (Tucson: University of Arizona Press, 1996), 43.

16. Gina Pérez, *The Near Northwest Side Story: Migration, Displacement, and Puerto Rican Families* (Berkeley: University of California Press, 2004), 9.

17. Emilio Pantojas-García, *Development Strategies as Ideology: Puerto Rico's Export-Led Industrialization Experience* (Boulder, CO: Lynne Rienner Publishers, 1990), 83.

18. See, for example, James Dietz, *Economic History of Puerto Rico: Institutional Change and Capitalist Development* (Princeton: Princeton University Press, 1986), 227–228.

19. For more information on population control measures in Puerto Rico, including sterilization campaigns during the Operation Bootstrap era, see Laura Briggs, *Reproducing Empire: Race, Sex, Science, and U.S. Imperialism in Puerto Rico* (Berkeley: University of California Press, 2002) and Iris Lopez, *Matters of Choice: Puerto Rican Women's Struggle for Reproductive Freedom* (New Brunswick, NJ: Rutgers University Press 2008).

20. Pantojas-García, *Development Strategies as Ideology*, 121.

21. James L. Dietz, *Puerto Rico: Negotiating Development and Change* (Boulder: Lynne Rienner Publishers, 2003), 27n22.

22. Emilio Pantojas-García, "'Federal Funds' and the Puerto Rican Economy: Myths and Realities," *Centro Journal* 19, no. 2 (2007): 209.

23. Edwin Melendez and Edgardo Melendez, introduction to *Colonial Dilemma: Critical Perspectives on Contemporary Puerto Rico*, ed. Edwin Melendez and Edgardo Melendez (Boston: South End Press, 1993), 8.

24. As sociologist Sudhir Vankatesh explains, "At its core, the underground economy is a widespread set of activities, usually scattered and not well integrated, through which people earn money that is not reported to the government and that, in some cases, may entail criminal behavior." See Sudhir Alladi Venkatesh, *Off the Books: The Underground Economy of the Urban Poor* (Cambridge, MA: Harvard University Press, 2009), 8.

25. For information on the informal economy, particularly the drug economy, and its impact, see Ileanexis Vera Rosado, "Imparable la economía informal en la Isla," *El Vocero*, May 9, 2014, http://elvocero.com/imparable-la-economia-informal -en-la-isla; "Economía subterránea de Puerto Rico ronda los $14,000 millones," *El Nuevo Día*, February 16, 2012, www.elnuevodia.com/negocios/consumo/nota/eco nomiasubterraneadepuertoricorondalosi4000millones-1192485; and "Si no mejora la economía no baja el crimen," *El Nuevo Día*, September 25, 2011, www.elnuevodia .com/noticias/locales/nota/sinomejoralaeconomianobajaelcrimen-1075677.

26. Ruth Wilson Gilmore points out that both crime and drug use were in decline when California embarked on its massive prison buildup. Thus, the state's investment in punitive technologies responded to political, economic, and social crises as opposed to increased levels of crime, violence, and/or drug use. See Gilmore, *Golden Gulag*, 17–24.

27. Stuart Hall et al., *Policing the Crisis: Mugging, the State, and Law and Order* (London: Macmillan, 1978), viii.

28. Hall et al., *Policing the Crisis*, viii.

29. Legal scholar and activist Dean Spade provides an excellent review of this literature in the introduction and first chapter of his book *Normal Life: Administrative Violence, Critical Trans Politics, and the Limits of Law* (Brooklyn: South End Press, 2011).

30. See Zaire Zenit Dinzey-Flores, *Locked In, Locked Out: Gated Communities in a Puerto Rican City* (Philadelphia: University of Pennsylvania Press, 2013).

31. For critiques of Puerto Rico's color-blind discourses, see Carlos Alamo-Pastrana, *Seams of Empire: Race and Radicalism in Puerto Rico and the United States* (Gainesville: University Press of Florida, 2016); Dinzey-Flores, *Locked In, Locked Out*; Isar P. Godreau, *Scripts of Blackness: Race, Cultural Nationalism, and U.S. Colonialism in Puerto Rico* (Urbana: University of Illinois Press, 2015); Ileana M. Rodríguez-Silva, *Silencing Race: Disentangling Blackness, Colonialism, and National Identities in Puerto Rico* (New York: Palgrave Macmillan, 2012); and Hilda Lloréns, *Imaging the Great Puerto Rican Family: Framing Nation, Race, and Gender During the American Century* (Lanham, MD: Lexington Books, 2014).

32. Rodríguez-Silva, *Silencing Race*, 1.

33. Lloréns, *Imaging the Great Puerto Rican Family*, 21.

34. Alamo-Pastrana, *Seams of Empire*, 7.

35. Alamo-Pastrana, *Seams of Empire*, 7–8.

36. For more on the concept of color-blind racism, see Eduardo Bonilla-Silva, *Racism without Racists: Color-Blind Racism and the Persistence of Racial Inequality in America*, 4th ed. (Lanham, MD: Rowman & Littlefield Publishers, 2013).

37. George Lipsitz, *How Racism Takes Place* (Philadelphia: Temple University Press, 2011), 5.

38. Lipsitz, *How Racism Takes Place*, 15.

39. Arlene Torres, "La gran familia Puertorriqueña 'ej prieta de bledá' (The Great Puerto Rican Family Is Really Really Black)," in *Blackness in Latin American and the Caribbean*, vol. 2, ed. Arlene Torres and Norman Whitten (Bloomington, Indiana University Press, 1998), 295–296.

40. Torres, "La gran familia Puertorriqueña 'ej prieta de bledá,'" 295–296.

41. Petra R. Rivera-Rideau, *Remixing Reggaetón: The Cultural Politics of Race in Puerto Rico* (Durham, NC: Duke University Press, 2015), 10.

42. Rivera-Rideau, *Remixing Reggaetón*, 11.

43. Godreau, *Scripts of Blackness*, 5.

44. This number is currently in flux with the combined catastrophes of the debt crisis and Hurricane María as police officers, like other Puerto Ricans, have left the archipelago in the past five years in search of greater stability and economic opportunity.

45. David Correia and Tyler Wall, *Police: A Field Guide* (Brooklyn: Verso, 2018), 6.

46. In 1842 Karl Marx wrote a series of articles about the theft of wood that show how definitions of crime and the subsequent enforcement of laws are foundational to the functions of capital. According to Marxist historian Peter Linebaugh, Marx's early writings demonstrate how crime functions as "capital's most ancient tool in the creation and control of the working class," helping us to recognize how, as a creation stemming from the needs of capital, policing as a structure is inherently opposed to working-class and low-income people, who are simultaneously seen as threats and essential to processes of capital accumulation. For more see Peter

Linebaugh, "Karl Marx, the Theft of Wood, and Working Class Composition: A Contribution to the Current Debate," *Crime and Social Justice* 6 (Fall–Winter 1976): 5–16.

47. For more on the concept of violence workers see Martha K. Huggins, Mika Haritos-Fatouros, and Philip G. Zimbardo, *Violence Workers: Police Torturers and Murderers Reconstruct Brazilian Atrocities* (Berkeley: University of California Press, 2002).

48. Sam Mitrani, *The Rise of the Chicago Police Department: Class and Conflict, 1850–1894* (Champaign: University of Illinois Press, 2014), 4.

49. Mitrani, *The Rise of the Chicago Police Department*, 11.

50. Mitrani, *The Rise of the Chicago Police Department*, 11.

51. Nikhil Pal Singh, "The Whiteness of the Police," *American Quarterly* 66, no. 4 (2014): 1092.

52. Singh, "The Whiteness of the Police," 1096.

53. Singh, "The Whiteness of the Police," 1093.

54. Spade, *Normal Life*, 27.

55. Mel Y. Chen, *Animacies: Biopolitics, Racial Mattering, and Queer Affect* (Durham, NC: Duke University Press, 2012), 234.

56. Donna Murch, "Who's to Blame for Mass Incarceration?," *Boston Review*, October 16, 2015, http://bostonreview.net/books-ideas/donna-murch-michael-javen -fortner-black-silent-majority.

57. Murch, "Who's to Blame for Mass Incarceration?"

58. Stuart Hall, "Encoding, Decoding," in *The Cultural Studies Reader*, 2nd ed., ed. Simon During (London: Routledge, 1993), 93 and 98–99.

59. Paul Chevigny, *Edge of the Knife: Police Violence in the Americas* (New York: The New Press, 1995), 33; and Didier Fassin, *Enforcing Order: An Ethnography of Urban Policing* (Cambridge, UK: Polity Press, 2013), 17–21.

CHAPTER 1. A WAR AGAINST THE VICTIMS

1. See Gino Ponti, "Group of UPR Professors Assail Police Ad on Housing Takeovers," *San Juan Star*, May 17, 1994, 3 and 6.

2. Lorraine Blasor, "Toledo Defends Force's $700,000 Ad Campaign," *San Juan Star*, August 10, 1994, 4.

3. Ponti, "Group of UPR Professors Assail Police Ad," 6.

4. Alfredo Carrasquillo Ramírez discusses Goachet's remarks on Carmen Jovet's show at length in "Los enemigos del orden: La mano dura contra el crimen y la legitimación del poder político en Puerto Rico, 1992–1995" (MA thesis, Centro de Estudios Avanzados de Puerto Rico y el Caribe, 2002).

5. Harvey Simon, "Mano Dura: Mobilizing the National Guard to Battle Crime in Puerto Rico (Epilogue)" (Kennedy School of Government Case Program, Case No. C109-97-1390.0, 1997), 4.

6. For a discussion of how colorblind rhetoric justifies racially disproportionate policing and incarceration, see Michelle Alexander, *The New Jim Crow: Mass Incarceration in the Age of Colorblindness* (New York: The New Press, 2012).

7. Scholar and activist Ruth Wilson Gilmore notes that racism must be understood as "the state-sanctioned or extralegal production and exploitation of group-differentiated vulnerability to premature death." I draw from her definition to understand how racial hierarchies of power and difference always structure conditions of harm, vulnerability, and proximity to death. For more see, Gilmore, *Golden Gulag: Prisons, Surplus, Crisis, and Opposition in Globalizing California.*

8. As is still the case, during the late 1980s the Puerto Rican press began to categorize gangland-style murders involving three or more people as "massacres." For more information see Jorge L. Giovannetti, "Puerto Rico: An Island of Massacres," *Global Dialogue: Newsletter for the International Sociological Association* 3, no. 5 (2013), http://isa-global-dialogue.net/puerto-rico-an-island-of -massacres.

9. Dinzey-Flores, *Locked In, Locked Out*, 39–41; and Luz Marie Rodríguez, "Suppressing the Slum! Architecture and Social Change in San Juan's Public Housing," in *San Juan Siempre Nuevo: Arquitectura y Modernización en el Siglo XX*, ed. Enrique Vivoni Falagio (Río Piedras: Archivo de Arquitectura y Construcción Universidad de Puerto Rico, 2000), 74–117.

10. José I. Fusté, "Colonial Laboratories, Irreparable Subjects: The Experiment of '(B)ordering' San Juan's Public Housing Residents," *Social Identities* 16, no. 1 (2010): 55.

11. Dinzey-Flores, *Locked In, Locked Out*, 41.

12. Ivelisse Rivera-Bonilla, "Divided City: The Proliferation of Gated Communities in San Juan" (PhD diss., University of California at Santa Cruz, 2003), 13.

13. The turn to gating in Puerto Rico mirrors similar trends in other societies with extreme wealth disparities. Gated residential enclaves became popular in US suburbs and gentrifying urban areas, especially in California and Florida, in the post–World War II period. Gating also became popular in Brazil, South Africa, and Israel/Palestine over the course of the late twentieth century as a way of managing unequal and increasingly volatile power relations rooted in racial and spatial domination. For information on gating in Puerto Rico, see Dinzey-Flores, *Locked In, Locked Out*. For information on gated communities in the United States, see Edward J. Blakely and Mary G. Snyder, *Fortress America: Gated Communities in the United States* (Washington, DC: The Brookings Institution, 1999); and Setha Low, *Behind the Gates: Life, Security, and the Pursuit of Happiness in Fortress America* (New York: Routledge, 2004). For information on gated communities in Brazil, South Africa, and Israel/Palestine, see Teresa Caldeira, *City of Walls: Crime, Segregation, and Citizenship in São Paulo* (Berkeley: University of California Press, 2000), Martin J. Murray, *Taming the Disorderly City: The Spatial Landscape of Johannesburg after Apartheid* (Ithaca, NY: Cornell University Press, 2008); and Stephan Graham, *Cities Under Siege: The New Military Urbanism* (London: Verso, 2010).

14. Fernando Picó, *De la mano dura a la cordura: Ensayos sobre el estado ausente, la sociabilidad y los imaginarios puertorriqueños* (Río Piedras, PR: Ediciones Huracán, Inc., 1999), 10. Translation by author.

15. Nilka Estrada Resto, "Descartar tirar a la calle la guardia nacional," *El Nuevo Día*, September 11, 1991, www.adendi.com/archivo.asp?num=46942&year=1991&month=9&keyword=.

16. Pedro Rosselló, *A mi manera*, vol. 1 (Gurabo, PR: Sistema Universitario Ana G. Méndez, 2012), 204.

17. Carmen Enid Acevedo, "Diecinueve arrestados en el operativo en las acacias," *El Nuevo Día*, June 6, 1991, www.adendi.com/archivo.asp?num=28994&year=1991&month=6&keyword=. Translation by author.

18. Keeanga-Yamahtta Taylor, *From #Blacklivesmatter to Black Liberation* (Chicago: Haymarket Books, 2016), 69.

19. Elizabeth Hinton, *From the War on Poverty to the War on Crime: The Making of Mass Incarceration in America* (Cambridge, MA: Harvard University Press, 2016), 9.

20. The death penalty was abolished in 1929 in Puerto Rico, and the Commonwealth Constitution explicitly forbids capital punishment. In 1994 President Bill Clinton signed the Federal Death Penalty Act, which federalized certain crimes, allowing them to be tried as capital offences regardless of states' or territories' positions on the death penalty. As César J. Ayala and Rafael Bernabe note, "The fact that federal courts in Puerto Rican can nonetheless impose the death penalty is a stark commentary on the limited reach of the insular constitution." For more see César J. Ayala and Rafael Bernabe, *Puerto Rico in the American Century: A History Since 1898* (Chapel Hill: University of North Carolina Press, 2007), 314.

21. For more on "talk of crime" see Caldeira, *City of Walls*, 1–2.

22. Joel A. Villa Rodríguez, *Crimen y criminalidad en Puerto Rico: El sujeto criminal* (San Juan: Ediciones SITUM, Inc., 2006), 252. Translation by author.

23. Legal scholar Jonathan Simon discusses the ways that lawmakers have implicitly and explicitly crafted laws that identify victims as idealized subjects whose needs and experiences increasingly stand in for the general good. For more see Jonathan Simon, *Governing Through Crime: How the War on Crime Transformed American Democracy and Created a Culture of Fear* (Oxford: Oxford University Press, 2007), 109–110.

24. Hall et al., *Policing the Crisist*, 21.

25. Pedro Rosselló, *Executive Order of the Governor of the Commonwealth of Puerto Rico to Order the Activation and Utilization of the Personnel and Equipment of the National Guard of Puerto Rico* (OE-1993-08), February 25, 1993.

26. Jorge Luis Medina, "Rosselló: I Have the People's Mandate, Not the Protestors," *San Juan Star*, January 26, 1993, 4.

27. Harvey Simon, "Mano Dura: Mobilizing the National Guard to Battle Crime in Puerto Rico," Kennedy School of Government Case Program, Case No. C109-97-1390.0 (1997), 8.

28. Simon, "Mano Dura."

29. Villa Rodríguez, *Crimen y criminalidad en Puerto Rico*, 238–239.

30. Alfredo Montalvo-Barbot, "Crime in Puerto Rico: Drug Trafficking, Money Laundering, and the Poor," *Crime & Delinquency* 43, no. 4 (1997): 535.

31. Rivera-Bonilla, "Divided City," 302. It should be noted that this figure does not include when police reoccupied public housing complexes, such as was the case with Nemesio Canales. In addition, this figure does not represent the police occupation of neighborhoods such as La Perla and Barrio Obrero, which also occurred during this period.

32. Trina Rivera de Ríos, "Caseríos: ¿Reservaciones nativas militares-policiacas?," *Claridad*, June 24, 1993, 14. Translation by author.

33. Larry Luxner, "Police Action in La Perla Prompts Legal Questions," *San Juan Star*, March 3, 1994, 5.

34. According to Zaire Dinzey-Flores, "Gated housing for the poor and the affluent has fostered a formal division of communities and has broken contact across class and race." See Dinzey-Flores, *Locked In, Locked Out*, xiii.

35. Dora Nevares-Muñiz, *El crimen en Puerto Rico: Tapando el cielo con la mano*, 3rd ed.(San Juan: Instituto para el Desarrollo del Derecho, 2008), 136. Translation by author.

36. Nevares-Muñiz, *El Crimen en Puerto Rico*, 135. Translation by author.

37. Irmarilis González Torres, "¡No hay cárcel pa' tanta gente!," *Masturbana*, December 1994, 17. Translation by author.

38. Montalvo-Barbot, "Crime in Puerto Rico," 542. See also Jorge Luis Medina, "Rossello Denies Bias in Anti-drug Tactic," *San Juan Star*, June 24, 1993, 7; and Miguel Rivera Puig, "Super sera dura en los 'puntos'; pondera cartas," *El Vocero*, June 26, 1993, 6.

39. Medina, "Rossello Denies Bias in Anti-drug Tactic," 7.

40. Andrea Martínez, "Advierte de 'estrategia criminal' contra la operación antidrogas," *El Nuevo Día*, June 11, 1993, 18. Translation by author.

41. José Rafael Reguero, "Ráfagas de indignación en el residencial," *El Nuevo Día*, June 5, 1993, 8. Translation by author.

42. Laura Candelas, "Rosselló dice ante criticas: 'Operativos están dentro ley,'" *El Vocero*, July 1, 1993, 18. Translation by author.

43. Karl Ross, "Animosity Toward Cops Is Order of the Day in Las Gladiolas," *San Juan Star*, July 16, 1995, 2.

44. Miguel Díaz Ramón, "Ecos de un pasado doloroso," *El NuevoDía*, February 7, 2010, www.elnuevodia.com/ecosdeunpasadodoloroso-668746.html. Translation by author.

45. Ross, "Animosity Toward Cops Is Order of the Day in Las Gladiolas."

46. Luxner, "Hundreds Protest La Perla closure," *San Juan Star*, March 5, 1994, 4.

47. Gino Ponti, "El Trebol Project Takeover Far from a Rousing Success," *San Juan Star*, March 3, 1994, 3.

48. Ross, "Animosity Toward Cops Is Order of the Day in Las Gladiolas."

49. Ross, "Animosity Toward Cops Is Order of the Day in Las Gladiolas."

50. Ross, "Animosity Toward Cops Is Order of the Day in Las Gladiolas."

51. This reconstruction of the events that occurred on September 8, 1993, and resulted in the death of José Rosario Díaz draws from the following news sources: Milvia Y. Archilla Rivera, "Caseríos: Victimas de la Mano Dura," *Claridad*, September 17–23, 1993, 4–5; Gino Ponti, "Officer Charged in Shooting Death," *San Juan Star*, May 20, 1994, 6; and Ingrid Ortega Borges, "Denuncian a los Jefes Policiacos," *El Nuevo Día*, September 4, 1994, 15. Information about officer Díaz Martínez's mental instability and long history of violence draws from the following court records: *Camilo-Robles v. Zapata*, 175 F.3d 141 (1st Cir. 1999); *Camilo-Roblez v. Hoyos*, 151 F.3d 1 (1st Cir. 1998); *Rosario Díaz v. González*, 140 F.3d 312 (1st Cir. 1998); and *Diáz v. Martínez*, 112 F.3d 1 (1st Cir. 1998).

52. Archilla Rivera, "Caseríos: Victimas de la Mano Dura," 4–5. Translation by author.

53. Nevares-Muñiz, *El crimen en Puerto* Rico, 135. Translation by author.

54. *The National Guard: Potential Uses in Crime-Fighting: Hearing before the Subcommittee on Crime and Criminal Justice, Committee on the Judiciary, House of Representatives* (October 5, 1994) (testimony of Nkechi Taifa, legislative counsel for the ACLU).

55. Judith Berkan, interview by the author, San Juan, Puerto Rico, November 30, 2011.

56. Berkan interview, November 30, 2011.

57. Díaz Ramón, "Ecos de un pasado doloroso." Translation by author.

58. Díaz Ramón, "Ecos de un pasado doloroso."

59. Zaire Dinzey-Flores, "Criminalizing Communities of Poor, Dark Women in the Caribbean: The Fight against Crime through Puerto Rico's Public Housing," *Crime Prevention and Community Safety* 13, no. 1 (2011): 65.

60. Dinzey-Flores, "Criminalizing Communities of Poor, Dark Women in the Caribbean," 67.

61. Dinzey-Flores, "Criminalizing Communities of Poor, Dark Women in the Caribbean," 68.

62. Edwin González, "La Maldad dentro de la bolsa," *Claridad*, April 7–13, 1995, 14.

63. While Puerto Rico's rural interior witnessed a growth of drug dealing and drug use during the mano dura era, the bulk of activity surrounding the informal, drug-based economy continued to occur in the metropolitan areas of San Juan, Ponce, and Mayagüez. The bloodiest battles over puntos continued to be seen in the San Juan area, due perhaps to sheer population density.

64. Speaking about Washington, D.C.'s Operation Clean Sweep, journalist and sociologist Christian Parenti notes, "[T]here is considerable evidence that Clean Sweep's mass arrests and constant police pressure merely fueled violence by stirring rivalries, destabilizing dealers' business networks, hierarchies, and turf arrangements, and setting off bloody power struggles, suspicions, and turf feuds." For more on the ghetto sweeps that wracked US cities, see Christian Parenti, *Lockdown America: Police and Prisons in the Age of Crisis*, 2nd ed. (New York: Verso Books, 2008), 58–60.

65. Gino Ponti, "Rio Piedras Project Taken over in 7th Police, Guard Raid," *San Juan Star*, June 16, 1993, 10.

66. Nilka Estrada Resto, "Cosecha fatal de plan anticrimen," *El Nuevo Día*, August 5, 1992, 5. Translation by author.

67. Estrada Resto, "Cosecha fatal de plan anticrimen," 5.

68. Michel Foucault, *The Birth of Biopolitics: Lectures at the Collège de France, 1978–1979* (New York: Picador, 2010).

69. John D. Márquez describes a similar logic and outcome in respect to im/migrant deaths along the US-Mexico border. Citing Doris Meissner, former commissioner of the US Immigration and Naturalization Service (INS), who said death and "violence will increase as the effects of the strategy are felt," Márquez notes: "This seems like a clear example that the state planned to not only let immigrants die, but to also encourage their death in large numbers as a means to secure the border from the transnational flow of laborers." See John D. Márquez, "Latinos as the 'Living Dead': Raciality, Expendability, and Border Militarization," *Latino Studies* 10, no. 4 (2012): 484–485.

70. As geographer Laura Pulido demonstrates in her work on environmental racism, an emphasis on intent rather than outcome often demands evidence of individual hostility or maliciousness, obscuring the structural forces at play that allow certain populations to be disproportionately exposed to harm. For more, see Laura Pulido, "Rethinking Environmental Racism: White Privilege and Urban Development in Southern California," *Annals of the Association of American Geographers* 90, no. 1 (2000): 17–19.

71. Kelly Lytle Hernández, *Migra! A History of the U.S. Border Patrol* (Berkeley: University of California Press, 2010), 132.

72. Villa Rodríguez, *Crimen y criminalidad en Puerto Rico*, 246–247. Translation by author.

73. Karl Ross, "Project Crime Spilling into Tamer Areas," *San Juan Star*, n.d., 3, 8.

74. "Al que no quiere caldo . . .," *El Nuevo Día*, August 22, 1993, 3.

75. Judith Butler, *Precarious Life: The Powers of Mourning and Violence* (New York: Verso, 2006), xv.

76. "Puerto Rico Uses National Guard to Fight Crime," *All Things Considered*, National Public Radio (NPR), December 7, 1993.

77. Carmen Enid Acevedo, "Parches a los aquejados residenciales," *El Nuevo Día*, May 6, 1994. Translation by author.

78. Díaz Ramón, "Ecos de un pasado doloroso." Translation by author.

79. Luz Zenaida Vélez Pérez, "Sitiado el Caserío," letter to the editor, *El Nuevo Día*, September 7, 1993. Translation by author.

CHAPTER 2. COLONIAL PROJECTS

1. United States Coast Guard, "Courageous, WMEC-622, Cutter History," www.uscg.mil/history/webcutters/Courageous1968.asp (accessed September 27, 2012; URL no longer active).

2. *The Rising Drug Threat and Some Recent Successes: Subcommittee on National Security, International Affairs, and Criminal Justice of the Committee on Government Reform and Oversight*, 104th Cong., 2nd sess. (Washington, DC: U.S. Government Printing Office, 1997).

3. Historian Michael Lapp notes that Puerto Rico's last US-appointed governor, Rexford G. Tugwell, popularized the idea of Puerto Rico as a "social laboratory" during the early 1940s. Tugwell, a New Dealer, sought to transform Puerto Rico into a social laboratory for projects of governance that could be put into practice in the United States. As Operation Bootstrap unfolded during the 1950s, urban planners, economists, sociologists, and other academic researchers flocked to Puerto Rico to experiment with models for Third World economic and social development. While the history of social policy experimentation in Puerto Rico is one of the reasons the idea of Puerto Rico as a laboratory holds particular resonance, many scholars have also researched its use as a literal testing ground for birth control, Agent Orange, and radiation treatment for cancer, producing studies that have shown how Puerto Rico has functioned as a laboratory for the United States. For more information see Michael Lapp, "The Rise and Fall of Puerto Rico as a Social Laboratory, 1945–1965," *Social Science History* 19, no. 2 (1995): 169–199.

4. Briggs, *Reproducing Empire*, 2.

5. Radley Balko, *Rise of the Warrior Cop: The Militarization of America's Police Forces* (New York: Public Affairs, 2013).

6. Scott Ware, "The Power of Change," *San Juan Star*, January 3, 1993, 41.

7. Ware, "The Power of Change," 41.

8. Ware, "The Power of Change," 41.

9. Dietz, *Puerto Rico*, 27n23.

10. Larry Rohter, "NAFTA Seen as Threat to P.R. Economy," *San Juan Star*, January 3, 1993.

11. Rohter, "NAFTA Seen as Threat to P.R. Economy."

12. Rohter, "NAFTA Seen as Threat to P.R. Economy."

13. Rohter, "NAFTA Seen as Threat to P.R. Economy."

14. Ivonne Garcia, "Rosselló, Salinas Meet to Stimulate Business Ties," *San Juan Star*, March 1, 1994, 3.

15. Garcia, "Rosselló, Salinas Meet to Stimulate Business Ties," 3.

16. Robert Friedman, "Rossello Describes P.R. as Asset to U.S. during Talks with Clinton," *San Juan Star*, May 17, 1994, 4.

17. Pedro Rosselló, "Address by Pedro Rosselló Delivered Before Executives and Guests of the Bank of Boston" (Boston, MA, July 15, 1994).

18. Rosselló, "Address by Pedro Rosselló Delivered Before Executives and Guests." . Emphasis in original.

19. Rosselló, "Address by Pedro Rosselló Delivered Before Executives and Guests."

20. Pedro Rosselló, "Discurso del Gobernador Pedro Rosselló ante los miembros de la Cámara de Comercio Americana en Republica Dominicana" (Hotel Lina, Santo Domingo, January 11, 1995).

21. Named for the "great liberator," Simón de Bolívar, the Bolivarian dream refers to the effort to create a unified Latin American confederation free from colonial rule. Rosselló invokes Bolivarianism in an attempt to cement Puerto Rico's place in Latin America, given the US capital interest in the region following the signing of NAFTA.

22. Of course this logic is deeply flawed, as Puerto Ricans have constantly been repaying their "debt" to the United States since the extension of American citizenship through the Jones Act in 1917. Puerto Ricans have fought in every American war since World War I; they have been a continuous source of low-waged labor for US industry; they have been guinea pigs for medical experimentation, including the development of radiation treatment for cancer and birth control; and the archipelago itself has provided a tax shelter for American capital since the early twentieth century.

23. Pedro Rosselló, "Discurso del Gobernador Pedro Rosselló en los actos de celebración del natalicio del Prócer José Celso Barbosa" (Bayamón, Puerto Rico, July 27, 1994). (Ellipses in original transcript of speech.) Translation by author.

24. As César Ayala and Rafael Bernabe put it: "For the PNP to insist on the pro-statehood discourse elaborated in the early 1970s was to set itself against the new dominant currents in U.S. politics. This it was not willing to do. Thus, the PNP that took office in 1992 was not a mere extension of the welfare-statehood populism of Romero Barceló but rather a party that had embraced the neoliberal gospel of entrepreneurial initiative, competition, deregulation, and privatization." See Ayala and Bernabe, *Puerto Rico in the American Century*, 291.

25. Friedman, "Rosselló Describes P.R. as Asset to U.S.," 4.

26. Michael H. Schill, "Privatizing Federal Low Income Housing Assistance: The Case of Public Housing," *Cornell Law Review* 75 (1990): 878.

27. James Fraser, Deirdre Oakley, and Joshua Bazuin, "Public Ownership and Private Profit in Housing," *Cambridge Journal of Regions, Economy and Society* 5, no. 3 (2012): 9.

28. Report of the President's Commission on Privatization, *Privatization: Toward More Effective Government*, March 1988, http://pdf.usaid.gov/pdf_docs /PNABB472.pdf.

29. Schill, "Privatizing Federal Low Income Housing Assistance," 879.

30. Lavonne Luquis, "P.R. to Privatize Public Housing," *San Juan Star*, May 6, 1992.

31. For more on the privatization of the HANO see John Arena, *Driven from New Orleans: How Nonprofits Betray Public Housing and Promote Privatization* (Minneapolis: University of Minnesota Press, 2012).

32. Salome Galib Bras, "Marcha el país a la vanguardia," *El Nuevo Día*, May 6, 1992, 4. Translation by author.

33. Nilka Estrada Resto, "Borran y cuenta nueva," *El Nuevo Día*, August 13, 1992, 7. Translation by author.

34. Estrada Resto, "Borran y cuenta nueva," 7.

35. Manny Suarez, "Housing Management Lawsuit Settled," *San Juan Star*, August 25, 1992, 3.

36. Rafael Matos, "HUD, Residents, Managers Unite to Tackle Problems," *San Juan Star*, August 3, 1992, 2.

37. Manny Suarez, "Housing Project Bids Being Sought," *San Juan Star*, August 27, 1992, 2.

38. P. J. Ortiz, "Hope Is Reborn in Llorens," *San Juan Star*, August 2, 1992, 8–9.

39. P. J. Ortiz, "Llorens Residents Still Feel Progress Slow in Coming," *San Juan Star*, January 12, 1993, 6–7.

40. Pedro Rosselló, "Mensaje especial a la legislatura y al pueblo de Puerto Rico sobre la criminalidad" (February 11, 1993).

41. 32 U.S.C. §112, "Drug Interdiction and Counter-drug Activities," Office of the Under Secretary of Defense for Policy, https://policy.defense.gov/portals/11/Documents/hdasa/references/32%20USC%20112.pdf.

42. Radley Balko, *Overkill: The Rise of Paramilitary Police Raids in America* (Washington, D.C.: The Cato Institute, 2006).

43. *The National Guard: Potential Uses in Crime-Fighting: Hearing before the Subcommittee on Crime and Criminal Justice, Committee on the Judiciary, House of Representatives* (October 5, 1994) (chair's opening remarks by Representative Charles "Chuck" Schumer [D-NY]).

44. *The National Guard: Potential Uses in Crime-Fighting, Hearing before the Subcommittee on Crime and Criminal Justice, Committee on the Judiciary, House of Representatives* (October 5, 1994) (prepared testimony by Pedro Rosselló).

45. *National Guard: Potential Uses in Crime-Fighting.*

46. Diego Ribadeneira, "Puerto Rico Employs Guard to Fight Drugs," *Boston Globe*, October 10, 1993, 1.

47. See Reuters, "Washington's Mayor Wants National Guard to Join Fight against City's Crime," *Gazette* (Montreal, Quebec), October 23, 1993, A20; and Times Wires, "Guard Called on to Help Police D.C.," *St. Petersburg Times*, October 23, 1993, 1A. The active D.C. National Guard figure is cited in Bernard W. Nussbaum and Clifford M. Sloan, "Memorandum for the President, Subject: D.C. National Guard," October 23, 1993 (The William J. Clinton Presidential Library, Clinton Presidential Records, Bruce Reed Collection, Crime Series, OA/Box Number 8413).

48. B. Drummond Ayres Jr., "Washington Mayor Seeks Aid of Guard in Combatting Crime," *New York Times*, October 23, 1993, 1.

49. Ayres, "Washington Mayor Seeks Aid of Guard in Combatting Crime," 1.

50. Bill Clinton, "Remarks by the President in NAFTA Meeting with Members of Congress," October 22, 1993 (The William J. Clinton Presidential Library, Clinton Presidential Records, Bruce Reed Collection, Crime Series, OA/Box Number 8413).

51. Clinton, "Remarks by the President in NAFTA Meeting with Members of Congress."

52. B. Drummond Ayres Jr., "Clinton Denies Washington's Request to Use Guard," *New York Times*, October 26, 1993, A14.

53. Clinton, "Remarks by the President in NAFTA Meeting with Members of Congress."

54. Nussbaum and Sloan, "Memorandum for the President, Subject: D.C. National Guard."

55. Nussbaum and Sloan, "Memorandum for the President."

56. Reuters, "Washington Mayor Wants National Guard to Join Fight against City's Crime."

57. Dinzey-Flores, *Locked In, Locked Out*, 30–32.

58. P.J. Ortiz, "Funds Will Cover Police, Drug Treatment Costs," *San Juan Star*, June 18, 1993, 2.

59. Gino Ponti, "Life Improves in Housing Projects," *San Juan Star*, January 23, 1994, 10.

60. Ponti, "Life Improves in Housing Projects," 10.

61. Jorge Luis Medina, "Multi-agency Group to Support Projects, Foster Self-help," *San Juan Star*, June 13, 1993, 11.

62. Arena, *Driven from New Orleans*, 60.

63. P.J. Ortiz, "Projects Thrive Year after Privatization," *San Juan Star*, August 9, 1993.

64. Nilka Estrada Resto, "A la raíz del problema en el residencial," *El Nuevo Día*, June 14, 1993, 4. Translation by author.

65. Mireya Navarro, "The Guard Takes on the Gangs," *New York Times*, July 13, 1994, A14.

66. Fraser, Oakley, and Bazuin, "Public Ownership and Private Profit in Housing," 3.

67. Sylvia Moreno, "Supporters Credit Military with Puerto Rico's Drop in Crime," *Dallas Morning News*, October 13, 1995, 43A.

68. Jorge Luis Medina, "Local Privatization of Public Housing Praised," *San Juan Star*, July 24, 1993, 4.

69. For information about these delegations, visits, and presentations see Luis García de la Noceda, "Mandatorios enfocan el narcotráfico," *El Vocero*, December 9, 1994, 32; Julio Ghigliotty, "Brown Tours 4 Projects Taken Over, Leaves with a Favorable Impression," *San Juan Star*, May 11, 1994; Manny Suarez, "Cuomo Lauds Rosselló, Reforms Arranged Tour," *San Juan Star*, August 16, 1994; Andrea Matinez, "Panamá también escucha," *El Nuevo Día*, October 6, 1994, 7; and "A Chicago Plan Anticrimen PRG," *El Vocero*, March 28, 1994, 48.

70. Julio Ghigliotty, "Brown Tours 4 Projects Taken Over."

71. Julio Ghigliotty, "U.S. Drug Control Czar Sees High Local, Federal Cooperation," *San Juan Star*, May 11, 1994, 4.

72. Zaire Dinzey-Flores notes that in her interviews with residents of Dr. Pila, a public housing complex in the southern city of Ponce, they often used language that indexed a feeling of punishment and incarceration within the space of their community

as a result of the perimeter fences built following mano dura. Dinzey-Flores recorded residents saying that they felt like "inmates" in a "prison" and that they were treated as so dangerous that "even the kitchen has bars on the windows." For more, see Dinzey-Flores, *Locked In, Locked Out*, 65.

73. Jasper Burnette, "If We're Going to Privatize Public Housing, We Ought to See How It's Done," editorial, *Washington Times*, August 5, 1994, A20.

74. Serge F. Kovaleski, "Housing Dept. Resort Trip Cost $10,800," *Washington Post*, July 13, 1994.

75. Kovaleski, "Housing Dept. Resort Trip Cost $10,800."

76. Burnette, "If We're Going to Privatize Public Housing."

77. Michael Grunwald, "Public Housing Reborn: Puerto Rico Takes Advantage of Privatization, Police," *Boston Globe*, December 31, 1995, 1.

78. Grunwald, "Public Housing Reborn," 1.

79. Pedro Rosselló, "La situación del estado, mensaje el honorable Pedro Rosselló Gobernador de Puerto Rico ante la séptima sesión ordinara de la Decimosegunda Asamblea Legislativa" (January 23, 1996). Translation by author.

80. Rosselló, "La situación del estado."

81. Rosselló, "La situación del estado."

82. *The Rising Drug Threat and Some Recent Successes*.

83. According to Rosselló, those were Villa Evangelina 3 and 4, Ramírez de Arellano, Antigua Vía, Felipe Sánchez Osorio, Alturas de Cibuco, Alturas de Vega Baja, Extensión Las Delicias, and Villa Los Santos 1 and 2.

84. Irmarilis González Torres, "¡No hay cárcel pa' tanta gente!," *Masturbana*, December 1994.Translation by author.

85. Karl Ross, "Prison Population May Soar to 20,000 by Year 2000," *San Juan Star*, May 8, 1995, 3.

86. *Guadarrama v. US Dept. of Housing and Urban Development*, U.S. District Court for the District of Puerto Rico, 74 F. Supp. 2d 127 (D.P.R. 1999), September 30, 1999, http://law.justia.com/cases/federal/district-courts/FSupp2/74/127/24 24365/.

87. Ivan Roman, "Puerto Rico vive su ano más violento," *El Nuevo Herald*, November 1, 1992, 1A. Translation by author.

88. *World Prison Brief Data, Puerto Rico* (USA), www.prisonstudies.org/country/puerto-rico-usa.

89. Patricio G. Martínez Llompart, "In the Custody of Violence: Puerto Rico Under La Mano Dura Contra el Crimen, 1993–1996," *Revista Jurídica UPR* 84, no. 2 (2015): 479.

90. Ross, "Prison Population May Soar to 20,000 by Year 2000."

91. Martínez Llompart, "In the Custody of Violence," 478.

92. Martínez Llompart, "In the Custody of Violence," 478.

93. Peter Wagner, "Blacks Are Overrepresented in Puerto Rico's Prisons and Jails" (graph), Prison Policy Initiative, May 2004, www.prisonpolicy.org/graphs/PR _Black.html.

94. Martínez Llompart, "In the Custody of Violence," 478.

95. P.J. Ortiz, "HUD to Pump $6 Million into Housing Projects," *San Juan Star*, June 18, 1993, 2.

96. Ortiz, "HUD to Pump $6 Million into Housing Projects," 2.

97. Jorge Luis Medina, "Rossello Urges Gates, Guards at Projects," *San Juan Star*, August 5, 1993, 3.

98. Gino Ponti, "Housing Takeovers Cost $1 Million," *San Juan Star*, June 27, 1993, 10.

99. Karl Ross, "'Mano Dura' Losing Favor of Project Residents," *San Juan Star*, August 27, 1995, 2.

100. Ross, "'Mano Dura' Losing Favor of Project Residents," 2.

101. Ross, "'Mano Dura' Losing Favor of Project Residents," 2.

102. Residents sometimes cut holes in the perimeter fences surrounding public housing in a refusal to accept how the gating has disrupted their normal patterns of movement and cut them off from the larger community. Often when management companies would repair the fences, they would find holes in the fences once again shortly afterward. As a result, some management companies decided not to repair sections of fencing that had been destroyed or altered. For more see Dinzey-Flores, *Locked In, Locked Out*, 89–90.

103. Ross, "'Mano Dura' Losing Favor of Project Residents."

104. Ross, "'Mano Dura' Losing Favor of Project Residents."

105. Gino Ponti, "Police Take Over Nemesio Canales for 2nd Time," *San Juan Star*, September 17, 1994, 6.

106. Ponti, "Police Take Over Nemesio Canales for 2nd Time," 6.

107. Ponti, "Police Take Over Nemesio Canales for 2nd Time," 6.

108. José Javier Pérez, "El Primer Grano de Arena," *El Nuevo Día*, April 7, 1994, www.adendi.com/archivo.asp?num=159171&year=1994&month=4&keyword=arena.

109. Gino Ponti, "Will Effort to Save Public Projects Go to Waste?," *San Juan Star*, June 27, 1993, 11.

110. Marta Font, "Respecto," *Claridad*, April 21–27, 1995, 39. Translation by author.

111. Font, "Respecto," 39.

112. Gerardo Cordero, "Inmutable la droga ante la presencia policiaca," *El Nuevo Día*, May 26, 1998, 28. Translation by author.

113. Cordero, "Inmutable la droga ante la presencia policiaca," 28.

114. Cordero, "Inmutable la droga ante la presencia policiaca," 28.

CHAPTER 3. UNDERGROUND

1. Mayra Santos Febres, "Geografía en decibeles: Utopías pancaribeñas y el territorio del rap," in *Caribe 2000: Definiciones, identidades y culturas regionales y/o nacionales*, ed. Lowell Fiet and Janette Becerra (San Juan: Facultad de Humanidades, Universidad de Puerto Rico, Recinto de Río Piedras, 1997), 123.

2. Wayne Marshall demonstrates this in "From Música Negra to Reggaeton Latino: The Cultural Politics of Nation, Migration, and Commercialization," in

Reggaeton, ed. Wayne Marshall, Raquel Z. Rivera, and Deborah Pacini Hernandez (Durham, NC: Duke University Press, 2009), 31–33.

3. Santos Febres, "Geografía en decibeles," 125.

4. Raquel Z. Rivera, "Rap Music in Puerto Rico: Mass Consumption or Social Resistance?." *Centro: Journal of the Center for Puerto Rican Studies* 5, no. 1 (1992–1993): 56.

5. Robin D. G. Kelley, *Yo' Mama's Disfunktional! Fighting the Culture Wars in Urban America* (Boston: Beacon Press, 1997), 75.

6. See, for example, Frank Bonilla and Ricardo Campos, *Industry and Idleness* (New York: Centro de Estudios Puertorriqueños, 1986); and History Task Force of the Centro de Estudios Puertorriqueños, *Labor Migration under Capitalism: The Puerto Rican Experience* (New York: Monthly Review Press, 1979). While *Labor Migration under Capitalism* was largely the work of Ricardo Campos, Frank Bonilla also formed part of the Centro History Task Force.

7. Frank Bonilla and Ricardo Campos, "A Wealth of Poor: Puerto Ricans in the New Economic Order," *Daedalus* 110, no. 2 (1981): 156.

8. Raquel Z. Rivera, "Rapping Two Versions of the Same Requiem," in *Puerto Rican Jam: Essays on Culture and Politics*, ed. Frances Negron-Muntaner and Ramon Grosfoguel (Minneapolis: University of Minnesota Press, 1997), 250.

9. Zaire Zenit Dinzey-Flores discusses the spatial aesthetics of reggaeton music in "De la Disco al Caserío: Urban Spatial Aesthetics and Policy to the Beat of Reggaetón," *Centro Journal* 20, no. 1 (Fall 2008): 35–69.

10. James C. Scott, *Weapons of the Weak: Everyday Forms of Peasant Resistance* (New Haven, CT: Yale University Press, 1987).

11. This practice was mentioned by various informants during the course of my research in Puerto Rico from 2011 to 2012.

12. Raquel Z. Rivera, "Policing Morality, *Mano Dura Stylee*: The Case of Underground Rap and Reggae in Puerto Rico in the Mid-1990s," in *Reggaeton*, ed. Wayne Marshall, Raquel Z. Rivera, and Deborah Pacini Hernandez (Durham, NC: Duke University Press, 2009), 117.

13. James Chankin and Leigh Savidge, dirs., *Straight Outta Puerto Rico: Reggaeton's Rough Road to Glory* (Xenon Pictures, 2008).

14. Daddy Yankee, "#tbt EL ORIGEN," Instagram post, December 17, 2015, www.instagram.com/p/_ZniagrK-a/. Translation by author.

15. Wayne Marshall, "From Música Negra to Reggaeton Latino"; and Raquel Z. Rivera, "Cultura y poder en el rap puertorriqueño," *Revista de Ciencias Sociales* 4 (1998): 139.

16. Chankin and Savidge, *Straight Outta Puerto Rico*.

17. Chankin and Savidge, *Straight Outta Puerto Rico*.

18. Rivera, "Policing Morality," 113–114.

19. For more see Tricia Rose, *Black Noise: Rap Music and Black Culture in Contemporary America* (Middletown, CT: Wesleyan University Press, 1994); Tricia Rose, *The Hip Hop Wars: What We Talk About When We Talk About Hip Hop—and Why It Matters* (New York: Basic Civitas Books, 2008); and Eithne Quinn,

Nuthin' but a 'G 'Thang: The Culture and Commerce of Gangsta Rap (New York: Columbia University Press, 2004).

20. Yolanda Rosaly, "¡Alto a la música 'underground!,'" *El Nuevo Día*, February 7, 1995, 79. Translation by author.

21. Rosaly, "¡Alto a la música 'underground!,'" 79.

22. John Marino, "Police Seize Recordings, Say Content Is Obscene," *San Juan Star*, February 3, 1995, 2.

23. For more see Peter Blecha, *Taboo Tunes: A History of Banned Bands & Censored Songs* (San Francisco: Backbeat Books, 2004).

24. Hilario De Leon, "'Tocan' a favor de la música 'underground,'" *El Nuevo Día*, February 17, 1995, 23.

25. De Leon, "'Tocan' a favor de la música 'underground,'" 23. Translation by author.

26. Chankin and Savidge, *Straight Outta Puerto Rico*.

27. Jaime Torres Torres, "Al rescate de un género," *El Nuevo Día*, June 18, 1999, 110–111.

28. Manny Suarez, "Order Established Drug-free Zones for Schools," *San Juan Star*, August 24, 1994, 3.

29. Superintendent Toledo repeatedly stressed that while police and school officials would encourage students to come forward with information about drugs or firearms on school property, the police would not be recruiting undercover agents. As Toledo put it, "The experience with that in the past has not been good," alluding to the Police Intelligence Office's practice of hiring students to infiltrate pro-independence student groups. The most notorious case involved Alejando González Malave, a student at Gabriel Mistral High School in San Juan, who was later involved in the brutal assassination of two young *independentisas* by police at Cerro Maravilla in 1978. For more see Julio Ghigliotty, "Drug-free School Plan to Begin in September," *San Juan Star*, July 21, 1994, 7.

30. Efe News Agency, "Schools Open to Frisking, Rationing Plans," *San Juan Star*, September 6, 1994, 7.

31. Lorraine Blasor, "Drug-free School Plan Being Expanded," *San Juan Star*, August 22, 1995, 9.

32. Jorge L. Giovannetti, "Popular Music and Culture in Puerto Rico: Jamaican and Rap Music as Cross-Cultural Symbols," in *Musical Migrations*, vol. 1: *Transnationalism and Cultural Hybridity in Latina/o America*, ed. Frances R. Aparicio and Cadida F. Jaquez (New York: Palgrave Macmillan, 2003), 87.

33. Translation of quote appears in Rivera-Rideau, *Remixing Reggaeton*, 43.

34. Rivera-Rideau, *Remixing* Reggaeton, 43.

35. Giovannetti, "Popular Music and Culture in Puerto Rico," 87.

36. Chankin and Savidge, *Straight Outta Puerto Rico*.

37. Karl Ross, "Toledo Defends Policy of Keeping Gays Off Force," *San Juan Star*, February 11, 1995, 2.

38. Georgie Irizarry Vizcarrondo, "Police's 'mano dura,'" readers' viewpoint, *San Juan Star*, February 23, 1995.

39. Rafael Bernabe and Nancy Herzig, "'Moralidad', censura y derechos," *Claridad*, September 7, 1995. Translation by author.

40. John Marino, "Killing the Messengers?," *San Juan Star*, February 26, 1995, 7.

41. Edwin Reyes, "Rapeo sobre el rap en Ciales," *Claridad*, December 29, 1995–January 4, 1996, 23. Translation by author.

42. Pedro T. Berríos Lara, "Underground: ¿Obscenidad o Realidad?," *la iupi* (January/February 1995): 4. Translation by author.

43. Karen Entrialgo, "Underground," *Poder Estudiantil*, January-February 1995, 11. Translation by author.

44. Jorge Luis Medina, "Words That Rhyme and Rhythmic Time; That the Map for Rap," *San Juan Star*, February 19, 1995, 6.

45. Jorge Luis Medina, "Rappers Rap Bum Rap and Hypocrisy," *San Juan Star*, February 19, 1995, 6.

46. Medina, "Rappers Rap Bum Rap and Hypocrisy," 7.

47. Juan Carlos Pérez, "Señor oficial, esto es rap," *El Nuevo Día*, October 10, 1997, www.adendi.com/archivo.asp?num=310036&year=1997&month=10&keyword=oficial.

48. Drug Enforcement Agency (DEA), "Operation SOS II: DEA Dismantles Seven Violent Drug Trafficking Organization in Ponce, Puerto Rico," press release, October 15, 2002.

49. DEA, "Operation SOS II."

50. Andrea Martínez, "Arrestado en el tribunal el rapero Tempo," *El Nuevo Día*, October 18, 2002.

51. Carmen Edith Torres, "Fallo de 24 años a Tempo," *El Nuevo Día*, April 23, 2005, www.adendi.com/archivo.asp?num=9872&year=2005&month=4&keyword=Tempo.

52. Torres, "Fallo de 24 años a Tempo."

53. J. Santos, "Interview with TEMPO," YouTube, www.youtube.com/watch?v=eiAXAvCAflM.

54. Jose Vazquez, "Tempo Returns to Puerto Rico," *La Mezcla*, October 10, 2013, www.lamezcla.com/home/tempo-returns-to-puerto-rico/.

55. "Reguetonero se declara culpable," *El Nuevo Día*, May 29, 2015, www.elnuevodia.com/noticias/tribunales/nota/reguetonerosedeclaraculpable-2053677/.

56. Oscar J. Serrano, "Reguetonero condenado por su lírica tendrá segunda oportunidad," *Noticel*, July 9, 2016, www.noticel.com/noticia/192410/reguetonero-condenado-por-su-lirica-tendra-segunda-oportunidad.html.

57. Rivera, "Policing Morality," 125.

CHAPTER 4. THE CONTINUED PROMISE OF PUNISHMENT

1. Mireya Navarro, "U.S. Says Officials in Puerto Rico Stole for Party and Profit," *New York Times*, January 24, 2002, www.nytimes.com/2002/01/24/us/us-says-officials-in-puerto-rico-stole-for-party-and-profit.html; and "Top 10 de la historia de corrupción local," *Elnuevodia.com*, March 19, 2014, www.elnuevodia.com/noticias/locales/nota/top10delahistoriadecorrupcionlocal-1735511/.

2. Sila María Calderón, "Proyecto puertorriqueño para el siglo 21," *Partido Popular Democrático Programa de Gobierno 2001–2004*, 49. Translation by author.

3. Calderón, "Proyecto puertorriqueño para el siglo 21."

4. New Orleans Police Department, "Crime and Police Problems in the City of New Orleans," Center for Problem Oriented Policing, www.popcenter.org/library /awards/goldstein/1999/99-41.pdf.

5. New Orleans Police Department, "Crime and Police Problems in the City of New Orleans."

6. The City of New Orleans, "New Orleans Police Chief Pennington Announces Complete Department Reorganization and Sweeping Reforms," press release, January 11, 1995 (Amistad Research Collection, Marc H. Morial Papers, Folder 7, New Orleans Police 1993–1995, Box 53).

7. City of New Orleans, "New Orleans Police Chief Pennington Announces Complete Department Reorganization."

8. "Report of the Volunteer Transition Task Force on the New Orleans Police Department Presented to the Morial Transition Office," April 1994 (Amistad Research Collection, Marc H. Morial Papers, Folder 4, Mayoral Transition: New Orleans Police Department, 1994, Box 33).

9. Lydia Pelot-Hobbs, "The Contested Terrain of the Louisiana Carceral State: Dialectics of Southern Penal Expansion, 1971–2016" (PhD diss., City University of New York Graduate Center, 2019).

10. "Report of the Volunteer Transition Task Force on the New Orleans Police Department."

11. New Orleans Police Department, "Crime and Police Problems in the City of New Orleans."

12. Pelot-Hobbs, "The Contested Terrain of the Louisiana Carceral State."

13. Pelot-Hobbs, "The Contested Terrain of the Louisiana Carceral State."

14. "Public Officials of the Year: Richard J. Pennington," *Governing*, 1998, www .governing.com/poy/Richard-Pennington.html.

15. "Public Officials of the Year."

16. José R. Negrón Fernández, Asesor de la Gobernadora, fax communication to Lcdo. Pierre E. Vivoni, Superintendente de la Policía de Puerto Rico, October 22, 2001 (Centro Para Puerto Rico, Archivo de la Fundación Sila M. Calderón, Box A-WN-9-a).

17. Negrón Fernández, fax communication to Lcdo. Pierre E. Vivoni.

18. "Agenda comentada para la gobernadora, Consejo de Seguridad," Oficina de la Gobernadora, October 30, 2001 (Centro Para Puerto Rico, Archivo de la Fundación Sila M. Calderón, Box A-WN-9-a). Translation by author.

19. Negrón Fernández, fax communication to Lcdo. Pierre E. Vivoni. Translation by author.

20. "Agenda comentada para la gobernadora, Consejo de Seguridad," October 30, 2001 (Centro Para Puerto Rico, Archivo de la Fundación Sila M. Calderón, Box A-WN-14-b); and "Agenda comentada para la gobernadora, Consejo de Seguridad," Oficina de la Gobernadora.

21. "Dura el crítica del pueblo," *El Nuevo Día*, May 1, 2002, 4; and Julio Ghigliotty Matos, "Cumbre por la 'C' a Sila Calderón," *El Nuevo Día*, May 6, 2002, 6.

22. Sandra Morales Blanes, "Calderón y Pereira afinan el Plan de Seguridad," *El Nuevo Día*, May 8, 2002, 59. Translation by author.

23. Morales Blanes, "Calderón y Pereira afinan el Plan de Seguridad," 59.

24. Nicholas Kristof, "A Neighborly Style of Police State," The World, *New York Times*, June 4, 1995, www.nytimes.com/1995/06/04/weekinreview/the-world-a
-neighborly-style-of-police-state.html.

25. Lynn A. Curtis, *Youth Investment and Police Mentoring*, The Milton S. Eisenhower Foundation, Washington D.C., 1997, www.eisenhowerfoundation.org
/docs/youth.pdf.

26. Elliott Currie, *Crime and Punishment in America* (New York: Henry Holt and Company, 1998), 178.

27. Waldo, D. Covas Quevedo, "Prioridad resolver casos," *El Nuevo Día*, May 10, 2002, 5.

28. Covas Quevedo, "Prioridad resolver casos,"5.

29. Covas Quevedo, "Prioridad resolver casos," 5.

30. "Se presenta el plan anti crimen tras quince meses de espera," *Associated Press*, May 9, 2002, www.puertorico-herald.org/issues/2002/vol6n19/Media1-es
.html. Translation by author.

31. "Se presenta el plan anti crimen tras quince meses de espera,"

32. Maribel Hernández, "Sila y un ambicioso proyecto anticrimen," *Primera Hora*, May 9, 2002. Translation by author.

33. Associated Press, "Control de acceso en 78 residenciales para octubre," *El Nuevo Día*, May 15, 2002, 52.

34. Associated Press, "Control de acceso en 78 residenciales para octubre," 52.

35. Associated Press, "Control de acceso en 78 residenciales para octubre," 52.

36. Associated Press, "Control de acceso en 78 residenciales para octubre," 52; and Carmen Edith Torres, "Cuestionado el control de acceso a los residenciales," *El Nuevo Día*, May 16, 2002, 52.

37. Associated Press, "Control de acceso en 78 residenciales para octubre," 52.

38. Torres, "Cuestionado el control de acceso a los residenciales."

39. Torres, "Cuestionado el control de acceso a los residenciales."

40. Daniel Rivera Vargas, "Desconfían los caseríos del plan de seguridad," *El Nuevo Día*, May 16, 2002, 53.

41. Daniel Rivera Vargas, "Recomendados controles a la medida del complejo," *El Nuevo Día*, May 16, 2002, 53. Translation by author.

42. Waldo, D. Covas Quevedo, "Defensa férrea al control de acceso," *El Nuevo Día*, May 20, 2002, 38. Translation by author.

43. Covas Quevedo, "Defensa férrea al control de acceso," 38.

44. Covas Quevedo, "Defensa férrea al control de acceso," 38.

45. Covas Quevedo, "Defensa férrea al control de acceso," 38.

46. Pepo Garcia, "'Nada nuevo' en el plan anticrimen," *El Nuevo Día*, May 11, 2002, 14. Translation by author.

47. Garcia, "'Nada nuevo' en el plan anticrimen," 14.

48. "Informe narrativo sobre las propuestas del Proyecto Puertorriqueño del Siglo 21 correspondientes a la Policía de Puerto Rico," Policía de Puerto Rico, July 1, 2002 (Centro Para Puerto Rico, Archivo de la Fundación Sila M. Calderón, Box A-WN-1-D); and "Agenda comentada, Consejo de Seguridad," July 23, 2002 (Centro Para Puerto Rico, Archivo de la Fundación Sila M. Calderón, Box A-WN-14-b).

49. "Informe narrativo sobre las propuestas del Proyecto Puertorriqueño." Translation by author.

50. "Agenda comentada, Consejo de Seguridad."

51. "Agenda comentada, Consejo de Seguridad."

52. "Agenda comentada, Consejo de Seguridad."

53. Waldo, D. Covas Quevedo, "Ocupa la policía tres residenciales," *El Nuevo Día*, October 22, 2002, 44.

54. Covas Quevedo, "Ocupa la policía tres residenciales," 44.

55. Covas Quevedo, "Ocupa la policía tres residenciales," 44. Translation by author.

56. Proviana Colon Diaz, "Public Housing Residents Skeptical of Long-Term Commitment," *Wow News*, October 22, 2002, www.puertorico-herald.org/issues /2002/vol6n43/Media2-en.html.

57. Colon Diaz, "Public Housing Residents Skeptical of Long-Term Commitment."

58. Daniel Rivera Vargas, "Denuncia de abuso en el operativo," *El Nuevo Día*, October 23, 2002, 46.

59. Rivera Vargas, "Denuncia de abuso en el operativo." Translation by author.

60. Rivera Vargas, "Denuncia de abuso en el operativo."

61. Colon Diaz, "Public Housing Residents Skeptical of Long-Term Commitment."

62. Israel Rodríguez, "Defensa a los operativos," *El Nuevo Día*, October 24, 2002, 54. Translation by author.

63. Rodríguez, "Defensa a los operativos," 54.

64. Manuel Ernesto Rivera, "Se distancia la gobernadora de la 'mano dura,'" *El Nuevo Día*, October 24, 2002, 54. Translation by author.

65. Rivera, "Se distancia la gobernadora de la 'mano dura,'" 54.

66. Geraldo Cordero, "Ocupado el residencial Juana Matos," *El Nuevo Día*, October 28, 2002, 40. Translation by author.

67. Geraldo Cordero, "Como sacado del cine el operativo," *El Nuevo Día*, October 28, 2002, 41. Translation by author.

68. Cordero, "Como sacado del cine el operativo."

69. Mario Santana, "Proyecto de policía comunitaria," *El Nuevo Día*, October 29, 2002, 46.

70. Santana, "Proyecto de Policía comunitaria," 46.

71. Miried González Rodríguez, "Ausente la seguridad en la lista de logros de la gobernadora," *Primera Hora*, December 23, 2002, http://corp.primerahora.com /archivo.asp?guid=2149F62F68C14E3CA4DE3A2D8030BB61&year=2002&key word=.

72. Abby Goodnough, "Two-Front Battle in Puerto Rico: Crime and Apathy," *New York Times*, December 28, 2003, www.nytimes.com/2003/12/28/us/two-front-battle-in-puerto-rico-crime-and-apathy.html; and "Informe final [sobre la seguridad] 19 de Diciembre de 2003," Policía de Puerto Rico, documento preparado para la gobernadora (Centro Para Puerto Rico, Archivo de la Fundación Sila M. Calderón, Box A-WN-1a).

73. Abby Goodnough, "Two-Front Battle in Puerto Rico."

74. "Informe final [sobre la seguridad] 19 de Diciembre de 2003." Policía de Puerto Rico, documento preparado para la gobernadora (Centro Para P Translation by author.

75. Waldo D. Covas Quevedo, "Acogida unánime a Cartagena Díaz," *El Nuevo Día*, January 18, 2004, 27. Translation by author.

76. Policía de Puerto Rico, Oficina del Superintendente Agustín Cartagena Díaz, "Plan de vigilancia estratégico para rescatar áreas de alta incidencia criminal," February 13, 2004 (Centro Para Puerto Rico, Archivo de la Fundación Sila M. Calderón, Box A-WN-12-a).

77. Policía de Puerto Rico, "Plan de vigilancia estratégico."

78. "Identificación de 500 puntos de drogas e implementación, plan para desarticularlos durante los próximos seis meses," Policía de Puerto Rico, February 25, 2004, SAECNCO-1-4-054 (Centro Para Puerto Rico, Archivo de la Fundación Sila M. Calderón, Box A-WN-12-c).

79. Hilario de Leon, "Toledo: PRNG Should Be Armed If Deployed to Public Housing Projects," *Associated Press*, July 15, 2004, www.puertorico-herald.org/issues/2004/vol8n29/Media1-en.html.

80. De Leon, "Toledo."

81. Rebecca Banuchi, "Calderon Activates National Guard to Aid Police," *Associated Press*, July 19, 2004, www.puertorico-herald.org/issues/2004/vol8n30/Media3-en.html.

82. Reuters, "Puerto Rico: Guard Called In," *New York Times*, July 21, 2004.

83. Reuters, "Puerto Rico: Guard Called In."

84. Banuchi, "Calderon Activates National Guard to Aid Police."

85. Banuchi, "Calderon Activates National Guard to Aid Police."

86. Policía de Puerto Rico, Oficina del Superintendente Agustín Cartagena Díaz, "Plan de seguridad de Julio a Octubre de 2004," July 21, 2004 (Centro Para Puerto Rico, Archivo de la Fundación Sila M. Calderón, Box A-WN-7-a). The areas identified by the PRPD as areas of "high criminal incidence" are the following: San Juan (Residenciales Nemesio Canales, Lloréns Torres, Los Peña, Julio Sellés Solá), Bayamón (Cataño, Barrio Amelia, Sector Puente Blanco, Calle Cucharilla, Residencial Las Vegas), Ponce (Santa Isabel, Barrio Las Hoyas, Juana Díaz, residencial Kennedy y Sector Los Mojaitos, Sector Villa Pueblo, La Cantera, Urb. Ferrán, Ponce), and Carolina (Distrito de Loíza, Distrito de Canóvanas). The overwhelming majority of these communities are low income, and many are racially marginalized and have been subjected to race-based segregation and discrimination. Many of these areas also saw joint PRNG and PRPD patrols and raids as part of mano dura contra el crimen during the 1990s.

87. "Public Housing Projects Leaders Voice Their Demands," *Associated Press*, July 21, 2004.

88. "Public Housing Projects Leaders Voice Their Demands."

89. "Public Housing Projects Leaders Voice Their Demands."

90. Melissa B. Gonzalez Valentin, "Rossello Promises to Fight Crime," *Wow News*, July 2004.

91. "Acevedo Vilá ofrece detalles de un plan anticrimen," *Associated Press*, May 10, 2004, www.puertorico-herald.org/issues/2004/vol8n20/Media3-es.html. Translation by author.

92. Aníbal Acevedo Vilá, "Mensaje sobre el estado de situación del país del gobernador del Estado Libre Asociado de Puerto Rico," January,30, 2006. Translation by author.

93. Acevedo Vilá, "Mensaje sobre el estado de situación del país."

94. United States Department of Justice, Civil Rights Division, "Investigation of the Puerto Rico Police Department," September 5, 2011, 5, www.justice.gov/sites/default/files/crt/legacy/2011/09/08/prpd_letter.pdf.

95. Aníbal Acevedo Vilá, "Mensaje sobre el estado de situación del país del gobernador del Estado Libre Asociado de Puerto Rico," February 6, 2007. Translation by author.

96. Jeannette Rivera-Iyles, "Puerto Rico Accepts Camera Surveillance While Florida Approaches It Cautiously," *Orlando Sentinel*, December 24, 2007, http://articles.orlandosentinel.com/2007-12-24/news/prcameras24_1_puerto-rico-rico-police-department-hatillo.

97. "Cámaras en residenciales: Desperdicio de $13 millones," Centro de Periodismo Investigativo, August 28, 2010, http://periodismoinvestigativo.com/2010/08/camaras-en-residenciales-desperdicio-de-13-millones/.

98. Lourdes C. Santiago Negron and Pedro Lugo Vázquez, interview by the author, Rio Piedras, Puerto Rico, March 6, 2011.

99. Naomi Murakawa, *The First Civil Right: How Liberals Built Prison America* (Oxford: Oxford University Press, 2014, 8).

100. Murakawa, *The First Civil Right*, 13.

CHAPTER 5. POLICING SOLIDARITY

1. I discuss this moment in relation to the long history of targeted political repression and harassment of political dissidents in Puerto Rico in "Carpeteo Redux: Surveillance and Subversion Against the Puerto Rican Student Movement," *Radical History Review* 128 (May 2017): 147–172.

2. Video footage of police intervention and brutality during the *pintata* can be seen in this two-part video report for *Diálogo*, the URP student newspaper: Editores Diálogo, "9 de febrero motín en UPR-RP," YouTube, February 9, 2011, http://youtu.be/_DVtAd5avqo; and Editores Diálogo, "Motín en UPR-RP–9 de febrero de 2011 (2da parte)," YouTube, February 9, 2011, http://youtu.be/LjBaWESdTjg.

3. "Editorial: The Police Must Leave Campus," *Puerto Rico Daily Sun*, February 10, 2011.

4. "Editorial: The Police Must Leave Campus."

5. Xiomara Caro, interview by the author, Río Piedras, Puerto Rico, March 7, 2012. It is worth noting that this circuitry of police practice that Caro points to, which moves from marginalized communities to the wider population, is not specific to this particular moment or to Puerto Rico. A number of scholars and theorists have described the ways in which police often "test" new technologies and practices in low-income communities and communities of color before they expand these technologies, which subsequently become normalized as simply *policing*. For an excellent primer, see Parenti, *Lockdown America*. See also Dylan Rodríguez, *Forced Passages: Imprisoned Radical Intellectuals and the U.S. Prison Regime* (Minneapolis: University of Minnesota Press, 2006).

6. "Ley especial declarando estado de emergencia fiscal y estableciendo plan integral de estabilización fiscal para salvar el crédito de Puerto Rico," Ley Núm. 7 del año 2009 (P. de la C. 1326). Translation by author.

7. Yarimar Bonilla and Rafael Boglio Martínez, "Puerto Rico in Crisis: Government Workers Battle Neoliberal Reform," *NACLA Report on the Americas* 43, no. 1 (January/February 2010): 6–8.

8. Yarimar Bonilla, "Caribbean Youth Battle for the Future of Public Education: General Strike at the University of Puerto Rico Goes into Its Fourth Week," *Stabroek News*, May 17, 2010, www.stabroeknews.com/2010/features/05/17/caribbean-youth-battle-for-the-future-of-public-education-general-strike-at-the-university-of-puerto-rico-goes-into-its-fourth-week/.

9. Bonilla, "Caribbean Youth Battle for the Future of Public Education."

10. Abner Y. Dennis Zayas, interview by the author, Río Piedras, Puerto Rico, March 8, 2012. Translation by author.

11. Roberto José Thomas Ramírez, interview by the author, Río Piedras, Puerto Rico, March 2, 2012. Translation by author.

12. "Radio Huelga: Conéctate a la resistencia," *Desde Adentro*, May 2, 2010, http://rojogallito.blogspot.com/2010/05/radio-huelga-conectate-la-resistencia.html. Translation by author.

13. Juan Laguarta Ramírez makes a similar point when he notes that, following the *paro nacional*, "widespread discontent and vocal protest failed to materialize into significant resistance, in part as a result of the weakness, fragmentation, or cooptation of the leadership of the traditional labor movement (itself a result of ongoing neoliberalization since the 1980s). In this context, UPR students were increasingly seen as (and imagined themselves to be) the last redoubt of popular opposition." See Juan Laguarta Ramírez, "Struggling to Learn, Learning to Struggle: Strategy and Structure in the 2010–11 University of Puerto Rico Student Strike" (PhD diss., Graduate Center, City University of New York, 2016), 34.

14. Lourdes C. Santiago Negrón and Pedro Lugo Vázquez, interview by the author, Río Piedras, Puerto Rico, March 6, 2011.

15. For the percentage of students studying at private versus public institutions of higher learning, see Jaime Calderón Soto, "Perfil del estudiantado universitario en Puerto Rico: Hallazgos del Consejo de Educación," Consejo de Educación de Puerto Rico, March 2012, www.edicion.pr.gov/agencias/cepr/inicio/Investigacion /Documents/Otros/PERFIL%20DEL%20ESTUDIANTADO%20UNIVERSI TARIO%20EN%20PUERTO%20RICO%20BW.pdf.

16. Dennis Zayas interview, March 8, 2012.

17. Alessandra M. Rosa, "Resistance Performances: (Re)constructing Spaces of Resistance and Contention in the 2010-2011 University of Puerto Rico Student Movement" (PhD diss., Florida International University, 2015), 87–88.

18. Isabel Picó Vidal, "Los orígenes del movimiento estudiantil universitario: 1903–1930," *Revista de Ciencias Sociales* 24, no. 1 (1985): 43.

19. Rosa, "Resistance Performances," 106–107.

20. José F. Paralitici, "A 85 años—situación del ROTC," in *Universidad y (Anti) Militarismo: Historia, Luchas y Debates*, ed. Anita Yudkin Suliveres (San Juan: Universitarios por la Desmilitarización, 2005).

21. Paralitici, "A 85 años—situación del ROTC."

22. Rosa, "Resistance Performances," 115.

23. "Policias y estudiantes heridos en motin en la Universidad," *El Vocero*, November 26, 1981, 3.

24. "¿Que se busca, un muerto?," *El Nuevo Día*, November 26, 1981, 4.

25. Rosa, "Resistance Performances," 120.

26. Waldemiro Vélez Soto, interview by the author, Río Piedras, Puerto Rico, April 26, 2012. Translation by author.

27. Vélez Soto interview, April 26, 2012.

28. For footage from the protest at the Sheraton, see primerahoravideos, "Motín en actividad de fortuño por huelga en la UPR- parte 1," YouTube, May 21, 2010, www.youtube.com/watch?v=o4TIgF6Cj_U; and primerahoravideos, "Motín en actividad de fortuño por huelga en la UPR- parte 2," YouTube, May 21, 2010, www .youtube.com/watch?v=XSimXwuJWfA. For more on José "Osito" Pérez Reisler, see Oscar J. Serrano, "Demanda por patada testicular," *Noticel*, May 16, 2011, www. noticel.com/noticia/104753/1346977531000.

29. Leila A. Andreu Cuevas, "Presidenta de la Cámara llama 'radicales' a los manifestantes del hotel Sheraton," *Primera Hora*, May 21, 2010, www.primerahora .com/noticias/gobierno-politica/nota/presidentadelacamarallamaradicalesalos manifestantesdelhotelsheraton-388935/.

30. Nydia Bauza, "Repudio a los excesos policiacos," *Primera Hora*, May 22, 2012, www.primerahora.com/noticias/gobierno-politica/nota/repudioalosexc esospoliciacos-388998/. Translation by author

31. Karol Joselyn Sepúlveda, "Inundan Facebook las expresiones de supuestos policías 'orgullosos' de macanear estudiantes de la UPR," *Primera Hora*, May 21, 2010, January 27, 2014, www.primerahora.com/noticias/gobierno-politica/nota /inundanfacebooklasexpresionesdesupuestospoliciasorgullososdemacanearestudi antesdelaupr-388928. Translation by author.

32. Sepúlveda, "Inundan Facebook las expresiones de supuestos policías."

33. Karol Joselyn Sepúlveda and Nydia Bauza, "Superintendente ordena investigación por expresiones desacertadas de policías," *Primera Hora*, May 22, 2012, www.primerahora.com/noticias/gobierno-politica/nota/superintendenteordena investigacionporexpresionesdesacertadasdepolicias-388999/.

34. Maritza Stanchich, "University of Puerto Rico Student Strike Victory Unleashes Brutal Civil Rights Backlash," *Huffington Post*, July 7, 2010, www.huffi ngtonpost.com/maritza-stanchich-phd/university-of-puerto-rico_b_635090.html.

35. Stanchich, "University of Puerto Rico Student Strike Victory Unleashes Brutal Civil Rights Backlash."

36. Maritza Stanchich, "More Violence in Puerto Rico as University Student Fee Is Imposed," *Huffington Post*, December 15, 2010, www.huffingtonpost.com/maritza -stanchich-phd/more-violence-in-puerto-r_b_810628.html.

37. Caro interview, March 7, 2012.

38. See Mariana Cobián, "Los recogen en Loíza y los meten de guardias en la UPR sin explicaciones," *Primera Hora*, December 13, 2010, www.primerahora.com /noticias/gobierno-politica/nota/losrecogenenloizaylosmetendeguardiasenlauprsin explicaciones-452612; and Giovanni Roberto, "De cuando el barrio entró a la UPR," *Socialismo Internacional*, October 26, 2013, https://latrincheraobrera.wordpress .com/2013/10/26/de-cuando-el-barrio-entro-a-la-upr/.

39. Cobián, "Los recogen en Loíza y los meten de guardias en la UPR sin explicaciones." Translation by author.

40. Giovanni Roberto makes this point clear in "De cuando el barrio entró a la UPR."

41. Cobián, "Los recogen en Loíza y los meten de guardias en la UPR sin explicaciones"; and Roberto, "De cuando el barrio entró a la UPR."

42. "Encubiertos de Capitol Security en huelga de la Universidad de Puerto Rico UPR," YouTube, December 7, 2010, http://youtu.be/xZPOrVvKwCM. Translation by author.

43. "Huelga UPR 2010—Me gusta dar cantazos (Capitol Security)," YouTube, December 10, 2010, http://youtu.be/Uv8pAXDZ-gA.

44. Benjamín Torres Gotay, "Los discípulos de Chicky Starr en la UPR," *Elnuevodia.com*, December 7, 2010, www.elnuevodia.com/blog-los_discipulos_de _chicky_starr_en_la_upr-832674.html (last accessed January 27, 2014; URL no longer valid).

45. Roberto, "De cuando el barrio entró a la UPR."

46. Ramírez interview, March 2, 2012.

47. For more information on the police occupation of Villa Cañona and the violence that followed, see the short documentary "El color de la justicia [2008]," YouTube, published March 24, 2011, http://youtu.be/H3CiyzJjSCo.

48. Cobián, "Los recogen en Loíza y los meten de guardias en la UPR sin explicaciones." Translation by author.

49. Cobián, "Los recogen en Loíza y los meten de guardias en la UPR sin explicaciones."

50. Huggins, Haritos-Fatouros, and Zimbardo, *Violence Workers*.

51. Cobián, "Los recogen en Loíza y los meten de guardias en la UPR sin explicaciones."

52. Santiago Negrón and Lugo Vázquez interview, March 6, 2011.

53. Roberto, "De cuando el barrio entró a la UPR." Translation by author.

54. Giovanni Roberto, interview by the author, Río Piedras, Puerto Rico, January 31, 2012.

55. Roberto interview, January 31, 2012.

56. Roberto interview, January 31, 2012.

57. Roberto interview, January 31, 2012.

58. "Giovanni Roberto—Discurso a Guardias Capitol—UPR 2010," YouTube, December 10, 2010, http://youtu.be/xXzpbYB7Ndo. Translation by author.

59. "Giovanni Roberto—Discurso a Guardias Capitol—UPR 2010."

60. "Giovanni Roberto—Discurso a Guardias Capitol—UPR 2010."

61. Historian Lauren Araiza defines bridge leaders as individuals within organizations or groups who cross divides to build coalitions that did not occur spontaneously with other organizations or groups. She notes, "But even with all of the necessary ingredients in place, individuals were needed to serve as catalysts. Bridge leaders had to recognize the potential in forming a coalition and convince their colleagues of its merits." For more see *To March for Others: The Black Freedom Struggle and the United Farm Workers* (Philadelphia: University of Pennsylvania Press, 2014), 9 and 170.

62. Juan A. Hernández, "Police Takes Over Campus after Stoppage," *Puerto Rico Daily Sun*, December 9, 2010.

63. y se quedará mientras sea necesario," *Primera Hora*, December 9, 2010, www.primerahora.com/noticias/gobierno-politica/nota/fortunoafirmapoliciarestablecio ordenenlauprysequedaramientrasseanecesario-451586. Translation by author.

64. "Fortuño afirma policía restableció orden en la UPR."

65. Javier Colón Dávila, "Se asoma un cuartel en la UPR," *El Nuevo Dia*, December 11, 2010, www.elnuevodia.com/seasomauncuartelenlaupr-835156.html. Translation by author.

66. Colón Dávila, "Se asoma un cuartel en la UPR."

67. Dennis Zayas interview, March 8, 2012.

68. The leaders represented Cantera in Santurce, the Luis Lloréns Torres public housing residence, Sonadora in Aguas Buenas, Piñones in Loíza, Mariana in Humacao, San Antonio in Caugas, and Los Filtros in Guaynabo.

69. Cristina del Mar Quiles, "Condena unánime a represión policiaca contra estudiantes UPR," InterNewsService, December 10, 2010. Translation by author.

70. del Mar Quiles, "Condena unánime a represión policiaca contra estudiantes UPR."

71. Nydia Bauza, Maritza Díaz, and Mariana Cobián, "Calma en la UPR—Minuto a minute," *PrimeraHora*, December 17, 2010, www.primerahora.com/noticias/gobier no-politica/nota/calmaenlaupr-minutoaminuto-454555/. Translation by author.

72. Caro interview, March 7, 2012.

73. Leysa Caro García, "Giovanni Roberto suspendido sumariamente de la UPR," *Primera Hora*, December 20, 2010, www.primerahora.com/noticias/gobier no-politica/nota/giovannirobertosuspendidosumariamentedelaupr-457077. Translation by author.

74. Caro García, "Giovanni Roberto suspendido sumariamente de la UPR."

75. Pedro Lugo, personal correspondence, December 9, 2013.

76. Lugo correspondence.

77. Caro interview, March 7, 2012.

78. Caro interview, March 7, 2012.

79. Caro interview, March 7, 2012.

80. Maritza Díaz Alcaide, "Se van a paro los profesores de la UPR," *Primera Hora*, February 10, 2011, www.primerahora.com/noticias/gobierno-politica/nota /sevanaparolosprofesoresdelaupr-472401/.

81. Gloria Ruiz Kuilan, "Miles marchan en 'Yo Amo la UPR,'" *El Nuevo Día*, February 15, 2011, www.elnuevodia.com/milesmarchanenyoamolaupr-889168.html.

82. Maribel Hernández Pérez, "Gobernador afirma que los policías deben estar en la calle y no en la universidad," *Primera Hora*, February 14, 2011, www.primera-hora.com/noticias/gobierno-politica/nota/gobernadorafirmaquelospoliciasdebene starenlacalleynoenlauniversidad-474453/.

83. The end date of the second strike is debatable. Some suggest that the strike did not end until May 2011; however, for many the end of the strike was marked by an incident in which UPR-RP chancellor Ana Guadalupe and the chief of campus security were assaulted by protesters on March 7, 2011. Although many students claim that the individuals who assaulted the chancellor and chief of campus security were not actually affiliated with the student movement and were police operatives, this moment soured the public's support, and the movement had difficulty mobilizing in the assault's wake.

84. Caro interview, March 7, 2012.

85. Vélez Soto interview, April 26, 2012.

86. Roberto interview, January 31, 2012.

87. Roberto interview, January 31, 2012.

88. Martha D. Escobar, *Captivity Beyond Prisons: Criminalization Experiences of Latina (Im)migrants* (Austin: University of Texas Press, 2016), 62.

89. Escobar, *Captivity Beyond Prisons*, 63.

90. Roberto, "De cuando el barrio entró a la UPR."

91. Roberto, "De cuando el barrio entró a la UPR."

CHAPTER 6. #IMPERFECTVICTIMS

1. Carlos Pabón, "Una Guerra social (in)visible," *80grados.net*, August 15, 2013, www.80grados.net/una-guerra-social-invisible. Translation by author.

2. "Internet Users (per 100 People)," The World Bank (last accessed June 9, 2016), https://datamarket.com/data/set/14ns/internet-users-per-100-people#!ds=1 4ns!gop=79.6y.20.67&display=line.

3. Michelle Kantrow, "88.1% of Local Social Media Users Connect Daily, Most Gravitate toward Facebook," *News Is My Business*, June 7, 2012, http://newsismybusiness.com/88-1-of-local-social-media-users-connect-daily-most-gravitate-toward-facebook.

4. For a popular critique of Internet activism, see Malcolm Gladwell, "Small Change: Why the Revolution Will Not Be Tweeted," *New Yorker*, October 4, 2010, www.newyorker.com/magazine/2010/10/04/small-change-malcolm-gladwell.

5. Anthropologist John Postill emphasizes the viral nature of social media and their potential to impact social change. According to Postill: "I am suggesting that social media are viral media. That is, they are designed and actively used to spread digital contents epidemically, from peer to peer, through routinized activities such as 'liking' a Facebook photograph, retweeting a political slogan, or emailing a You-Tube hyperlink to friends. From an epidemiographic vantage point, social media 'sharing' is synonymous with spreading." See John Postill, "Democracy in an Age of Viral Reality: A Media Epidemiography of Spain's Indignados Movement," *Ethnography* 15, no. 1 (2014): 55.

6. Yarimar Bonilla and Jonathan Rosa, "#Ferguson: Digital Protest, Hashtag Ethnography, and the Racial Politics of Social Media in the United States," *American Ethnologist* 42, no. 1 (2015): 10.

7. Bonilla and Rosa, "#Ferguson," 10.

8. John Postill, "Democracy in an Age of Viral Reality," 57.

9. Original tweet: *Esto no puede seguir así ya me da miedo salir hasta al trabajo #TodosSomosJoseEnrique*. Translation by author.

10. "Exitosa vigilia mundial en reclamo de paz en Puerto Rico," *El Nuevo Día*, December 8, 2012, www.elnuevodia.com/exitosavigiliamundialenreclamodepazenp uertorico-1403653.html.

11. Cristina Costantini, "After the Arab Spring, Comes a Boricua Winter," *ABC News*, December 7, 2012, https://abcnews.go.com/ABC_Univision/News/arab-spring-boricua-winter/story?id=17897909.

12. José A. Delgado, "Con más boricuas afuera que adentro," *El Nuevo Día*, September 29, 2013, www.elnuevodia.com/conmasboricuasafueraqueadentro -1606985.html.

13. Delgado, "Con más boricuas afuera que adentro."

14. Delgado, "Con más boricuas afuera que adentro." The total number of people living in Puerto Rico is 3.67 million; excluding foreign populations, the figure decreases to 3.51 million, the number cited by *El Nuevo Día* in its discussion of the Census data.

15. Costantini, "After the Arab Spring, Comes a Boricua Winter."

16. The original Facebook note reads: "Esta cabrón, y perdonen la palabra pero es la única que le cae, las cosas q vemos en nuestra isla. Hombre profesional, compañero de clase durante mas de 10 años de mi hermana. Es un asco ver como los criminales aquí hacen lo que les da la gana con la vida de las personas y todo por unos trapos de 500 dolares. . . Aveces por menos le quitan la vida a personas que aportan algo positivo al 100x35 que se ha convertido en una jungla de sobrevivientes sucumbiendo ante el temor, la opresión y ante las cabronerias de los que se creen que pueden

faltarle el respecto a la vida humana. Dicen que la mejor justicia es la justicia divina. Yo espero q asi sea. Pq ya de vdd q me da asco lo que vemos en nuestra isla todos los días. No podemos dejarle la isla a los delincuentes y encerarnos nosotros. No podemos restringirnos para dejarles a ellos los espacios y calles que desde pequeños corríamos bicicleta hasta la noche y pasaba nada. Eso es lo que quieres para ti? Para tu famila? Espero que no! Pq yo no lo quiero! A ponerse los calzoncillos y calzones en su sitio y a meter mano por nuestra isla!!!! YA ESTA BUENO!" Translation by author.

17. Statistic cited in Carlos Pabón, "Una Guerra social (in)visible."

18. "Padre de una de las detenidas en caso publicista afirma que es inocente," *PrimeraHora.com*, December 4, 2012, www.primerahora.com/noticias/policia-tribunales/nota/padredeunadelasdetenidasencasopublicistaafirmaqueesinocente-730942/.

19. Spawn 7896, "SuperXclusivo 12/6/12—Nuevos detalles sobre el asesinato del publicista 1/2," YouTube, January 8, 2013, https://youtu.be/QprTZeUdu9E; and Spawn 7896, "SuperXclusivo 12/6/12—Nuevos detalles sobre el asesinato del publicista 2/2," YouTube, January 8, 2013, https://youtu.be/om7UQbRZrOk.

20. Spawn 7896, "SuperXclusivo 12/6/12 . . . 1/2." Emphasis added.

21. Spawn 7896, "SuperXclusivo 12/6/12 . . . 2/2."

22. Ed Morales, "In Puerto Rico, the Political Discourse Is Dictated by a Female Puppet Called La Comay," *ABC News*, September 7, 2012, http://abcnews.go.com/ABC_Univision/Entertainment/puerto-rico-television-la-comay-super-xclusivo-tv/story?id=17213898.

23. Melissa Camacho, " La Comay: An Examination of the Puerto Rican Comadre as a Feminist Icon, Patriarchal Stereotype, and Television Tabloid Host," *Studies in Latin American Popular Culture* 30 (2012): 129.

24. Camacho, "La Comay," 132.

25. Manuel G. Avilés-Santiago, "No Puppet's Land: The Role of Social Media in Puerto Rico's Mainstream Television," *Journal of Latin American Communication Research* 4, no. 2 (2014): 58–59.

26. Avilés-Santiago, "No Puppet's Land," 59–60.

27. Erik Carrion, "La Comay & Me: What a Puerto Rican Creative Director Living in the U.S. Thinks of the Controversial Gossip Show," *HispanicAd.com,* November 17, 2012, http://hispanicad.com/blog/news-article/had/television/la-comay-me-what-puerto-rican-creative-director-living-us-thinks.

28. Frances Rosario, "Exigen investigación de crímenes de odio," *El Nuevo Día*, November 16, 2009, www.elnuevodia.com/exigeninvestigaciondecrimenesdeodio-638327.html.

29. Julio Ricardo Varela, "Opinion: Puerto Rico Needs More Than Hate Crime Laws to Change Intolerant Culture," *NBC Latino*, January 3, 2013, http://nbclatino.com/2013/01/03/opinion-puerto-rico-needs-more-than-hate-crime-laws-to-change-intolerant-culture.

30. Original tweet: *Jose Enrique era el tipico macho boricua embustero que le pegaba cuernos a su mujer con putas y patos en la calle. #TodosSomosJoseEnrique.* Translation by author.

31. Original tweet: #*TodosSomosJoseEnrique Ustedes quieren ser un tipo que le engañaba a la esposa y chingaba con maricones mmmm?? Yo no soy el, aya ustedes.* Translation by author.

32. Original tweet:*¿Ahora que saben que dije todo como era ya no me tiran? ¿Ah cabrones? Ese tipo se buscó la muerte por PUERCO. #YoNoSoyJoseEnrique.* Translation by author.

33. "'Nadie merece, ni se busca ser asesinado,'" *El Nuevo Día,* December 4, 2012, www.elnuevodia.com/nadiemerecenisebuscaserasesinado-1401098.html. Translation by author.

34. "'Nadie merece, ni se busca ser asesinado.'"

35. "Carta abierta del grupo 'Boicot a La Comay' exigiendo cancelación de SuperXclusivo," December 7, 2012, www.facebook.com/notes/boicot-a-la-comay /carta-abierta-del-grupo-boicot-a-la-comay-exigiendo-cancelación-de-superxclusivo /476827455693484.

36. Michelle Kantrow, "Latest Boycott of 'La Comay' Could Be Costly for WAPA TV," *News Is My Business,* December 5, 2012, http://newsismybusiness.com /latest-boycott-of-la-comay-could-be-costly-for-wapa-tv.

37. "Walmart se une al boicot a La Comay," *El Nuevo Día,* December 6, 2012, www.elnuevodia.com/walmartseunealboicotalacomay-1402320.html. Translation by author.

38. 40viajero, "Nuevas Voces diciendo 'NO a la comay,'" *YouTube,* www.you tube.com/watch?feature=player_embedded&v=3Jw8uROhqDg. Translation by author.

39. Nancy Scheper-Hughes, "Coming to Our Senses: Anthropology and Genocide," in *Annihilating Difference: The Anthropology of Genocide,* ed. Alexander Laban Hinton (Berkeley: University of California Press, 2002), 373.

40. This description of the hit and run that caused Ivania Zayas Ortiz's death draws from information provided by Javier Colón Dávila, "Muere cantautora impactada por un auto," *El Nuevo Dia,* February 8, 2015, www.elnuevodia.com/noticias /seguridad/nota/muerecantautoraimpactadaporunauto-2005227/.

41. "Redes sociales inundadas de mensajes contra el machismo en caso de Ivania Zayas," *Primera Hora,* February 9, 2015, http://www.primerahora.com/tecnologia /nota/redessocialesinundadasdemensajescontraelmachismoencasodeivaniazayas -1064523/.

42. Dalissa Zeda Sánchez, "Indignación y molestia por declaraciones sexistas de teniente de la policía," *El Nuevo Dia,* February 9, 2015, www.elnuevodia.com/noticias /locales/nota/indignacionymolestiapordeclaracionessexistasdetenientedelapolicia -2005708/. Translation by author.

43. Zeda Sánchez, "Indignación y molestia por declaraciones sexistas de teniente de la policía."

44. Feminist scholars and activists have long criticized the ways in which both the police and the public often criminalize and blame women who experience sexual violence and/or domestic violence. For arguably the most foundational example of this feminist critique for the discipline, see Kimberlé Crenshaw "Mapping the

Margins: Intersectionality, Identity Politics, and Violence against Women of Color," *Stanford Law Review* 43, no. 6 (1991): 1241–1299.

45. Zeda Sánchez, "Indignación y molestia por declaraciones sexistas de teniente de la policía." Translation by author.

46. Original Facebook post: *Aquí andando la calle solo. Supongo que si me atropellan y soy un hombre gay algo estaba hacienda a esta hora en la calle y me lo estaba buscando #andandolacallesola #necessitamosperspectivadegenero.* Translation by author.

47. Original text: *#andandolacallesoda desnuda, con ropa como de da la gana!* Translation by author.

48. All of the following tweets in the paragraph were posted on February 9, 2015, unless otherwise noted.

49. Original tweet: *#andandolacallesola y no por eso merezco ser victíma de caulquier tipo de violencia #Equidad #Mujer.* Translation by author.

50. Original tweet: *Me paso todo el día #andandolacallesola y no por eso alguien tiene que alsaltarme o atropellarme. #igualdad.* Translation by author.

51. Original tweet: *Soy Culpable, Irresponsable, Inepta. . .yo tomo guagua y el tren sola. . . y cruzo varias calles todos los días! #andandolacallesola.* Translation by author.

52. Original tweet: *De los creadores del gran éxito 'Si te violan es culpa tuya', ahora llega 'Si te atropellan te lo has buscado'. #andandolacallesola.* Translation by author.

53. Original tweet: *Razón # 1,000,000 para defender la educacion con #perspectivadegenero: Andar solas de noche sin que nos cuestione. #andandolacallesola.* Translation by author.

54. Original Instagram post: *#AndandolaCalleSola Porque soy libre de andar con quien quiera y a la hora que quera sin que sea algo pervertido y NADIE tiene que preguntar, y mucho menos tengo que someterme al estrutinio público si mis acciones no afectan a los demás. Otra de las muchas razones por las que necesitamos entender lo que es #PerspecitivadeGénero.* Translation by author.

55. Original tweet: *La ignorancia se combate con educación. No pospongamos más. Para que nunca más a una mujer la juzguen por estar #andandolacallesola.* Translation by author.

56. Movimiento Amplio de Mujeres de Puerto Rico, "Repudian expresiones machistas del Teniente Bauzó ante muerte de Ivania," Centro de Medios Independientes de Puerto Rico, February 11, 2015, http://pr.indymedia.org/news/2015/03/57636.php. Translation by author

57. Laura M. Quintero, "Perspectiva de género ya es ley en Educación," *Noticel*, February 26, 2015, www.noticel.com/noticia/172767/perspectiva-de-genero-ya-es-ley-en-educacion-documento.html.

58. George Rivera, "¿No les cansa?," *QiiBO*, February 10, 2015, www.qiibo.com/2015/02/10/columna-sobre-ivania-zayas/. Translation by author

59. Luis Daniel Hernández, "Reacciona a pruebas de alcohol en caso de Ivania Zayas," *El Vocero*, April 8, 2015, http://elvocero.com/reacciona-a-pruebas-de-alcohol-en-caso-de-ivania-zayas/ (last accessed; URL no longer valid).

60. Rebecca Banuchi, "No irá preso Tyrone Rohena por muerte de Ivania Zayas," *Primera Hora*, December 10, 2015, www.primerahora.com/noticias/policia-tribuna les/nota/noirapresotyronerohenapormuertedeivaniazayas-1125787/.

CHAPTER 7. SECURITY FROM BELOW

1. American Civil Liberties Union, *Island of Impunity: Puerto Rico's Outlaw Police Force* (June 2012), 12, www.aclu.org/report/island-impunity-puerto-ricos -outlaw-police-force.

2. ACLU, *Island of Impunity*, 49.

3. ACLU, *Island of Impunity*, 54.

4. ACLU, *Island of Impunity*, 54.

5. ACLU, *Island of Impunity*, 53.

6. ACLU, *Island of Impunity*, 53.

7. For footage and discussion of the Loizazo, see the documentary film *Aquel Rebaño Azul*, directed by Guillermo Gómez Álvarez (Comisión de Derechos Civiles de Puerto Rico, 2010).

8. Milvia Archilla, "Acusarán policías de los macanazos,'" *Primera Hora*, July 13, 2001, http://corp.primerahora.com/archivo.asp?guid=9E37E277773E11D5A2D80 0508B124842&year=2001&keyword=.

9. For an institutional history of Cure Violence see, Gary Slutkin, Charles Ransford, and R. Brent Decker, "Cure Violence: Treating Violence as a Contagious Disease," in *Envisioning Criminology: Researchers on Research as Process of Discovery*, ed. Michael D. Maltz and Stephen K. Rice (Basel: Springer International Publishing, 2015).

10. Slutkin, Ransford, and Decker, "Cure Violence," 43.

11. For instance, see Andrew V. Papachristos, "Too Big to Fail: The Science and Politics of Violence Prevention," *Criminology & Public Policy* 10, no. 4 (2011): 1056.

12. John D. Márquez, "The Black Mohicans: Representations of Everyday Violence in Postracial Urban America," *American Quarterly* 64, no. 3 (2012): 646.

13. "Masacran a tres jóvenes en Loíza," *Primera Hora*, October 1, 2009, www .primerahora.com/noticias/policia-tribunales/nota/masacranatresjovenesenloiza -334398/.

14. Zinnia Alejandro, interview by the author, Loíza, Puerto Rico, June 15, 2015.

15. Alana Feldman Soler, interview by the author, Río Piedras, Puerto Rico, June 3, 2015.

16. Feldman Soler interview, June 3, 2015.

17. Feldman Soler interview, June 3, 2015.

18. For more information on the police occupation of Villa Cañona and the violence that followed, see the short documentary, "El color de la justicia [2008]," YouTube, published March 24, 2011, http://youtu.be/H3CiyzJjSCo.

19. "Tiembla Loíza con la batalla entre bandos," *El Nuevo Día*, October 29, 2009, www.elnuevodia.com/noticias/locales/nota/tiemblaloizaconlabatallaen trebandos-631837/.

20. "Golpe Policial a Narcos en Loiza," *Notiuno*, www.notiuno.com/golpe -policial-a-narcos-en-loiza/.

21. "Golpe Policial a Narcos en Loiza."

22. Feldman Soler interview, June 3, 2015.

23. Feldman Soler interview, June 3, 2015.

24. Feldman Soler interview, June 3, 2015.

25. Feldman Soler interview, June 3, 2015.

26. Slutkin, Ransford, and Decker, "Cure Violence," 49.

27. Papachristos, "Too Big to Fail," 1056.

28. Papachristos, "Too Big to Fail," 1056.

29. Papachristos, "Too Big to Fail," 1056.

30. Alejandro interview, June 15, 2015.

31. Feldman Soler interview, June 3, 2015.

32. Feldman Soler interview, June 3, 2015.

33. Alejandro interview, June 15, 2015.

34. Alejandro interview, June 15, 2015.

35. Alejandro interview, June 15, 2015.

36. Alejandro interview, June 15, 2015.

37. Alejandro interview, June 15, 2015.

38. Alejandro interview, June 15, 2015.

39. According to Feldman Soler, police representatives participated in community panels less than a handful of times over the three years of the pilot program.

40. Alejandro interview, June 15, 2015.

41. Feldman Soler interview, June 3, 2015.

42. Feldman Soler interview, June 3, 2015.

43. Feldman Soler interview, June 3, 2015.

44. Feldman Soler interview, June 3, 2015.

45. Alejandro interview, June 15, 2015.

46. Alejandro interview, June 15, 2015.

47. Feldman Soler interview, June 3, 2015.

48. Cure Violence, "CureViolence—Puerto Rico," YouTube, May 27, 2015, https://youtu.be/aWcHbxJkXK8.

49. Laura M. Quintero, "Taller Salud, un escudo humano contra la violencia en Loíza," *Noticel*, October 27, 2013, www.noticel.com/noticia/150430/taller-salud-un -escudo-humano-contra-la-violencia-en-loiza.html.

50. Alejandro interview, June 15, 2015.

51. Feldman Soler interview, June 3, 2015.

52. Alejandro interview, June 15, 2015.

53. Alejandro interview, June 15, 2015.

54. Alejandro interview, June 15, 2015.

55. Feldman Soler interview, June 3, 2015.

56. Angela P. Harris, "Gender, Violence, Race, and Criminal Justice," *Stanford Law Review* 52, no. 4 (2000): 779.

57. Harris, "Gender, Violence, Race, and Criminal Justice," 779. Emphasis in the original.

58. Michael S. Kimmel and Matthew Mahler, "Adolescent Masculinity, Homophobia, and Violence: Random school shootings, 1982–2001," *American Behavioral Scientist* 46, no. 10 (2003): 1452.

59. Alejandro interview, June 15, 2015.

60. Alejandro interview, June 15, 2015.

61. Victor Ríos, *Punished: Policing the Lives of Black and Latino Boys* (New York: New York University Press, 2011), 129.

62. Feldman Soler interview, June 3, 2015.

63. Feldman Soler interview, June 3, 2015.

64. Feldman Soler interview, June 3, 2015.

65. Feldman Soler interview, June 3, 2015.

66. Alejandro interview, June 15, 2015.

67. Alejandro interview, June 15, 2015.

68. Alejandro interview, June 15, 2015.

69. Cherríe Moraga, Preface to *This Bridge Called My Back: Writings by Radical Women of Color*, 2nd ed., ed. Cherríe Moraga and Gloria Anzaldúa (New York: Kitchen Table: Women of Color Press, 1983), xiv.

70. Alejandro interview, June 15, 2015.

71. Inter News Services, "Cierre de Programa Acuerdo de Paz Aguadiza la Incidencia Criminal en Loíza," *Univision*, September 12, 2016, www.univision.com /noticias/violencia/cierre-de-programa-acuerdo-de-paz-agudiza-la-incidencia -criminal-en-loiza.

POSTSCRIPT: BROKEN WINDOWS AND FUTURE HORIZONS AFTER THE STORM

1. Puerto Rico Oversight, Management, and Economic Stability Act or PROMESA, H.R. 4900, 114th Cong. (2015–2016), www.congress.gov/bill/114th -congress/house-bill/4900/.

2. Hidla Lloréns, "Ruin Nation," *NACLA Report on the Americas* 50, no. 2 (2018): 154–159.

3. Marga Parés Arroyo and Sara Del Valle Hernández, "Hallan causa contra siete estudiantes por interrumpir reunión de la UPR," *El Nuevo Día*, May 9, 2017, www .elnuevodia.com/noticias/tribunales/nota/hallancausacontrasieteestudiantesporin terrumpirreuniondelaupr-2319269/; and "Causa para arresto por delitos graves contra universitarios por incidentes en la Junta de Gobierno de la UPR," Departamento de Justicia de Puerto Rico, May 9, 2017, www.justicia.pr.gov/causa-para-arresto-por -delitos-graves-contra-universitarios-por-incidentes-en-la-junta-de-gobierno-de -la-upr/.

4. "Woman Arrested for Use of Arson or Explosives," Department of Justice, United States Attorney's Office District of Puerto Rico, May 2, 2017, www.justice .gov/usao-pr/pr/woman-arrested-use-arson-or-explosives.

5. Comité de Amigos y Familiares de Nina Droz Franco, www.facebook.com/ NinaNoEstaSola/.

6. Eric De León Soto, "Policía atropella a manifestante contra la junta," *Noticel*, February 20, 2018, www.noticel.com/ahora/politica/desatan-furia-contra -maniquis-de-polticos/704798074.

7. Carla Minet and Luis J. Valentín Ortiz, "Protest Faceoff at Puerto Rico Control Board Meeting," *Village Voice*, February 2, 2018, www.villagevoice.com/2018 /02/02/protest-faceoff-at-puerto-rico-control-board-meeting/.

8. Minet and Valentín Ortiz, "Protest Faceoff at Puerto Rico Control Board Meeting."

9. Hilda Lloréns, "In Puerto Rico, Environmental Injustice and Racism Inflame Protests over Coal Ash," *Conversation*, December 8, 2016, https://theconversation. com/in-puerto-rico-environmental-injustice-and-racism-inflame-protests -over-coal-ash-69763.

10. Rob Nixon, *Slow Violence and the Environmentalism of the Poor* (Cambridge, MA: Harvard University Press, 2011).

11. Javier Arbona and Marisol LeBrón, "Resisting Debt and Colonial Disaster in Post-Maria Puerto Rico," *Funambulist*, no. 16: 6–8.

12. Associated Press, "Adoptan 'tolerancia cero' por homicidios," *El Vocero*, January 16, 2018, www.elvocero.com/ley-y-orden/adoptan-tolerancia-cero-por-homici dios/article_437205a8-fb21-11e7-9182-b73da895f53c.html. Translation by author.

13. Syrmarie Villlalobos, "Comerse la luz será delito a perseguir fuertemente," *WAPA TV*, January 16, 2018, www.wapa.tv/noticias/locales/comerse-la-luz-sera -delito-a-perseguir-fuertemente_20131122421369.html.

14. "Domestic Violence Soared Following Puerto Rico Hurricane," *Crime Report*, February 1, 2018, https://thecrimereport.org/2018/02/01/domestic-violence -soared-following-puerto-rico-hurricane/.

15. A. J. Vicens, "After the Hurricane, Puerto Rico's Suicide Rates Spike," *Mother Jones*, February 12, 2018, www.motherjones.com/politics/2018/02/after-the -hurricane-puerto-ricos-suicide-rates-spike/.

BIBLIOGRAPHY

Alamo-Pastrana. Carlos. *Seams of Empire: Race and Radicalism in Puerto Rico and the United States*. Gainesville: University Press of Florida, 2016.

Alexander, Michelle. *The New Jim Crow: Mass Incarceration in the Age of Color-blindness*. New York: The New Press, 2012.

Araiza, Lauren. *To March for Others: The Black Freedom Struggle and the United Farm Workers*. Philadelphia: University of Pennsylvania Press, 2014.

Arbona, Javier, and Marisol LeBrón. "Resisting Debt and Colonial Disaster in Post-Maria Puerto Rico." *Funambulist* 16 (2018): 6–8.

Arena, John. *Driven from New Orleans: How Nonprofits Betray Public Housing and Promote Privatization*. Minneapolis: University of Minnesota Press, 2012.

Avilés-Santiago, Manuel G. "No Puppet's Land: The Role of Social Media in Puerto Rico's Mainstream Television." *Journal of Latin American Communication Research* 4, no. 2 (2014): 52–70.

Ayala, César J., and Rafael Bernabe. *Puerto Rico in the American Century: A History Since 1898*. Chapel Hill: University of North Carolina Press, 2007.

Balko, Radley. *Overkill: The Rise of Paramilitary Police Raids in America* (Washington, DC: The Cato Institute, 2006).

———. *Rise of the Warrior Cop: The Militarization of America's Police Forces*. New York: Public Affairs, 2013.

Berman Santana, Déborah. *Kicking Off the Bootstraps: Environment, Development, and Community Power in Puerto Rico*. Tucson: University of Arizona Press, 1996.

Blakely, Edward J., and Mary G. Snyder. *Fortress America: Gated Communities in the United States*. Washington, DC: The Brookings Institution, 1999.

Blecha, Peter. *Taboo Tunes: A History of Banned Bands & Censored Songs*. San Francisco: Backbeat Books, 2004.

Bonilla, Frank, and Ricardo Campos. *Industry and Idleness*. New York: Centro de Estudios Puertorriqueños, 1986.

———. "A Wealth of Poor: Puerto Ricans in the New Economic Order." *Daedalus* 110, no. 2 (1981): 133–176.

Bonilla, Yarimar, and Rafael A. Boglio Martínez. "Puerto Rico in Crisis: Government Workers Battle Neoliberal Reform." *NACLA Report on the Americas* 43, no. 1 (2010): 6–8.

Bonilla, Yarimar, and Jonathan Rosa. "#Ferguson: Digital Protest, Hashtag Ethnography, and the Racial Politics of Social Media in the United States." *American Ethnologist* 42, no. 1 (2015): 4–17.

Bonilla-Silva, Eduardo. *Racism without Racists: Color-Blind Racism and the Persistence of Racial Inequality in America.* 4th ed. Lanham, MD: Rowman & Littlefield Publishers, 2013.

Briggs, Laura. *Reproducing Empire: Race, Sex, Science, and U.S. Imperialism in Puerto Rico.* Berkeley: University of California Press, 2002.

Butler, Judith. *Precarious Life: The Powers of Mourning and Violence.* New York: Verso, 2006.

Cacho, Lisa Marie. *Social Death: Racialized Rightlessness and the Criminalization of the Unprotected.* New York: New York University Press, 2012.

Caldeira, Teresa. *City of Walls: Crime, Segregation, and Citizenship in São Paulo.* Berkeley, University of California Press, 2000.

Camacho, Melissa. "La Comay: An Examination of the Puerto Rican Comadre as a Feminist Icon, Patriarchal Stereotype, and Television Tabloid Host." *Studies in Latin American Popular Culture* 30 (2012): 124–137.

Carrasquillo Ramírez, Alfredo. "Los enemigos del orden: La mano dura contra el crimen y la legitimación del poder político en Puerto Rico, 1992–1995." MA thesis, Centro de Estudios Avanzados de Puerto Rico y el Caribe, 2002.

Chankin, James, and Leigh Savidge, dirs. *Straight Outta Puerto Rico: Reggaeton's Rough Road to Glory.* Xenon Pictures, 2008.

Chen, Mel Y. *Animacies: Biopolitics, Racial Mattering, and Queer Affect.* Durham, NC: Duke University Press, 2012.

Chevigny, Paul. *Edge of the Knife: Police Violence in the Americas.* New York: The New Press, 1995.

Correia, David, and Tyler Wall. *Police: A Field Guide.* Brooklyn, NY: Verso, 2018.

Crenshaw, Kimberlé. "Mapping the Margins: Intersectionality, Identity Politics, and Violence against Women of Color." *Stanford Law Review* 43, no. 6 (1991): 1241–1299.

Currie, Elliott. *Crime and Punishment in America.* New York: Henry Holt and Company, 1998.

Dietz, James. *Economic History of Puerto Rico: Institutional Change and Capitalist Development.* Princeton, NJ: Princeton University Press, 1986.

Dietz, James L. *Puerto Rico: Negotiating Development and Change.* Boulder, CO: Lynne Rienner Publishers, 2003.

Dinzey-Flores, Zaire Zenit. "Criminalizing Communities of Poor, Dark Women in the Caribbean: The Fight against Crime through Puerto Rico's Public Housing." *Crime Prevention and Community Safety* 13, no. 1 (2011): 53–73.

———. "De la Disco al Caserío: Urban Spatial Aesthetics and Policy to the Beat of Reggaetón." *Centro Journal* 20, no. 2 (2008): 35–69.

———. *Locked In, Locked Out: Gated Communities in a Puerto Rican City*. Philadelphia: University of Pennsylvania Press, 2013.

Escobar, Martha D. *Captivity Beyond Prisons: Criminalization Experiences of Latina (Im)migrants*. Austin: University of Texas Press, 2016.

Fassin, Didier. *Enforcing Order: An Ethnography of Urban Policing*. Cambridge, UK: Polity Press, 2013.

Figueroa, Judith Rodríguez, and Alma Irizarry Castro. *El homicidio en Puerto Rico: Características y nexos con la violencia*. San Juan: Universidad Carlos Albizu, 2003.

Foucault, Michel. *The Birth of Biopolitics: Lectures at the Collège de France, 1978–1979*. New York: Picador, 2010.

Fraser, James, Deidre Oakley, and Joshua Bazuin. "Public Ownership and Private Profit in Housing." *Cambridge Journal of Regions, Economy and Society* 5, no. 3 (2011): 397–412.

Fusté, José I. "Colonial Laboratories, Irreparable Subjects: The Experiment of '(B)ordering' San Juan's Public Housing Residents." *Social Identities* 16, no. 1 (2010): 41–59.

Gilmore, Ruth Wilson. *Golden Gulag: Prisons, Surplus, Crisis, and Opposition in Globalizing California*. Berkeley: University of California Press, 2007.

Giovannetti, Jorge L. "Puerto Rico: An Island of Massacres." *Global Dialogue: Newsletter for the International Sociological Association* 3, no. 5 (2013). http://isa -global-dialogue.net/puerto-rico-an-island-of-massacres.

———. "Popular Music and Culture in Puerto Rico: Jamaican and Rap Music as Cross-Cultural Symbols." In *Musical Migrations*, vol. 1, *Transnationalism and Cultural Hybridity in Latina/o America*, edited by Frances R. Aparicio and Cadida F. Jaquez, 81–98. New York: Palgrave Macmillan, 2003.

Godreau, Isar P. *Scripts of Blackness: Race, Cultural Nationalism, and U.S. Colonialism in Puerto Rico*. Champaign: University of Illinois Press, 2015.

González Torres, Irmarilis. "¡No hay cárcel pa' tanta gente!" *Masturbana* (independently distributed 'zine), December 1994.

Graham, Stephan. *Cities Under Siege: The New Military Urbanism*. London: Verso, 2010.

Hall, Stuart. "Encoding, Decoding." In *The Cultural Studies Reader*, 2nd ed., edited by Simon During, 507–517. London: Routledge, 1993.

Hall, Stuart, Chas Critcher, Tony Jefferson, John Clarke, and Brian Roberts. *Policing the Crisis: Mugging, the State, and Law and Order*. London: Macmillan Press, 1978.

Harris, Angela P. "Gender, Violence, Race, and Criminal Justice." *Stanford Law Review* 52, no. 4 (2000): 777–807.

Hinton, Elizabeth. *From the War on Poverty to the War on Crime: The Making of Mass Incarceration in America*. Cambridge, MA: Harvard University Press, 2016.

History Task Force of the Centro de Estudios Puertorriqueños. *Labor Migration under Capitalism: The Puerto Rican Experience*. New York: Monthly Review Press, 1979.

Huggins, Martha K., Mika Haritos-Fatouros, and Philip G. Zimbardo. *Violence Workers: Police Torturers and Murderers Reconstruct Brazilian Atrocities.* Berkeley: University of California Press, 2002.

Kelley, Robin D. G. *Yo' Mama's Disfunktional! Fighting the Culture Wars in Urban America.* Boston: Beacon Press, 1997.

Kimmel Michael S., and Matthew Mahler. "Adolescent Masculinity, Homophobia, and Violence: Random School Shootings, 1982–2001." *American Behavioral Scientist* 46, no. 10 (2003): 1439–1458.

Laguarta Ramírez, Juan. "Struggling to Learn, Learning to Struggle: Strategy and Structure in the 2010–11 University of Puerto Rico Student Strike." PhD diss., Graduate Center, City University of New York, 2016.

Lancaster, Roger. *Sex Panic and the Punitive State.* Berkeley: University of California Press, 2011.

Lapp, Michael. "The Rise and Fall of Puerto Rico as a Social Laboratory, 1945–1965." *Social Science History* 19, no. 2 (1995): 169–199.

LeBrón, Marisol. "Carpeteo Redux: Surveillance and Subversion Against the Puerto Rican Student Movement." *Radical History Review* 128 (2017): 147–172.

———. "Neocolonial Policing in Puerto Rico." *NACLA Report on the Americas* 45, no. 1 (2011): 12–16.

Linebaugh, Peter. "Karl Marx, the Theft of Wood, and Working Class Composition: A Contribution to the Current Debate." *Crime and Social Justice* 6 (Fall–Winter 1976): 5–16.

Lipsitz, George. *How Racism Takes Place.* Philadelphia: Temple University Press, 2011.

Lloréns, Hilda. *Imaging the Great Puerto Rican Family: Framing Nation, Race, and Gender During the American Century.* Lanham, MD: Lexington Books, 2014.

———. "Ruin Nation." *NACLA Report on the Americas* 50, no. 2 (2018): 154–159.

Lopez, Iris. *Matters of Choice: Puerto Rican Women's Struggle for Reproductive Freedom.* New Brunswick: Rutgers University Press, 2008.

Low, Setha. *Behind the Gates: Life, Security, and the Pursuit of Happiness in Fortress America.* New York: Routledge, 2004.

Lytle Hernández, Kelly. *Migra! A History of the U.S. Border Patrol.* Berkeley: University of California Press, 2010.

Márquez, John D. "The Black Mohicans: Representations of Everyday Violence in Postracial Urban America." *American Quarterly* 64, no. 3 (2012): 625–651.

———. "Latinos as the 'Living Dead': Raciality, Expendability, and Border Militarization." *Latino Studies* 10, no. 4 (2012): 473–498.

Marshall, Wayne. "From Música Negra to Reggaeton Latino: The Cultural Politics of Nation, Migration, and Commercialization." In *Reggaeton*, edited by Wayne Marshall, Raquel Z. Rivera, and Deborah Pacini Hernandez, 19–78. Durham, NC: Duke University Press, 2009.

Martínez Llompart, Patricio G. "In the Custody of Violence: Puerto Rico Under La Mano Dura Contra el Crimen, 1993–1996." *Revista Jurídica UPR* 84, no. 2 (2015): 477–493.

Melendez, Edwin, and Edgardo Melendez, eds. *Colonial Dilemma: Critical Perspectives on Contemporary Puerto Rico*. Boston: South End Press, 1993.

Mitrani, Sam. *The Rise of the Chicago Police Department: Class and Conflict, 1850–1894*. Champaign: University of Illinois Press, 2014.

Montalvo-Barbot, Alfredo. "Crime in Puerto Rico: Drug Trafficking, Money Laundering, and the Poor." *Crime & Delinquency* 43, no. 4 (1997): 533–547.

Moraga, Cherríe, and Gloria Anzaldúa, eds. *This Bridge Called My Back: Writings by Radical Women of Color*. 2nd ed. New York: Kitchen Table/Women of Color Press, 1983.

Murakawa, Naomi. *The First Civil Right: How Liberals Built Prison America*. Oxford: Oxford University Press, 2014.

Murray, Martin J. *Taming the Disorderly City: The Spatial Landscape of Johannesburg after Apartheid*. Ithaca, NY: Cornell University Press, 2008.

Nevares-Muñiz, Dora. *El crimen en Puerto Rico: Tapando el cielo con la mano*. 3rd ed. San Juan: Instituto para el Desarrollo del Derecho, 2008.

Nixon, Rob. *Slow Violence and the Environmentalism of the Poor*. Cambridge, MA: Harvard University Press, 2011.

Pantojas-García, Emilio. *Development Strategies as Ideology: Puerto Rico's Export-Led Industrialization Experience*. Boulder, CO: Lynne Rienner Publishers, 1990.

———. "'Federal Funds' and the Puerto Rican Economy: Myths and Realities." *Centro Journal* 19, no. 2 (2007): 206–223.

Papachristos, Andrew V. "Too Big to Fail: The Science and Politics of Violence Prevention." *Criminology & Public Policy* 10, no. 4 (2011): 1053–1061.

Paralitici, José F. "A 85 años—situación del ROTC." In *Universidad y (Anti)Militarismo: Historia, Luchas y Debates*, edited by Anita Yudkin Suliveres, 28–49. San Juan: Universitarios por la Desmilitarización, 2005.

Parenti, Christian. *Lockdown America: Police and Prisons in the Age of Crisis*. 2nd ed. New York: Verso Books, 2008.

Pelot-Hobbs, Lydia. "The Contested Terrain of the Louisiana Carceral State: Dialectics of Southern Penal Expansion, 1971–2016." PhD diss., City University of New York Graduate Center, 2018.

Pérez, Gina. *The Near Northwest Side Story: Migration, Displacement, and Puerto Rican Families*. Berkeley: University of California Press, 2004.

Picó, Fernando. *De la mano dura a la cordura: Ensayos sobre el estado ausente, la sociabilidad y los imaginarios puertorriqueños*. Río Piedras, PR: Ediciones Huracán, 1999.

Picó Vidal, Isabel. "Los orígenes del movimiento estudiantil universitario: 1903–1930." *Revista de Ciencias Sociales* 24, no. 1 (1985): 36–77.

Postill, John. "Democracy in an Age of Viral Reality: A Media Epidemiography of Spain's Indignados Movement." *Ethnography* 15, no. 1 (2014): 51–69.

Pulido, Laura. "Rethinking Environmental Racism: White Privilege and Urban Development in Southern California." *Annals of the Association of American Geographers* 90, no. 1 (2000): 12–40.

Quinn, Eithne. *Nuthin' but a 'G 'Thang: The Culture and Commerce of Gangsta Rap.* New York: Columbia University Press, 2004.

Ríos, Victor. *Punished: Policing the Lives of Black and Latino Boys.* New York: New York University Press, 2011.

Rivera, Raquel Z. "Cultura y Poder en el rap puertorriqueño." *Revista de Ciencias Sociales* 4 (1998): 124–146.

———. "Policing Morality, *Mano Dura Stylee*: The Case of Underground Rap and Reggae in Puerto Rico in the Mid-1990s." In *Reggaeton*, edited by Wayne Marshall, Raquel Z. Rivera, and Deborah Pacini Hernandez, 111–134. Durham, NC: Duke University Press, 2009.

———. "Rap Music in Puerto Rico: Mass Consumption or Social Resistance?" *Centro: Journal of the Center for Puerto Rican Studies* 5, no. 1 (1992–1993): 52–64.

———. "Rapping Two Versions of the Same Requiem." In *Puerto Rican Jam: Essays on Culture and Politics*, edited by Frances Negron-Muntaner and Ramon Grosfoguel, 243–256. Minneapolis: University of Minnesota Press, 1997.

Rivera-Bonilla, Ivelisse. "Divided City: The Proliferation of Gated Communities in San Juan." PhD diss., University of California at Santa Cruz, 2003.

Rivera-Rideau, Petra R. *Remixing Reggaetón: The Cultural Politics of Race in Puerto Rico.* Durham, NC: Duke University Press, 2015.

Rodríguez, Dylan. *Forced Passages: Imprisoned Radical Intellectuals and the U.S. Prison Regime.* Minneapolis: University of Minnesota Press, 2006.

Rodríguez, Luz Marie. "Suppressing the Slum! Architecture and Social Change in San Juan's Public Housing." In *San Juan siempre nuevo: Arquitectura y modernización en el siglo XX*, edited by Enrique Vivoni Falagio, 74–117. Río Piedras: Archivo de Arquitectura y Construcción Universidad de Puerto Rico, 2000.

Rodríguez-Silva, Ileana M. *Silencing Race: Disentangling Blackness, Colonialism, and National Identities in Puerto Rico.* New York: Palgrave Macmillan, 2012.

Rosa, Alessandra M. "Resistance Performances: (Re)constructing Spaces of Resistance and Contention in the 2010–2011 University of Puerto Rico Student Movement." PhD diss., Florida International University, 2015.

Rose, Tricia. *Black Noise: Rap Music and Black Culture in Contemporary America.* Middletown, CT: Wesleyan University Press, 1994.

———. *The Hip Hop Wars: What We Talk About When We Talk About Hip Hop—and Why It Matters.* New York: Basic Civitas Books, 2008.

Rosselló, Pedro. *A mi manera.* Vol. 1. Gurabo, PR: Sistema Universitario Ana G. Méndez, 2012.

Santos Febres, Mayra. "Geografía en decibeles: Utopías pancaribeñas y el territorio del rap." In *Caribe 2000: Definiciones, identidades y culturas regionales y/o nacionales,* edited by Lowell Fiet and Janette Becerra, 121–137. San Juan: Facultad de Humanidades, Universidad de Puerto Rico, Recinto de Río Piedras, 1997.

Scheper-Hughes, Nancy. "Coming to Our Senses: Anthropology and Genocide." In *Annihilating Difference: The Anthropology of Genocide,* edited by Alexander Laban Hinton, 348–381. Berkeley: University of California Press, 2002.

Schill, Michael H. "Privatizing Federal Low Income Housing Assistance: The Case of Public Housing." *Cornell Law Review* 75 (1990): 878–948.

Scott, James C. *Weapons of the Weak: Everyday Forms of Peasant Resistance.* New Haven, CT: Yale University Press, 1987.

Simon, Harvey. "Mano Dura: Mobilizing the National Guard to Battle Crime in Puerto Rico." Kennedy School of Government Case Program (Case No. C109-97-1390.0), 1997.

———. "Mano Dura: Mobilizing the National Guard to Battle Crime in Puerto Rico (Epilogue)." Kennedy School of Government Case Program (Case No. C109-97-1390.0), 1997.

Simon, Jonathan. *Governing Through Crime: How the War on Crime Transformed American Democracy and Created a Culture of Fear.* Oxford: Oxford University Press, 2007.

Singh, Nikhil Pal. "The Whiteness of the Police." *American Quarterly* 66, no. 4 (2014): 1091–1099.

Slutkin, Gary, Charles Ransford, and R. Brent Decker. "Cure Violence: Treating Violence as a Contagious Disease." In *Envisioning Criminology: Researchers on Research as Process of Discovery*, edited by Michael D. Maltz and Stephen K. Rice, 43–56. Basel, Switzerland: Springer International Publishing, 2015.

Spade, Dean. *Normal Life: Administrative Violence, Critical Trans Politics, and the Limits of Law.* Brooklyn, NY: South End Press, 2011.

Taylor, Keeanga-Yamahtta. *From #Blacklivesmatter to Black Liberation.* Chicago: Haymarket Books, 2016.

Torres. Arlene. "La gran familia Puertorriqueña 'ej prieta de bledá' (The Great Puerto Rican Family Is Really Really Black)." In *Blackness in Latin American and the Caribbean*, Vol. 2, edited by Arlene Torres and Norman Whitten, 285–306. Bloomington: Indiana University Press, 1998.

Venkatesh, Sudhir Alladi. *Off the Books: The Underground Economy of the Urban Poor.* Cambridge, MA: Harvard University Press, 2009.

Villa Rodríguez, Joel A. *Crimen y Criminalidad en Puerto Rico: El sujeto criminal.* San Juan: Ediciones SITUM, Inc., 2006.

INDEX

abjection, 14

Las Acacias, 27–29, 86, 88

accountability, 2, 4, 140–141, 167, 171, 187, 195, 204, 217–220, 228

Acevedo Vilá, Aníbal, 115–116, 134, 138, 141–143, 187, 198; *Puerto Rico sin miedo* (Puerto Rico without fear), 139–140; 2006 State of the Nation address, 140

activism, 5, 18, 75, 126, 143, 233, 242n11, 246n7; antiviolence, 4, 83, 122, 176–201, 204–231, 272n44; hashtag, 22, 176–201; mano dura and, 20–21, 36, 115; student, 1, 21, 144–175, 239, 265n13, 269n83. *See also* anticolonialism; Arab Spring; Boricua Winter; boycotts; decolonization; feminism; May Day Protest (2017); Paro Nacional del Pueblo (People's National Stoppage); pintatas (paintins); strikes

Acuerdo de Paz, 22, 205–208, 211–222, 224–231

AES, 234

Africa, 12, 182, 205. *See also individual countries*

African American studies, 30. *See also* Black studies

Aguas Buenas, 268n68

AIDS, 100, 205

Alamo-Pastrana, Carlos, 12

Los Alamos, 126

@alejandrat67, 198

Alejandro, Zinnia, 208, 212–216, 219–225, 227–229, 233

Alemán, Laura: "Un Abrazo Para Puerto Rico" ("A Hug for Puerto Rico"), 181–182

Alexander Hamilton Building, 233

@Alexandrita_03, 197

Al Grano, 92–93

Al Jazeera, 180

Al Rojo Vivo, 112

Alturas de Cibuco, 255n83

Alturas de Vega Baja, 255n83

Álvarez Núñez, Neftalí "Pacho," 112; "Como Grita el Palo," 113

American Chamber of Commerce of the Dominican Republic, 58

American Civil Liberties Union (ACLU), 2, 41, 158, 209, 220; *Island of Impunity: Puerto Rico's Outlaw Police Force*, 202–204

Americanization, 12, 150

American studies, 13, 18

Americas, 6, 34, 36, 57–59. *See also individual countries and territories*

Ana Marie (@Anamarierr), 181

#AndandoLaCalleSola, 179, 194–201. *See also* #WalkingTheStreetsAlone

annexation, 12, 58, 147, 150

anthropology, 12, 14–15, 19, 27, 178, 193, 232, 242n10, 270n5

anticolonialism, 12. *See also* decolonization

apartheid boricua, 35–36

Aponte, Lenisse: murder of Enrique Gómez Saladín, 180

Arab Spring, 180

Araiza, Lauren, 268n61
Archilla Rivera, Milvia Y., 40
archipelago, explanation, 241n7
Arecibo, 98
Arena, John, 69
Arístides Chavier, 132
arrabales, 14
Asia: Southeast, 151
Asociación de Miembros de la Policía, 135–136
Asociación Ñeta, 79
Association of Puerto Rican University Professors, 149
ATH, 191
AT&T, 191
austerity, 172, 232–233, 236. See also neoliberalism
autogestión (self-management), 238–239
Avilés-Santiago, Manuel G., 188
Ayala, César J., 247n20, 252n24
Ayala Rivera, José Amaury: murder by PRPD, 203
Ayala Rivera, Luis, 203

Banco Popular Center, 233
Bank of Boston, 57–58
Barbés, Scott, 233
Barbosa, José Celso, 58, 83
Barceló, Carlos Romero, 151, 252n24; "Statehood Is for the Poor," 59
Barrio Amelia, 263n86
Barrio Las Hoyas, 263n86
Barrio Obrero, 248n31; police precinct, 48
#BastaYa, 180, 184
Bauzó Carrasquillo, Félix J., 179, 194–196, 198–199
Bayamón, 39–40, 137, 263n86
Bazuin, Joshua, 69
Beethoven: Ode to Joy, 24
Berkan, Judith, 41
Berman Santana, Déborah, 7
Bernabe, Rafael, 100, 247n20, 252n24
Berríos, Rubén, 117
Berrios Cotto, Alejandra: murder of Enrique Gómez Saladín, 180
Berrios Martínez, Pedro, 63
Betancourt Lebrón, Ismael, 28, 48
bichotes, 29, 83

biopolitics, 4
Black studies, 14, 18. See also African American studies
blue flu, 28
Boglio Martínez, Rafael, 146
#BoicotLaComay, 179, 190
Boicot La Comay (Boycott La Comay) Facebook Group, 190–191
Bolívar, Simón, 55, 58, 60, 252n21
Bonilla, Frank, 86–87
Bonilla, Yarimar, 146, 178
Borden Dairy, 191
Boricua Winter, 180–181, 185, 192, 194
Boston Globe, 65, 73–74
boycotts, 179, 191–193. See also #BoicotLaComay; Boicot La Comay (Boycott La Comay) Facebook Group
Bratton, William J., 120
Brazil, 246n13
Brazil, Harold, 67
Brewley MC: "La Voz del Crimen," 89–90
Brigada Solidaria del Oeste, 239
Briggs, Laura, 53
broken windows policing, 82, 232, 236–237
Brotherhood of Non-Teaching Employees, 149
Brown, Lee P., 71
Brown, Michael: police murder of, 178
Bureau of Alcohol, Tobacco, and Firearms, 129
Burnette, Jasper, 73
Bush, George H.W., 56, 60
Bush, Laura, 211
B.W. Cooper, 119

Cacho, Lisa Marie, 3
Caguas, 98, 186
Caimito, 124
Calas, Manuel, 76
Calderón, Sila María, 115–118, 120–127, 133–140, 143; Policía y Comunidad program, 132; Puerto Rican Project for the Twenty-First Century, 128. See also mano firme
California, 243n26, 246n13; Los Angeles, 45, 67; Orange County, 45

Calle Cucharilla, 263n86
Calle Padial, 186–187, 190
Camacho, Melissa, 188
Camilo-Robles, Grancid: attack by Miguel
  Díaz Martínez, 40
Campos, Ricardo, 86–87, 257n6
Canada, 56
Candelas, Luara, 195–196
Canóvanas, 223, 263n86
La Cantera, 263n86, 268n68
capitalism, 7, 47, 86, 160; colonial, 8, 10–12,
  16–17, 22, 59, 87, 104–105, 110, 143, 150,
  233, 236, 239, 242n10; policing's role in,
  6, 16–17, 174, 204. *See also* austerity;
  class; neoliberalism; poverty; trade
  liberalization
Capitol Security, 155–163, 173–174
carceral state, 5, 55, 143. *See also* incarcera-
  tion; prisons
carceral studies, 18
Caribbean, 7, 52–53, 55–57, 59, 61, 68, 78, 82,
  177, 212, 242n11. *See also individual
  countries and territories*
Caribbean Basin Initiative, 56
Caribbean Sea, 52
Caribe Hilton, 72
Caro, Xiomara, 145–146, 155, 160, 166–167,
  169–170, 172, 265n5
Carolina, 38, 137, 161–162, 263n86
Carrasquillo, José A. Rosa: attack on José
  "Osito" Pérez Riesler, 153
Carrasquillo Carrasquillo, Jonathan:
  murder of, 207
Cartagena Díaz, Agustín, 135–137
caseríos, 14–15, 88, 108, 166, 170. *See also*
  public housing
casetas, 126
castigo seguro (certain punishment), 116,
  139–140, 142, 185
Castillo, Lourdes, 129–130
Cataño, 40, 113, 131–132, 263n86
Caugas, 268n68
Cayey, 99, 180, 188
CeaseFire. *See* Cure Violence
cementerio de los jóvenes (cemetery of the
  young), 207
Census Bureau, 182, 270n14
Centro de Periodismo Investigativo, 142

Centro Medico, 39
Centros de Apoyo Mutuo (mutual aid
  centers), 239
Centro Sor Isolina Ferre, 124
Centro Vocacional de la Unión Independi-
  ente Auténtica, 203
Cerro Maravilla, 151, 258n29
Chárriez, Max, 196–197
Chen, Mel Y., 18
Chevigny, Paul, 19
Chevrolet, 191
Chicago Housing Authority, 71
La Chiwinha, 1–2
Christianity, 95, 102, 198
citizenship, 3, 11, 17, 33, 58–59, 176, 232, 235;
  citizen-as-victim rhetoric, 181
citizen soldiers, 53
civil rights, 1, 36, 38, 41, 87, 140, 158, 209,
  242n11
Clark, Anne, 72
Claro Cellular, 191
classism, 21, 33, 36, 100, 104, 146, 157–158,
  160, 162, 209, 217, 222, 230
Clinton, Bill, 57, 59, 65–66, 75, 247n20
CNN, 65
Coca-Cola, 191
Cold War, 33, 53, 55–56, 59, 64–65, 73
Coleman Federal Prison, 112
Colon, Cristóbal, 88
Colón, José Luis, 138
@colongil, 189
colonialism, 6, 47, 113, 204, 252n21; colonial
  capitalism, 8, 10–12, 16–17, 22, 59, 87,
  104–105, 110, 143, 150, 233, 236, 239,
  242n10; Spanish, 12, 14; US, 4–5, 7–8,
  12–14, 53, 58–59, 85, 150, 232–234, 238,
  242n9. *See also* anticolonialism;
  decolonization
Columbus, Christopher. *See* Colon,
  Cristóbal
La Comay (The Godmother), 186, 188–189,
  201; #BoicotLaComay, 179, 190; Boicot
  La Comay (Boycott La Comay) Facebook Group, 190–191; La Reina de la
  Bochinche (queen of gossip), 187; *Nuevas Voces diciendo "NO a la Comay,"*
  192–193
Comedores Sociales, 239

commonwealth status of Puerto Rico, 4, 7–8, 29, 55–56, 80–81, 88, 104, 116, 134, 140, 150, 232–234, 236, 238. *See also* Estado Libre Asociado (Associated Free State)

communism, 54

community policing, 21, 39, 67, 70–72, 115, 118–121, 123–124, 127, 137, 143

CompStat, 120

Concepcion, William, 154

La Concha, 180

Condado, 34, 100, 161, 180, 186

Condomanía, 100

contact zones, 36

controlled access (housing), 27, 78, 125–126. *See also* gated communities; Law 21 (Controlled Access Law)

Controlled Access Law. *See* Law 21 (Controlled Access Law)

CoreCivic. *See* Corrections Corporation of America (CoreCivic)

corillos, 90, 206, 219, 222–223, 222–227. *See also* gangs

Corona Extra, 191

Corrections Corporation of America (CoreCivic), 76

Correia, David, 16

Costa Rica, 71, 74

Courageous, 52

credit rating of Puerto Rico, 146

crime rates, 10, 21, 41, 115, 118, 124, 132–134, 136–138, 140

criminalization, 3, 18, 140, 165, 173–174, 190, 237; classed, 21, 24, 26, 33, 42–43, 77, 115, 117, 125–127, 130–132, 136–137, 142–143, 146, 157, 202; gendered, 42–43, 226, 272n44; mano dura and, 25, 30, 33, 76–77, 96, 115, 117, 125–127, 130–132, 139; racialized, 2, 17, 19, 21, 24–26, 33–36, 42–49, 72, 77, 85, 88, 96–103, 110, 113, 116–117, 120, 136, 142–143, 145–146, 152, 156–157, 202–206, 209, 219; of underground music, 86, 96

criminology, 9, 35, 41, 44, 83, 124, 205

crisis, 18–19, 100, 105, 122, 147, 160, 210, 230; colonial crisis management, 6–11; debt, 22, 232–234, 238, 244n44; policing as solution to, 20, 30, 32, 49, 175, 207

critical ethnic studies, 18. *See also* ethnic studies

critical geography (academic field), 6–7, 119, 250n70

Cruz, Juanquina, 80–81

Cruz, Orlando, 180

Cruz Pizarro, Joaquina, 37, 49

Cuban American National Council, 71

Cuevas, Adriana (@lagitanita17), 197

Culebra, 241n7

culture of illegality, 83

culture of poverty myth, 42, 68, 103

Cuomo, Mario, 71

Cupey, 124, 194

Cups, 99–100

Cure Violence, 205–206, 210–214, 221, 229

Currie, Elliott, 124

Daddy Yankee, 93–94; *Playero 39:* "Abuso Oficial," 104, 106–107

death penalty, 32, 184, 187, 247n20

debt, 22, 149, 232–233, 236, 238, 244n44; US citizenship as, 58–59, 252n22

decoding, 19

decolonization, 6. *See also* anticolonialism

Dee, Eddie: "Señor Oficial," 107–109

Delgado Ortiz, Ruben: murder of Enrique Gómez Saladín, 180

delitos tipo 1 crimes, 43

democracy, 7, 16, 26, 53, 65, 67, 130, 154, 242n10; racial, 12

Dennis Zayas, Abner Y., 147–148, 150, 165

Desire, 119

development (economic), 4, 6–8, 10–11, 15, 53, 56–59, 71, 85, 115, 117, 143, 236, 251n3

diaspora: Puerto Rican, 20, 22, 86–87, 95, 164, 172, 178, 180–183, 181–182, 185, 190, 192, 196, 233, 241n7

Diaz, Mercedes, 69

Díaz-Colón, Emilio, 34

Diaz de Leon, Zulma: role in Miguel Cáceres's death, 141

Díaz Martínez, Miguel: attack on Grancid Camilo-Robles, Grancid, 40; hostage taking in Cataño police station, 40; murder of José Rosario Díaz, José, 39–42

Dickie, 105
Dinzey-Flores, Zaire, 26, 42, 248n34, 254n72
dirty economies, 234
DISH network, 191
DJ Joe: *Playero 37:* "Original Si Soy Yo," 90–91; *Underground Masters,* 106
DJ Playero, 93; *Playero 34,* 94; *Playero 37,* 97; "Original Si Soy Yo," 90–91; *Playero 38,* 95; *Playero 39,* 106
DJ Ruben: "La Escuela," 89
domestic violence, 40, 237, 272n44. *See also* gender violence; sexual violence
Dominguez, Daniel, 112
Dominican Republic, 56, 58, 145, 188, 202, 242n11
Dominican Republic-Central America-United States Free Trade Agreement (CAFTA-DR), 56
Dorado, 161
Droz Franco, Nina, 233
Dr. Pila, 254n72
drug economy, 2, 71, 125, 129, 131, 135–136, 138, 158, 164, 165, 167, 184–185, 199, 204, 206–210, 237, 243n26, 249n63, 258n29; antiviolence activism and, 221–226, 230; Drug Free Schools, 117; as informal economy, 4, 9–10, 25–26, 31, 42, 47–49, 79, 87–88, 91, 95, 112; mano dura target-ing, 5, 21, 23–52, 64, 74, 79; mano firme targeting, 115–117; role in US–Puerto Rican relations, 53–54, 60–83; under-ground music and, 21, 84–100, 104–112. *See also* puntos (drug points); war on drugs; zero tolerance policies
Drug Enforcement Agency (DEA): Opera-tion SOS II, 110–111

El Flamboyán, 129
El Hormiguero, 239
El Nuevo Día, 27, 41, 50, 61, 97–98, 123, 151, 157, 270n14
El Nuevo Herald, 76
El Salvador, 212
El Trebol, 38
El Vlade, 189
Emanuel R. (@emarosario), 182–183
emplacement, 14–15

enclosure, 5, 27–28, 31, 35–36, 48, 71, 86, 125, 127, 130, 157
England, 10; London, 33. *See also* Great Britain
Entrialgo, Karen, 105
environmental racism, 250n70, 251n3
Escobar, Martha, 173
Estado Libre Asociado (Associated Free State), 7. *See also* commonwealth status of Puerto Rico
Esteves, José, 156–157
ethnic studies, 3, 26, 205; critical ethnic studies, 18. *See also* critical ethnic studies
Europe, 182. *See also individual countries*
eviction, 55, 75–76
exceptionalism, 6, 15, 102, 185, 193; racial, 13
Extensión Las Delicias, 255n83

Facebook, 22, 154, 176–177, 180–183, 196, 229, 270n5; Boicot La Comay (Boycott La Comay) Facebook Group, 190–191
Fajardo, Victor, 98
Falo: "Pal Cruce," 92–93
Fassin, Didier, 19
Fat Joe, 112
Febles, Magali, 188
Federal Bureau of Investigation (FBI), 128
Federal Control Board (la junta), 232–233, 236
Federal Death Penalty Act, 247n20
Feldman Soler, Alana, 208–214, 216, 218–219, 221, 224, 226–227, 229, 275n39
femininity, 133, 196
feminism, 22, 103, 107, 194–195, 201, 204, 212, 224, 230, 239, 272n44; intersec-tional, 228–229, 231; Third World, 228
feminist studies, 18
Fernández, Gisela Alfonso, 200
Figueres, Jose Maria, 71
Figuero Sancha, José, 154, 164–165, 209
Los Filtros, 268n68
Fiscal Control Board, 233–234, 236
Florida (housing complex), 119
Florida (state), 112, 246n13; Miami, 45, 67, 71, 95, 97
Ford, 191

foreign policy: Puerto Rico as US "laboratory" for, 53
La Fortaleza, 114, 133
Fortuño, Luis, 41, 146–149, 153–154, 164, 170–171, 187
Foucault, Michel, 46
Fox News Latino, 180
fracaso de la mano dura, 5. *See also* mano dura contra el crimen
Fraser, James, 69
Frente Unido de Policías Organizados (FUPO), 204
Fusté, José A., 113
Fusté, José I., 26

G4S Secure Solutions. *See* Wackenhut (G4S Secure Solutions)
Gabriel Mistral High School, 258n29
gangs, 28, 30, 37, 45, 53, 78–80, 156, 214, 219, 221, 246n8; territorial disputes, 46, 204–211, 215, 222, 224, 230, 237. *See also* corillos; puntos (drug points)
gangsta rap, 95
García, Jesús, 96
García, José, 166
gated communities, 27, 35, 126, 256n102; segregated, 11, 246n13, 248n34. *See also* controlled access (housing); Law 21 (Controlled Access Law)
Gateway to the Americas, 57
gatilleros, 78
Gay Officers Action League (GOAL), 100
gender, 3, 11, 19, 22, 185, 200, 207, 212, 221, 224–227, 230–231, 235, 272n44; perspectiva de genero (gender-inclusive education), 179, 194–196, 198–199, 201; policing and, 16, 39–43, 99–100, 167, 176; racialized, 101, 228–229. *See also* gender violence; heteropatriarchy; machismo; patriarchy; perspectiva de genero; sexism; transphobia
gender violence, 224–231. *See also* domestic violence; sexual violence
General Agreement on Tariffs and Trade (GATT), 58
gente decente, 32, 185–186
Georgie, 101–102

"ghetto sweeps," 45, 82
Gillette, 191
Gilmore, Ruth Wilson, 6, 243n26, 246n7
Giuliani, Rudolph, 120
Las Gladiolas, 37–38, 80
Global North, 58
Global South, 53–54, 58
Goachet, Alberto, 24, 70
Godreau, Isar, 15
Gómez Saladín, José Enrique: murder of, 178–193, 197, 201; #TodosSomosJoseEnrique, 178, 183, 189; #YoNoSoyJoseEnrique, 189
Gonzalez, Jennifer, 154
Gonzalez Malave, Alejandro, 258n29
Gonzalez Meza, Choco, 71
González Ortiz, Ulises: murder of, 78
González Rosa, Nirvana, 199
González Torres, Irmarilis, 36, 75
Goodyear, 191
Governing, 120
Government Communications Office, 24
Great Britain, 96. *See also* England
Great Migration, 182, 233
grievability, 48, 178–179, 184–201
Guadalupe, Ana, 269n83
Las Guanabanas, 103; *The Noise I:* "Maldita Puta," 101; "Pa/l carajo las mente sana," 91; "Un Día Con Carlitos," 101–102
Guayama, 234
Guaynabo, 77, 126, 268n68
Gulf of Mexico, 52
gun violence, 11, 32, 39, 89, 107, 125, 141, 150, 151, 205–206
Gurabo, 34

Haiti, 242n11
Hall, Stuart, 10, 19, 33
Hardiman, Tio, 205
Harris, Angela P., 224–225
Hastert, J. Dennis, 52
Hato Rey, 28, 124
Hernández Colón, Rafael, 30–32, 46, 48, 50, 61–63, 75, 90, 126
Hernández Marrero, Damián, 233
Herzig, Nancy, 100
heteropatriarchy, 103, 195. *See also* heterosexism; machismo; patriarchy

heterosexism, 102–103, 196–197, 200. *See also* heteropatriarchy; homophobia; transphobia
Hinton, Elizabeth, 31
hip-hop, 83–113. *See also* underground rap
Hispanic identity, 12
homophobia, 101–103, 179, 186–193, 197. *See also* heteropatriarchy; heterosexism
hospitalillos, 135
Hostos, Eugenio María de, 83
hot-spot policing, 34, 40, 46, 115–120, 135, 138, 157, 165
Housing Authority of New Orleans (HANO), 61
Housing Opportunity for People Everywhere (HOPE VI), 60, 62
Humacao, 98, 141, 268n68
Hurricane Irma, 235
Hurricane María, 22, 234–239, 244n44

IDEBAJO/Coqui Solar, 239
Illinois, 52; Chicago, 61, 67, 71, 124, 205, 210, 212–213; West Garfield Park, 211
Immigration and Naturalization Service (INS), 250n69
incarceration, 3, 75–77, 112, 200, 205, 214, 230, 254n72. *See also* carceral state; prisons
independentistas, 117, 150–151
indignado movement, 178
industrialization, 7, 26, 87
informal economy, 4, 9–10, 25–26, 46, 49, 79, 86, 88, 99, 104, 110, 173. *See also* dirty economies
innocence, 36, 89, 106, 173, 184–186, 190, 193, 242n10
insecurity, 10–11, 15, 25, 46, 113, 115, 123, 132, 139, 180, 181, 183, 194, 206–207, 221, 237; community, 230; personal, 4, 138; public, 136
Instagram, 22, 93–94, 176–177, 180, 198
Interactive Advertising Bureau, 177
Inter-Island Rental P.R. Corp., 69
The Interrupters, 211
intersectionality, 228–229, 231
In the House, 94
Los Intocables: "Vive y Aprede," 89
Irizarry, Alma, 44

Irizarry Vizcarrondo, Georgie, 100
Island of Impunity: Puerto Rico's Outlaw Police Force, 202–204
Israel/Palestine, 246n13
Ivy Queen, 106

Japan, 123–124
Jardines de Country Club, 41
Jet Blue, 187
Jones Act, 252n22
José Celso Barbosa, 39, 58, 83
journalism, 40, 100, 126, 157, 187–188, 195, 211, 234, 249n64
Juana Díaz, 263n86
Juana Matos, 78–79, 113, 131
Julio Sellés Solá, 263n86
la junta. *See* Federal Control Board (la junta)

Kantrow, Michelle, 191
Kelley, Robin D.G., 86
Kelly, Sharon Pratt, 65–67
Kemp, Jack, 60–61
Kimmel, Michael S., 225
Koban model of policing, 123–124, 132
Kotolwitz, Alex, 211

Lafontaine, Bienvenida, 39
Lancaster, Roger, 242n10
Lapp, Michael, 251n3
Las Carreras, 207, 209
Latin America, 57–59, 61, 70, 82, 177, 182, 212, 252n21. *See also individual countries*
Latinx studies, 18
Law 7 (Public Law 7), 146–147
Law 21 (Controlled Access Law), 27
law and order politics, 10, 32, 237
legal studies, 19, 83
León, Eduardo, 79
liberalism, 116, 140, 142–143, 242n10
Linebaugh, Peter, 244n46
líos de falda, 227
Lipsitz, George, 13
Lizardi, David, 99
Lloréns, Hilda, 12, 232
Lloréns Torres, 69, 85, 263n86, 268n68; Parents Recreational Council, 63; Residents Council, 81

Loicano, Felix, 121–123, 134
Loíza, 22, 98, 155–164, 169, 174, 202–231, 235, 263n86, 268n68
Loizazo, 203–204
López, Roberto, 80
López Meléndez, Luis Joel: murder of, 207
López Mercado, Jorge Steven: murder of, 188–189
Lora, Ricardo Olivero, 148
#LosBuenosSomosMas, 180
Louisiana, 118–122; New Orleans, 60–61; Ninth Ward, 119
Lugo, Pedro, 168
Luina, Alexander, 154
Luquillo, 98
Lytle Hernández, Kelly, 47

machismo, 198–199. See also heteropatriarchy; patriarchy
Machuca, Felix, 126
Mahler, Matthew, 225
Maldonado, Roberto "Junior," 130
mano dura contra el crimen, 18, 100, 140, 143, 158, 170, 176, 185, 201, 241n7, 249n63; fracaso de la mano dura, 5; increasing murder rates, 44–47, 104, 184; increasing segregation, 5, 32, 36; legacy, 2–3, 5, 20–21, 35–36, 115–117, 120–121, 125, 127–134, 137, 139, 145–146, 167, 206, 213; mano amiga seguia la mano dura, 70; public housing and, 14, 23–55, 54–55, 60, 63–85, 96, 99, 103, 116–117, 132, 165, 167, 254n72, 263n86; role in US–Puerto Rico relationship, 53–82; targeting drug economy, 5, 21, 23–52, 64, 74, 79; underground music and, 21, 84–85, 88, 90, 93, 96–97, 99, 103–106, 109–114
mano firme, 115, 127, 129–130
Manso, Eddie, 220
Manuel A. Pérez (housing complex), 50, 124, 167–168
Manuelle, Victor, 180
Mariana, 268n68
@marilola, 198
Marino, John, 100
Márquez, Francisco, 137
Márquez, John D., 205, 250n69

Martin, Ricky, 180
Martínez, Antonia: killing by PRPD, 151
Martinez-Cabello, Belen, 188
Marx, Karl, 244n46
Maryland: Baltimore, 124
masculinity, 42, 92, 133–134, 185, 212, 224–228, 230
Master Joe, 94; Playero 37: "Original Si Soy Yo," 90–91
Mayagüez, 249n63
May Day Protest (2017), 233
media coverage, 18–19
Mediania Alta, 208
Meissner, Doris, 250n69
Melilla, 207, 209
methodology, of book, 18–20. See also participant observation
Mexicano, 97
Mexico, 56; Mexico City, 57; US–Mexico border, 250n69
Miami bass, 95
Michigan: Detroit, 67
militarization of policing, 23, 54, 64–67, 73, 134, 137–138, 157, 230. See also Puerto Rico National Guard; Puerto Rico Police Department (PRPD): Tactical Operations Unit (Fuerza de Choque/ Shock Force)
Milton S. Eisenhower Foundation, 124
Miñi Miñi, 214
Miranda, Beatriz, 170
Miranda, César, 130, 137, 230
Miss Puerto Rico pageant, 188
Mitrani, Sam, 16–17
mixtapes, 90, 93–94, 97–98, 101. See also The Noise I; Playero 34; Playero 38; Playero 39
Los Mojaitos, 263n86
Monte Hatillo, 38, 41, 50, 129, 167–168
Monte Park, 129
Moody's, 146
Moraga, Cherríe: This Bridge Called My Back, 228
Morales, Ada Estel, 38–39, 42
Morales, Ed, 187
Morales, Karl William, 104
Morales Pérez, José: murder of, 78
Morality in Media, 95–96, 106

Morial, Marc H., 118–120
Mother Teresa, 70
Movimiento Amplio de Mujeres de Puerto
  Rico, 198–199
Mr. G, 105
muggings, 10, 33, 113
Mulroney, Brian, 56
Muñoz Marín, Luis, 7, 26. *See also* Opera-
  tion Bootstrap (Operación Manos a la
  Obra)
Muñoz Rivera, Luis, 83
Murakawa, Naomi, 143
Murch, Donna, 18–19
music, 21, 23, 83–113, 84, 124. *See also* hip-
  hop; Miami bass; mixtapes; punk;
  rap; reggae; reggaeton; ska; under-
  ground rap

Narváez, Mari Mari, 195–196
National Center for Housing Management,
  71, 74
nationalism, 12, 150
National Public Radio (NPR), 65
National Puerto Rican Coalition, 56
Negrón Fernández, José R., 122, 128
Nemesio Canales, 28–29, 79, 248n31,
  263n86
neoliberalism, 5, 11, 30, 58–59, 64, 68, 73,
  81–82, 85, 88, 142, 146, 148, 154, 210,
  229, 252n24, 265n13; neoliberal carceral
  state, 55. *See also* austerity; capitalism;
  class; poverty; privatization; trade
  liberalization
Nevares-Muñiz, Dora, 35, 41
New Deal, 7, 55
New Orleans Police Department (NOPD):
  Citizens Academy, 119; Community
  Oriented Police Squad (COPS), 119;
  Pennington Plan, 116, 118–123
newspapers, 19, 27, 96, 98, 102, 105, 145,
  181
New York City, 45, 61, 67, 71, 86, 105, 120,
  190, 233–234
New York Police Department (NYPD),
  134–135, 234
New York Times, 65, 134; *Magazine,* 211
Nixon, Richard, 9
Nizzie, 105–106

The Noise I: "Maldita Puta," 101; "Pa/l
  carajo las mente sana," 91; "Un Día Con
  Carlitos," 101–102
@noralissoe, 183
North American Free Trade Agreement
  (NAFTA), 56–58, 66–67, 252n21
Nuevas Voces diciendo "NO a la Comay,"
  192–193
Nuñez, Lou, 56
Nuyoricans, 86

Oakley, Deidre, 69
Obama, Barack, 232
ola criminal, 102
O'Neill Carrasquillo Cirino, Luis: murder
  of, 207
OPEC oil embargo (1973), 9
Operation Bootstrap (Operación Manos a
  la Obra), 7–8, 29–30, 49, 55–56, 71, 87,
  182, 251n3
Operation Centurion, 33–34, 67
Operation Clean Sweep, 45, 249n64
Operation Force Against Crime (Oper-
  ación Fuerza Contra el Crimen), 123
Operation Hammer, 45
Operation Pressure Point, 45
Operation Snow Ball, 45
Operation SOS II, 110–111
Operation Sting, 45
Orff, Carl: *Carmina Burana,* 23
Organización Socialista Internacional
  (International Socialist Organization),
  166
Ortiz Dalliot, José, 138

Pabón, Carlos, 176
Pacho y Cirilo, 113; "Como Grita el Palo,"
  113. *See also* Álvarez Núñez, Neftalí
  "Pacho"
Pagán, Amárilis, 196
Pagán, Javier: murder of Miguel Céaceres,
  141
Las Palmas, 131
Panama, 71, 74
Pantojas-García, Emilio, 8
Parenti, Christian, 249n64
Paro Nacional del Pueblo (People's
  National Stoppage), 147–149

participant observation, 18
Partido Indepenentista Puertorriqueño (PIP), 117
Partido Nacionalista de Puerto Rico (PNPR, Puerto Rican Nationalist Party): Río Piedras massacre (1935), 150
Partido Nuevo Progresista (PNP), 116–117, 127, 134, 139–140, 142–143, 232, 252n24
Partido Popular Democratico (PPD, Popular Democratic Party), 7, 115–116, 130, 133–134, 138–140, 142–143, 232
patriarchy, 194–196, 200–201, 228
pejes gordos, 49
Pelot-Hobbs, Lydia, 119
Los Peña, 263n86
penepe, 80
Pennington, Richard J.: Pennington Plan, 116, 118–123
Pennsylvania: Philadelphia, 124
Peñuelas, 234
Pereira, Miguel, 123, 125–129, 131–133
Pérez, Charles, 48
Perez, Hazael, 221
Pérez, Hector, 41
Pérez, Juan José, 38, 50
Pérez, Mariem: "Un Abrazo Para Puerto Rico" ("A Hug for Puerto Rico"), 181–182
Pérez Reisler, José "Osito": attack by José A. Rosa Carrasquillo, 153
La Perla, 38, 130, 248n31
perspectiva de genero (gender-inclusive education), 179, 194–196, 198–199, 201
Pesquera, Carlos, 117
Picó, Fernando, 27
Picón, Milton, 95–96
Los Pies Negros: "Niño de sangre azul," 28
Piñones, 268n68
pintatas (paint-ins), 144–145, 169–171
Pita Boom, 105
Pizarro, Cruz, 49
Pizarro Rivera, Edgar: attack by police, 202–203
Playero 34, 94
Playero 37, 90–91, 95, 97
Playero 38, 95
Playero 39, 104, 106–107
Plaza Las Américas, 34, 36
plebiscite on Puerto Rico's status, 59

Poder Estudiantil, 105
Policía y Comunidad program, 132
Ponce, 26, 83, 111, 132, 137, 139, 249n63, 254n72, 263n86
Pontificia Universidad Católica de Puerto Rico, 83
populares, 80
population control, 47; sterilization, 8
pornography, 97, 100
Posse Comitatus Act, 66
Postill, John, 178, 270n5
poverty, 2, 4, 7, 8, 14, 26, 30, 31–32, 45–46, 59, 77, 86–87, 116, 120, 124–125, 147, 149, 223, 231, 233, 248n34; criminalization of, 21, 24, 27, 42, 77, 84, 97, 115, 117, 126–127, 130, 136–137, 142–143, 157, 202; culture of poverty myth, 42, 68, 103; private security forces demographics and, 156–161; racialized, 2, 24, 42, 77, 85, 100, 103, 158, 217
premature death, 5, 25, 51, 193, 219, 246n7. See also social death
President's Commission on Privatization, 60, 62
prisons, 35, 51, 72, 77, 79, 112, 113, 180, 217, 233, 243n26, 254n72; private, 76. See also Asociación Ñeta; carceral state; Coleman Federal Prison; Corrections Corporation of America (CoreCivic); incarceration; Wackenhut (G4S Secure Solutions)
private security forces, 1, 27, 35, 76–78, 152, 155–163, 173–174
privatization, 54, 89, 146, 165, 210, 232, 252n24; of education, 144, 171; of public housing, 21, 26–27, 55, 60–63, 67–82
public health, 22, 83, 114, 204–206
public housing, 2, 4–5, 15, 21, 61–62, 86, 92–94, 104, 111, 113, 118–119, 124–132, 136–138, 142, 145, 157, 163, 166, 168–170, 193–194, 223, 248n31, 254n72; mano dura and, 14, 23–52, 23–55, 60, 63–85, 69–85, 96, 99, 103, 116–117, 132, 165, 167, 254n72, 263n86. See also caseríos; eviction; public housing authorities (PHAs)
public housing authorities (PHAs), 54, 61, 71, 73. See also Chicago Housing Authority; Housing Authority of New

Orleans (HANO); Puerto Rico Housing Authority (PRHA); Washington DC Department of Public and Assisted Housing

pueblo puertorriqueño, 25, 48, 187

Puente Blanco, 263n86

Puerta de Tierra, 27, 31

Puerto Rican Project for the Twenty-First Century, 128

Puerto Rico Civil Rights Commission, 158, 209

Puerto Rico Congress: House of Representatives, 130; Senate, 130, 138, 154

Puerto Rico Constitution, 7, 32, 97, 247n20

Puerto Rico Daily Sun, 145

Puerto Rico Department of Corrections, 133

Puerto Rico Department of Education, 98, 199

Puerto Rico Department of Health, 44

Puerto Rico Department of Public Security, 236

Puerto Rico Drugs and Vice Control Bureau, 96

Puerto Rico Fire Department, 135

Puerto Rico Governor's Security Council, 121–122, 127–128

Puerto Rico Housing Authority (PRHA), 61–62, 73, 77, 124, 213

Puerto Rico Industrial Development Company (PRIDCO), 57

Puerto Rico Lesbian and Gay Coalition of the Human Rights Project, 100

Puerto Rico National Guard (PRNG), 32–35, 37–39, 41, 49, 52–54, 64–66, 68, 72–73, 77–79, 116, 125, 137–138, 263n86

Puerto Rico Oversight, Management, and Economic Stability Act (PROMESA), 232–233

Puerto Rico Penal Code: Article 113, 96

Puerto Rico Police Department (PRPD), 1–2, 28, 41, 77, 117, 120–124, 127–129, 133–134, 136–140, 165, 210, 212, 263n86; attacks at Loizazo, 203–204; attacks on students, 144–175; corruption in, 20; demographics, 15–17; Education and Training Division, 135; Homicide Investigation Division, 179, 194; Intelligence Office, 258n29; Internal Affairs, 118, 141; *Island of Impunity: Puerto Rico's Outlaw Police Force,* 202–203; killing of Alejandro Medina Colón, 233; killing of Antonia Martínez, 151; motivational video, 23–24; murder of José Amaury Ayala Rivera, 203; murder of José Rosario Díaz, 39–42; murder of Miguel Cáceres, 141; nonconfrontation policy with the Univ. of Puerto Rico, 149–153, 156, 158, 165, 171; Policía y Comunidad program, 132; Public Housing Division, 79; Public Integrity Division, 118; Review Board, 40; shooting of María Rosario Díaz, 39–40, 42; Tactical Operations Unit (Fuerza de Choque/Shock Force), 141, 151, 153–154, 203–204, 230. *See also* Asociación de Miembros de la Policía; community policing; hot-spot policing; *Island of Impunity: Puerto Rico's Outlaw Police Force;* mano dura contra el crimen; militarization of policing

Puerto Rico sin miedo (Puerto Rico without fear), 139–140

puertorriqueñizar la Universidad, 151

Pulido, Laura, 250n70

punitive governance, 3, 11, 18, 20, 22, 110, 140, 143, 199, 239, 242nn10–11, 306

punk, 96–97

puntos (drug points), 25–26, 29–30, 41, 43, 45–51, 62, 88–94, 135–137, 158, 165, 184, 209, 222, 249n63. *See also* gangs

QiiBo, 199

Quality of Life Congress (QLC), 68–71, 77, 80–81

quality of life policing, 68–71, 77, 80–81, 118, 120–121, 132

queerness, 3, 18–19, 99, 102–103, 181, 189–190, 193, 195, 197

queer studies, 18

queer theory, 18

race, 3–5, 10–11, 14–17, 20, 30–33, 59, 84, 149, 158–163, 166–169, 173–175, 184–185, 229, 234, 236, 246n7, 246n13, 263n86; classed, 13–15; color-blind discourse, 13,

race *(continued)*
24; gendered, 101, 228–229; poverty
and, 2, 24, 42, 77, 85, 100, 103, 158, 217;
racial capitalism, 17; racial democracy,
12; racial exceptionalism, 13; racialization of crime, 2, 17, 19, 21, 24–26, 33–36,
42–49, 72, 77, 85, 88, 96–103, 110, 113,
116–117, 120, 136, 142–143, 145–146, 152,
156–157, 202–206, 209, 219; sexuality
and, 14. *See also* racism; segregation
racial profiling, 21, 97
racism, 12–13, 17, 21, 33, 36, 47, 100, 104,
157–162, 160, 188, 192, 202–203, 209,
217, 222–223, 230–231, 246n7; environmental, 250n70, 251n3. *See also* racial
profiling; slavery; white supremacy
radio, 19, 64–65, 75, 84, 94, 96, 137, 148,
159, 168
Radio Huelga (Strike Radio), 148, 155, 159,
168
Rambo, 70
Ramírez, Juan Laguarta, 265n13
Ramírez, Roberto José Thomas, 148, 158
Ramírez, William, 2
Ramírez de Arellano, 255n83
Ramos, Rosario María del Pilar, 39
rap. *See* gangsta rap; underground rap
raperos, 84–85, 94, 97–98, 100, 103–110. *See
also* underground rap
Reagan, Ronald, 56
reasonable perception, 2
recession, 9, 146
Recinto de Ciencias Medicas, 149
Red de Apoyo Mutuo Autogestionada
(Self-Managed Mutual Aid Network),
239
reempowerment, 68–69, 77
reggae, 85, 90
reggaeton, 84, 93–94, 110, 113. *See also*
underground rap
reggaetoneros, 84, 93, 112. *See also* underground rap
Renta, Carlos, 80
Reserve Officers' Training Corps (ROTC),
150–151
Residencial Las Vegas, 263n86
Rexach Construction Corp.: Rexset Enterprises Inc., 62

Rexach Management Corp., 79
Reyes, Edwin, 102
Rindiendo Cuentas, 75
Río Grande, 223
Río Piedras, 1, 38, 124, 129–131, 144–145,
148, 151, 155, 159, 163, 165, 170–171,
179, 194; Río Piedras massacre (1935),
150
Ríos, Monserate, 63
Ríos, Victor, 226
Rivera, Carlos, 190
Rivera, Carmen, 126
Rivera, Evelyn, 202–203
Rivera, George, 199
Rivera, José Luis, 38
Rivera, Joshua (@Im_Freshh), 189
Rivera, Raquel Z., 86–87, 113
Rivera-Bonilla, Ivelisse, 27
Rivera Clemente, Maricruz, 159
Rivera González, Víctor, 133–135
Rivera-Rideau, Petra R., 14–15, 98
Rivera Vázquez, Joredimar, 203
Roberto, Giovanni, 1–3, 11, 157, 160–164,
167, 172, 174
Rodríguez, Ángel, 188–189
Rodríguez, Benjamin, 158–159
Rodriguez, Blanca (@bandarrita), 197–198
Rodríguez, Judith, 44
Rodríguez, María, 129
Rodríguez, Tomasa, 41
Rodríguez Nazario, Annie, 81
Rodríguez-Silva, Ileana, 12
Rohena Vélez, Tyrone: killing of Ivania
Zayas Ortiz, 194, 200
Rosa, Alessandra, 151
Rosa, Jonathan, 178
Rosario, Orlando, 41
Rosario Díaz, José
Rosario Díaz, María: shooting by Miguel
Díaz Martínez, 39–40, 42
Rosselló, Pedro, 5, 31, 48, 50, 98, 134–135,
143, 255n83; role in mano dura contra el
crimen, 5, 21, 32–39, 43–44, 52–60,
63–67, 70–71, 74–82, 90, 104, 114–117,
125–127, 129, 132, 137, 138–140. *See also*
mano dura contra el crimen; Operation
Centurion
@_rubimarie, 197

Ruiz, Carlitos: "Un Abrazo Para Puerto Rico" ("A Hug for Puerto Rico"), 181–182
Russia, 33. *See also* Soviet Union

sacrifice zones, 234
Salinas, Carlos, 56–57
San Antonio, 268n68
Sánchez Badillo, David. *See* Tempo
Sanes, David, 114
San Juan, 1, 26, 37, 52, 84, 90, 95–101, 111, 116, 124, 127, 129, 131, 133, 137–139, 147, 179–180, 233, 249n63, 258n29, 263n86; 1992 sniper attacks in, 28–29; class in, 26–27; Old San Juan, 38, 181
San Juan Star, 31, 55, 79, 100, 105
San Juan Vice Squad, 95
San Martín, 65
San Sebastían, 235
Santa Isabel, 263n86
Santa Rita, 151
Santarrosa, Antulio "Kobbo," 186–188; #BoicotLaComay, 179, 190; Boicot La Comay (Boycott La Comay) Facebook Group, 190–191; *Nuevas Voces diciendo "NO a la Comay,"* 192–193. *See also* La Comay (The Godmother)
Santiago, León, 37
Santiago Negrón, Lourdes, 149, 159
Santini, Jorge, 127
Santos Febres, Mayra, 85
Santurce, 100, 181, 197, 268n68
scapegoating, 102–104, 113, 161
Scheper-Hughes, Nancy, 193
Schumer, Charles, 65
Schwarzenegger, Arnold, 70
S.C. Johnson, 191
Scott, James C., 91
Se Acabaron las PROMESAS (The PROMISES Are Over), 233
segregation, 3, 11, 13, 19, 30–31, 34, 146, 162, 174, 229, 231, 263n86; mano dura increasing, 5, 32, 36. *See also* apartheid boricua; gated communities
Serrano, Pedro Julio, 190
sexism, 101–103, 133–134, 179, 193–201, 224, 227, 230, 272n44
The Sex Pistols, 97

sexuality, 3, 11, 31, 84–85, 99–103, 176, 179, 185–190, 193, 197, 225, 227, 235; racialized, 14. *See also* heterosexism; homophobia
sexual violence, 23, 40–43, 92, 196–198, 200–201, 272n44. *See also* domestic violence; gender violence
sex work, 9, 100, 186–187, 189–190, 195, 199
@sharonclaudia, 197
Shell, 180
Sheraton Hotel, 153–154
Simon, Jonathan, 181, 247n23
Singh, Nikhil, 17
ska, 28
slavery, 12–13, 17
slow violence, 234
Slutkin, Gary, 205, 211
sniper attacks, 28–29
social abandonment, 45, 221
social death, 4, 36, 171. *See also* premature death
social justice, 36
social media, 18–19, 94, 153, 156, 163, 270n5; hashtag activism, 22, 176–201. *See also individual platforms* 176
Somalia, 205
Sonadora, 268n68
South Africa, 246n13
Soviet Union, 55, 65. *See also* Russia
Spade, Dean, 17
Spain, 178; Spanish colonialism, 12, 14
spatial engineering, 26
Standard & Poor's, 146
Starfleet, 105–106
sterilization, 8
Stevens, Roger, 74
Stockholm Syndrome, 163
Straight Outta Puerto Rico: Reggaeton's Rough Road to Glory, 93
strikes: general, 147–149; student, 1, 21, 144–175, 239, 265n13, 269n83. *See also* activism; Paro Nacional del Pueblo (People's National Stoppage)
"students not criminals" ("somos estudiantes, no somos criminales"), 146, 173
Suárez, José, 79
Sundance Film Festival, 211
Superior Court of San Juan, 97

SuperXclusivo, 179, 186–189, 199, 201; #BoicotLaComay, 179, 190; Boicot La Comay (Boycott La Comay) Facebook Group, 190–191; *Nuevas Voces diciendo "NO a la Comay,"* 192–193. *See also* La Comay (The Godmother)

Sustache, Carlos, 141; role in Miguel Cáceres's death, 141

Taboada de Jesús, José, 135–136, 204

Taifa, Nkechi, 41

Taínos, 12

Taller Sauld, 22, 204, 209–210, 239; Acuerdo de Paz, 22, 205–208, 211–222, 224–231

Taylor, Keeanga-Yamahtta, 30

Telenoticias, 156

television, 19, 23, 47, 64, 92, 112, 144, 156, 160, 186–194, 188. *See also individual networks and shows*

Tempo (David Sánchez Badillo), 110; "Narcohampon," 111–112

Terror Squad Records, 112

Third World, 53, 56, 64, 67, 71, 251n3; Third World feminism, 228

This Bridge Called My Back, 228

Tirado, Cirilo, 130

#TodosSomosJoseEnrique, 178, 183, 189

Toledo, Pedro, 23–24, 33–34, 36, 38–39, 43, 46, 52–54, 78–80, 97–100, 104, 111, 116–117, 137, 140–141. *See also* Operation Centurion

Toro, Ana Teresa, 195–196

Torres, Arlene, 14

Torres, Carmen Edith, 126

Torres, Lina, 35

Torres Gotay, Benjamín, 157

Torres Osorio, Edwin: murder of Enrique Gómez Saladín, 180

trade liberalization, 53, 81–82. *See also* neoliberalism

transdisciplinarity, 18

transnationalism, 50, 56, 250n69

transphobia, 101–103, 188–189. *See also* heteropatriarchy; heterosexism

Travieso, Héctor, 186

Triple-S, 191

Tugwell, Rexford G., 251n3

Tumblr, 177

Twitter, 22, 176–183, 189–190, 196–198, 270n5. *See also individual hashtags*

2 Live Crew, 97

"Un Abrazo Para Puerto Rico" ("A Hug for Puerto Rico"), 181–182

underground rap, 4, 21, 83–113, 84

unemployment, 4, 8–9, 49, 59, 62, 84, 87, 113, 124, 156

University of Puerto Rico (UPR), 105, 208, 233; Aguadilla campus, 235; Cayey campus, 99; nonconfrontation policy with the PRPD, 149–153, 156, 158, 165, 171; Río Piedras campus (UPR-RP), 1, 144–175, 269n83; strikes, 21, 144–175, 239, 265n13, 269n83

urbanizaciones, 14, 35–36, 50

Urb. Ferrán, 263n86

US Coast Guard, 52

US Congress, 7, 9, 41, 52–53, 64–66, 134, 232; House of Representatives, 52, 60; Subcommittee on National Security, International Affairs, and Criminal Justice, 52; Senate, 60

US Department of Homeland Security, 234

US Department of Housing and Urban Development (HUD), 60, 63, 71, 77; Caribbean Office, 61, 68, 78; "troubled housing" list, 61–62

US Department of Justice (DOJ), 20, 64, 141–142, 211, 229; Civil Rights Division, 1–2, 140

US Internal Revenue Code: Section 936, 9, 55

US Marshals Service, 129

US Navy, 114

utopia, 162–163

Vankatesh, Sudhir, 243n24

Vázquez, Miguel, 81

Vázquez, Wanda, 237

Vélez Pérez, Luz Zenaida, 50

Vélez Soto, Waldemiro, 153, 172

Vico C, 86; "La Recta Final," 88–89; "Xplosión," 96

Vieques, 114, 241n7

Vietnam War, 37

Villa Cañona, 155, 157–159, 202–203, 209
Villa Cristiana, 207
Villa España, 34–35, 37, 49, 64, 80, 126;
    Residents Council, 81
Villa Esperanza, 124
Villa Evangelina 3 and 4, 255n83
Villa Kennedy, 93, 263n86
Villalonga, Rosa C., 61–62, 68, 78
Villa Los Santos 1 and 2, 255n83
Villanueva, Richie, 94
Villa Pueblo, 263n86
Villa Santos, 208
Villas de Lomas Verdes, 194
violence interrupters, 205–206, 211, 213–
    214, 218, 229; *The Interrupters,* 211. *See
    also* Cure Violence; Taller Sauld: Acu-
    erdo de Paz
Vivoni, Carlos, 52, 54, 68–69
Vivoni del Valle, Pierre, 117, 120–123

Wackenhut (G4S Secure Solutions), 76
#WalkingTheStreetsAlone, 179, 197–198.
    See also #AndandoLaCalleSola
Walkmans, 99
Wall, Tyler, 16
Wall Street, 146
Walmart, 191
WAPA-TV, 156, 186–187, 190–191
Ware, Scott, 55
war on crime, 24, 42, 119
war on drugs, 4, 21, 23, 25, 30, 35–36, 45,
    53–54, 63, 65, 95–96, 98, 110, 137, 184–
    185, 193, 221, 230. *See also* drug economy;
    puntos (drug points)
Washington, DC, 45, 61, 65–66, 71,
    249n64; City Council, 67; Department
    of Public and Assisted Housing,

72–73; Resident Council Advisory
    Board, 72
Washington, DC Metropolitan Police
    Department, 118
Washington DC Department of Public and
    Assisted Housing, 72
Washington DC National Guard, 67
Washington Post, 65, 72
weapons of the weak, 91
Welch's, 191
#WeNeedGenderEducation, 197
White House, 67
white supremacy, 12–13, 17
Wiso G: *Sin Parar,* 95
World Bank, 177
World War I, 252n22
World War II, 6, 246n13

xenophobia, 188, 192–193

Yo amo la UPR (I love the UPR) march,
    170–171
#YoNoSoyJoseEnrique, 189
YouTube, 141, 176

Zambrana, Carmelo, 38
Zayas Ortiz, Ivania: #AndandoLa-
    CalleSola, 179, 194–201; killing by
    Tyrone Rohena Vélez, 194–201
zero tolerance policies, 82, 121
Zervigón, Pedro, 92
zombie policies, 236
zonas calientes (crime hot spots), 34, 40,
    46, 118–120, 157, 165, 173
Zonas Escolar Libre de drogas y Armas
    (ZELDAs, School Zones Free of Drugs
    and Firearms), 98